Lecture Notes in Computer Science

Lecture Notes in Computer Science

Vol. 23: Programming Methodology. 4th Informatik Symposium, IBM Germany Wildbad, September 25–27, 1974. Edited by C. E. Hackl. VI, 501 pages. 1975.

Vol. 24: Parallel Processing. Proceedings 1974. Edited by T. Feng. VI, 433 pages. 1975.

Vol. 25: Category Theory Applied to Computation and Control. Proceedings 1974. Edited by E. G. Manes. X, 245 pages. 1975.

Vol. 26: GI-4. Jahrestagung, Berlin, 9.–12. Oktober 1974. Herausgegeben im Auftrag der GI von D. Siefkes. IX, 748 Seiten. 1975.

Vol. 27: Optimization Techniques. IFIP Technical Conference. Novosibirsk, July 1–7, 1974. (Series: I.F.I.P. TC7 Optimization Conferences.) Edited by G. I. Marchuk. VIII, 507 pages. 1975.

Vol. 28: Mathematical Foundations of Computer Science. 3rd Symposium at Jadwisin near Warsaw, June 17–22, 1974. Edited by A. Blikle. VII, 484 pages. 1975.

Vol. 29: Interval Mathematics. Procedings 1975. Edited by K. Nickel. VI, 331 pages. 1975.

Vol. 30: Software Engineering. An Advanced Course. Edited by F. L. Bauer. (Formerly published 1973 as Lecture Notes in Economics and Mathematical Systems, Vol. 81) XII, 545 pages. 1975.

Vol. 31: S. H. Fuller, Analysis of Drum and Disk Storage Units. IX, 283 pages. 1975.

Vol. 32: Mathematical Foundations of Computer Science 1975. Proceedings 1975. Edited by J. Bečvář. X, 476 pages. 1975.

Vol. 33: Automata Theory and Formal Languages, Kaiserslautern, May 20–23, 1975. Edited by H. Brakhage on behalf of GI. VIII, 292 Seiten. 1975.

Vol. 34: GI – 5. Jahrestagung, Dortmund 8.–10. Oktober 1975. Herausgegeben im Auftrag der GI von J. Mühlbacher. X, 755 Seiten. 1975.

Vol. 35: W. Everling, Exercises in Computer Systems Analysis. (Formerly published 1972 as Lecture Notes in Economics and Mathematical Systems, Vol. 65) VIII, 184 pages. 1975.

Vol. 36: S. A. Greibach, Theory of Program Structures: Schemes, Semantics, Verification. XV, 364 pages. 1975.

Vol. 37: C. Böhm, λ-Calculus and Computer Science Theory. Proceedings 1975. XII, 370 pages. 1975.

Vol. 38: P. Branquart, J.-P. Cardinael, J. Lewi, J.-P. Delescaille, M. Vanbegin. An Optimized Translation Process and Its Application to ALGOL 68. IX, 334 pages. 1976.

Vol. 39: Data Base Systems. Proceedings 1975. Edited by H. Hasselmeier and W. Spruth. VI, 386 pages. 1976.

Vol. 40: Optimization Techniques. Modeling and Optimization in the Service of Man. Part 1. Proceedings 1975. Edited by J. Cea. XIV, 854 pages. 1976.

Vol. 41: Optimization Techniques. Modeling and Optimization in the Service of Man. Part 2. Proceedings 1975. Edited by J. Cea. XIII, 852 pages. 1976.

Vol. 42: James E. Donahue, Complementary Definitions of Programming Language Semantics. VII, 172 pages. 1976.

Vol. 43: E. Specker und V. Strassen, Komplexität von Entscheidungsproblemen. Ein Seminar. V, 217 Seiten. 1976.

Vol. 44: ECI Conference 1976. Proceedings 1976. Edited by K. Samelson. VIII, 322 pages. 1976.

Vol. 45: Mathematical Foundations of Computer Science 1976. Proceedings 1976. Edited by A. Mazurkiewicz. XI, 601 pages. 1976.

Vol. 46: Language Hierarchies and Interfaces. Edited by F. L. Bauer and K. Samelson. X, 428 pages. 1976.

Vol. 47: Methods of Algorithmic Language Implementation. Edited by A. Ershov and C. H. A. Koster. VIII, 351 pages. 1977.

Vol. 48: Theoretical Computer Science, Darmstadt, March 1977. Edited by H. Tzschach, H. Waldschmidt and H. K.-G. Walter on behalf of GI. VIII, 418 pages. 1977.

Vol. 49: Interactive Systems. Proceedings 1976. Edited by A. Blaser and C. Hackl. VI, 380 pages. 1976.

Vol. 50: A. C. Hartmann, A Concurrent Pascal Compiler for Minicomputers. VI, 119 pages. 1977.

Vol. 51: B. S. Garbow, Matrix Eigensystem Routines – Eispack Guide Extension. VIII, 343 pages. 1977.

Vol. 52: Automata, Languages and Programming. Fourth Colloquium, University of Turku, July 1977. Edited by A. Salomaa and M. Steinby. X, 569 pages. 1977.

Vol. 53: Mathematical Foundations of Computer Science. Proceedings 1977. Edited by J. Gruska. XII, 608 pages. 1977.

Vol. 54: Design and Implementation of Programming Languages. Proceedings 1976. Edited by J. H. Williams and D. A. Fisher. X, 496 pages. 1977.

Vol. 55: A. Gerbier, Mes premières constructions de programmes. XII, 256 pages. 1977.

Vol. 56: Fundamentals of Computation Theory. Proceedings 1977. Edited by M. Karpiński. XII, 542 pages. 1977.

Vol. 57: Portability of Numerical Software. Proceedings 1976. Edited by W. Cowell. VIII, 539 pages. 1977.

Vol. 58: M. J. O'Donnell, Computing in Systems Described by Equations. XIV, 111 pages. 1977.

Vol. 59: E. Hill, Jr., A Comparative Study of Very Large Data Bases. X, 140 pages. 1978.

Vol. 60: Operating Systems, An Advanced Course. Edited by R. Bayer, R. M. Graham, and G. Seegmüller. X, 593 pages. 1978.

Vol. 61: The Vienna Development Method: The Meta-Language. Edited by D. Bjørner and C. B. Jones. XVIII, 382 pages. 1978.

Vol. 62: Automata, Languages and Programming. Proceedings 1978. Edited by G. Ausiello and C. Böhm. VIII, 508 pages. 1978.

Vol. 63: Natural Language Communication with Computers. Edited by Leonard Bolc. VI, 292 pages. 1978.

Vol. 64: Mathematical Foundations of Computer Science. Proceedings 1978. Edited by J. Winkowski. X, 551 pages. 1978.

Vol. 65: Information Systems Methodology, Proceedings, 1978. Edited by G. Bracchi and P. C. Lockemann. XII, 696 pages. 1978.

Vol. 66: N. D. Jones and S. S. Muchnick, TEMPO: A Unified Treatment of Binding Time and Parameter Passing Concepts in Programming Languages. IX, 118 pages. 1978.

Vol. 67: Theoretical Computer Science, 4th GI Conference, Aachen, March 1979. Edited by K. Weihrauch. VII, 324 pages. 1979.

Vol. 68: D. Harel, First-Order Dynamic Logic. X, 133 pages. 1979.

Vol. 69: Program Construction. International Summer School. Edited by F. L. Bauer and M. Broy. VII, 651 pages. 1979.

Vol. 70: Semantics of Concurrent Computation. Proceedings 1979. Edited by G. Kahn. VI, 368 pages. 1979.

Vol. 71: Automata, Languages and Programming. Proceedings 1979. Edited by H. A. Maurer. IX, 684 pages. 1979.

Vol. 72: Symbolic and Algebraic Computation. Proceedings 1979. Edited by E. W. Ng. XV, 557 pages. 1979.

Vol. 73: Graph-Grammars and Their Application to Computer Science and Biology. Proceedings 1978. Edited by V. Claus, H. Ehrig and G. Rozenberg. VII, 477 pages. 1979.

Vol. 74: Mathematical Foundations of Computer Science. Proceedings 1979. Edited by J. Bečvář. IX, 580 pages. 1979.

Vol. 75: Mathematical Studies of Information Processing. Proceedings 1978. Edited by E. K. Blum, M. Paul and S. Takasu. VIII, 629 pages. 1979.

Vol. 76: Codes for Boundary-Value Problems in Ordinary Differential Equations. Proceedings 1978. Edited by B. Childs et al. VIII, 388 pages. 1979.

Lecture Notes in Computer Science

Edited by G. Goos and J. Hartmanis

126

Microcomputer System Design

An Advanced Course
Trinity College Dublin, June 1981

Edited by M.J. Flynn, N.R. Harris, and D.P. McCarthy

Springer-Verlag
Berlin Heidelberg New York 1982

Editors

Michael J. Flynn
Computer Systems Laboratory
Stanford University
Stanford, CA 94305, USA

Neville R. Harris
Department of Computer Science
School of Engineering
Trinity College
University of Dublin
Dublin 2
Ireland

Daniel P. McCarthy
Department of Computer Science
School of Engineering
Trinity College
University of Dublin
Dublin 2
Ireland

AMS Subject Classifications (1979): 68-02, 68A05, 68B20
CR Subject Classifications (1981): 4.1, 4.2, 4.3, 6.1, 6.2, 6.3

ISBN 3-540-11172-7 Springer-Verlag Berlin Heidelberg New York
ISBN 0-387-11172-7 Springer-Verlag New York Heidelberg Berlin

2145/3140-543210

PREFACE

The main European tradition is for computer people to be educated in either the software or the hardware side of computing. The Computer Scientist graduates with his knowledge of operating systems, compilers, data structures, etc. and happily enters the field of software and has no contact with computer hardware except as a user. Engineers generally graduate with a knowledge of Electronics and very little knowledge of the software side.

The advent of microcomputers has seen the Computer Scientist trying to increase his hardware knowledge in order to implement systems. It has also seen the Engineer implementing large systems using assembly language or struggling with interfaces to operating systems and high level languages. It is now evident that in order to use microcomputers effectively system designers require a broad knowledge of computer hardware, interfacing, software, and design tools.

Because of this we proposed a microcomputer system design course which would integrate the hardware and software sides of microcomputers and bring together academics/practitioners from both disciplines. In 1979 a course proposal was made to the National Board of Science and Technology (N.B.S.T.) Ireland and to the Informatics Training Group of the EEC Scientific and Technical Research Committee (CREST). The proposal was enthusiastically received and supported.

Lecturers were chosen to cover the main areas of the syllabus and during the last week of September 1980 a week-long meeting took place in County Wicklow for the detailed planning. It was agreed that the syllabus should "span development from silicon technology to software and should bring together current techniques in LSI/VLSI design, computer structures and languages and show their application to, and implication for, microcomputer system designs". A detailed syllabus was prepared resulting in this set of course notes.

The course ran in July 1981 and had approximately 75 attendees from ten countries whose enthusiasm and interest made the program all the more interesting for all. A preliminary version of these notes was published at Trinity College for use in the course. This Springer-Verlag edition includes revisions based on presentations, corrections and some new material.

Acknowledgements:

With great pleasure we take this opportunity to express our gratitude and appreciation to:

- the EEC for their financial sponsorship and to the Informatics Training Group of the EEC Scientific and Technical Research Committee (CREST) for their support and encouragement.
- the National Board of Science and Technology for their financial sponsorship, advice and encouragement. In this regard special thanks are due to Dr. B. O'Shea.
- the lecturers for their full co-operation during the preparatory seminar, planning of the course, and submission of course notes and the course itself.
- Mrs. Janet Hogan, our Administrative Secretary, for her cheerful organisation of these course notes and her efficient, willing administration of the course.
- Professor J. G. Byrne, Head of Department of Computer Science, Mrs. H. Smith and Miss Susie Pakenham-Walsh, and to all the members of our staff who have helped in the organisation of this course.
- Prof. F. Sumner of the University of Manchester who provided early council on the course organization and lecturers. Events conspired to prevent him from a later, more direct involvement with the course.
- The course presentation was assisted by the use of several video taped lectures originally presented at Stanford University. We are grateful to the Stanford Computer Systems Laboratory for making these available and to the TCD Communications Centre for use of its video facilities during the course.

M. J. Flynn

N. R. Harris

D. P. McCarthy

TABLE OF CONTENTS

HIGH LEVEL SEQUENTIAL AND CONCURRENT PROGRAMMING

R. H. Perrott, Department of Computer Science, The Queen's University, Belfast.

MICROCOMPUTER OPERATING SYSTEMS

N. R. Harris, Department of Computer Science, Trinity College, University of Dublin, Dublin 2.

NOTES ON DISTRIBUTED SYSTEMS OF MICROPROCESSORS
G. J. Popek, University of California at Los Angeles

LILITH : A PERSONAL COMPUTER FOR THE SOFTWARE ENGINEER
N. Wirth, Federal Institute of Technology (ETH), Zurich.

PERSPECTIVE ON MICROCOMPUTERS

Michael J. Flynn
Department of Computer Science
Trinity College, Dublin
(on leave - Stanford University)

It is the thesis of this introduction, and indeed this Course, that the study of Microcomputers is not simply the study of very small computers. It is that the radical decrease in the cost of technology has significantly altered the designer's and user's view of realizing systems' applications.

From the point of view of the designer the Microcomputer is an integrated computer engineering discipline encompassing and relating such studies as:

- technology
- computer aided design (CAD)
- computer architecture
- operating systems
- language
- environment/function

From the users' point of view the Microcomputer is an amplifying systems component. Unlike simple signal amplifiers, the Microcomputer amplifies behaviour - or "intelligence" (Fig. 1). Given an input, i, the output is any response based on the behaviour of (i), (B(i)); not just a simple gain multiplier as in more familiar amplifiers. These components (designated μBj on Fig. 2 - representing the jth behaviour or programmed response to an input signal) may be connected in arbitary patterns to create complex system interactions. The reader will note the need for a new "circuit theory" - a theory of complex behaviour interaction.

Coupling these views is the realization that the more integration of function (behaviour) that occurs during the design the better the response (i.e. performance) of the system's component. Offsetting this is that the very integration specializes the resultant design, limiting its overall applicability and increasing effective per unit cost - since design costs are fixed. Only by reducing design costs (through CAD) can we hope to realize the potential inherent in the technology.

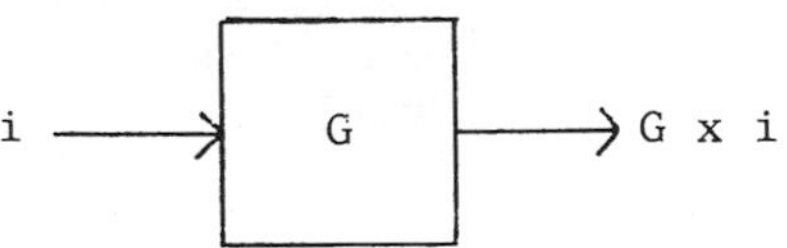

A familiar amplifier increase signal energy

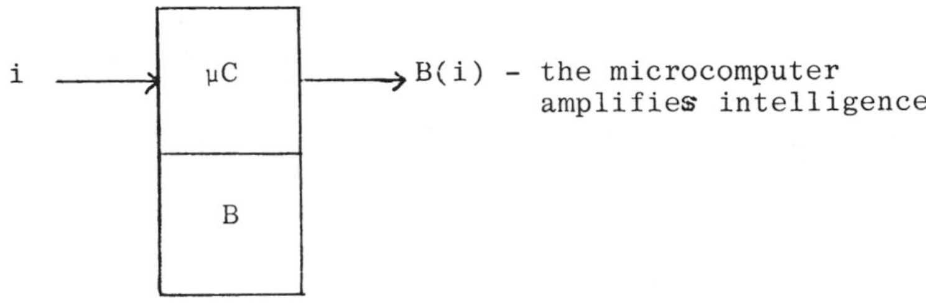

Figure 1 : Microcomputer : An intelligence amplifying component

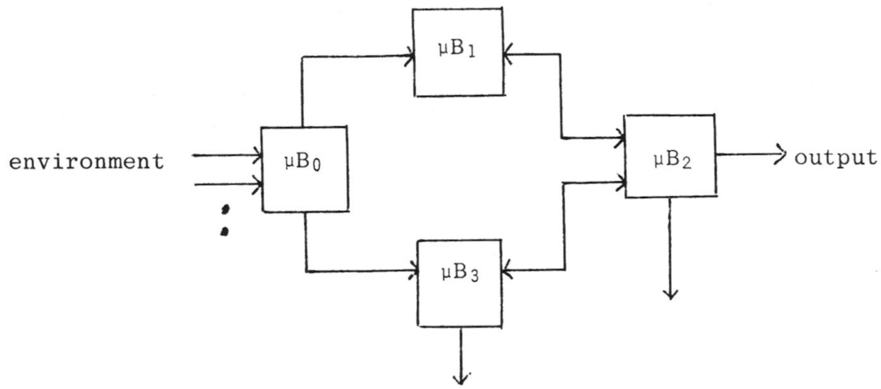

Figure 2 : Interconnected microcomputers

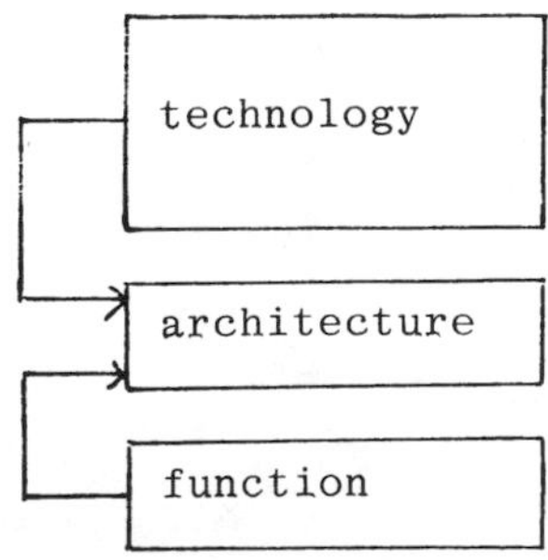

Figure 3 : Early computers

It is useful to review the changing nature of computer design in an historical perspective; to situate the Microcomputer environment.

Early computer development (pre-transistor)

Perhaps one might even call this the "classical period" of computer design because there was a relatively high degree of inter-disciplinary understanding on design (Fig. 3). With cost dominated by technology the architecture closely reflected the particular function within severe technological limitations: the "form closely followed the function". Of course designers considerations were much simplified by modern standards - there were no CAD, language or operating systems considerations. In these early systems the user was required to display considerable familiarity with the technology for efficient functional execution. For example, in many drum based computers proper placement of the next instruction depended on the execution time of the current instruction.

The Middle Ages - Batch Computing (Fig. 4)

As technology evolved and the cost per computation decreased secondary functions were taken over by the computer, viz. high level languages to improve programmer productivity, operating systems to manage system resources. By the early 1960's the "batch processing system" had fully evolved. In this environment the programmer would write a complete program in a suitable higher level language (only two were in really common use: Fortran and Cobol), submit it to the system which would translate all programs written in a particular language at the same time, then one by one load and execute them (batched together), and finally print all the results. The batch system was a further evolution in the recognition of the decreasing cost of the computer vis-a-vis the human being.

A few points about these early systems are worth recalling to mind.

The costs were dominated by the "system"; including processor technology, input-output equipment and the supporting management facilities. In fact, because the (human) management function was so important at this time it was very slow to respond to technology which would decentralize this responsibility. Even today the residue of this centralized "computer centre" management philosophy still persists.

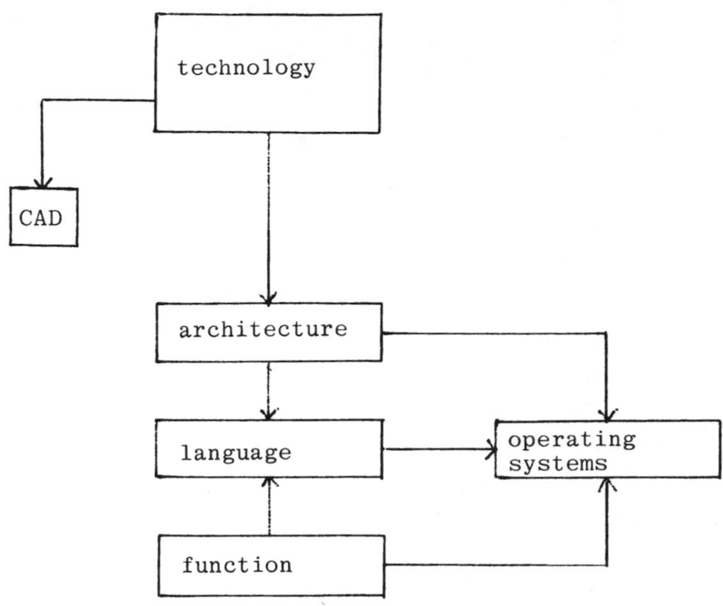

Figure 4 : Middle Ages - Batch Computing

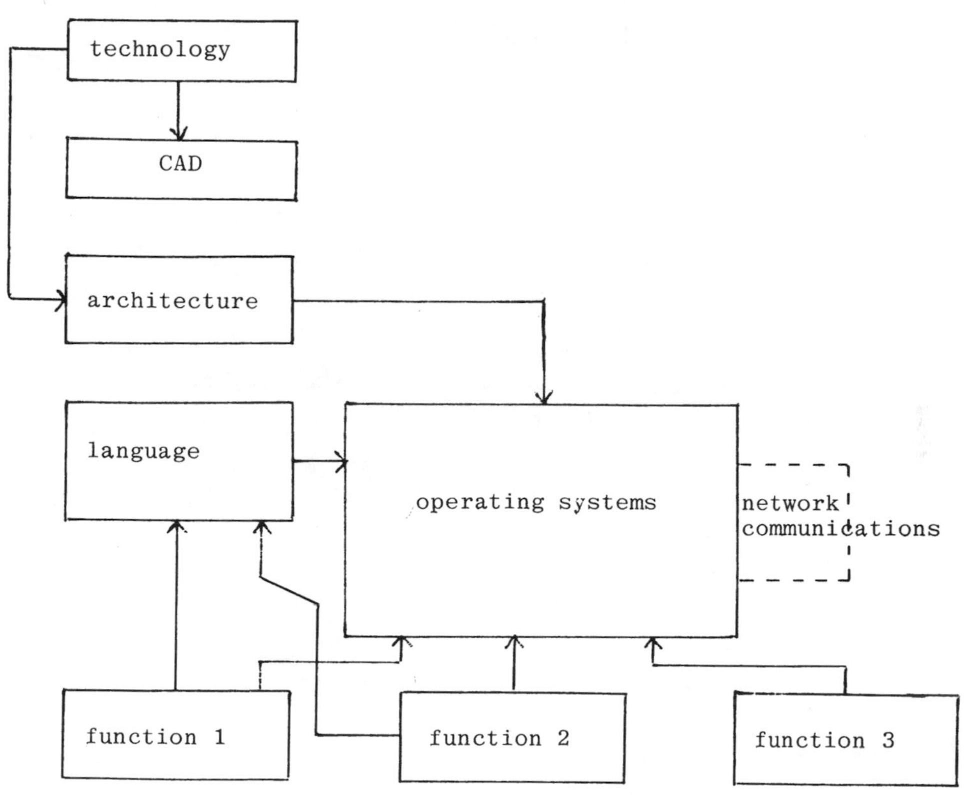

Figure 5 : Later Ages - Time Sharing

The genesis of CAD was developed at this time - mainly for the rather unglamorous role of production control. "Unglamorous", perhaps, but a number of otherwise successful commercial ventures failed due to the lack of systematic production (quality) control.

Early higher level languages were "low level" by latter standards - they were sensitive to machine architecture and execution performance.

The latter ages - "time sharing" and beyond (Fig. 5)

Within ten years the batch model had largely been replaced by the time sharing system. As processor technology costs continued to decline, the relative emphasis on direct user costs increased. Thus time sharing was introduced as an aid to programmer productivity accompanied by increasing diversity and sophistication in high level languages. Quick response to multiple users using diverse languages/functional environments required still further sophistication in operating systems. One may truly speak of this age as the "baroque" era of system design. The very complexity of such systems - especially the operating systems - designed to serve a universal user - is its great weakness. Again many commercial ventures failed because of inability to constrain the complexity and universality of the system.

Language design became almost as complex; with some (nameless) efforts proving to be equally unsuited to man or machine ("man and machine independent").

At the same time, CAD tools improved at a modest pace to include many useful hardware design aids - simulation, test, wiring printed circuit layout, etc.

VLSI - The era of distributed intelligence

Question : How does one design a system with a very low cost technology?
Answer : Use as much of it as you can.

The message for today's designers is to distribute function/capability through low cost technology while sharing only expensive resources (e.g. centralized data banks). But, as many have already noticed, neither a small computer or program is "small" when fully situated with interface hardware and software. Clearly, the interface problem limits the applicability of the technology. And design costs limit the use of the technology in solving the interface problem. The CAD of earlier times is inadequate in coping with the complex requirements of modern technology. Linear improvements in minimizing a feature dimension result in a squared improvement in logic per unit area. Increases in logic gates increase the CAD complexity (for layout, simulation, test, etc.) by a power function.

Some problems (and opportunities) for the VLSI era

The growth in complexity illustrated by CAD (above) continues the higher one goes into the design process - architecture, operating systems, language - but it is basically also an increase in design opportunity, the ability to realize complex design which would have been otherwise infeasible.

We can summarize some of these problems/opportunities as follows:

1. CAD tools to allow ready use (verified and testable) of the technology.
2. Architectural designs which are optimized to the execution of particular language/operating system environments.
3. Operating systems which provide efficient local services as well as reliable communications to central resources.
4. Languages which are matched to function (comprehensible by both man and machine).
5. Data communications networks which are flexible and reliable and allow a variable balance between distributed and central intelligence.

The above is certainly not a comprehensive list - it is a departure point for those participating in the use of these notes and lectures.

The ant

We are frequently concerned with the limits of technology - the ultimate number or speed of logic gates per unit volume or energy. A more interesting question concerns the limits of design - independent of technology: our ability to represent ideas, languages and architectures. If we confront today's technologist with the possibility of a 100,000 gate chip, each gate switching with energy of 1pJ(1×10^{-12}

watt-seconds), he would certainly regard this as highly probable, if not now, then in the not far distant future. Yet the brain of the common ant consists of 100,000 neurons, each switching with energy of about 1pJ. And the architect/designer would not be at all sanguine about duplicating anything like the sophistication or complexity of such a creature. Thus even with the advantage of over a million times in speed (logic gates are much faster and use correspondingly more power than neurons giving the same energy product), we - the users of technology - have a long way to go before approaching a design limit.

Well, perhaps with several hundred million years of engineering effort ......

INTEGRATED CIRCUIT PHYSICS AND TECHNOLOGY

J. F. Gibbons and J. D. Shott
Stanford Electronic Laboratories
Stanford University

Stanford, CA 94305/USA

Our purpose in these lectures is to introduce the physical principles on which integrated circuit behavior depends and to show how semiconductor technology is employed to fabricate integrated circuits that behave according to these principles. Our presentation of this subject will necessarily be highly condensed and oversimplified. However, the analysis to be offered is conceptually correct and in any case is intended to provide only a broad understanding of the role that semiconductor physics and technology play in the solution of electronic systems problems. References are provided for those wishing a deeper appreciation of the topics to be presented.

We will begin with a discussion of the basic principles of MOS integrated circuits, leading to a discussion of both CMOS gate arrays and the "sticks" approach to IC chip design that has been so successfully pioneered by Mead and Conway. We follow this discussion with an outline of the fabrication processes that are used to make integrated circuits. We conclude with a discussion of bipolar digital technology and some remarks that compare this technology with its MOS counterpart.

1. Basic Principles of MOS Devices and Integrated Circuits

1.1 What is a Semiconductor ?

Solid state materials can be divided broadly into three categories: conductors (i.e., metals), semiconductors, and insulators. Integrated circuits contain representatives of each of these types of material. However it is the special properties of crystalline semiconductors that provide the signal amplification and switching characteristics that are necessary for the construction of electronic systems. It is therefore appropriate to begin with a brief description of those properties of crystalline semiconductors that are essential to the operation of integrated circuits.

The Conduction Process. On a microscopic scale, current consists of a flow of charged particles, called carriers. The flow of electrons in a metal in response to an applied electric field is a familiar example. Metals have an abundance of free electrons, that is, electrons which can readily move within the material. Because the number of free electrons is large, metals can conduct currents readily with the application of very small electric fields.

At the opposite extreme is the class of solids called insulators, in which the electrons form highly localized bonds that hold the solid together. These electrons are not free to move in response to an electric field.

A semiconductor is intermediate between these two extremes. In semiconductors, the vast majority of the electrons are involved in insulator-like bonding configurations and are not free to conduct a current. However, electrons are occasionally released from these bonding configurations, and they are then free to move away from their bonding sites, providing that the crystal itself is sufficiently ideal (i.e., the atoms that comprise the solid are in regular crystalline positions over very large distances). Furthermore, it is possible to control the relative number of free and bound electrons by chemical doping of the material. This control is the basis for semiconductor device operation. Hence it is profitable to examine more closely the nature of free and bound electrons in semiconductors and the process of chemical doping by which this ratio is controlled.

Bonding Electrons and Free Electrons. A single silicon atom has an effective nuclear charge of +4q and four valence electrons (q is the charge on an electron). The geometry of a silicon crystal follows a tetrahedral pattern, with each atom sharing one valence electron with each of four neighboring atoms. The covalent bonds required in this configuration are shown schematically in Fig. 1. At temperatures close to absolute zero, all of the valence electrons for silicon are utilized in the formation of these covalent bonds and are thus unavailable for carrying a current: i.e., silicon is an insulator at T = 0°K. To make current flow possible, it is necessary to either add electrons not involved in crystal bonding, or else to free some of the electrons from their bonds by some means.

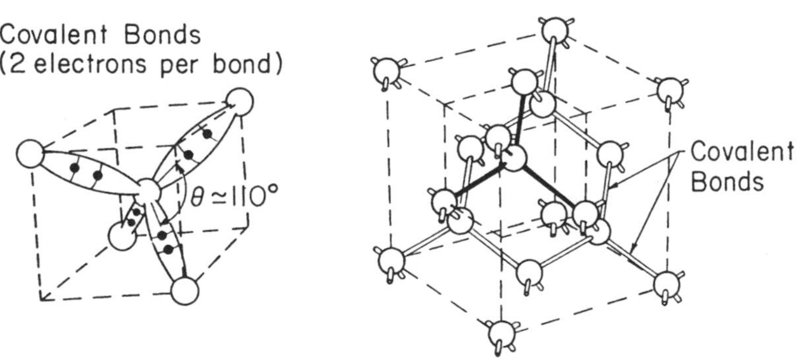

Figure 1 Silicon Crystal Structure.

If sufficient energy is supplied to a bonding electron in the form of either heat or light, that bonding electron can be set free as suggested in Fig. 2. The resulting free electron, because it is not now confined to a local bond, can move through the crystal in much the same way that an electron moves through a metallic crystal. Furthermore, when a covalent bond is ionized (Fig. 2), a vacancy or hole is left in the original bond. The region in which this vacancy exists has a net positive charge. Then, if a valence electron from a nearby covalent bond fills the hole (without first gaining sufficient energy to become "free"), the vacancy will appear in a new place in the crystal. The effect is then as if a positive charge (of magnitude q) has moved through the crystal.

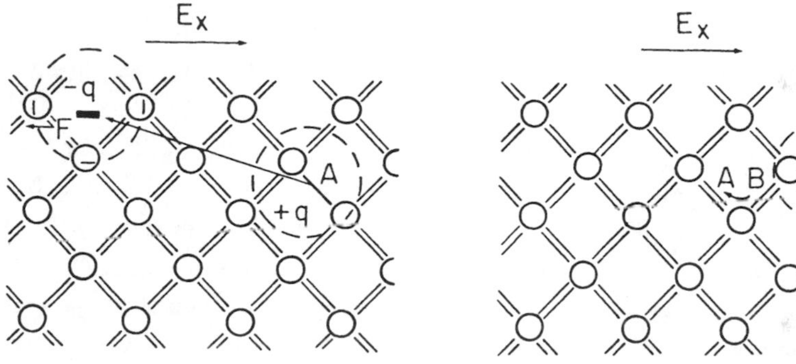

(a) Creation of free electron and hole by bond-breaking event.

(b) Hole motion obtained by transport of valence electrons.

Figure 2 Illustrating the creation and motion of free electons and holes.

We see then that when a bond is broken, two kinds of carriers are produced: both free electrons and holes are created, and both are able to move through the crystal in response to an applied electric field and thus carry a current. The process of creation of electrons and holes (whether by thermal, optical or some other process) is called carrier generation. It should be realized that there is a corresponding reverse process called recombination, in which a free electron hops into a hole in the valence structure, annihilating both particles. At any given temperature, covalent bonds are constantly being broken by thermal excitation, and free electrons and holes are constantly recombining. These processes balance each other at some particular concentration of holes and electrons.

Quantitatively, the average thermal energy of each atom and electron in a crystal at absolute temperature T is $\sim$ kT, where k is Boltzmann's constant. The value of kT at room temperature (300°K) is $\sim$ 0.026 eV. Since the energy of an electron in a covalent bond in silicon is 1.1 eV at room temperature, or about 40 times larger than kT, it follows that very few bonding electrons can gain enough thermal energy to escape. Hence the bond breaking process will occur very infrequently at room temperature. The number of free electrons and holes in a pure silicon crystal at room temperature will therefore be small (a factor of $\sim 10^{13}$ smaller than the concentration of electrons in a metal).

<u>Doping Chemistry</u>. In practical applications, chemical impurities, called <u>dopants</u>, are introduced into the silicon to increase the concentration of electrons or holes. Elements from Group Va of the periodic table are introduced to increase the concentration of free electrons, while elements from Group IIIa may be introduced to increase the concentration of holes. Figure 3 illustrates the effect of adding an element from Column Va. Such a doping agent has five valence electrons and an effective nuclear charge of +5q. When this atom replaces a silicon atom in the crystal lattice, only four of the five valence electrons are used to complete covalent bonds. The remaining electron still experiences a Coulomb attraction to its parent nucleus, though the effects of all the other surrounding nuclei and electrons are such that this fifth electron can be separated from its parent nucleus with the addition of only a small amount of energy (typically 0.01 eV as compared to the 1.1 eV required to break a covalent bond). More precisely, since the binding energy E_d for this fifth electron is $\lesssim$ kT, it can be set free at the temperature at which silicon operates in an integrated circuit. Hence, to a first approximation, we obtain one free electron for each phosphorus atom introduced into the crystal. Doping with phosphorus thus succeeds in creating a silicon crystal with an abundance of <u>n</u>egatively charged carriers, which we call an n-type semiconductor. It is important to emphasize that each electron that is set free from its parent atom leaves behind a net <u>immobile</u> charge of +q (the extra unit of positive charge on the Group V nucleus compared to the silicon nucleus it replaced).

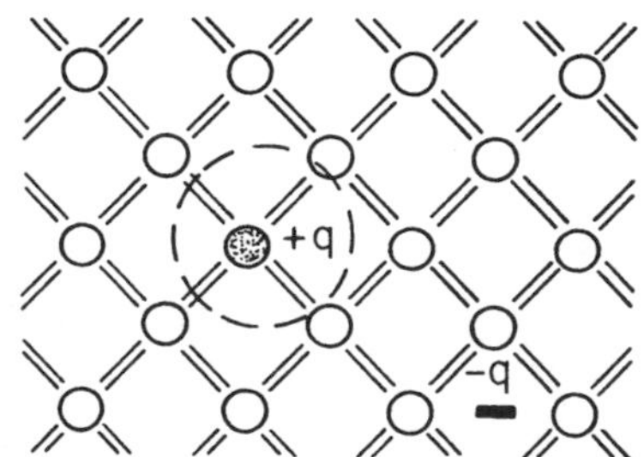

Figure 3 Group Va impurity atom (bound in the lattice) and fifth valence electron.

If a small amount of an element from Column III is added (aluminum, boron, gallium or indium), a p-type semiconductor is obtained. For example, when boron replaces silicon in the crystal lattice (Fig. 4), only three valence electrons are available to complete covalent bonds. If the remaining unfilled covalent bond is filled by a valence electron from a neighboring atom, a mobile hole is introduced into the lattice. The region surrounding the doping atom then has a fixed charge of -q, while the region surrounding the hole contains a charge of +q.

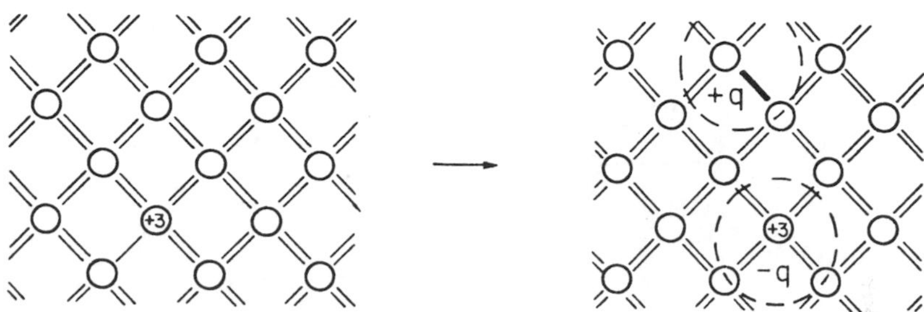

(a) Group IIIa atom (bound in lattice) and hole at absolute zero.

(b) Group IIIa atom (bound in lattice) with hole moved.

Figure 4 Creation of holes by Group IIIa Doping of Silicon.

From the preceding discussion we see that it is possible to produce two <u>different</u> types of conductivity by incorporating appropriate dopants. In an n-type silicon crystal, phosphorus or arsenic (Group Va) doping will produce a high concentration of free electrons and fixed positive charge (the phosphorus or arsenic atoms). The recombination process will cause the hole density to be low in such a crystal. Similarly, in a p-type silicon crystal, boron (Group IIIa) doping produces a large hole concentration and the recombination process assures that the electron concentration will be very small. Hence, while an intrinsic (undoped) crystal has equal numbers of holes and electrons, the doping process produces a situation in which one of these carrier types is far more numerous than the other. A doped semiconductor is thus, for most purposes, either n-type or p-type, depending on the selection of the dopant.

1.2 The MOS Capacitor: Depletion Mode

With these ideas in mind, we turn now to a description of the basic device which controls current flow in MOS transistors. This device is an MOS capacitor, and is shown schematically in Fig. 5. For illustration, we study a capacitor fabricated on a p-type single crystal substrate. To make the capacitor we first grow a thin layer of silicon dioxide (SiO_2) on the silicon crystal. A metal film or a very heavily doped layer of polycrystalline silicon is then deposited on the oxide and patterned to form the control electrode for the MOS capacitor. The procedures used to fabricate the oxide and the control electrode will be discussed in more detail in Section 3.

The operation of the capacitor can be deduced from an application of Gauss' law, taken together with the properties of a semiconductor just discussed. For this purpose, let us first suppose that we apply a negative voltage between the semiconductor and the

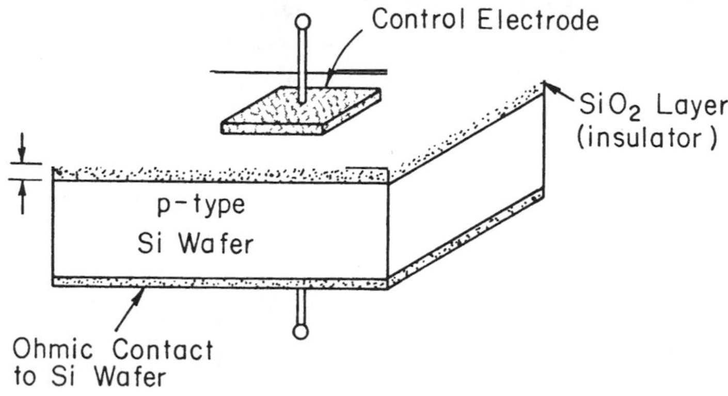

Figure 5 Structure of an MOS Capacitor on p-type Si.

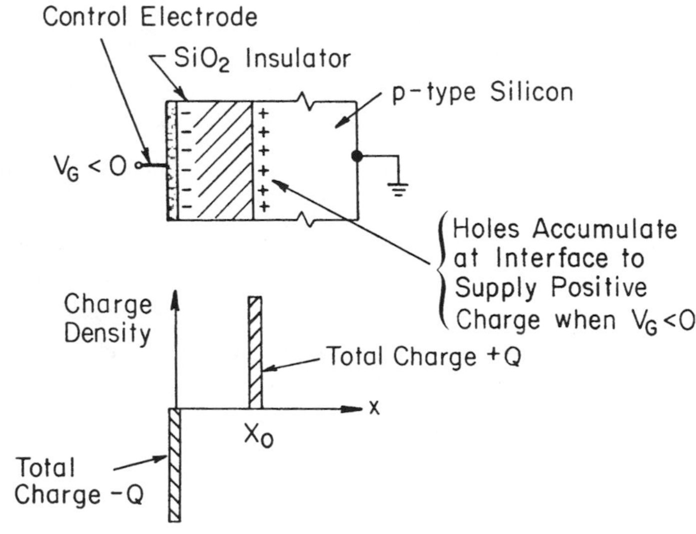

Figure 6 An MOS Capacitor as Simple Parallel Plate Capacitor.

control electrode, as shown in Fig. 6. Application of such a voltage will result in a negative charge -Q appearing on the metal plate. A positive charge (equal in magnitude to the negative charge) must then be developed within the semiconductor. Since the semiconductor is p-type, and therefore has a large number of mobile holes, this positive charge can be obtained by simply letting holes flow from the semiconductor to the interface between the silicon and the silicon dioxide. Since the silicon dioxide is an insulator (so cannot pass a current), holes will not be able to flow through it but will simply accumulate at the interface. Hence, application of the voltage produces a dipole layer of charge, just as would occur in a normal parallel plate capacitor.

If we reverse the polarity of the applied voltage, then we will introduce a positive charge +Q on the control electrode, and we must then find a <u>negative</u> charge of equal magnitude in the semiconductor. Now, since the semiconductor is p-type, the principal sources of charge within it are the boron doping atoms and the mobile holes introduced by these doping atoms. As suggested in Fig. 4, in the process of creating a hole, each boron atom contributes a net charge of -q to the semiconductor crystal. We may therefore obtain the necessary negative charge by pushing holes away from the interface so as to reveal the negative charge associated with the boron atoms. Briefly, we say that holes have to be <u>depleted</u> from a layer of the silicon near the interface to a depth x_d that is sufficient to produce a net negative charge in the semiconductor of magnitude Q (Fig. 7). The force causing this depletion is the electric field originating on the positive charge supplied to the control electrode. It follows from this description that if the charge on the control electrode is doubled, then the <u>thickness</u> of the depletion region will be doubled, so that the negative charge in the semiconductor is once again equal to the positive charge on the control electrode. (An alternative view is that the applied voltage creates an electric field in the SiO_2 layer that requires a positive charge on the control electrode and an equal negative charge in the semiconductor. The positive charge is then obtained by hole flow from the semiconductor through the battery to the control electrode.)

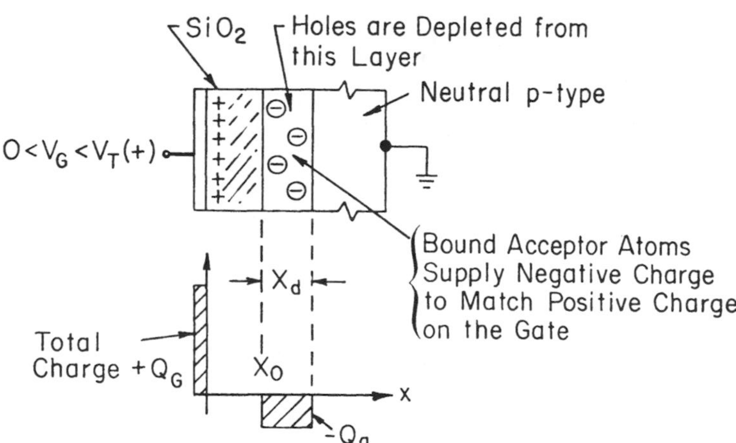

Figure 7 MOS Capacitor in Depletion Mode.

1.3 A Depletion Mode MOSFET

It is important to realize that the material lying beneath the depletion region in in Fig. 7 is unaffected by the electric fields created by the charge on the control electrode; that is, the hole concentration in the undepleted portion of the semiconductor has the same value that it did in the absence of the applied bias. This fact can be used to explain the operation of an MOS <u>depletion mode</u> transistor. A schematic illustration of the structure is shown in Fig. 8. The device is essentially an MOS capacitor with "side contacts" made to the p-type semiconductor region. These contacts permit current to flow through the undepleted region of the semiconductor. The contacts are visualized as being "p+", which means they are very heavily doped with boron so as to readily supply holes for current flow in the p-type silicon.

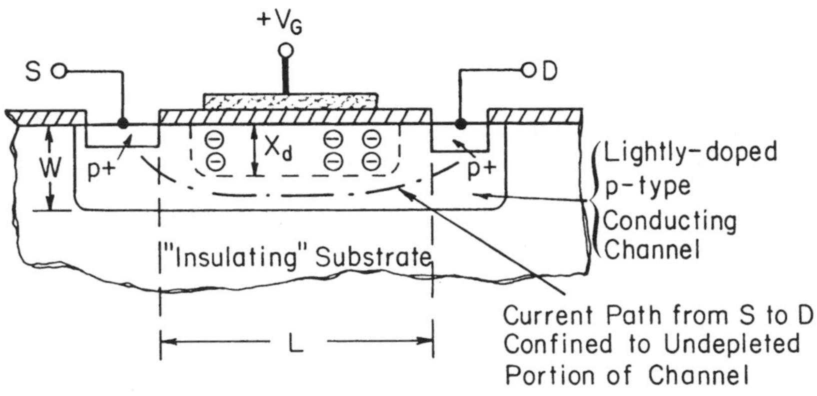

Figure 8 Depletion Mode MOSFET.

If the control electrode in this structure is left unbiased (floating), then the entire width of the p-type conducting channel is available for conduction between the source S and the drain D. If, however, a positive voltage is applied to the gate (with respect to the semiconductor), then a depletion layer is produced. The flow of holes from one contact to the other is then restricted to the undepleted portion of the semiconductor. It follows that the resistance of the conducting channel connecting the source and drain contacts is increased (because the thickness of the conducting channel is reduced by an amount equal to the thickness of the depletion layer). If the depletion layer is made to extend all the way across the semiconductor, the device is said to be pinched off, and no current will flow between the two contacts. In effect, then, application of a positive voltage between the gate and the semiconductor (in practice between the gate and source terminals of the device) controls the flow of current from source to drain by controlling the thickness of the region through which the carriers may flow. Depletion mode transistors will be used as load resistors in the NMOS IC technology to be described later. They are called MOS field effect transistors (MOSFETS) because the electric field created on the control electrode controls the channel resistance.

1.4 The MOS Capacitor: Inversion Mode

In the previous discussion we have neglected one possible source of negative charge in the silicon; i.e., electrons. Neglecting electrons is permissible in a neutral p-type semiconductor because the hole concentration is sufficiently large to keep the electron concentration low by means of the electron-hole recombination process. However, in the depletion region just discussed, the hole concentration has been reduced well below its equilibrium value. This suppresses the recombination process, so it may no longer be a permissible to neglect electrons as a source of negative charge.

To give a somewhat more refined view, we show in Fig. 9(a) an MOS capacitor in the depletion mode, where the hole concentration is depicted as decreasing rapidly but not abruptly as we proceed from the semiconductor body toward the Si/SiO_2 interface. In the depletion approximation, holes are considered to be fully depleted from the interface to a depth x_d; and at their equilibrium concentration for $x > x_d$ [dashed line in Fig. 9(a)]. Such an abrupt change in hole concentration at x_d is, however, nonphysical, because holes can diffuse from the undepleted material back in the depletion layer. Thus an equilibrium must be established between the electric field (which tends to push holes out of the depletion region) and the diffusion tendency (which transports holes from regions of high concentration to region of lower concentration). The result is the hole concentration profile shown by the solid line in Fig. 9(a). In this case the hole density at the Si/SiO_2 interface is reduced significantly below its equilibrium value, but not to zero. The effective width of the depletion layer is still x_d.

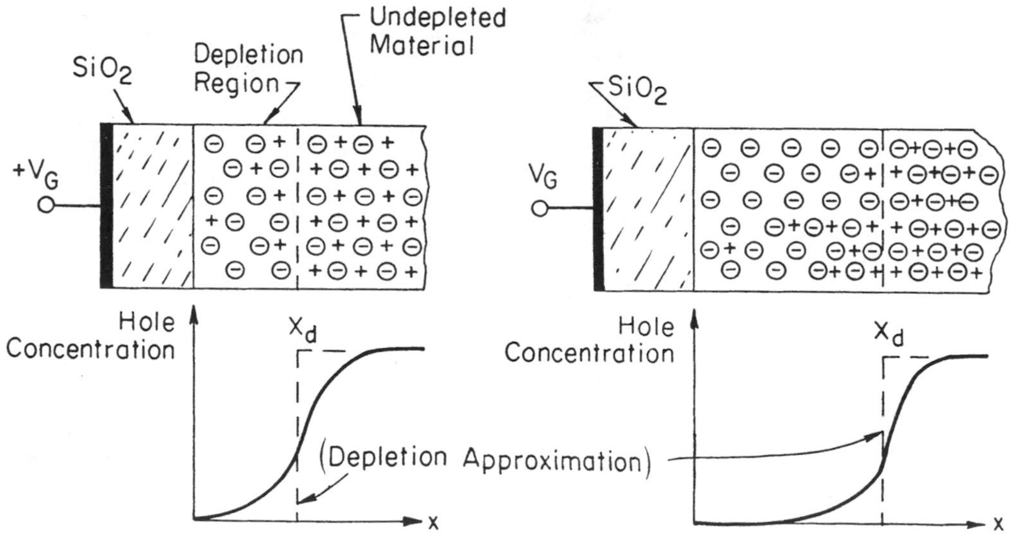

(a) Depletion Mode: low V_G (b) Depletion Mode for larger V_G.

Figure 9 Hole Concentration Profiles in the Depletion Region.

If we now increase the charge on the control electrode, the effective width of the depletion layer will increase as suggested in Fig. 9(b) and the mobile hole concentration at each point in the depletion layer will be reduced. In particular, the hole concentration at the Si/SiO_2 interface decreases continuously (and rapidly) as the charge on the control electrode is increased.

Electron-hole pairs are of course always being generated in the semiconductor by thermal processes. As indicated above, when the hole concentration is high, the electron concentration will be low because of recombination. However, when the hole concentration is reduced at the Si/SiO_2 interface sufficiently, the recombination process will also be suppressed, and it then becomes possible for electrons to build up a substantial charge density at this interface. In the quantitative theory of the MOS capacitor, it can be shown that this <u>surface accumulation</u> of electrons becomes an important source of negative charge when the voltage drop across the depleted portion of the silicon reaches approximately 0.7 V. The voltage that must be applied between the control electrode and the semiconductor to produce this condition is called the <u>threshold voltage</u> and given the symbol V_T. The exact value of V_T will depend on the thickness of the oxide as well as the doping conditions within the semiconductor and can be controlled by the fabrication technology.

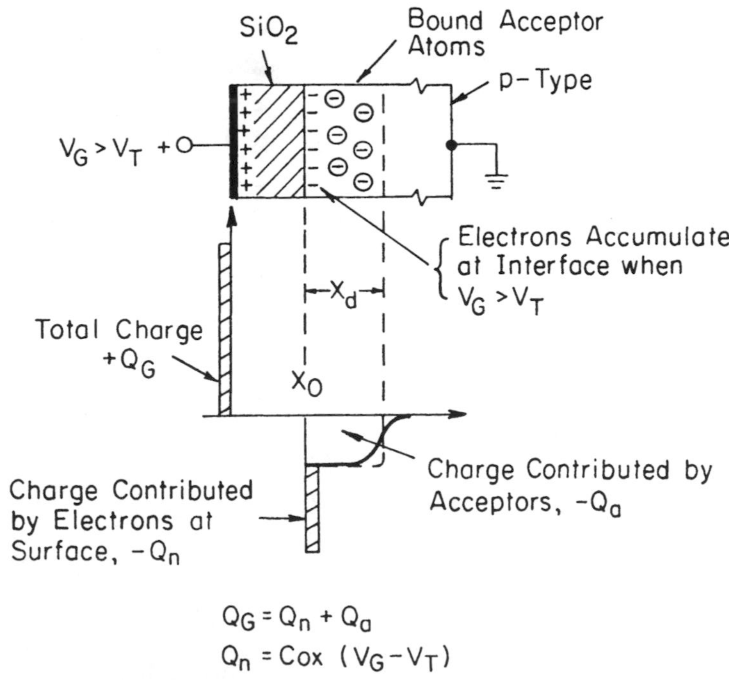

$$Q_G = Q_n + Q_a$$
$$Q_n = Cox\ (V_G - V_T)$$

Figure 10 MOS Capacitor in Inversion Mode.

The essential result of the description just given is summarized in Fig. 10, where we show an MOS capacitor operating with an applied voltage in excess of the threshold voltage. For this case some of the negative charge required in the semiconductor is obtained from boron atoms in the depletion layer, as before; and the remainder of the negative charge is obtained by the accumulation of electrons in a thin layer at the Si/SiO_2 interface. There are thus two components of negative charge in the semiconductor when the voltage applied across the MOS capacitor exceeds the threshold value. The capacitor is then said to be operating in the inversion mode.

To summarize:

- When $V_G < V_T$, all of the negative charge required in the semiconductor comes from hole depletion over a thickness x_d
- when $V_G > V_T$, all of the additional negative charge comes from electron accumulation at the Si/SiO_2 interface.

1.5 The Enhancement Mode MOSFET

By analogy with the depletion mode device, we can make an enhancement mode device by simply arranging to make "ohmic contact" to the electrons that accumulate at the Si/ SiO_2 interface. We can accomplish this objective in the manner shown in Fig. 11, by introducing two heavily doped n-type regions (phosphorus or arsenic doping) at either end of the MOS capacitor surface where electron accumulation occurs. In effect, these source and drain contact wells are isolated from each other in the absence of voltage applied to the gate of the device, since they are separated by a p region that contains very few electrons. However, when sufficient voltage is applied between the gate and the p-type semiconductor to produce substantial electron accumulation at the Si/SiO_2 interface, then electrons can flow from the source along this surface-oriented electron

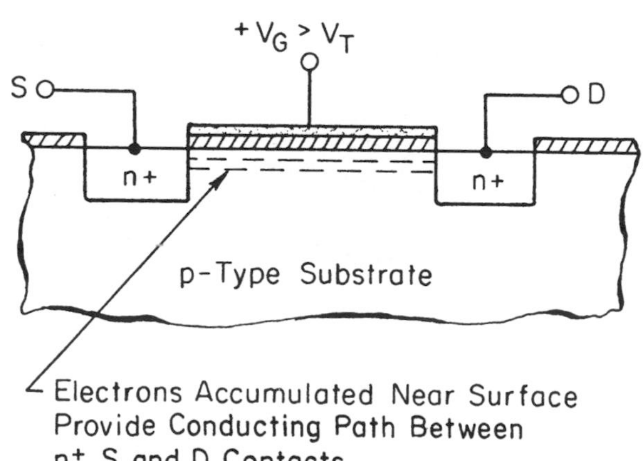

Figure 11 Enhancement Mode MOSFET.

channel to the drain. In effect, the MOS capacitor has provided a surface conduction channel that permits current to flow between source and drain contacts that are otherwise isolated. Such a device is OFF until a sufficient voltage is applied to the gate ($> V_T$), after which conduction is possible. The resistance in the conduction path can be reduced as far as is desired by applying a sufficient gate voltage and thereby accumulating a sufficient number of electrons in the source-drain channel region. In practice, the source terminal and the semiconductor body are connected together so that the voltage required to form the electron accumulation layer may be applied between the gate and the source.

It is of course also possible to make complementary devices to those just discussed by starting with an n-type semiconductor. This will lead to an n-type depletion mode device, in which electrons rather than holes are the (majority) carriers that flow in the undepleted channel; and an enhancement mode device in which holes are accumulated at the surface. p+ source and drain contact wells must then be fabricated to permit current to flow in this surface-oriented p-type channel.

1.6 Fabrication of Compatible Enhancement-Depletion Pairs

Frequently, we use an n-type depletion mode device as a load resistor for an n-channel enhancement mode switch. We wish to fabricate these two devices as close to each other as possible on the silicon chip, and therefore have the problem of providing n-type doping for the depletion mode device in a semiconductor that must be basically p-type for the enhancement mode device. This problem is normally solved by introducing n-type dopants directly into the surface regions of a p-type crystal by a process called ion implantation (to be described later). In Fig. 12, we show an n-channel depletion mode device which is geometrically very similar to its companion enhancement

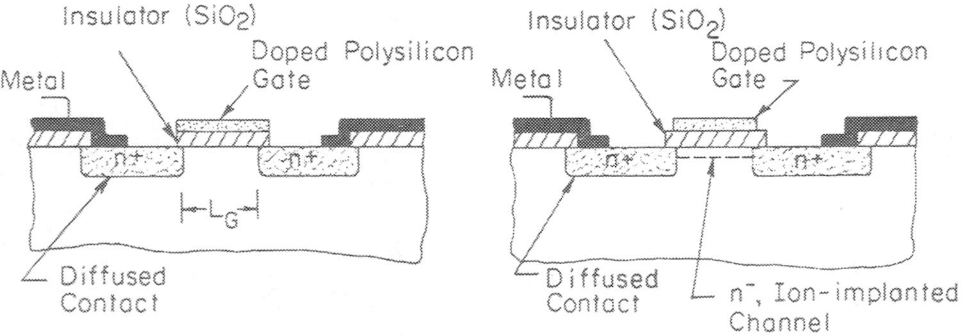

mode device with the exception that the electrons that form the channel between the n+ source and drain regions are now introduced by <u>surface doping</u> rather than electron accumulation in the surface regions. In practice, the ion implantation step is performed first over a limited area where the depletion device is to be fabricated. Source and drain contact wells are then fabricated for both enhancement and depletion mode devices at a later step in the process.

1.7 Drain Characteristics for MOS Transistors (MOSFETS)

A relatively simple derivation of the electrical characteristics of these devices at their terminals can be obtained by considering the charge that moves between the source and drain when a voltage is applied. To facilitate this development we show first (Fig. 13) an enhancement mode device in which the gate has a length L (between source and drain) and a width W.

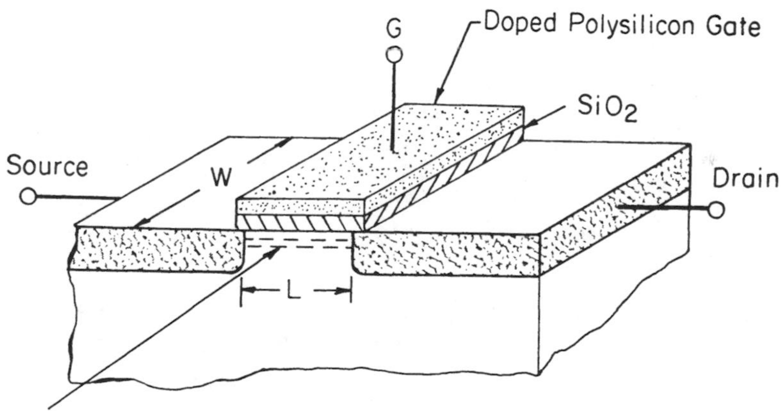

Figure 13 Enhancement Mode MOSFET With Gate Length L and Width W.

In the absence of any charge on the gate, the drain-to-source path along the surface is like an open switch. The gate, separated from the substrate by the thin layer of oxide, forms a capacitor. If the voltage applied to this capacitor between gate and source, V_{GS}, exceeds the threshold voltage V_T, then electrons will accumulate in the surface regions and will contribute a charge Q_n, where

$$Q_n = C_{ox} (V_{GS} - V_T) \tag{1}$$

C_{ox} is the capacitance of the oxide layer that lies between the gate electrode and the semiconductor.

The charge Q_n forms a conducting channel from source to drain so that a current can flow when a voltage V_{DS} is applied between these two terminals. The current which flows is equal to

$$I = Q_n/\tau \tag{2}$$

where τ is the transit time or the average time required for an electron to move from source to drain. The transit time is in turn the distance the electron has to move (L) divided by its average velocity, v_n. When the drain-to-source V_{DS} voltage is small, this average velocity is proportional to the electric field that exists along the channel between source and drain. Formally,

$$v_n = \mu_n E = (\mu_n V_{DS})/L \tag{3}$$

where in the last equality we have expressed the electric field E as being the drain to source voltage V_{ds} divided by the gate length L. The parameter μ_n is the carrier mobility and is known for each semiconductor and carrier type.

Combining Eqs. (1-3), we see that (for small values of the drain to source voltage), the drain to source current can be written in the form

$$I_{DS} = \frac{\mu_n C_{ox}}{L^2} (V_{GS} - V_T) V_{DS} \tag{4}$$

This equation suggests that for a given value of V_{DS}, the current flowing along the channel will increase in proportion to the charge that exists in the channel as a result of applied gate to source voltage. However this formula proves to be inaccurate for large values of V_{DS}. In particular, when V_{DS} is increased to the value $(V_{GS} - V_T)$, the drain current is found to saturate at the value

$$I_{DS} = \frac{\mu_n C_{ox}}{2L^2} (V_{GS} - V_T)^2 \tag{5}$$

The source-to-drain transit time is also found to saturate, placing a limit on the device speed that is obtainable in MOS circuits of given geometry.

The drain characteristics of an n-channel enhancement mode device that follow from the above analysis are shown in Fig. 14, assuming a 5V operating supply voltage and a threshold voltage of 1V.

A similar analysis can be applied to a depletion mode device by simply observing that the surface doping process (ion implantation) introduces a total charge Q_0 into the channel, thereby contributing Q_0 electrons in the absence of applied gate voltage. If a negative voltage is applied to the gate, this implanted channel is partly depleted so that the residual mobile charge is

$$Q_n' = Q_o - C_{ox} V_{GS}$$

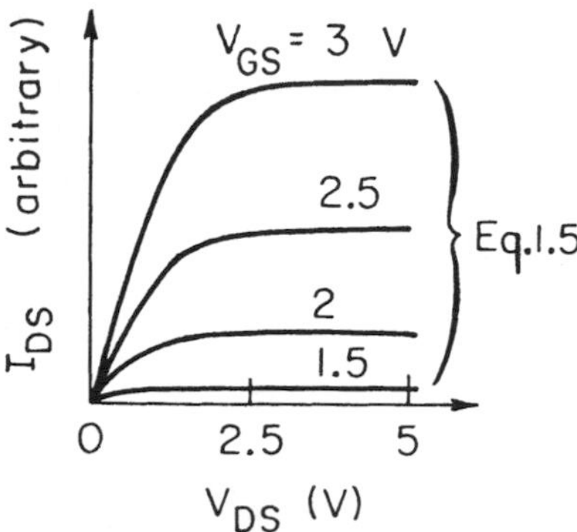

Figure 14 Drain Characteristics MOSFET. of n Channel Enhancement Mode MOSFET. V_T = 1V.

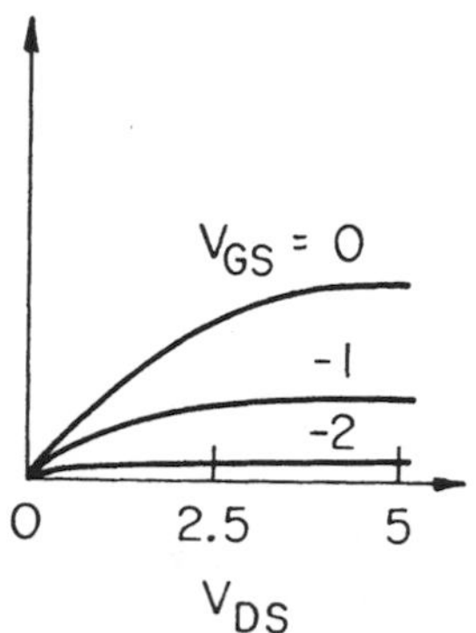

Figure 15 Drain Characteristics for n Channel Depletion Mode MOSFET. V_p = 4V.

The corresponding current for low values of drain to source voltage is

$$I_{DS} = (Q_o - C_{ox} V_{GS})/$$

A saturation phenomenon similar to that described for the enhancement device also occurs as V_{DS} is increased, leading to the I-V characteristics shown in Fig. 15.

1.8 Basic MOS Integrated Circuit Inverters

There are two common MOSFET inverter circuits around which the vast majority of MOS technology is presently developed. These are called CMOS and NMOS inverters, respectively. Their operation can be understood by first discussing a simple inverter made from an enhancement mode MOSFET switch and a resistive load, as shown in Fig. 16. When the input voltage to the inverter is less than the threshold voltage, the enhancement mode device is OFF (no conducting channel is formed) and the output voltage will

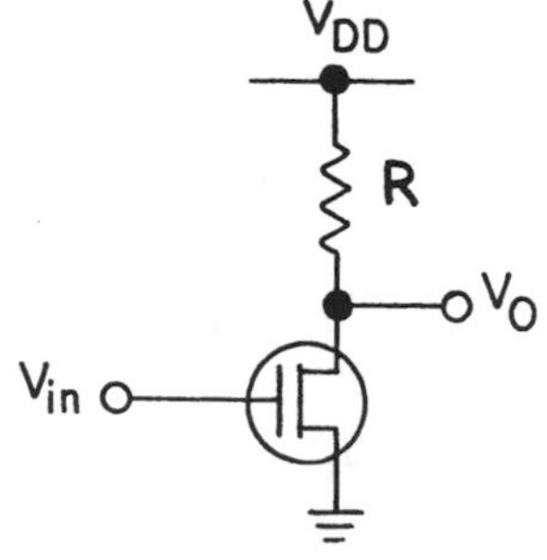

Figure 16 Logic Inverter With n-Channel Enhancement Mode MOSFET and Resistor.

be equal to the supply voltage, V_{DD}. If the input voltage exceeds the threshold voltage for the enhancement device by a sufficient amount to accumulate a substantial charge in the channel, then the channel resistance will be low compared to R and the output voltage will drop significantly. By appropriate design, the output voltage in this circuit can be made to be well below the threshold voltage for the next enhancement mode device, so the output of the inverter can be considered as the complement of its input.

The fabrication of large value resistors such as are required in this circuit is, however, difficult except by the ion implantation process, so in fact the resistor shown in Fig. 16 is realized by fabricating a depletion mode transistor as the load element. This pair of transistors is called an <u>NMOS inverter</u>. Its transfer characteristic can be obtained by appropriately combining the drain characteristics for the two devices in the manner illustrated in Fig. 17. The gate of the depletion mode device is connected to its source during fabrication so V_{GS} = 0. The vertical axis in this figure is left in arbitrary units since the relative dimensions of the depletion and enhancement mode device have not been specified.

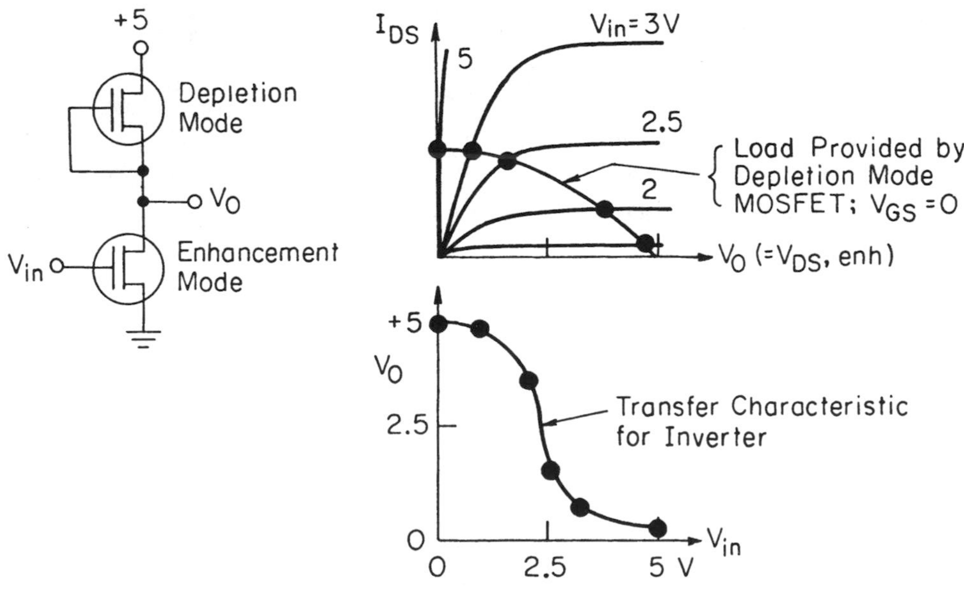

Figure 17 Illustrating the Development of the Transfer Characteristic of an NMOS Inverter.

A variety of transfer characteristics can be obtained by adjusting the geometry of the devices in the NMOS inverter. From a fabrication standpoint such an adjustment is made by making the length of the depletion mode gate several times that of the enhancement mode gate. Since the depletion mode device causes the output of the inverter to be pulled up to the power supply voltage when the enhancement mode device is OFF, the depletion mode device is called the "pull-up", while the enhancement mode device is called the "pull-down". The transfer characteristics are thus a function of L_{pu}/L_{pd}. Analysis of the inverter shows that $L_{pu} \sim 4L_{pd}$ will produce a reasonably symmetrical transfer characteristic.

An alternative to the use of a depletion mode pull-up is to fabricate a p-channel enhancement mode pull-up and to operate it with its gate connected to that of the n-channel enhancement mode pull-down, as suggested in Fig. 18. For this connection, if the input voltge is LOW, then the p-channel enhancement mode device has $V_{GS} > V_T$. This device is therefore ON and the inverter output is connected to the supply voltage through the p channel. Alternatively, if the input voltage is high, then the n-channel pull-down device is ON, the p-channel pull-up is OFF, and the output of the inverter is connected through the n-channel pull-down to ground. Such an inverter is called a CMOS inverter since it uses two complementary devices (one p channel and the other n channel) to obtain the desired transfer characteristic. A central advantage of this circuit over its NMOS counterpart is that in the steady state there is no connection from V_{DD} to ground, and hence no steady state power dissipation. There is of course power consumed during switching operations (in either inverter). However, this is the only (or at least the major) source of power consumption in a CMOS integrated circuit and therefore these circuits are selected when power dissipation is critical. This may be because the power source is limited (a battery); or because we wish to minimize heat dissipation in the chip itself, a problem which will be increasingly important as the number of devices packed into a given chip area increases.

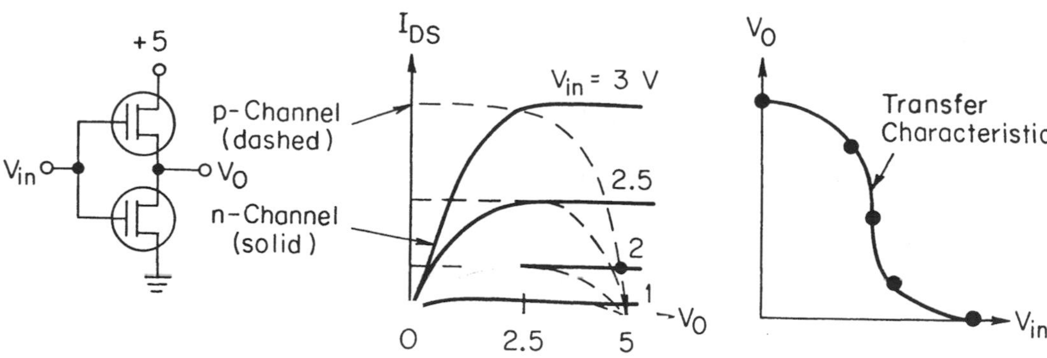

Figure 18 CMOS Inverter.

2. Introduction to MOS Chip Design

We turn now to a brief description of how the basic inverters just discussed are combined to form an MOS integrated circuit. We begin with a consideration of the NMOS alternative.

2.1 A Conceptual Framework for NMOS Chip Design (Mead and Conway "sticks")

NMOS integrated circuits can be visualized as containing three levels of conducting material separated by two layers of dielectric (insulating) material, as in Fig. 19. Proceeding from top to bottom, the conducting levels are typically aluminum, heavily doped polysilicon, and heavily doped single crystal silicon, respectively. When current flow in one of these paths is to be transferred to another one, a "window" is opened in the appropriate dielectric layer as suggested in Fig. 19 so that the two layers of conducting material can come into contact at the desired point.

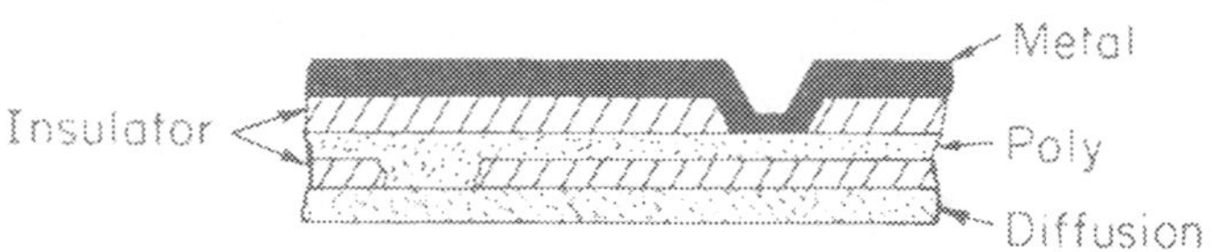

Fig. 19 Conceptual Framework for NMOS IC Design.

As discussed in Sec. 1, the basic NMOS inverter consists of an enhancement mode switch with a depletion mode load (Fig. 17). In Fig. 20, we show a top view of the inverter as it might appear in an NMOS integrated circuit. The diffusion line runs between V_{DD} and ground with a right angle path between the two devices to provide an output connection. The diffusion line is interrupted underneath the pull-up and pull-down as suggested. The gates for the two devices are fabricated in polysilicon; and if long connections are to be made between this device and those that interact with it, metal connections may be made to the input "poly" line and output diffusion line as suggested.

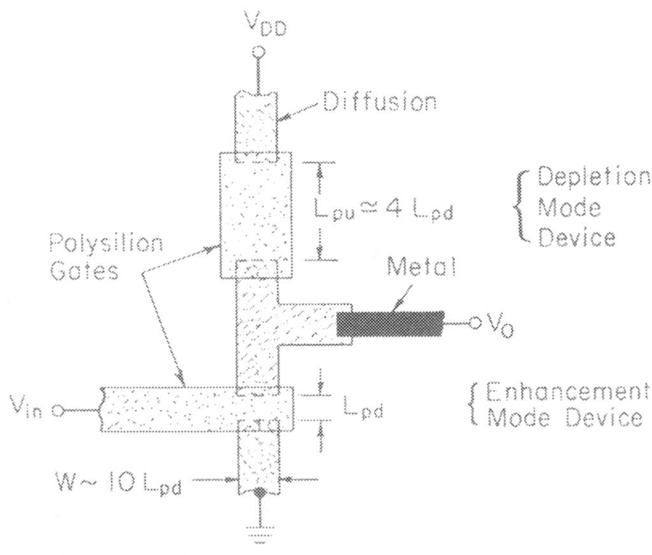

Figure 20 Top View of NMOS IC Inverter.

Two points that are worth noting with regard to this structure are as follows:

(a) The inverter has a simple, regular geometry.

(b) The "minimum feature size" in the inverter is L_{pd}, the length of the pull-down gate. All other dimensions are scaled to this length; for example, the width of the diffusion line, W, is typically 10 L_{pd}; and the length of the pull-up gate, L_{pu} = 4 L_{pd}.

Two input NAND and NOR gates are shown in Fig. 21 to emphasize the regularity of the geometry and the scaling of feature sizes to L_{pd} in more complicated logic circuits.

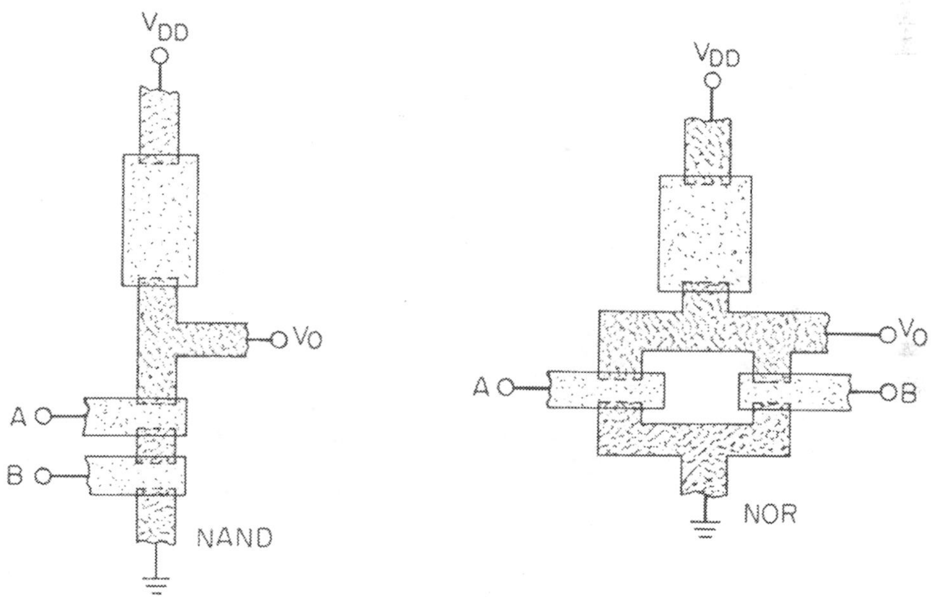

Figure 21 NMOS NAND and NOR Gates.

2.2 Programmable Logic Arrays (PLA)

To give a somewhat more elaborate example of an NMOS logic circuit that will be useful for our subsequent discussion of fabrication, we consider in this section the development of an NMOS programmable logic array for a seven segment decoder. For simplicity we will develop only that portion of the PLA that is required to drive segment C of the display device (Fig. 22). The truth table shown in that figure indicates that the logic equation for segment C is, in a sum of products form,

$$C = \overline{A}\,\overline{B}\,\overline{C}\,\overline{D} + \overline{A}\,\overline{B}\,C\,\overline{D} + \overline{A}\,B\,C\,\overline{D} + A\,\overline{B}\,\overline{C}\,\overline{D}$$

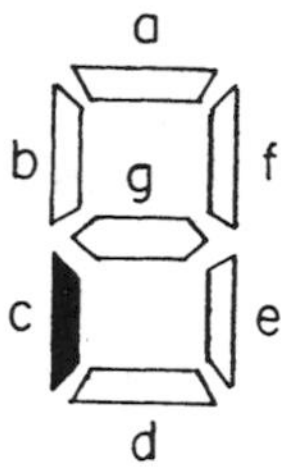

Decimal Number	(8) A	(4) B	(2) C	(1) D	Segment C
	Binary Code				
0	0	0	0	0	yes (1)
1	0	0	0	1	no (0)
2	0	0	1	0	yes (1)
3	0	0	1	1	no (0)
4	0	1	0	0	no (0)
5	0	1	0	1	no (0)
6	0	1	1	0	yes (1)
7	0	1	1	1	no (0)
8	1	0	0	0	yes (1)
9	1	0	0	1	no (0)

$$C = \overline{A}\,\overline{B}\,\overline{C}\,\overline{D} + \overline{A}\,\overline{B}\,C\,\overline{D} + \overline{A}\,B\,C\,\overline{D} + A\,\overline{B}\,\overline{C}\,\overline{D}$$

Figure 22 Truth Table for Segment C of Seven Segment Decoder.

Since we are contemplating building an integrated circuit with a very large number of transistors available to us, we need not concern ourselves with minimizing this expression. Rather, we can easily afford to implement the sum of products expression directly. For this purpose we show in Fig. 23 a regular arrangement of poly lines that carry the input signals A, B, C, D, and their complements along the AND plane of the array. Running parallel to these lines is a set of continuous diffusion lines, each of which is connected to ground. Threading across these paths is a series of metal lines, each of which is connected to a depletion load device on the left hand column of the PLA. All of these lines are independent of each other with regard to signal conduction because of the dielectric layers that are interposed between each of the conducting paths.

Taking the top metal line of the PLA for illustration, we have inserted an interrupted diffusion line leading from the metal underneath the poly line carrying the A signal and on to the adjacent diffused line that is connected to ground. This succeeds in producing an enhancement mode transistor that connects the metal line to one of the

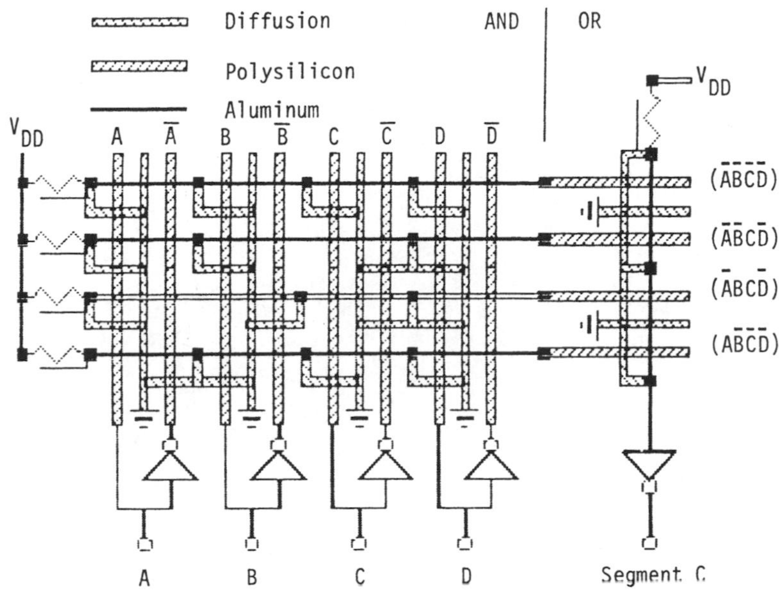

Figure 23 Programmable Logic Array for the Seven Segment Decoder.

grounded diffusion lines when A = 1. Three other similar transistors are placed on the array such that, for the metal line to carry logic level 1, we require A = B = C = D = 0, which is the first term in the sum of products function to be implemented. A brief study of the figure will show that the remaining three metal lines implement the other terms in the logic expression.

To add these individual terms together we build an OR plane in the PLA, as follows. First we transfer the signals from the metal lines in the AND plane to poly lines to provide gate drives for the enhancement mode devices in the OR plane. Grounded diffusion lines run parallel to these poly gate lines, and metal lines run in the perpendicular direction as suggested. Each metal line has a depletion mode load device at the top connected to V_{DD}. The placement of transistors between the first metal line in the OR plane and the grounded diffusion lines insures that the first OR metal line will be LOW when any of the poly lines transmitting signals from the AND plane is HIGH. An inverter on the output of the metal line in the OR plane will then implement the required logic expression. Clock lines and driver transistors must be added to this PLA to make a more practical integrated circuit of it.

Notice once again that the architecture of the PLA is highly regular, which makes layout, checking and fabrication relatively simple. It is also worth noting that in a large PLA the metal, poly and diffusion lines may become rather long, and the RC charging time for these lines then contributes a substantial component to the circuit delay. The physical limits on sheet resistance of useable materials thus set a limit on the practical size of such an array, at least in the simple form suggested above. The chip designer thus faces a trade-off between array size (which translates to logic function complexity) and speed. Nevertheless this approach proves to be extremely useful for custom IC design and is a cornerstone of the system design philosophy pioneered so successfully by Mead and Conway.

2.3 CMOS Gate Arrays

To discuss a popular alternative to the custom NMOS technology just discussed, we describe briefly in this section the general structure of a CMOS gate array and show what the user must do to employ these arrays in a system design.

For concreteness we consider the implementation of two and three input NAND gates in CMOS technology. As shown in Fig. 24, the n-channel devices for the 2 input configuration are operated in series while the p-channel devices are operated in parallel.

The CMOS gate array itself can be thought of as a "kit" of n-channel and p-channel enhancement mode transistors fabricated in a regular array in the manner suggested in Fig. 25. Chips are available from a variety of manufacturers with, for example, 300, 500, 700 and 1000 gates per chip. The chip is fully fabricated with all diffusion and gate lines defined, after which the entire surface of the chip is covered with metal. The circuit designer then has the task of specifying the patterning the metal layer that will produce the required circuit function.

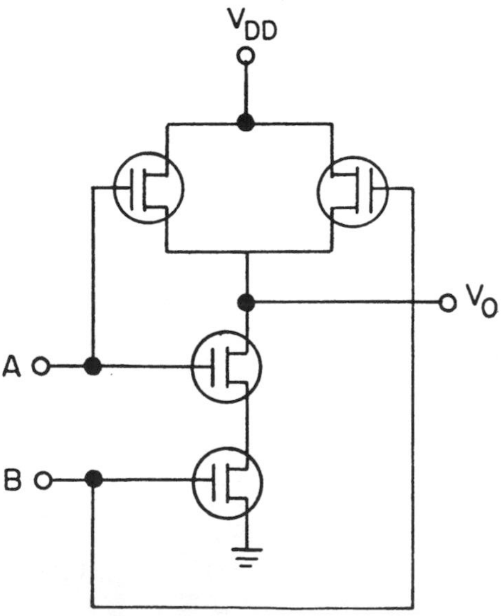

Figure 24 Two Input NAND Gate in CMOS.

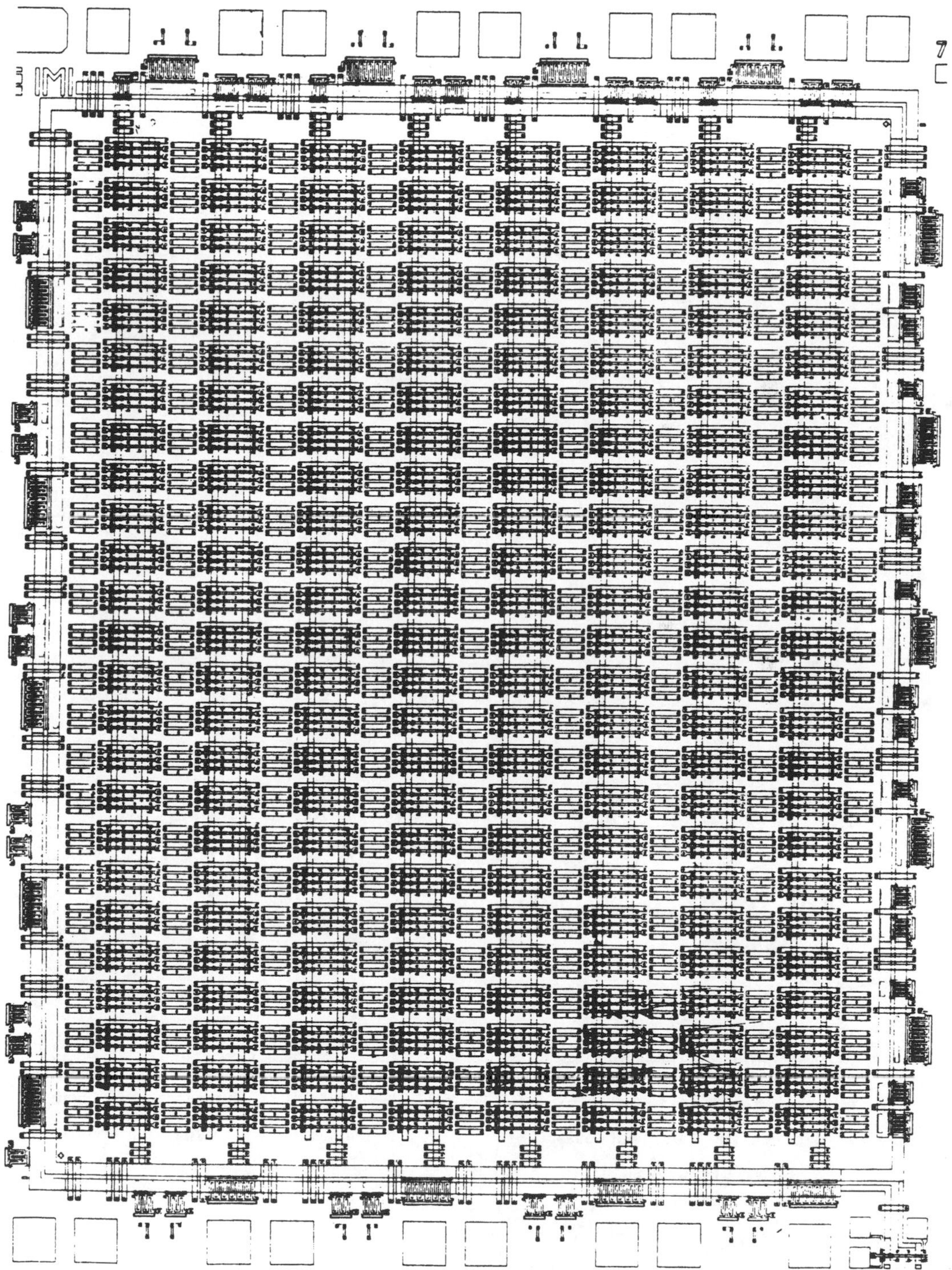

Figure 25 200 Gate. Si-Gate CMOS Gate Array.

<u>What The Circuit Designer (or CAD) Must Do</u>. The metal pattern that is required for the two input NAND gate is shown in Fig. 26. In effect the metal surface layer has been removed everywhere except where metal connections are required to connect the devices appropriately. The fabrication of such a circuit proceeds by providing the chip manufacturer with the single mask (see Sec. 4) that defines the areas where metal is to be retained. There will of course be other metal lines to connect the output of this circuit to other circuits on the same chip. The length of these lines will be based on the prudent choice of transistor combinations, from which it follows that the principal problems encountered in the utilization of gate arrays has to do with keeping interconnection lines short, utilizing the transistor potential of the chip efficiently and ensuring that the final logic function implemented is both correct and will operate with the necessary speed...clearly a job for CAD.

In practice the ease of customizing CMOS gate arrays leads to an increasing use of these types of circuits (with their bipolar counterparts) to interface a number of large standard chips in a system design.

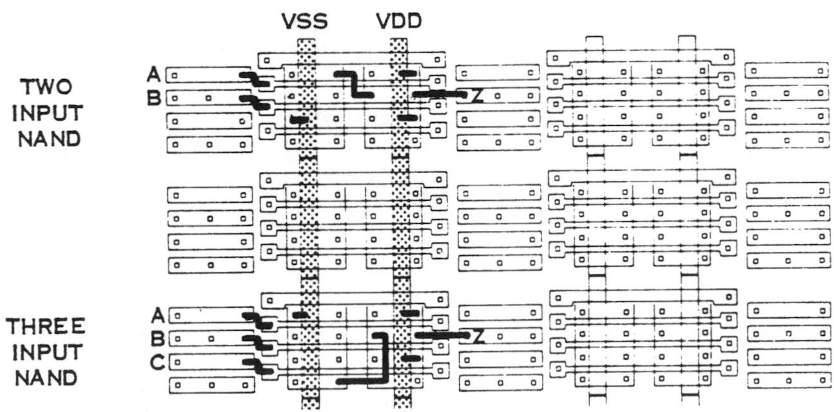

Figure 26 Silicon-gate CMOS Gate Array Metal Interconnects.

3. Basic IC Fabrication Principles

In this section we will briefly describe the basic technology used to fabricate integrated circuits. Our purpose is to provide a technological overview which can be used by a circuit/system designer to better understand some of the capabilities and limitations of the fabrication process. Because the simple, regular geometry of NMOS is attractive from a design and layout standpoint, our discussion will concentrate on NMOS enhancement/depletion technology. Many of the individual process steps in the fabrication sequence are similar to those employed in CMOS or even bipolar process technologies, however, so much of this discussion is applicable to silicon integrated circuits in general.

A typical enhancement mode MOSFET transistor such as is used in semiconductor memory and logic circuits is shown in Fig. 27. The device consists of a lightly doped p-type substrate into which heavily doped n-type contact wells (designated as n^+ source and drain contacts) have been introduced from the surface of the device . An oxide (insulating) layer is then prepared on the surface between the source and drain, and metallizations are applied to provide external connection to the source, gate and drain regions. Although this view of a MOSFET is somewhat oversimplified, it correctly suggests the four main technological problems which must be solved to fabricate an MOS integrated circuit:

1. Dopant incorporation--we must arrange for the controlled introduction of impurity atoms into the silicon crystal to produce the desired electrical conductivity in the source and drain contacts and in the depletion channels.
2. Silicon oxidation--we must fabricate the gate insulator material. The naturally occurring oxide of silicon (SiO_2) is the insulator which is almost universally used as the gate dielectric in MOS devices. In addition SiO_2 is often used to select the areas where dopants are introduced into the silicon crystal.
3. Thin film deposition--we must fabricate low resistance gate electrodes and transistor-to-transistor interconnections required on the integrated circuit.
4. Precision pattern definition--we must be able to accurately control the locations and dimensions of these various regions, including especially accurate layer-to-layer registration.

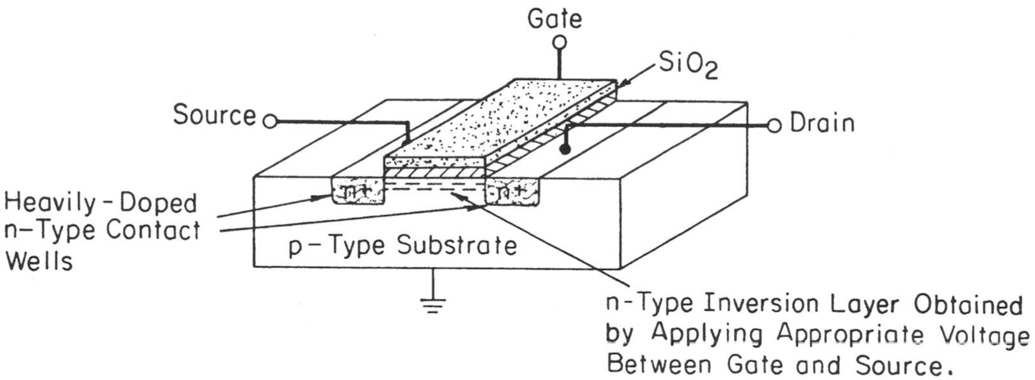

Figure 27 Basic Geometry of an n-channel MOS Transistor (MOSFET).

The remainder of this section will be devoted to a discussion of techniques used to solve these problems. We will then describe the application of these techniques in a straightforward, but nonetheless reasonably complete, NMOS enhancement/depletion fabrication sequence and will show how a system/circuit designer might proceed from a circuit or logic design to a working circuit.

3.1 Surface Doping Processes

There are two processes by which dopants can be introduced from the surface into the interior of a semiconductor wafer. These processes are called solid state diffusion and ion implantation, respectively, and will be described briefly below.

The solid state (or thermal) diffusion of impurities into a semiconductor is in most instances carried out in a series of two steps:

1. A very highly concentrated layer of impurity atoms (e.g., P or B) is introduced into the surface layers of the semiconductor. This is called the predeposition step.
2. Conditions are then set up to permit the deposited impurity to diffuse from the thin surface layer into the body of the semiconductor. This impurity redistribution step is called the drive-in diffusion.

At sufficiently high temperatures an impurity atom can move through a silicon crystal in a way that is analogous to the motion of a dye molecule through a jar of water. This basic (random) motion can give rise to a net transport of impurity atoms through a crystal if there is an impurity concentration gradient to drive the process.

The net rate at which impurity atoms move is determined by the impurity species and by the temperature of the diffusion process. Mathematically, one may characterize the diffusive motion of impurities in silicon by specifying a diffusion coefficient D_I for the impurity (in $\mu m^2/hr$); the concentration of the impurity at the silicon surface; and the duration of the diffusion process. The most striking (and commercially significant) feature of D_I is its exponential temperature dependence, which permits one to vary D_I over a wide range with only a moderate change in temperature. For example, D_I for phosphorus in silicon has a value of about $.02\mu^2/hr$ at a temperature of 1050°C, increasing to $0.55\mu^2/hr$ at a temperature of 1200°C. Hence D_I changes by more than an order of magnitude for a 150°C change in temperature. Controllable thermal diffusion therefore requires a very precisely controlled thermal environment --it turns out to be quite reasonable, however, to control a furnace to within ±0.5°C. In order to accurately control the number of impurities introduced in the silicon, we must accurately control the concentration of that impurity at the silicon surface.

One means of controllably introducing impurities into silicon is shown in Fig. 28 for the case of phosphorus. Here phosphine gas (PH_3) is mixed with a slightly oxidizing carrier gas ($N_2 + O_2$) and permitted to flow into a reaction tube where the chemical reaction

$$2PH_3 + 4O_2 \rightarrow P_2O_5 + 3H_2O$$

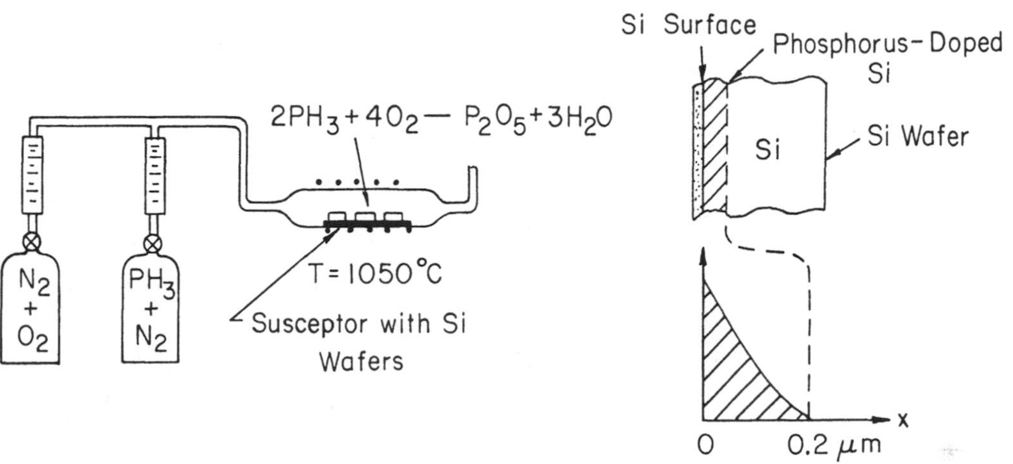

Figure 28 Illustrating the Predeposition of P on Si.

takes place as the gases heat up. A second reaction of the form

$$P_2O_5 + Si\ (solid) \rightarrow P + SiO_2$$

occurs at the silicon surface, in which SiO_2 is formed and phosphorus is liberated. The net result is that a high concentration of phosphorus is produced at the semiconductor surface. The silicon absorbs as much of the liberated phosphorus at its surface as the laws of thermodynamics permit. This limit is called the <u>solid solubility</u> of the impurity and is a weakly temperature dependent quantity, being about 3×10^{20} P atoms/cm^3 at a temperature of $T \simeq 1050°C$. The solid solubility is denoted by N_s.

It is usually more important to know the total number of impurities introduced into the silicon during predeposition ($N_\square$ impurities per cm^2) than to know the precise concentration profile of those impurities. If the impurity concentration is high enough to maintain the surface impurity concentration at the solid solubility limit then the total number of impurities introduced during the predeposition ($N_\square$) is approximately:

$$N_\square \simeq N_s\ (Dt)^{1/2} \qquad (6)$$

where N_s is the solid solubility limit, D is the diffusion coefficient evaluated at the predeposition temperature, and t is the predeposition time. A half-hour predeposition of phosphorus at 1050°C will introduce 3×10^{15} atoms/cm^3 in a shallow heavily doped region near the silicon surface.

In most cases we would also like to tailor the shape of the impurity concentration profile (particularly the peak impurity concentration and the penetration depth of the impurities) more precisely than we can by using predeposition techniques alone. In other words, without adding additional impurities to the silicon, we would like to redistribute those impurities that are already present. To perform this drive-in diffusion, as it is called, we transfer the wafer to a furnace in which the temperature is maintained at a temperature generally higher than that of the predeposition (e.g., 1200°C). The gas flowing through the drive-in furnace is usually either pure N_2 or O_2. No phosphorus-bearing species is present for this step.

Under these conditions, the pre-deposited phosphorus will diffuse into the silicon in much the same way as dye molecules diffuse from a surface layer into a jar of water. Analysis of the drive-in diffusion process shows that under proper conditions, the phosphorus concentration P(x) can be represented by the equation

$$P(x) = \frac{N_{\square}}{2(Dt)^{1/2}} e^{-x^2/4Dt} \qquad x > 0 \qquad (7)$$

in which P(x) is the phosphorus concentration as a function of x for $x > 0$, $N_{\square}$ is the total (predeposited) phosphorus concentration per cm^2 of surface area, D is the diffusion coefficient at the drive-in temperature and t is the time duration of the drive-in. The (Dt) product must be expressed in $(cm)^2$ to obtain P(x) in atoms/cm^3 (the units usually desired).

From a strict mathematical standpoint, Eq. (7) is precisely correct only in the limiting case where the initial (predeposited) phosphorus profile is an impulse. However, if the drive-in diffusion length, (or $2(Dt)^{1/2}$ with D evaluated at the drive-in temperature) is large compared to the predeposition diffusion length (e.g., $2(Dt)^{1/2}$) under the predeposition conditions), then Eq. (7) gives a reliable estimate of the impurity profile after drive-in.

The Gaussian profile of Eq. (7) indicates that during the drive-in cycle we may achieve deeper impurity penetration into the silicon at the expense of a modestly reduced peak impurity concentration. Impurity profiles that result from sequential pre-deposition and drive-in diffusion steps can therefore produce the heavily doped regions which are well suited for use as drain and source contacts in MOS transistors.

As just explained, thermal predeposition leads to surface doping at the limit of solid solubility (which is very heavy doping). As a result predeposition techniques are unsuitable in those cases requiring a shallow, lightly doped region of silicon. However, lightly doped regions are required to precisely adjust the threshold voltages and to form the depletion load in virtually all NMOS enhancement/depletion fabrication processes. Ion implantation is a process in which impurity atoms are introduced into a semiconductor by simply bonbarding the silicon with an energetic ion beam containing the desired impurity species, and is ideally suited to fabrication of those lightly doped, shallow layers that are difficult to achieve using thermal predeposition.

Suppose that by some means we have been able to produce a beam of impurity ions (boron, for example) that has been accelerated to an energy (or through a potential) of 60 keV. We now let this ion beam strike a target of crystalline Si, as shown schematically in Fig. 29. The energetic B atoms will penetrate the target, colliding with Si atoms as they go and losing energy with each collision. Ultimately the B ions will have lost all of their initial energy in these collisions and will then come to rest. A possible set of trajectories for the boron ions during the stopping process is shown in Fig. 29(a), where we also show a number of displaced Si atoms that are created along the track of the B ion as it comes to rest. A thermal annealing step (performed at a temperature of ~ 1000°C in a furnace similar to that used for a drive-in diffusion) must follow the ion implantation process to restore the crystallinity of the crystal (i.e., return the boron and the displaced Si atoms to regular sites in the silicon crystal).

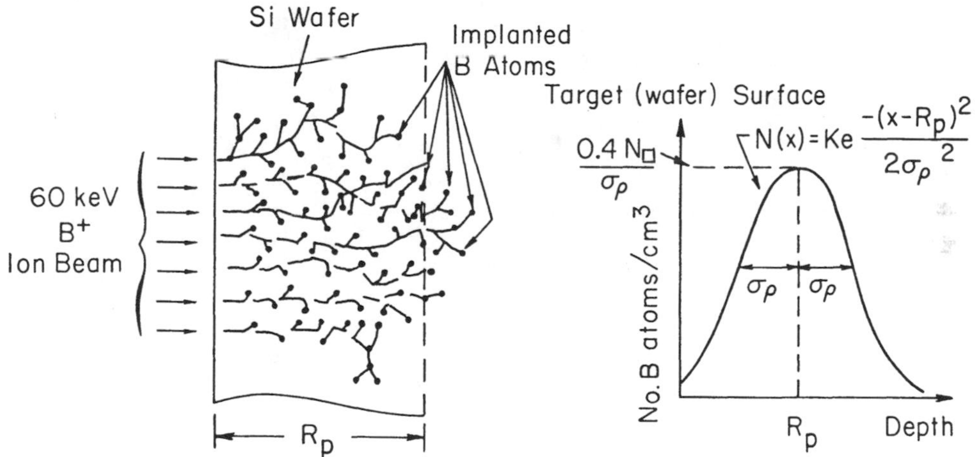

Figure 29 Illustrating the Ion Implantation Process and the Approximate Impurity Distribution Obtained From It.

Naturally each ion that is injected will follow a different trajectory so that when the implantation has been completed the injected ions will be distributed around some average depth in the semiconductor. The distribution law can, to a first approximation, be represented by a Gaussian curve which has the form

$$N_I\ (x) = N_{peak}\ \exp - [(x - R_p)^2/2\sigma_p^2] \qquad 0 < x < \infty \qquad (8)$$

where N_I is the impurity density as a function of distance from the surface (at x = 0), R_p is the mean penetration depth of the ions and σ_p is the standard deviation in penetration depth. The pre-exponential factor N_{peak} can be written as

$$N_{peak} = \frac{0.4N_\square}{\sigma_p} \qquad (9)$$

where $N_\square$ is the total number of ions implanted per unit area of target surface. $N_\square$ is also called the ion dose. The general form for this distribution is shown in Fig. 29(b).

Values of R_p and σ_p can be worked out from a consideration of the collisions that occur as the particle slows down. Representative values for B, P and As in Si are shown in Table 1 for initial energies from 30 keV to 300 keV.

Table 1

VALUES OF THE AVERAGE PENETRATION DEPTH (R_p) AND STANDARD DEVIATION IN PENETRATION DEPTH (σ_p) FOR COMMON IONS IN SILICON.* VALUES IN Å.

		Energy, keV				
		30	50	100	200	300
B	R_p	987	1608	3000	5300	7245
	σ_p	371	504	710	921	1040
P	R_p	368	607	1238	2539	3812
	σ_p	116	256	456	775	1017
As	R_p	215	322	582	1114	1671
	σ_p	80	118	207	374	533

*Data taken from J. F. Gibbons, W. S. Johnson and S. W. Mylroie, "Projected Range Statistics in Semiconductors", Dowden, Hutchinson and Ross, Publishers, Distributed by John Wiley and Sons.

The implanted impurity distribution shown in Fig. 29(b) together with the values of R_p and σ_p lead to several consequences that are of considerable interest for device fabrication. Specifically,

1. The form of the implanted impurity distribution depends only on the initial energy E_0 through R_p and σ_p. In particular, the maximum of the impurity density occurs at $x = R_p$, not $x = 0$ as is the case for thermal predispositions and diffusions. This characteristic of implanted distributions is of considerable use since it permits us to produce doped layers in which the peak doping concentration occurs at a well controlled depth beneath the surface of the target. This possibility makes it feasible to adjust the threshold voltage of MOS devices after many of the other steps in the fabrication sequence have been completed, which is a very important application.

2. While the form of the implanted impurity distribution depends only on the initial energy E_0 through R_p and σ_p, the actual impurity concentration at each value of x also depends on the implanted dose $N_\square$. $N_\square$ can in turn be controlled by controlling the ion beam currrent and/or the time of implantation.

The outstanding advantage which the ion implantation process has over thermal predeposition is that E_0 and $N_\square$ can both be controlled _independently_ and _electronically_, rather than thermodynamically. Hence the process is insensitive to surface contaminants that may affect the thermal predeposition of impurities. Additionally, ion implantation is ideally suited to applications requiring impurity profiles which are both shallow and yet lightly doped because the depth of the implant is determined by energy E_0 whereas the doping level is largely determined by the implanted dose $N_\square$.

3.2 Thermal Oxidation of Silicon

Both the diffusion and ion implantation processes are of course _un_selective; i.e., they operate on any silicon surface that is exposed to the process. To fabricate the isolated n^+ source and drain wells required for the MOS transistor shown in Fig. 27, we need a procedure by which we can _mask_ those areas of the semiconductor where the introduction of impurities is undesired. Furthermore, for MOS transistor operation, we need a high quality dielectric layer between the gate electrode and the active channel region of this transistor.

SiO_2 (the naturally occurring oxide of silicon) has a number of properties which make it almost ideally suited for these applications:

1. It is an extremely good insulator.
2. It is chemically rugged and stable, even at the elevated temperatures required for diffusion.
3. The diffusion coefficient of impurities in SiO_2 is generally less than that of the same impurity in silicon--it may thus be used as a _diffusion_ _mask_ (provided that we can define a pattern in the SiO_2 layer--the topic of section 3.4.)
4. Thin, controllable films of SiO_2 can be readily produced by directly _oxidizing_ the silicon in an O_2 or H_2O ambient at elevated temperatures.

The apparatus used to oxidize silicon, shown in Fig. 30, consists of a quartz tube inserted into a precisely controlled, resistance-heated furnace. Oxygen (i.e., "dry oxygen") and nitrogen bubbled through a heated flask of water (i.e., steam or "wet") are generally provided as two oxidizing ambients. Figure 31 schematically shows a cross-section of an oxidizing silicon wafer and indicates that the oxidant (either O_2 or H_2O) first must diffuse through the existing oxide where it may then react with silicon at the silicon/silicon dioxide interface to form additional SiO_2. The oxidation rate for a given set of conditions may be limited by either the diffusion of

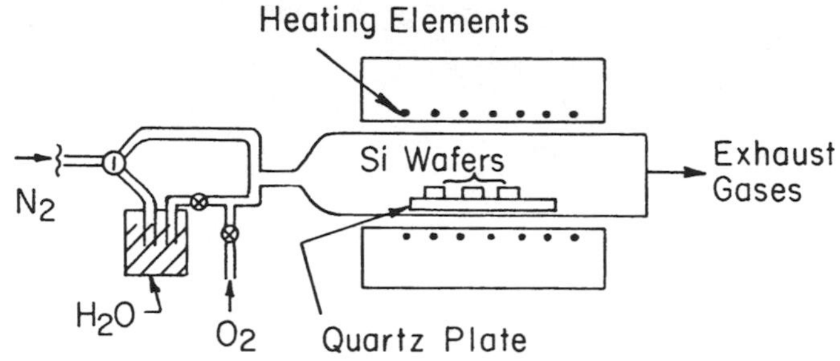

Figure 30 Oxidation Furnace.

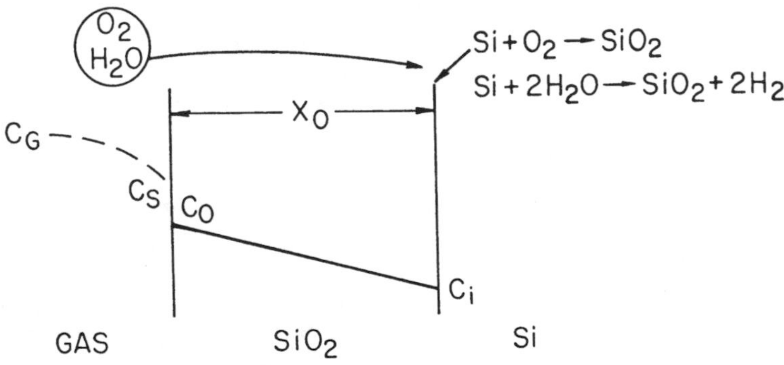

Figure 31 Thermal Oxidation of Silicon.

oxidant through the oxide or the surface reaction rate of silicon and oxidant at the silicon/silicon dioxide interface.

The oxidation rate can be described mathematically by the relation

$$\frac{x_o^2}{B} + \frac{x_o}{B/A} = t$$

where x_o is the oxide thickness, t is the oxidation time, and B and B/A are chemical rate constants which are functions of the oxidant species and exponential functions of the absolute temperature.

Figure 32 is a plot of resulting oxide thickness as a function of time for different temperatures in a dry O_2 ambient. It is evident in this plot that the thermal oxidation process allows us to precisely control the thickness of the resulting silicon dioxide layer--this is particularly important for controlling the threshold voltage of MOS transistors. In modern day MOS technology gate oxides are typically in the range of 700 Å (i.e., 70 nm) thick with the trend going toward thinner gate oxides. Thin gate oxides are generally desirable because this results in an active channel

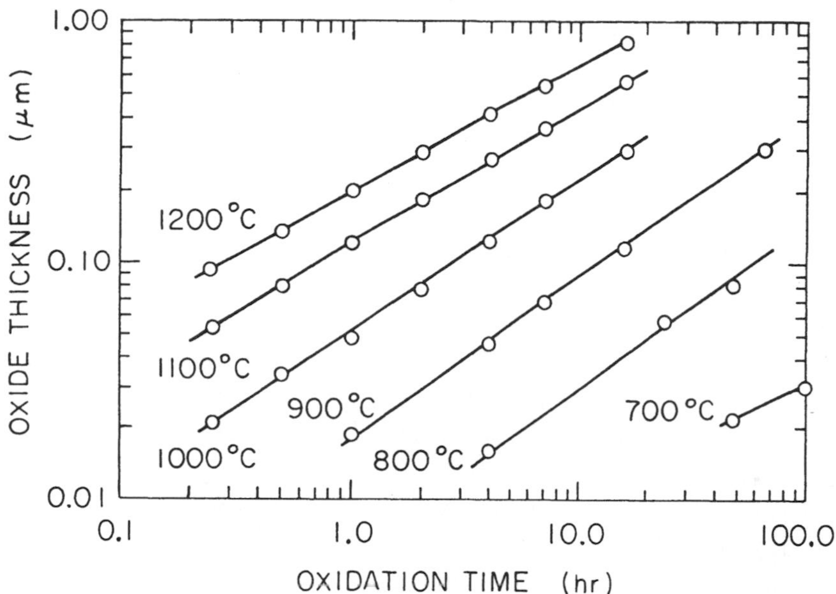

Figure 32 Oxide Thickness Vs Oxidation Time for the Oxidation of (100) Silicon in Dry Oxygen at Various Temperatures.

region of a transistor which is more responsive to variations in gate voltage and thus results in faster circuit switching (particularly if this is accompanied by geometrical reduction of the feature size in the circuits, which in turn results in reduced capacitive loading of the nodes of the circuit).

3.3 Thin Film Deposition

Although silicon and silicon dioxide are undoubtedly the two most important materials used in integrated circuit fabrication, one must also be able to deposit and delineate other materials on the silicon substrate. Of particular importance are the materials which are used to form the gate electrode of the MOS transistor and those which are used to interconnect the various transistors in the desired circuit configuration.

Thin films of metal are obvious candidates for these functions, and, in fact, aluminum is the most widely used material for the interconnection of transistors on integrated circuits. Thin films of aluminum (and many other metals) may be controllably produced through a variety of vacuum deposition techniques. Most metals, however, are unable to withstand the high temperatures and/or corrosive environments commonly encountered during an integrated circuit fabrication sequence and are therefore required to be deposited and patterned virtually at the end of the fabrication sequence. While this is often acceptable for the interconnection layer, we shall see in Section 4 that this constraint is undesirable when the material is to be used as the actual gate electrode of the MOS transistor.

An alternative to vacuum deposition techniques is the use of chemical vapor deposition to produce the desired films. Chemical vapor deposition is accomplished by heating the wafers in the presence of precisely controlled partial pressures of reactant gases which combine to deposit a film of the appropriate composition. The partial pressures of the reactant gases may be controlled either through dilution with inert gases or by operating the entire system at sub-atmospheric pressure.

Of particular interest to MOS technology is the decomposition of silane (SiH_4) at elevated temperatures, a process which produces a thin film of polycrystalline silicon on the wafers. Although undoped polycrystalline silicon has a very high resistivity, it can be heavily doped to produce a film with a (low) resistivity approaching that of heavily doped single crystal silicon. Unlike most metals, however, polycrystalline silicon can readily withstand high process temperatures such as those encountered during diffusion and oxidation. Polycrystalline silicon itself can also be oxidized to electrically isolate it from an interconnecting film of aluminum where desired, thus producing the general three conductor-two insulator system shown in Fig. 19. The benefits of using doped polysilicon as a gate electrode will be described in more detail in Section 4.

3.4 Precision Pattern Delineation

To precisely control the location of the diffused regions when fabricating an integrated circuit we make use of a process known as photolithography or photoengraving to "cut windows" in an oxide film where source and drain regions are to be formed. As we shall see in Section 4, the fabrication of an integrated circuit or other semiconductor device requires a number of separate photolithographic cycles (one for each diffusion, ion implantation, etc.) to complete a particular device. In general, each photolithographic step requires the use of a separate photomask to define where a given diffusion or contact hole will occur with respect to the previously diffused regions. Photomask preparation will be described in Section 4.

Photoresist Coating [Fig. 33(a)]. The photolithographic process starts by coating the oxidized silicon wafer with a thin layer of photoresist. Photoresist is normally an organic photosensitive polymer which is suspended in a solvent.

Drying or Soft-bake [Fig. 33(b)]. After coating, the wafer is heated to evaporate the solvent from the resist.

Mask Alignment [Figure 33(c)]. Next a photomask containing the pattern where windows are to be cut for a particular step in the process is placed above the wafer. Using a system consisting of high magnification microscopes and precise micromanipulators, the mask is aligned with respect to the previous oxide cuts visible on the wafer

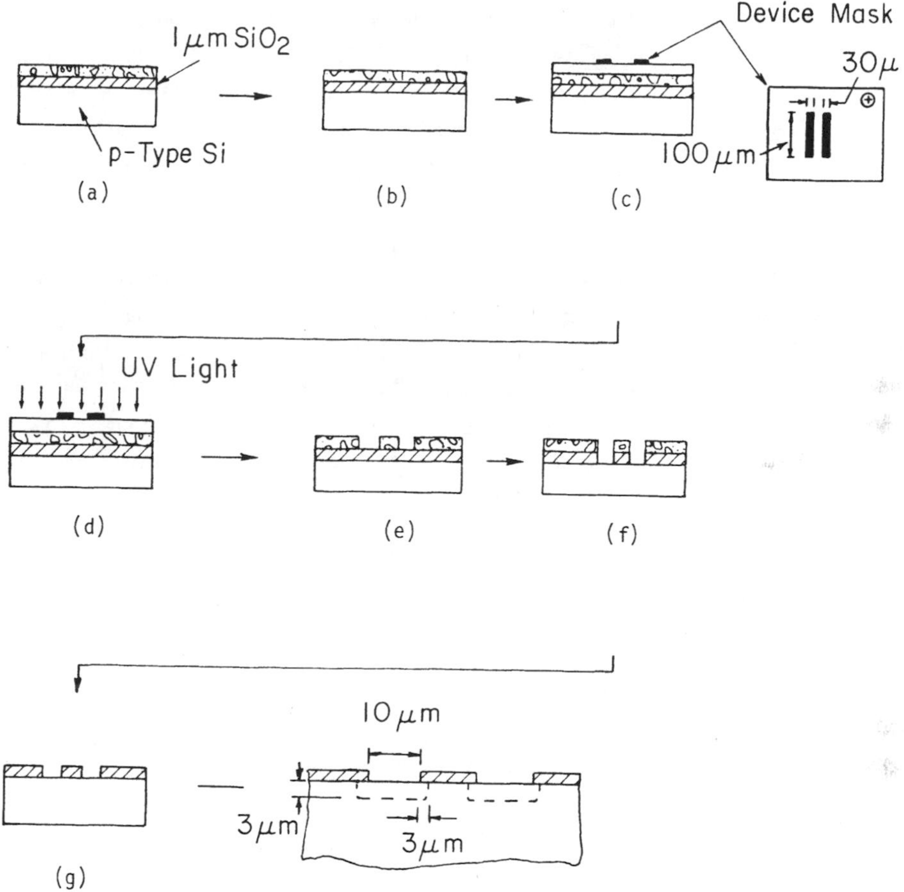

Figure 33 Use of Photoengraving Technique to Prepare an Oxide Mask for Subsequent Impurity Diffusion.

surface. Although mask alignment equipment is very precise, it is unreasonable to expect that alignment will be perfect from layer to layer; the integrated circuit designer must be aware of the limitations of his fabrication capabilities and account for the proper <u>alignment tolerance</u> during photomask design. The impact of these alignment tolerances will be examined further in Section 4.

In many mask alignment systems, the wafer and the mask are placed very close to one another during the alignment procedure. Then, when the alignment is complete, the wafer and mask are clamped together prior to photoresist exposure. Although this type of system is still widely used, it suffers from the drawback that something as small as a speck of dust can get between the wafer and the mask, which may result in a flaw in the photoresist pattern at that point, and more importantly may create a permanent flaw in the mask itself. For applications requiring very low defect densities during photolithography (such as microprocessors or high density memory chips), sophisticated optical systems are used to project an image of the mask onto the wafer. The use of projection alignment systems reduces the defect density on the wafer and also increases the usable lifetime of a particular mask almost indefinitely. This allows the mask maker to put great effort (and thus great expense) into the generation of virtually defect-free masks.

Photoresist Exposure [Figure 33(d)]. After alignment, the photoresist-coated wafer and photomask are now exposed to a source of ultraviolet light (usually contained in the mask alignment equipment). If the photoresist is a negative working resist, the ultraviolet light induces cross-linking of the polymer which makes the exposed resist insoluble in the solvents used as developers. There are also positive resists which will remain beneath the opaque portions of the mask and will be developed away where it is exposed to UV illumination.

Development [Figure 33(e)]. After exposure the wafer is immersed in xylene (for negative resists) to remove the unexposed resist. Following this step, the wafer is rinsed and baked at a temperature of about 130°C for 30 minutes to further harden the resist and to improve its chemical resistance.

Etching [Figure 33(f)]. The oxide covered wafer is now covered with a patterned, chemically resistant film of photoresist. We may now place the wafer in a liquid etchant (such as a buffered hydroflouric acid) that attacks SiO_2 but not the photoresist or the silicon underlying the oxide. This step replicates the photoresist pattern in the silicon dioxide. The use of wet chemicals as the etchants in this process, however, suffers from two main limitations. First, most of the chemicals used as etchants in the fabrication of integrated circuits are highly corrosive chemicals which pose serious industrial safety problems. Secondly, liquid chemicals generally display isotropic etching characteristics (i.e., their etch rate is equal in all directions). This results in an increase in the size of the window opened in the SiO_2 as compared to that in the photoresist. This undercutting of the photoresist obviously becomes an increasingly serious problem as the feature sizes in the photoresist pattern become smaller.

To circumvent the problem associated with wet chemical etching, the use of "dry" etching techniques is becoming increasingly popular in the fabrication of integrated circuits. In most dry etching systems, the photoresist-patterned wafers are placed in a vacuum system containing a small partial pressure of an etchant gas (usually a mixture of flourocarbon or halocarbon gases). The etchant gas is chemically "excited" by the application of RF (radio frequency) power. Under the appropriate conditions, "dry" etching can be quite anisotropic (i.e., the vertical etch rate is much greater than the lateral etch rate), which implies that the photoresist pattern will be faithfully replicated in the silicon dioxide without significant undercutting. Dry etching can be anisotropic largely because (a) the electric field resulting from the applied RF power can be directed normal to the wafer surface, which will tend to accelerate any ionic species present in the etching atmosphere toward the horizontal surfaces of the wafer; and (b) the mean free path length of a gas molecule is inversely proportional to the total system pressure. Therefore, by operating the etching system at a reduced pressure we will more effectively collimate the gas molecules so that they will impinge on the wafer surface in a nearly perpendicular fashion.

Photoresist Stripping [Figure 33(g)]. After cutting the holes in the SiO_2, the photoresist may be removed from the wafer by placing it in either hot H_2SO_4 or a reactor similar to that used in the dry etching process and exposing it to an "excited" oxygen ambient which very slowly and controllably reacts with the organic photoresist to form volatile CO_2 and H_2O. Regardless of the method of stripping the photoresist, it is generally wise to subject the wafer to additional acid cleaning step prior to any subsequent high temperature diffusion or oxidation steps.

4. The IC Fabrication Process

In the previous section we described a number of the individual process steps that are employed in the fabrication of NMOS integrated circuits. In this section we will begin by describing a simplified but conceptually correct fabrication sequence for an enhancement/depletion NMOS process. We will then discuss some of the principal aspects of photomask preparation. The photomask is critical because it embodies the geometry and topology of the circuit design and must at the same time reflect the constraints imposed by the fabrication process itself. In state-of-the-art designs (which tend to push circuit and fabrication constraints to the limit), preparation of the photomask can become highly involved. By making some simplifying assumptions once again, we hope to indicate the manner in which the circuit/process interface will generally be bridged.

4.1 Enhancement/Depletion NMOS

In the (simplified) NMOS process, we begin by oxidizing a lightly doped p-type single crystal wafer of silicon with a relatively thick ($\sim 1.0\mu m$) layer of SiO_2 which will ultimately prevent the formation of unwanted conduction channels between adjacent transistors. We will then perform a sequence of photolithography and etching steps to open holes in the SiO_2 down to the bare silicon in the areas where we wish to fabricate MOS transistors. We then remove the photoresist and reoxidize the wafer to grow a thin (700 Å) gate oxide in the active regions. The cross-sectional view of a simple inverter after this step is shown in Fig. 34. Note that this mask will have defined the widths (normal to the page) of the pulldown and load devices.

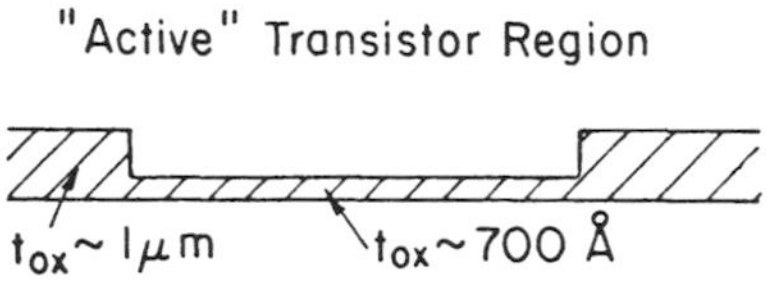

Figure 34 NMOS Inverter After Gate Oxidation.

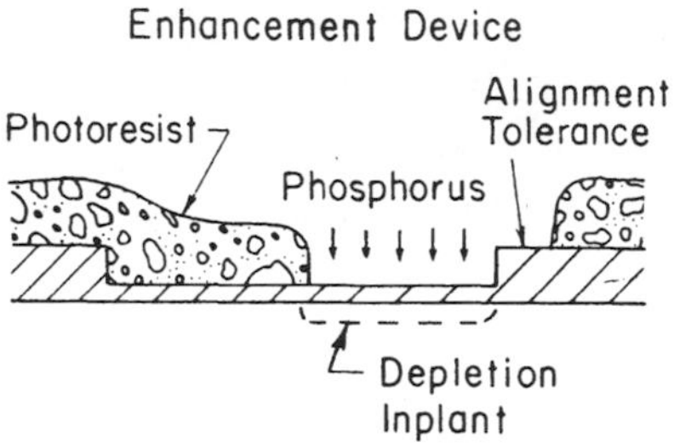

Figure 35 NMOS Inverter After Depletion Implant.

The next step of the process is to perform another photolithography step, opening holes in the photoresist where we wish to fabricate the depletion-mode transistor (i.e., the load device). In Fig. 35 we see that we have to allow an alignment tolerance between levels 1 and 2 so that the entire depletion load thin-oxide region is exposed even if our alignment and lithography are not perfectly accurate. Both photoresist and SiO_2 can be used as masking materials for ion implantation, so if we select our ion implantation energy (and hence range) correctly, we can implant phosphorus through the thin oxide of depletion transistors only but be well assured that it will be stopped by either the thick field oxide or by the photoresist elsewhere.

After stripping the depletion implant photoresist, we deposit a thin (~ 0.5μm) layer of undoped polycrystalline silicon over the entire wafer and then use a third photomask to etch the polysilicon, leaving it in only those regions where we wish to form the gate electrodes to the two transistors (this defines the length of the two transistors). Note that on this layer (and on all layers in general) we will have certain limitations due to imperfections in the lithography and etching process which constrain us to use feature sizes and distances between features which are larger than some mininum value. The exact value of these minimum sizes will be a strong function of the capabilities of any given fabrication facility.

Now, using an etchant that will etch SiO_2 but not Si, we etch roughly 1000 Å of SiO_2 off the wafer (without using an additional mask). This will reduce the field oxide thickness to 9000 Å, not touch the gate oxide that is protected by the polycrystalline silicon, and remove all of the gate oxide in the transistor drain and source regions. We can then do a phosphorus predeposition and drive-in diffusion (see Fig. 36) which will form heavily doped source and drain regions which are self-aligned to the edges of the polysilicon gate electrodes. This process clearly requires a gate electrode material (polycrystalline silicon) which can withstand high temperatures without adverse effects. Furthermore, the phosphorus diffusion will simultaneously dope the polysilicon gate electrodes to make them highly conductive as well. Finally, during the drive-in portion of the phosphorus diffusion, we can oxidize the gate, source, and drain so that we can run metal interconnects over the transistors without contacting them if need be.

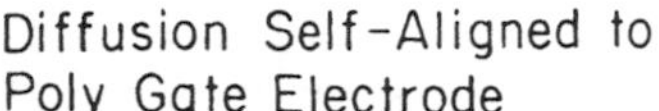

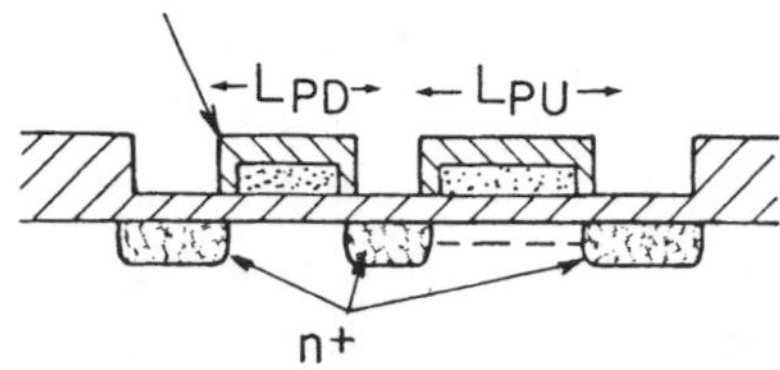

Figure 36 NMOS Inverter After Poly Etch, Drain/Source Predeposition and Drive-In.

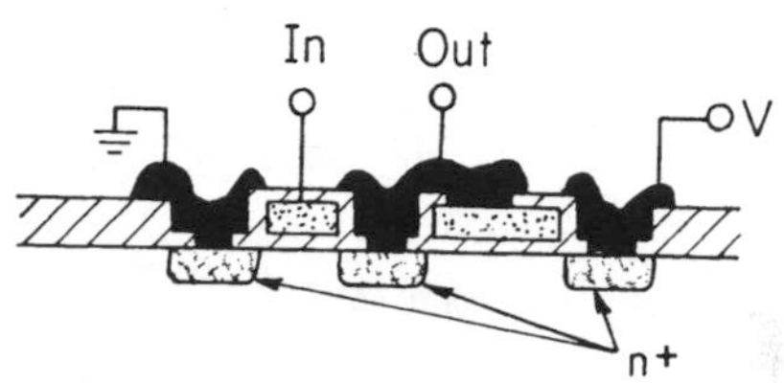

Figure 37 Completed NMOS Inverter.

As shown in Fig. 37, a fourth mask is used to define contact holes through which the aluminum metallization (which is patterned with a fifth mask) may make contact to the various gate, source, or drain regions as desired. Of course it is not necessary that all interconnections be done with the aluminum. For example, the input of this inverter could be connected via poly to the output node of a previous gate (in NMOS the gate of the depletion load is normally connected to its source so we can often route an output in either poly, diffusion or metal layers).

We therefore have succeeded in "fabricating" an NMOS enhancement/depletion inverter with as few as five photolithographic mask levels. If we were actually fabricating high performance NMOS chips (in silicon instead of on paper) we would likely use as many as 8 or 10 masking levels, but conceptually this NMOS process "works".

Before we can design masks and produce circuits using these chips there are three major questions which must be addressed:

1. For specified drain characteristics of these devices (worst case), what are the width-to-length ratios of the various transistors which will be required to make the circuits function properly?
2. On any given mask layer, what are the minimum feature sizes and the minimum separation between features which can be reliably produced? In general, these numbers will vary for each masking level in the process. For simplicity, we will assume that the same number applies to all levels and that the minimum feature size equals the minimum separation distance.

3. What is the layer-to-layer registration accuracy which can be maintained? Note that, in general, this must include not only the actual alignment accuracy of the processing system but wafer shrinkage or expansion due to the thermal coefficient of expansion.

The answers to these questions will normally only be formulated after careful study of statistically significant numbers of processed wafers. When these answers are known they will usually be incorporated into the design as a set of complex design rules for each masking step. As a rough indication of the degrees of control required to fabricate a sophisticated integrated circuit, we will grossly simplify the situation and say that a process can be characterized by 3 numbers: a minimum linewidth, an alignment tolerance, and a total number of transistors on a single chip. As a matter of interest, the field of very large scale integration (VLSI) requires a fabrication process with a linewidth of 2.0μm or less, an alignment tolerance of 0.5μm or less, and containing more than 10^5 transistors on a single chip. The precision required to achieve these objectives cannot be underestimated.

4.2 Photomask Preparation

In our discussion of photolithography in the previous section we assumed that we would have available a set of masks which determine where each particular diffusion, ion implantation, etc. will occur with respect to other regions of that particular level, and, through precise mask alignment, with respect to previously defined areas of interest. Although the preparation of these patterned masks is conceptually a simple task, we shall see that mask making has necessarily evolved into a very sophisticated technology to keep pace with the demands of large scale integration (LSI) of the late 1970's (see Fig. 38).

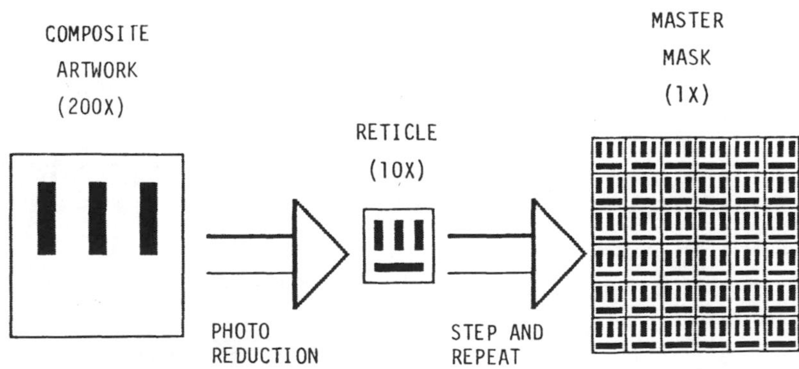

Figure 38 Illustrating a Mask Making Process.

To fix ideas, we begin with a discussion of the mask making procedure as it was practised until the mid-1970's (for circuits with a few thousand transistors or less). The first step is to prepare a large composite drawing of the chip showing each of the diffused regions, contact holes, etc. Such a drawing can be made at a conveniently large magnification (for example, 200:1) compared to the final size of the chip itself. From this drawing, an individual pattern consisting of opaque and clear regions (not unlike a stencil pattern) can be prepared for each masking step in the process. This set of drawings is then photographically reduced and printed on a glass plate coated with high resolution photographic emulsion or a thin layer of chrome covered with photoresist. After developing the image in the emulsion or the photoresist (and, in the case of the chrome covered plate, etching the chrome using the photoresist as a mask), we are left with a reduced image of the original artwork. The image on this glass plate (known as a reticle) is still ten times larger than the final circuit size and is the object of a second photoreduction, this time in an instrument known as a step-and- repeat camera. As the name implies, a step-and-repeat camera projects a 10X reduction of the reticle onto a second chrome and photoresist coated glass plate, steps the plate laterally a distance corresponding to the dimension of the chip, and repeats this process until the second photomask is covered with a two-dimensional array of the desired image. This second plate, known as the master copy, might be roughly 10 cm on a side and might contain several hundred or even several thousand identical images of the pattern for one level of a particular integrated circuit fabrication sequence. In this way, when we align a silicon wafer beneath this photomask we are actually fabricating many copies of the same integrated circuit simultaneously. This batch fabrication process largely explains why complex integrated circuits can be manufactured and sold so cheaply.

As the complexity and size of integrated circuits increases and the minimum feature size decreases, however, the manual preparation of composite drawings rapidly becomes far too time consuming and inaccurate a process. As a result, integrated circuit engineers have developed a highly automated mask fabrication process to turn the pattern information (usually contained on a magnetic tape) into a 10X reticle using a piece of equipment known as a pattern generator. A pattern generator is a very precise, computer controlled X-Y table coupled with a high intensity, variable aperture ultraviolet light source. The computer-controlled X-Y table holds a chrome and photoresist coated photomask which is precisely moved to the proper position beneath the optical column prior to the exposure of each rectangle. Simultaneously, a pair of computer-controlled slits open or close to provide the desired length and width of each rectangle. When all is in position, the UV source is flashed on to expose each rectangle individually. Although it might appear to be painfully slow to generate a complex pattern one rectangle at a time, modern pattern generators can expose photomasks at rates in excess of 25,000 flashes per hour, which leads to acceptable times for preparation of a complex reticle. Once the reticle is generated, the step-and-repeat process proceeds as before to generate the master plate.

Even these very sophisticated optical methods of mask generation do not have sufficient speed or resolution to keep pace with increases in chip complexity or reductions in minimum feature size. Hence faster and more accurate techniques have been developed for the most complex chips. One such technique, which avoids the resolution limits imposed by the wavelength of light, is to use a precisely focused beam of electrons to "write" the pattern on a mask. Very sophisticated electron beam exposure systems are, in fact, capable of producing a 1X master plate directly from the pattern information without the need for the intermediate reticle or the step-and-repeat process.

Stepping back one level from the actual preparation of a mask, the successful design and fabrication of an integrated circuit requires the translation of a circuit/system idea from either a block or a "sticks" diagram into pattern information data that is suitable for pattern generation and subsequent wafer fabrication. This task becomes increasingly difficult as the circuit becomes more complex and as the process tolerances (i.e., minimum linewidth, alignment accuracy, etc.) become more stringent. Computer-aided layout systems are then essential to keep track of the proper mask layers required for each component and to allow the designer to build a circuit from a library of previously designed and debugged circuits. By way of analogy to computer software, a computer-aided layout system may be thought of as a "high-level language" for circuit design as opposed to the "machine code" of individual pattern generator rectangles.

The geometrical regularity of NMOS (discussed in Sec. 2) makes it particularly well suited for highly automated layout systems. Among the features that are available on some of the most sophisticated layout systems is design rule checking to make sure that the designer doesn't make features or alignment tolerances too small. Even though the sticks diagram may be easy to "read" from a logic standpoint, the mask layout is much more difficult to check because the designer will usually pack the design as tightly as possible in order to minimize the size of the circuit. For example (in Fig. 39) the diffusion areas often run directly beneath the aluminum lines, making it difficult to check for design rule violations. Equally important is the fact that is very easy to misplace a diffusion region and implement an incorrect logical expression in the PLA. Computer automation is being used to eliminate these problems as well. Systems are under development that will directly translate a "sticks" diagram into a mask layout based on a complete set of design rules.

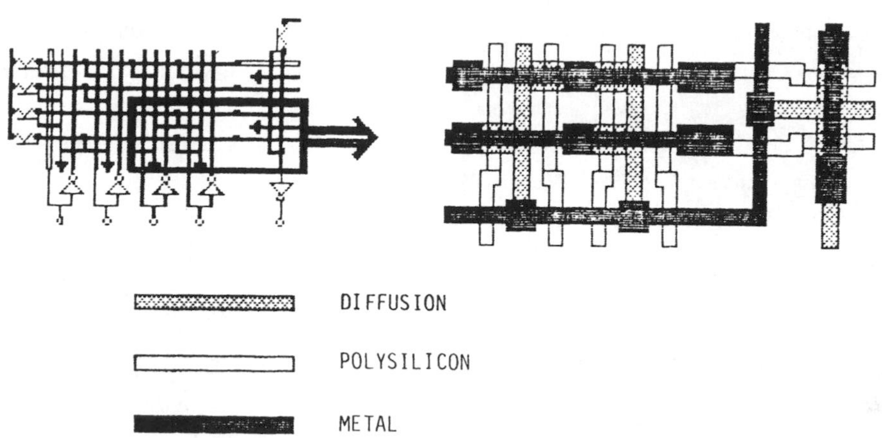

Figure 39 Automatic Layout of PLA From Sticks Diagram.

Other systems under development will extract the logical circuit from a completed set of mask pattern information and compare it to the desired logical function. Despite these advances in automated design tools, it is still highly desirable for the system/circuit designer to be well informed on the topics of device operation and fabrication technology in order to be a skillful user of these computerized tools.

4.3 System Implementation with NMOS

We have now described the basic elements of the fabrication of integrated circuits and of the preparation of photomasks. With these tools in hand, we would like to address the question: What are some of the options available to us if we wish to design a system using integrated circuit technology? For any given system, the correct technological implementation requires us to consider not only the desired electrical performance of the system but also such factors as the expected number of systems to be built, the anticipated system design time, acceptable limits of design cost, etc. In other words, we must always search for an appropriate technology for any particular problem from a wide variety of potential solutions. In particular, if we are considering designing an integrated circuit to perform a particular system function we must ask ourselves the question: What will be gained by designing an integrated circuit to perform this function as opposed to constructing the system from commercially available components?

Once we have decided that the design of an integrated circuit is the appropriate system solution we are by no means done answering difficult questions. We must next select the appropriate technology based on system considerations such as speed, power consumption, and packing density. We have been concentrating on NMOS integrated circuits in this discussion because of their straightforward mapping from circuit function to mask layout; however, complementary MOS (CMOS) technology must be kept in mind, particularly if power consumption is an important consideration; and one of the many bipolar technologies (see Sec. 5 for a discussion of emitter coupled logic, for example) should be considered if high speed operation is desired.

Let us assume, however, that we have decided that NMOS is the proper technology for the system task at hand. Before we can begin designing a circuit we must know a number of things about the actual process that we will be using to fabricate these circuits. In particular, we must know such things as the minimum allowable feature size on any given mask layer, minimum separation between features on the same mask layer, and the alignment tolerance between features on different mask layers. In general, the engineers in charge of wafer fabrication will distribute a set of DESIGN RULES to the circuit/system designers. These design rules constitute one of the major interfaces between the process environment and the designer and tell him how closely he can pack his circuitry without exceeding the resolution and/or registration capabilities of the fabrication process--failure to heed the design rules will generally result in a nonfunctional circuit. A complete set of design rules for a state of the art process may be a lengthy document. However, it is generally more instructive to adopt a simplified set of design rules such as that proposed by Mead and Conway. We must bear in mind that by adopting a loose set of design rules we are trading design simplicity in favor of higher speed and higher packing density--in many real system designs this is an acceptable trade-off and certainly within the educational environment design simplicity is a desirable feature.

In the extreme case, we may simplify a set of design rules down to two numbers: the minimum allowed feature size (and the minimum spacing between features) on each mask level and the worst-case alignment tolerance between any two mask levels. As one further simplification, it is often conservative to assume that the level-to-level alignment tolerance is one-half of the minimum feature size. In 1981 a conservative number for minimum feature size on any mask level is 5 microns and an equally conservative number for level-to-level alignment tolerance is 2.5 microns. The use of conservative design rules is particularly important if one hopes to have the wafers fabricated at one of a number of custom wafer fabrication houses--certainly the system designer doesn't want to re-layout his circuit for each possible vendor of wafer fabrication services. A state of the art NMOS process in 1981 has minimum feature sizes of roughly 2 microns (and alignment tolerances of roughly 0.5 microns), but, as we indicated earlier, it would be unwise to assume that a simplified set of design rules would be appropriate for this state of the art process--attempts to blindly apply these rules to all mask levels in the process sequence, for example, would likely result in shorting of features together which would ultimately result in a nonfunctional circuit.

Let us assume that we have selected NMOS technology to fabricate a particular circuit, and that we have the appropriate set of design rules from the wafer fabrication engineers who will actually fabricate our completed design. We are now faced with a difficult choice: What is the appropriate circuit design approach to implement the desired system function? Among the possible choices are:

1. The use of custom, random logic. This has been the dominant solution adopted by the high-volume producers of integrated circuits for the past 20 years.
2. The use of gate arrays (uncommitted logic arrays). CMOS gate arrays were introduced in Sec. 2.
3. The use of REGULAR logic structures such as programmable logic arrays (PLAs), read-only memories (ROMs), and to some extent random access read/write memories (RAMs). PLAs were also introduced in Sec. 2.

The remainder of this section will be devoted to a discussion of each of these approaches. We will pay particular attention to aspects relating to the packing density (area consumption), speed performance, and design complexity because these three performance criteria generally play a dominant role in the selection of a particular circuit implementation.

For those designers who have built digital circuitry using bipolar TTL (transistor-transistor logic) circuit families, the use of random logic to implement a desired system will seem to be a natural approach. In general, the use of random logic diagram starts with a logic diagram consisting of inverters, NAND gates, NOR gates, etc., translates those gates into a particular technology (NMOS in our case), and then optimizes the location of each of these components on the chip to achieve maximum speed or minimum area consumption. As indicated above, this is the primary approach which has been adopted by the integrated circuit industry for a number of years; however, it is misleading to think of a large scale NMOS integrated circuit such as a microprocessor as being simply a translation of a board full of TTL logic packages into a single chip. In particular, we make considerable use of the fact that the MOS transistor is a high-impedance, voltage controlled device (as opposed to the current controlled bipolar device) by using the charge stored on the gate of the transistor as a short term type of memory. The use of such "dynamic" memory makes it possible to realize certain logical functions in considerably less area than would be required if we were simply to translate a TTL design into its MOS NAND/NOR equivalent form.

We can estimate the area required for a custom random logic design by first examining the NAND and NOR gates shown in Fig. 21. If we call the minimum feature size L, then it is possible to lay out either a 2-imput NAND gate or a 2-input NOR gate in an area of roughly 80 L^2 (i.e., 80 minimum sized squares). Of course if we are designing a real circuit using this technology, it is unreasonable to expect that we would be able to completely pack the chip area with such gates because each gate must be wired to the appropriate input and output nodes as well as power supply and ground connections. It is difficult to make an accurate estimate of the silicon chip area that must be devoted to wiring, but in many designs the average chip area per gate including the overhead of wiring the circuit together is a factor of 2 or 3 greater than the area consumed by the gate alone. Therefore for a custom design, we would expect to require an area of 160 - 240 L^2 per gate in the fully wired circuit. The actual placement and orientation of each gate has a great impact on the overall ease of interconnecting the complete circuit. A carefully packed circuit will be much smaller and much faster (because the parasitic capacitances associated with the interconnections wiil be smaller) than a less well optimized layout. Additionally, in a custom design one has the freedom to optimize the size of each transistor to match the drive requirements of a particular circuit node. In particular, in a microprocessor one often finds buses which have a large parasitic capacitance and yet must be driven rapidly if the target machine cycle time is to be met. In this instance one would definitely design a set of bus drivers with ample drive capability to meet this performance specification; however, we would not want ALL transistors to be this large in the circuit because it would needlessly increase the area and the power consumption of the circuit without increasing the overall performance of the chip which will usually be limited by delays through one or more critical paths through the chip.

A custom designed chip of random logic potentially offers very high levels of performance in terms of packing density and speed. These potential advantages are often offset, however, by the large amounts of time required to design and to de-bug. Specifically, NMOS technology has evolved so rapidly that it is impractical to consider "hand packing" a new microprocessor design which might contain 100,000 transistors or more. The design of a large chip must rely on the availability of sophisticated computer aided design tools if the overall design time of a new system is to be less than the useable lifetime of that system. Unfortunately, in the case of a custom logic design, the number of possible gate locations and wiring patterns is so large that it difficult to create a powerful, general purpose set of computer aided design tools.

One alternative to the custom design of logic chips is the use of the gate array approach which was introduced in Sec. 2.3 in the context of CMOS technology. As shown in Fig. 2.3, a gate array (sometimes called an uncommitted logic array) consists of a number of individual logic gates which are pre-positioned and prefabricated on a chip except for the final level of metal interconnection. The task of the circuit designer is then reduced to simply interconnecting the existing gates together in the desired fashion. The gate array approach has the great advantage that the design time and the fabrication time are quite short because the designer only has to design and define one level as opposed to the 6 to 12 mask levels required for a fully custom design. Furthermore, once the position of the gates is known, the interconnection problem becomes sufficiently constrained than one can rely on computer aided wiring of gate arrays. The use of gate arrays is not totally free from difficulties, however: Because the individual logic gates are placed on the chip without any knowledge of the ultimate use of that chip, one must depopulate the gate array as compared to a comparable custom design to allow for the fact that we cannot move the individual gates to minimize the interconnection difficulties. Furthermore, it would be exceedingly unlikely that one would be able to interconnect all of the available gates into a particular circuit design--it is common to only be able to interconnect roughly 50 to 60 percent of the available gates in the array into a particular circuit. For these reasons, the packing density of a gate array is not as good as an equivalent custom design--the gate array approach generally requires roughly 300 - 500 L^2 per WIRED gate. The performance of a gate array design is also usually lower than that of an equivalent custom design because the parasitic capacitance associated with the interconnection wiring is larger in a gate array and one does not have the flexibility to selectively increase the size of drive transistors to minimize the time delays in a critical timing path.

A gate array design will generally offer lower performance than a custom design in terms of speed and packing density, but it offers the distinct advantages of reduced design time and improved computer aided design tools. Unless one is designing a chip which will be produced in very high volume, the reduced design time couples with the fact that one only has to define the metal interconnection layer result in a lower overall cost for a gate array implementation than the equivalent custom design. These features make the gate array approach particularly attractive for creating an interface circuit between two existing sub-systems. This function of creating the "glue" to hold a system together has been dominated until very recently by printed circuit boards of small scale and medium scale TTL circuitry. Gate arrays now make it possible to incorporate more system performance into a smaller area at a reduced system cost and are therefore receiving great amounts of attention from system designers.

In Sec. 2.2 we introduced the programmable logic array which is a highly STRUCTURED means of implementing AND-OR logic. Structured logic forms have a number of advantages, particularly as the number of logical functions per chip becomes very large:

1. Structured logic tends to result in regular layout geometries. Regular geometries tend to have lower overhead in terms of interconnection wiring. As we have already seen, interconnections can totally dominate the overall packing density of a circuit.
2. Structured logic is generally amenable to design with sophisticated computer aided design tools. For example, there are CAD tools which will accept the desired logical expression for a PLA and automatically generate the mask layout using the appropriate set of mask design rules.
3. Structured logic results in fewer circuit design flaws because the circuit operation and parasitic capacitances associated with the circuit are rigidly controlled by the topology of the regular layout.

These features of structured logic designs can be seen by examining the programmable logic array shown in Fig. 39. Programming the array in this instance consists simply of making a transistor/no transistor decision at each logical node and affects only one masking level. Because the array is so regular, there is virtually no interconnection problem associated with the PLA other than determining where the inputs come from and where the outputs go to. The end result of this highly regular structure is the impressive packing densities commonly associated with PLAs. Under the set of design rules we have been considering a single bit of a PLA requires only 12 - 13 L^2

Table I summarizes some of the important characteristics of the competing means of realizing a desired logical function: custom designed random logic, gate array logic, and the programmable logic array. Read-only memory and random-access memories have been included in this table for comparison.

Structure	Area	Regularity	CAD Aides
Custon MOS	160-240 L^2/gate	Poor-good	Poor
Gate array	300-500 L^2/gate	Poor	Good
PLA MOS	12-13 L^2/bit	High	Excellent
ROM	12-13 L^2/bit	High	Excellent
RAM	50-75 L^2/bit	High	Poor

Table I: Comparison of different MOS logic types. L = minimum mask feature size. Note: As a rough rule of thumb multiply area numbers by 2 for bipolar technology.

silicon surface area. The programmable logic array is highly desirable because it has a high packing density, it is easily programmed, and can be checked and programmed automatically. The designer must be prudent, however, in his use of PLAs because a large PLA can be quite slow; the designer must therefore take speed and size requirements into account early in the design of the PLA.

The system designer must make a large number of decisions between the time that he decides to build a chip to perform a desired system function and the time that he has a packaged chip in hand. As the complexity of these systems increases, we must be increasingly concerned with the availability of powerful CAD tools in order to reduce the time required to go from system concept to a functioning silicon chip. In this regard, the use of PLA and ROM based designs is desirable for large systems and the use of gate arrays is advantageous for smaller sub-systems because both of these approaches offers significant CAD support when compared to a fully custom logic implementation. Many systems, however, are constrained by speed limitations. The next section of this discussion focuses on the speed of MOS and bipolar technologies.

5. Propagation Delay and ECL

To conclude this introduction to integrated circuit physics and technology, we will calculate the propagation delay to be expected for integrated NMOS inverters of the type described in Sec. 2, both to provide an estimate of the speed that may be expected and the potential increases in speed that are possible with advanced technology. We then conclude with a brief discussion of ECL bipolar logic circuits to show why (in the present state of technology) they are used when speed is of utmost importance.

5.1 Propagation Delay for the Basic NMOS Inverter

We show in Fig. 40 the basic NMOS inverter driving a capacitive load C_L. For the time being we take the load to consist of the gate and interconnection line capacitance for F identical inverters, where F is the fanout. In Fig. 40(b) we show the drain characteristics for the pull up and pull down transistors and the path that is followed by each of them during a switching transient.

If the gate is OFF, then $V_O = V_{DD}$. If an input voltage step is applied, taking V_{in} from zero to V_{DD}, the current through the pull down transistor at $t = 0^+$ becomes [Eq. (10)]

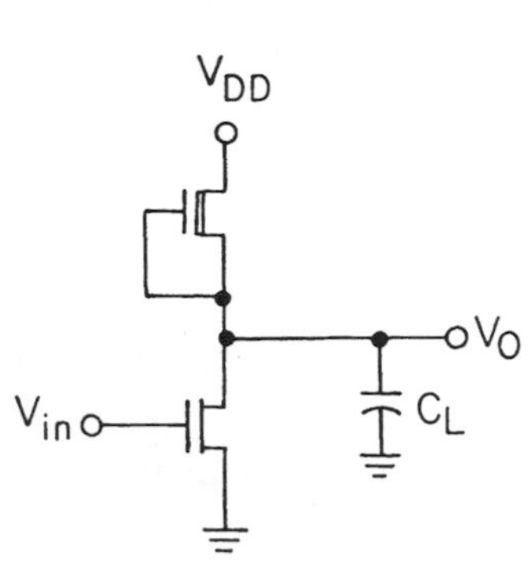

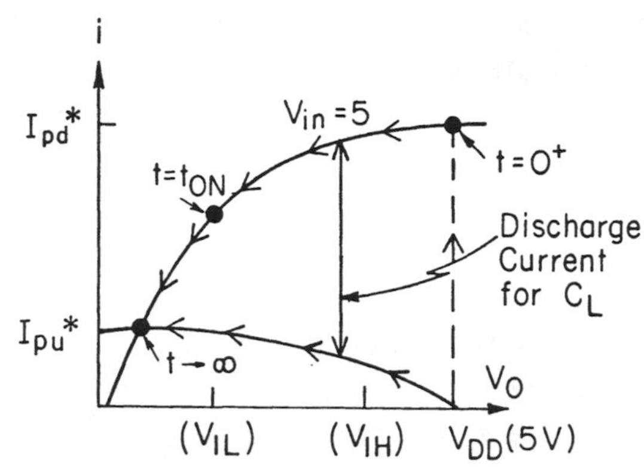

(a) Capactively-loaded inverter

(b) Drain characteristics and switching path.

Figure 40 NMOS Inverter With Capacitive Load.

$$I_{pd} = \frac{\mu_n C_{ox}}{2L^2_{pd}} (V_{DD} - V_T)^2 \tag{10}$$

where C_{ox} is the capacitance between the gate and the underlying channel.

This current begins to discharge C_L from its initial value of V_{DD}. As C_L discharges, current flow through the pull up transistor will reduce the discharge rate, so that the equation governing the discharge is

$$-C_L \frac{dV_O}{dt} = (I_{pd} - I_{pu}) \tag{11}$$

The discharge current is illustrated graphically in Fig. 40(b).

The physical significance of Eq. (11) is simple but nonetheless very important: to make V_O change rapidly (i.e., dV_O/dt large), we want to discharge as small a capacitance as possible with as large a current as we can obtain. At the same time, we do not want to get large currents by making I_{pu} too small, because this will adversely affect the turn OFF process.

As mentioned earlier, we normally choose $L_{pu} \sim 4\ L_{pd}$ for symmetry in the inverter characteristic, which leads to $I^*_{pu} \sim I^*_{pd}/4$. If we further describe each device interconnect line as having a capacitance C_i, then for a fanout F the total capacitance loading the output node of the inverter is

$$C_L = F\left(1 + \frac{C_i}{C_{ox}}\right) C_{ox} \tag{12}$$

Using these results the turn ON time can be calculated from Eq. (11). The approximate result is

$$t_{ON} \simeq \frac{16L_{pd}^2 F(1 + C_i/C_{ox})}{3\mu_n (V_{DD} - V_T)} \tag{13}$$

from which we can see that the principal geometrical feature of interest is L_{pd} (the minimum feature size possible for a given process). Reducing L_{pd} will decrease the capacitance and increase the discharge current, as required. It is also clear that reductions in L_{pd} (and therefore C_{ox}) must be matched by reductions in the interconnect capacitance C_i if their full effect on t_{ON} is to be realized.

Using numerical values typical of present technology (V_{DD} = 5V, V_T = 1V, μ_n = 600 cm^2/V-sec), we obtain

$$t_{ON} \sim 2 \times 10^{-3} L_{pd}^2 F$$

For a fanout F = 3 and $C_i \ll C_{ox}$, we find $t_{ON} \sim 6 \times 10^{-3} L_{pd}^2$, leading to a turn ON time of about 6 ns for a device with a gate length of 10 μm.

A turn off transient is initiated by an input step that takes V_{in} from V_{DD} to zero. The pull down is turned off, and C_L charges through the pull up transistor to V_{DD}. Since we have chosen $L_{pu} = 4L_{pd}$, we obtain a turn off time of about 4 t_{ON}, or 24 ns for the parameters listed earlier. The propagation delay, $(t_{ON} + t_{OFF})/2$, is therefore ~15 ns, which is typical of both NMOS and CMOS circuits presently available.

If the analysis just given continues to hold as L_{pd} is reduced, then decreasing L_{pd} to 1 μm would lead to a propagation delay of ~150 ps. Unfortunately, as L_{pd} is reduced, a number of parasitic factors become increasingly important. We have already mentioned the importance of C_i, which will usually not scale with C_{ox}. In addition, if we launch a signal along an interconnection electrode that has a sheet resistance $R_\square$ (= material resistivity ÷ thickness), then the time required for this signal to propagate a distance L is approximately

$$t_l \sim (2.2\, R_\square\, \varepsilon_{ox}\, L^2)/x_o$$

where x_o is the oxide thickness. This propagation time from device to device is already a significant part of the overall cycle time in the fastest microprocessor chips and leads to the necessity of both reducing interconnection length as much as possible and employing gate and interconnect materials with as low sheet resistance as possible. In addition there are of course a number of other materials and fabrication limitations that will determine the ultimate speed of MOS integrated circuits and are described in Ref. 4.

5.2 Bipolar Alternatives

When circuit speed is important it is often necessary, in the current state of the art, to employ bipolar rather than MOS digital technology. The speed advantage of the bipolar transistor arises principally from its current dimensional superiority over its MOS counterpart.

To provide a vastly oversimplified explanation of this advantage, we show in Fig. 41 an npn transistor having a geometry that can be obtained by appropriate use of the process technology described in Section 3. A space charge layer is formed at each pn junction in which an electric field is developed that tends to confine electrons to the n regions and holes to the p regions. This tendency can be controlled by voltages applied to the junctions. The voltage V_{BE} shown in Fig. 41 has a polarity that will reduce the electric field in the emitter space charge layer, thus permitting electrons to flow more readily from the n^+ emitter into the p type base. This polarity of voltage is called forward bias. The polarity of V_{CB}, on the other hand, increases the electric field in the collector space charge layer, further confining electrons to the n-type collector body and holes to the p type base region. This polarity of voltage is called reverse bias.

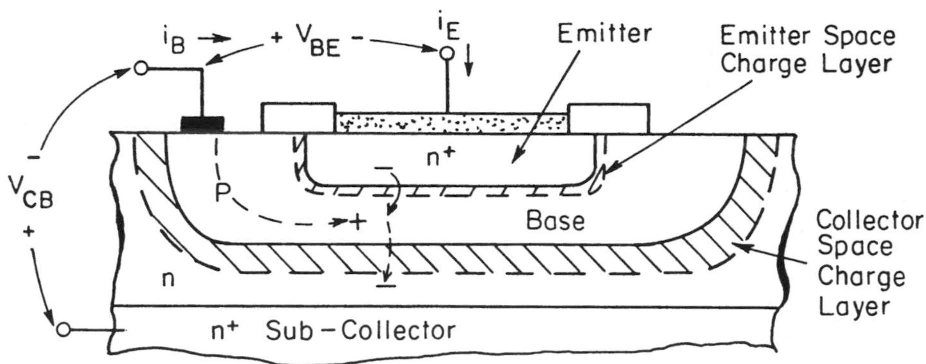

Figure 41 The Basic npn Transistor.

Base current (i_B) in such a device will consist of holes flowing into (or out of) the base layer as a result of an external drive. When a hole enters the base region (see Fig. 41), it will provoke the injection of an electron across the emitter-base space charge layer to maintain space charge neutrality in the base. However, this electron is free to diffuse across the base layer and enter the collector space charge layer. It can then be swept across the collector space charge layer and into the collector body to contribute to the collector current. When this is accomplished a second electron must be injected from the emitter into the base to continue to provide space charge neutralization for the hole. This process will continue until the hole recombines with one of the transiting electrons. The number of electrons that flow in the emitter-collector loop per hole introduced into the base is the (common emitter) current gain of the device, β. The essential speed of a bipolar transistor is determined by the time taken for a single electron to move from the emitter body to the collector body. This time τ_t has three components, as suggested in the analysis given above:

$$\tau_t = \tau_e + \tau_B + \tau_c$$

where τ_e is the time required to inject the electron across the emitter-base space charge layer, τ_B is the time required for the electron to diffuse across the base, and τ_c is the time required to move across the collector space charge layer. For transistors in modern digital integrated circuits, the total transit time τ_t is on the order of 0.5-1 ns. In the fastest microwave transistors, transit times may be ~15 ps. These very short transit times are possible primarily because the total thickness of the base and space charge layers is about 1 µm, rather than the 10 µm spacing (L_{pd}) that is characteristic of MOS devices. From a fabrication standpoint diffusion and ion implantation offer techniques for producing sub-micron vertical dimensions independent of the ability of photolithography to make sub-micron surface features. In effect, the bipolar technology is already scaled to the limits required by VLSI, at least as far as the basic transit time is concerned.

This speed advantage requires that the base current be suitably limited, however. In the (basic TTL) circuit shown in Fig. 42, for instance, the maximum collector current that can flow is $I_c(max) = (V_{CC}/R_L)$; and if the base current exceeds $I_c(max)/\beta$, then the voltage at the collector terminal will be essentially zero. This permits holes to flow from the base into the collector body. The transistor is then said to be saturated. Removal of these holes during a turn off transient takes time and increases the propagation delay significantly.

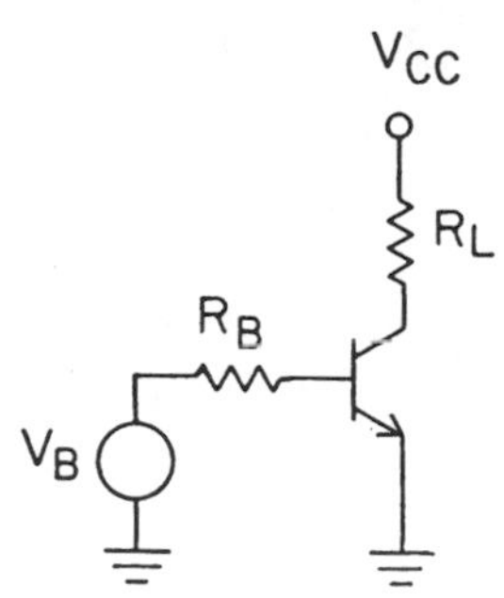

(a) Saturating.

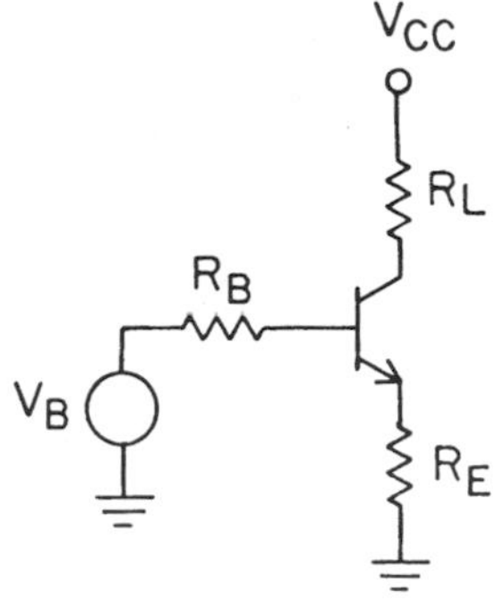

(b) Non-saturating.

Figure 42 Basic Logic Circuit Configurations.

To avoid this problem, we limit the base current by (1) limiting the size of the voltage swing between logic levels (V_B in Fig. 42) and (2) including a resistor in the emitter circuit, which tends to make the collector current less sensitive to the value of V_B [see Fig. 42(b)]. With these modifications, the saturation condition just described ($I_B > I_C(max)/\beta$) can be avoided and the inherent speed of the bipolar transistor realized.

5.3 The Basic ECL Gate

The basic ECL gate, shown in Fig. 43, builds on the nonsaturating circuit shown in Fig. 43. The number of inputs can be more than the three shown. The control transistor is Q_4. Together, V_{EE} and R_E constitute an effective current source that is divided between Q_4 and the input transistors. Transistor Q_5 and its associated circuitry provide a reference voltage to the base of the control transistor. The components and acceptable input voltages are selected to insure that all transistors always operate in the high speed (nonsaturated) mode.

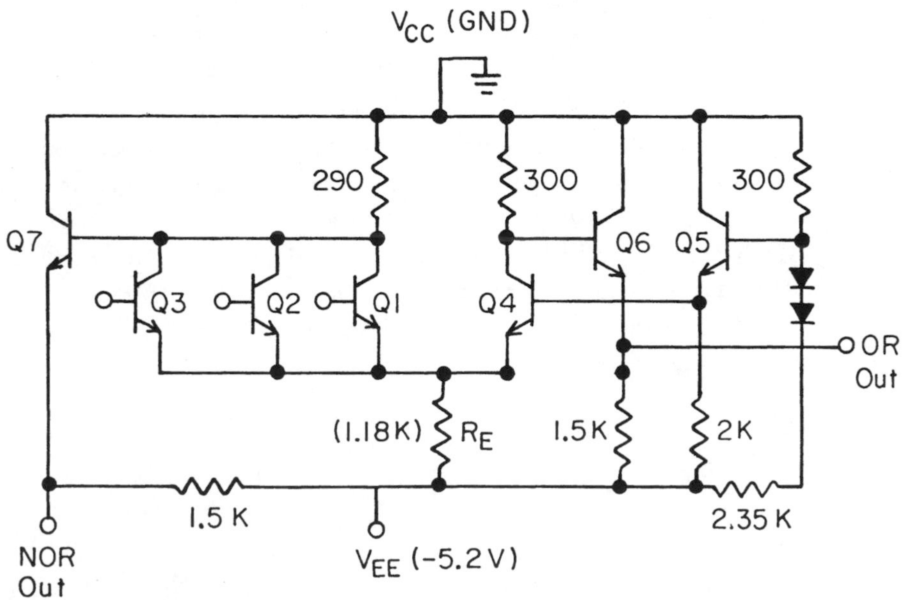

Figure 43 Emitter Coupled Logic (ECL) Gate.

Both NOR and OR outputs are provided by transistors Q_6 and Q_7; multiple outputs are also available. It is perhaps useful to compare this circuit with the NMOS NOR gate shown in Fig. 21. The NMOS circuit is clearly simpler (in fact, deceptively so). Bipolar circuits are certainly more complicated than their NMOS counterparts, and their design requires substantial experience.

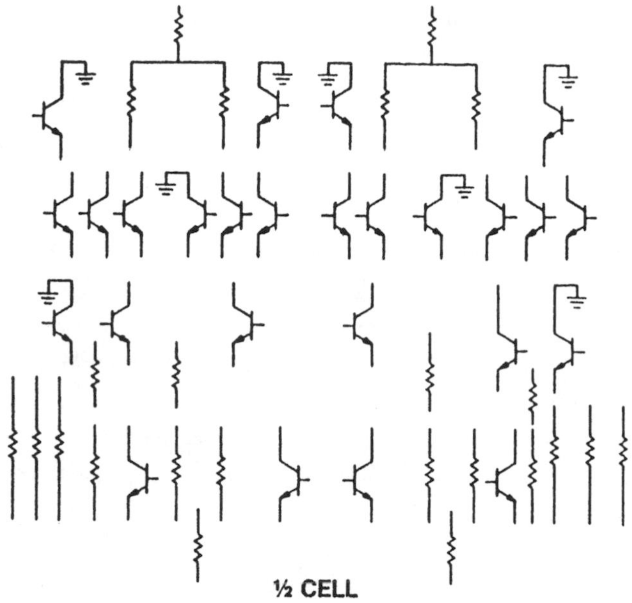

Figure 44   MECL 10,000 Half Macrocell; Uncommitted Components.

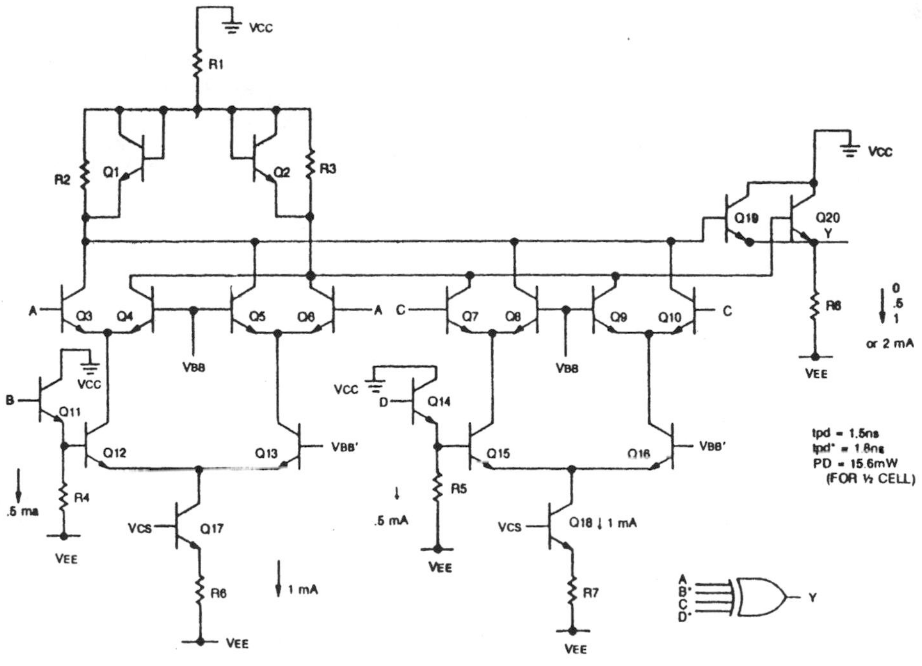

$$Y = A\bar{B}CD + \bar{A}BCD + AB\bar{C}D + ABC\bar{D} + A\bar{B}\bar{C}\bar{D} + \bar{A}B\bar{C}\bar{D} + \bar{A}\bar{B}C\bar{D} + \bar{A}\bar{B}\bar{C}D$$

Figure 45   MECL 10,000 Half Macrocell; Interconnects Defined by CAD.

The propagation delay of this gate is about 2 ns compared to 25 ns for the best NMOS and CMOS available. Hence, as suggested above, ECL is presently the technology of choice for fast circuits.

5.4 ECL Gate Arrays

Because of this speed advantage, gate arrays in ECL are also available for system designers who wish to build interface chips that operate at higher speeds than their MOS counterparts. A schematic illustration of an MECL 10,000 Half Macrocell array is shown in Figure 44 and a connection of the gate array components in a 4 input exclusive OR is shown in Fig. 45. The propagation delay for the exclusive OR is 1.5 ns. There are of course a number of resistors in this gate, which consume space, and hence reduce functional packing density. Also the power dissipation is relatively high. However, until advances in MOS technology are made, these are the prices that must be paid for fast circuits.

REFERENCES

1. J. F. Gibbons, Semiconductor Electronics, (McGraw-Hill, 1966). Chapters 2-4 provide a discussion of basic physics to supplement Section 1.

2. Carver Mead and Lynn Conway, Introduction to VLSI Systems, (Addison-Wesley, 1980). The pioneering book on VLSI design principles with special emphasis on the "sticks" approach.

3. A. S. Grove, Physics and Technology of Semiconductor Devices (John Wiley, 1967). Excellent text on basic physics and process technology for silicon devices.

4. J. A. Cooper, Jr., "Limitations on the Performance of Field Effect Devices for Logic Applications," Proc. IEEE, Feb. 1981, pp. 226-232. Excellent discussion of material requirements and limitations using simple circuit models and concepts.

COMPUTER AIDED DESIGN FOR MICROCOMPUTER SYSTEMS

Douglas Lewin

DEPARTMENT OF ELECTRICAL ENGINEERING AND ELECTRONICS
Brunel University, Uxbridge

1. Introduction

Current digital and computer systems have now reached such a high level of sophistication that conventional design methods are rapidly becoming inadequate. The major and fundamental problem is the complexity of the systems which are now feasible using LSI and VLSI sub-systems modules such as microprocessors, microcomputers, PLA's, UCLA's, ROM's, RAM's etc. Moreover future computer systems will be structured from parallel arrays of microcomputers and other programmable modules to give a distributed architecture.

In order to control and manage this complexity, for both software and hardware realisations, it has become necessary to use computer-aided design techniques and software design tools are now regarded as essential to the design process.

Digital systems can take many forms and it is important to broadly classify these application areas in order to put into perspective the design methods to be discussed in this paper. Current applications can be considered as falling into four main categories:

a) Small special purpose control logic
b) VLSI chip design
c) Computer architecture
d) Computer systems for control and real-time systems

The most important area of interest and the main concern of this paper is d) above - computer systems design - since applications of this kind will provide the impetus for future VLSI microcomputer systems. Note that both c) and d) above require hardware and software implementations to be considered in the design phase whereas with VLSI chips designs must inevitably result in a hardware realisation. However many of the design problems are common and software tools developed for the systems level, which should be implementation independent, are still pertinent to the design of VLSI.

The objective of this paper is to critically review the current methods of specifying, evaluating and synthesising digital structures with particular reference to microcomputer systems. In so doing the major theoretical problems which still remain to be solved will be highlighted together with some views on the research areas which need to be persued in order to establish viable software design tools.

2. The Design Problem

The design of any digital or microcomputer systems commences with the specification of the system in terms of its required behaviour as defined by the user. The design then proceeds towards a detailed realisation of the specification in terms of hardware and/or software.

There are in general two main methods of designing digital systems, these are:

a) the top-down approach where a behavioural specification, derived from user requirements, is decomposed into less complex functional modules which are then transformed into a structural form prior to realisation in a given LSI/VLSI technology (the physical form) or code for a specific host machine.

b) the bottom-up approach in which structural and physical modules are combined to realise a given behavioural specification.

In practice the design process is a combination of both top-down and bottom-up approaches (sometimes even middle-out!) but it is essential always to start with the user specification.

The top-down method constitutes what is essentially a hierarchial mode of working where complexity is handled by enforcing a multilevel structure using modules or sub-system components with well defined characteristics and inter-level communication protocols; note the similarity to structured programming techniques. Note also that the degree of detail required in the sub-system modules increases the deeper one goes down the hierarchy.

In general there are four major design levels as shown in Table 1: these are the behavioural level, functional level, structural level and the physical level. The mapping of a behavioural (algorithmic) specification into the functional (architectural)level is normally called systems design; the translation of a functional description into the structural (logic) level logic design, while the realisation of a structural representation at the physical level is called the physical design process.

As an illustration of this procedure let us consider the design of a microprocessor chip; this is shown diagramatically in figure 1. The first step is to specify the behaviour of the microprocessor in terms of its application requirements and performance, including the instruction set, after which the hardware architecture is defined and a rough estimate made of chip size and the overall layout topology; this constitutes the systems design stage of the design process.

The next step is the translation of the proposed architecture into the macro-micro orders necessary to execute the instruction set and their implementation in terms of state-transition tables and logic equations - this is the logic design phase.

The final stage is the physical design involving the derivation of the actual MOS (or an alternative technology such as I^2L) circuits and chip layout required to realise the microprocessor architecture. Note that the design procedure is not a

TABLE 1 - Hierarchial Design Levels

Design Stages	Design Procedures
System Design	*Behavioural* - system described in terms of interconnection of processes specifying required behaviour. Also called *algorithmic* level; note description independent of method used for implementation. *Functional* - system partitioned into sub-system
Logic Design	components with details of logic processes to be performed; also called *architectural* level *Structural* - description of actual hardware/software
Physical Design	realisations to be used in implementing sub-system functions; also called *Logic* level. *Physical* - translation of structural representation into physical realisation; also called *circuit* level.

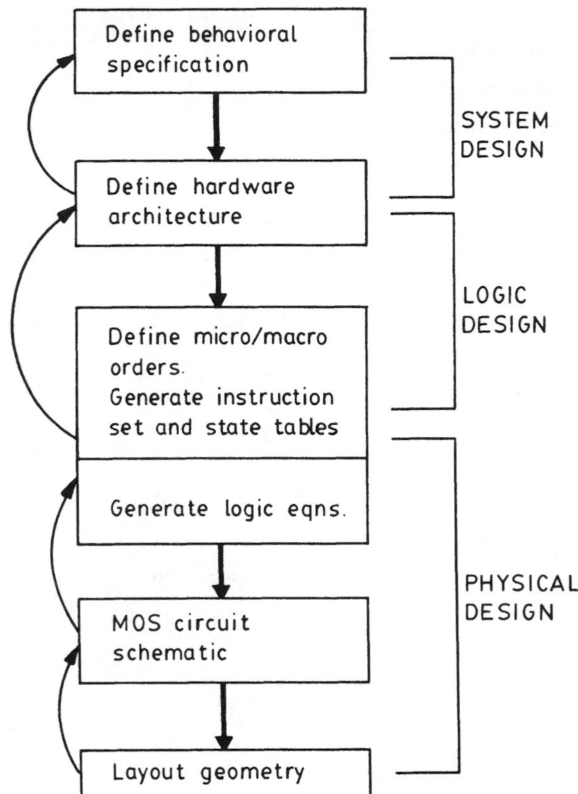

Figure 1 - Design of Microprocessor

a simple linear top-down progression, it is essential to be able to reiterate between all levels of the process. For example, it is important to be able to visualise the final layout in terms of MOS circuits and area at all stages of the design including the initial design specification stages. Again it is essential to back-track from the MOS circuit realisation to check that the control logic algorithms as specified by the state-tables and logic equations are still satisfied and to eliminate errors generated in the transformation process.

Thus it is essential that any computer-aided design scheme should be capable of describing and evaluating a specified hierarchial configuration, retaining autonomy at each level whilst preserving the algorithmic content during the required transformation between levels. It is highly unlikely that one general purpose design language would be able to serve all these purposes and it will require specific software tools to be made available for each level in the design hierarchy.

The range of software tools required for the design of microcomputer systems, including VLSI circuits, is shown in figure 2. Note the two-way iteration between each level and stage in the design process and that it is necessary for the evaluation procedures to extend across the design boundaries. For example, it should be possible to simulate both at the register (or bus) transfer levels and the logic gate levels and again at the logic gate and circuit levels (as for instance, with HILO[(1)] and SPLICE[(2)] respectively). Similar software tools can be used at the behavioural and functional levels when parts of the system are to be realised in software, the major difference occurs at the structural and physical levels when means must be provided to evaluate source and object code using for example static analysis and dynamic testing techniques[(3)].

With the advent of VLSI circuits it has become painfully obvious that CAD tools are absolutely vital in order to cope with the complexity and to exploit the possibilities of highly distributed concurrent processing systems.

One major problem is that of synthesis since most existing design techniques rely heavily on classical switching theory with the emphasis on reducing the number of gates and input terms and realisation in terms of discrete gates and bistables. Unfortunately when designing at the systems level using available LSI and VLSI modules as basic sub-system components these techniques are strictly limited in their application. It is more cost effective, for example, for a designer to use a LSI module such as a ROM or PLA to implement combinational logic even though there could be considerable redundancy than to apply minimisation techniques and implement in gates.

Again though finite-state machines are still used they would be employed to describe the control structure only, rather than the total machine which would also include the data-structure, and implemented using PLA's and shift registers in place of an optimal configuration of gates and bistables.

Thus using LSI modules the design goals have changed, the reduction of module types

Design Procedure / Design Stage	SPECIFICATION AND ANALYTIC TOOLS			
	Behavioural Level	Functional	Structural	Physical Level
System	Formal methods: Directed graphs, Petri Nets etc. ——— Algorithmic evaluation	System design Languages: PMS, SARA, LOGOS, etc. ——— System simulation		
Logic		Hardware descriptive languages, RTL's ISP etc. Logic eqns State machines ——— Logic simulation at function level	Logic diagrams Assigned machines ——— Logic simulation at gate level: test generation	
Physical			MOS transistor logic circuits etc. Circuit analysis	Layout, sticks diagrams etc. Design rule checker

Increasing level of Abstraction ↑

→ Increasing degree of detail

Figure 2 - Design tools for Digital Systems

and the number of interconnections is now far more important than minimising the total component count. It is apparent that a major problem exists due to the lack of a suitable design theory at the subsystem level, for instance algorithmic techniques are required for the cost effective realisation of systems using LSI modules such as UCLA's,PLA's etc. and including programmable devices such as microprocessors.

Even at the chip design level, where component count still has some meaning in terms of silicon area, the conventional theory is mostly inadequate. It is also important to realise that the complexity obtainable with VLSI is rapidly approaching that of a small minicomputer, thus we have all the problems of system design at the chip level.

A further complication in chip design is that the use of conventional logic design techniques produce circuit designs in terms of gates, bistables and/or standard LSI modules which must then be translated into the appropriate technology, say MOS circuits, before they can be realised on the chip. With very complex circuits, and certainly with VLSI, this process of transformation can and does lead to errors and the inefficient use of silicon area. It is essential that methods be developed to allow logic and system designers to relate the logic design process to the actual technology to be employed in the realisation of the system. Such techniques should take into account the physical design rules for layout geometries (for example, the line widths and separation of the diffused regions)and employ relevant logic structures.

The problem has been solved to some extent by Mead and Conway[(4)] who have proposed a procedure based on structured design and the use of stick diagrams (relating logic function to layout) and a simplified set of design rules; unfortunately this is only a beginning and a formal design methodology together with the relevant software tools still remains to be established.

An interesting approach to the problem that is receiving serious attention is based on the concept of a silicon compiler analogous to the normal high-level language compiler but in this case producing a mask-set for VLSI circuits. This rather over ambitious approach to designing VLSI has been brought about by the realisation that it is possible to derive a set of paramatised design rules for a particular technology, as described for example by Mead and Conway for NMOS, which can render the electronics "transparent" to the designer. Consequently by the use of suitable software design tools based on high-level functional programming languages[(5)] (such as LISP) the designer is able to specify and evaluate computer structures which can ultimately be realised as a silicon chip design. The feasibility of such an approach has been demonstrated by Sussman at MIT[(6)] who has developed his own software tools to design and implement a single chip microcomputer which directly interprets SCHEME a dialect of the LISP language.

Note that the use of simplified design rules will produce a circuit which is generously toleranced and easy to manufacture. However if optimum performance is required in terms of speed, packing densities etc., then it is necessary for the designer to have a much deeper understanding of the physical processes. Nevertheless in many cases, and of course depending on the system requirements, the Mead/Conway approach is perfectly adequate.

2.1. The Problem of Complexity

The limiting factor in the design of digital and microcomputer systems is that of complexity which arises due to the ever increasing ability and desire to design systems with a very large number of logic processes. Problems due to complexity, which in many cases are directly proportional to the number of state and input variables, can emerge in the following ways:

a) in the handling and control of the logistics of manufacture and production - layout, wiring, mask making, documentation etc.
b) in the design of the system - specification, evaluation synthesis, testing etc.
c) as computational inefficiency in the CAD algorithms.

The major problem that arises out of the inherent complexity of digital systems is the difficulty in achieving an error-free and reliable design, and the associated problems of testing and evaluation. There are two main causes of malfunction in a system, these are failures due to logical errors in the hardware/software design process and failure due to hardware faults. Though design errors will in general emanate as hardware faults and be detected in the same way they are fundamentally different and it is important to distinguish between these two categories if a reliable design is to be achieved.

The problems of testing digital systems are particularly acute and in many cases it is no longer cost effective to test complex logic chips. Deriving test sequences for large unstructured designs which have been developed intuitively is an extremely difficult procedure, particularly so in the case of VLSI chips. In fact unless cost-effective methods can be devised for testing VLSI the development of chips could be severely limited simply because complex designs cannot be produced and tested in production quantities. The solution lies in the design of testable or self-testing circuits using if necessary a high level of redundancy[(7)]. This approach has been adopted by IBM in the LSSD technique[(8)] which uses a structured design consisting of shift register latch (SRL) circuits which are used both to store information in the usual way but can also be reconfigured into a serial shift register network. The system can now be tested by applying tests to the primary inputs and examining the shift register outputs; note that the system can be considered, for test generation purposes, as a combinational network.

It would seem absolutely essential, in order to overcome the problems of complexity in designing reliable systems, that failure-tolerant computing techniques[(9)] be employed in future design work.

However the fundamental limitation imposed by complexity on the design process, especially in the development of software tools, is the efficiency of the computational process. In theory any problem in design or manufacture for which an algorithmic solution can be devised can be solved using a computer, that is with a software implementation of the algorithm. Unfortunately in many cases although in the limit the algorithm will always generate a solution they require an inordinate amount of computing time which renders them impracticable even with the fastest computers.

Algorithms can be broadly classified into two types[10][11]:

a) those whose execution time increases exponentially as a function of the number of input variables, called <u>exponential-time</u> algorithms, and
b) those whose execution times are a polynomial function of the input variables, called <u>polynomial-time</u> algorithms.

In general polynomial-time algorithm lead to an efficient machine implementation whereas exponential-time algorithms are highly inefficient and are generally considered intractable.

Problems with <u>known</u> polynomial-time solutions are said to be members of the class P, which is itself a sub-set of the class NP (non-deterministic polynomial). The class NP includes <u>all</u> problems which are soluble in principle, though in many cases only exponential-time solutions are known, though it is possible that polynomial-time algorithms <u>could</u> exist for these problems.

The class NP includes a wide variety of problems encountered in the evaluation and design of digital systems, for instance, algorithms for the minimisation of multiple output logic functions, the evaluation of Petri Nets, interconnection and layout etc. It is because many of these problems can only be solved using exponential-time algorithms that the design of complex systems, with very large input sets, is proving such a formidable task.

An alternative method of defining the class of NP problems is in terms of a non-deterministic machine, that is one in which its outcome is unpredictable, which traverses the paths of a tree structure on the basis of <u>guessing</u> the outgoing route at each node point. For example, let a computational problem be represented by a tree structure with N nodes as shown in figure 3, at each node P alternative branches may be taken and thus there are P^N possible outcomes. If there was sufficient information available at each node to decide which branch to take a sequential machine could complete the computation in KN cycles where K is the average number of computation cycles per node; the problem is said to be linear in N or of order N called O(N). However if there is not enough information at node P to positively decide which branch to take, a branch is chosen at random and the procedure back-tracked to the original node if the path is found to be incorrect; the procedure is repeated until the information gathered is sufficient to enable the correct branch to be selected.

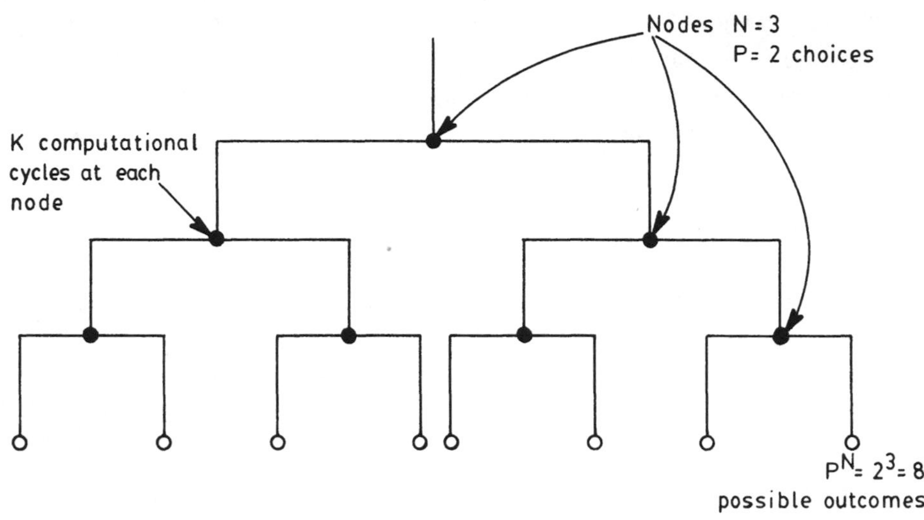

If problem order O(N) then computation complete KN cycles

Figure 3 - Class of NP Problems

Now imagine a sequential non-deterministic machine which can always select the correct branch at each node, such a machine could solve the problem in O(N) cycles. Thus NP problems can be defined as those which an imaginary non-deterministic sequential machine can solve in a bounded number (N) of cycles.

It has been shown that within the class NP there exists some general problems (called NP-complete) to which all other problems in the class NP may be reduced. Thus it follows if an efficient algorithm can be found for any one problem of this type that the algorithm would hold for every similar problem in NP.

Moreover, since NP complete problems exhibit the difficulties associated with all other problems in NP they are widely considered to be computationally intractable. NP-complete problems can be explained in terms of our tree searching example by considering a class of problems such that working one path through to the end gives no information concerning the outcome of other paths, thus the algorithm degenerates into an exhaustive search procedure.

Thus it follows that if the problems encountered in the design and evaluation of computer systems are NP - complete it would be pointless to search for an efficient machinable algorithm which yields an optimal solution. Moreover there is another class of difficult problems which contain NP, this is the polynomial-space-bounded problem which limits a solution in terms of storage and hardware. However it is possible in some cases to perform a time-space transformation which could for specific problems render an intractable problem soluble, for example by using ultra parallel processing techniques, a method which is being investigated for VLSI[12]. Note however that in general an NP-complete problem would require, using our tree example, an exponential number of processors situated at each node!

With these apparently insurmountable difficulties what can be done to devise suitable design procedures which can be implemented as software tools? The answer lies in developing heuristic algorithms which generate a good but not optimal (or error free?) solution and in accepting the limitations imposed by such algorithms. While designers attempt to obtain definitive and theoretically correct solutions to design problems little will be achieved and a more realistic approach whereby a "best solution" is generated together with some statistical estimate of the operational limits must be adopted. In this respect the problem solving methods which have evolved in the field of artificial intelligence could be directly applicable to the development of design aids[13]

2.2. Summary

Thus we may summarise the major problems in the design of microcomputer systems as follows:

a) currently there are very few viable software tools for the specification and synthesis of digital and computer systems. This is especially true at the behavioural design level where formal specification and evaluation methods are urgently required.

b) conventional synthesis methods are no longer applicable. The availability of LSI/VLSI modules has required a change from design at the binary level using gates and bistables to design at the digital level using hardware/software modules in a structured manner.

c) as a consequence of increasing complexity and the fact that most CAD algorithms tend to be NP-complete the generation of efficient algorithms presents a very difficult problem.

d) There is a need to consider the total system including the analogue and transducer elements. Too much emphasis is being placed on the processor architectures; real-time microcomputer systems depend for their very existence on the input of data and the need to perform useful work with the processed output.

e) A further area that has been neglected is the man-machine interface. The study of human factors as related to the requirements for controlling and operating complex computer systems is extremely important and operator errors can invalidate (sometimes with disastrous results) an otherwise good systems design.

It will be apparent that there are a large number of unsolved problems for which solutions must be obtained if viable and effective CAD design tools are to be developed. Moreover it is essential that the process of designing microprocessor systems be considered as a total engineering activity requiring both software and hardware expertise.

3. Methods of Specification and Evaluation

The need for specification and evaluation exists at all levels in the design hierarchy but it is at the behavioural level where software tools, in the form for example of descriptive languages, are most urgently required. The importance of the behavioral level is that it is here that the user's requirements are translated into a formal statement which will determine the overall design of the system. If errors or misunderstandings occur at this stage the repercussions will be felt throughout the entire design process. Moreover it is also essential to demonstrate to the customer that the proposed interpretation of his requirements does in fact meet his actual needs (and form the basis for a contract) hence the vital importance of evaluation procedures.

An ideal specification language at the behavioural level should have the following characteristics:

a) able to represent logical processes in algorithmic form and independent of any eventual implementation.

b) facility to formally evaluate the information flow in large variable systems, considering both input and state values.

c) capable of handling concurrent processes and providing an insight into alternative partitionings of the system.

d) possible to proceed from the behavioural description to the functional level without loss of algorithmic content.
e) can act as a means of communication between customers, designers and implementers.
f) able to interact directly with the designer in a conversational mode and with graphic facilities.

Most of these properties will of course also apply to design languages used further down the design hierarchy at the functional and structural levels. Moreover in these cases the languages can be more specific and directly related to actual hardware/software realisations. Note the relevance and importance of the specification languages to the synthesis function and as such they form the integral basis for a total design methodology.

One of the more important functions of a specification language is to aid the designer in investigating various decompositions of the system thus providing the insight and corroborative evidence necessary for the allocation of hardware/software processes. The partitioning of systems has been studied by Parnas(15) and the criteria proposed have been adopted for use in a number of design schemes, these are:

a) Decomposition may be performed in two ways:
   i) according to the independent user functions which need to be implemented, in this case the sub-system modules will correspond to user requirements and provide a direct mapping for evaluation.
   ii) according to the system functions which are required to satisfy user requirements; this approach normally leads to a better utilisation of shared resources.
b) A partitioning may be chosen such that the set of modules are estimated to have the same degree of complexity, or an equal influence on performance; in both cases the objective would be to achieve a balanced system.
c) Modules may be selected because they are readily constructed from known and available elements and therefore will avoid another partition step.
d) Modules may also be selected because they simplify refinements of higher level behavioural models in a manner which guarantees preservation of desired properties in particular the algorithmic content.

The proposed partitioning of the system must of course be capable of evaluation either by formal analysis or, less satisfactorily, simulation methods.

Numerous methods have been proposed for the description and design of digital systems; these techniques may be broadly classified as follows:

a) <u>Functional Descriptive Programming Languages</u>, such as computer hardware description languages (CHDL) including register transfer languages (RTL), simulation languages like GASP-PL/1 and general purpose languages like APL,ALGOL68 and PL/1.
b) <u>Graph Theoretic Methods</u>, employing transition graphs, Petri nets, computation

schemata etc.

c) Finite State Machine techniques, such as state-tables, regular expressions algorithmic state machines (ASM) etc.

These methods will now be considered in more detail in the following sections.

3.1 Computer Hardware Descriptive Languages(16)(17) The intuitive procedures used in the design of computer systems are normally centred around a predefined register and highway configuration. The execution of a required system function such as a machine code instruction is then interpreted in terms of a sequence of micro-orders (called a control or micro-program) which controls the required transfers and logic and arithmetic operations between registers. The same basic technique is employed in the design of VLSI systems where a finite state machine is used to generate the macro-micro orders. Register transfer languages are based on this heuristic design procedure and are similar to high level programming languages in that both carry out register assignments and allow the specification of algorithm. Register transfer languages allow the declaration of register configurations (the data structure) and the specification, using program statements, of the required data flow and processing operation between these registers. Thus the declarative section of the program in essence forms a linguistic description of the block diagram of a machine while the RTL program statements specify the control programs for executing particular instructions. The timing of the operations in a set of RT statements is represented by the order in which the operations are evaluated without regard to the actual real-time delays involved in the register transfers. The order in which the operations are evaluated depends on whether the RT language is procedural or non-procedural in nature. In procedural languages an explicit ordering is imposed on the statements with a statement or operation being evaluated on the completion of the preceding one. Non-procedural languages have no meaning associated with the lexographical ordering of their statements and a conditional global or clock period prefixes each statement which governs the sequence of evaluation.

Register transfer languages are mainly used for documentation and simulation. In addition they can also be employed for the generation of Boolean equations for the processing and transfer logic using a special translator for the RTL descriptions.

The Computer Design language, CDL(18), is a typical example of an early register transfer language which has been used extensively in teaching computer structures. A CDL description for the LOAD instruction is shown in Table 2. Note the initial declaration of the data structure which allows main memory, registers, register fields and flags to be specified. For example, after declaring register R to be of 18-bits in length it is possible to declare a field of this register consisting of bits 0 - 5 and called R(OP). Note also that in declaring main memory both the total number of words and word length need to be specified. CDL is a non-procedural language and permits the use of timing control signals such as /F(6)*P(1)/ which

TABLE 2 - CDL Description for LOAD Instruction

```
Comment,        Data Structure
Register,       R(0 - 17)                Buffer register memory M
                A(0 - 17)                Arithmetic register
                C(0 - 11)                Address register memory M
                D(0 - 11)                Program counter
                F(1 - 18)                Buffer register control memory CM
                G                        Stop/start control bistable
                H(1 - 5)                 Address register memory CM
Subregister     R(OP)=R(0-5)             op. code digits register R
                R(ADD)=R(6-17)           address digits register R
                F(ADD)=F(1-5)            address digits register F
Memory          M(C)=M(0-4095, 0-17)     main memory
                CM(H)=CM(0-31, 1-18)     control memory
Clock           P(1 - 3)                 Three phase clock
Comment         Control Structure
                /F(6)*P(1)/ R←M(C)
                /F(7)*P(2)/ H←R(OP),C←R(ADD),D←D+1
                /F(8)*P(3)/ IF(G) THEN (F←CM(H))
                            ELSE (H←0, C←0, D←0, R←0)
                END
```

dictates that the transfer operation R ← M(C) (that is the location in M given by the contents of Address register C is transferred to the Buffer register R) takes place when bit 6 of the Control Memory buffer register is high in clock phase one. Note also the use of the ALGOL like conditional statement IF-THEN-ELSE. The control section of the program may also be used to describe a finite-state machine controller which can be either synchronous or asynchronous in operation.

A more recent register transfer language which has been used to describe and simulate computer architectures[19] and in particular to perform comparison studies of computers for military use[20] is ISP (Instruction-Set-Processor). ISP was originally developed to precisely describe primitive at the programming level of design in the PMS/ISP descriptive system due to Bell and Newell[21]. Thus an ISP description can be considered as a programming language for the algorithmic description of instruction sets and architectures; it also contains however a number of constructs which can be used to describe a wide range of digital systems.

Computer architectures are usually described in ISP by a fixed format composed of declarations and procedures. The declarations consist of the following:

a) Memory - physical components which hold coded information these may be:
   Main Memory, described as an array of registers, for example, Memory \MP[0:255]<0:7> which is a memory of 256 8-bit words. Constants are by default decimal numbers unless otherwise specified by the ↓ (base) operator as, for example, [0:7777↓8] which is 4096 words expressed in octal. Bits are named from left to right; the slash \ operator allows alternative names to precede the declaration.
   Registers are declared in a similar manner, for instance, Accumulator \AC<0:15> is a 16-bit register AC; it is also possible to specify individual named bits ie: R < R_1;R_2;R_3;R_4;R_5;R_6;R_7;R_8> is a 8-bit register.
   Flags - individual bits or status flags indicating processor states may be defined as, for instance, Linkbit\L.

b) Data Operators - Data operators work on data types as defined in terms of registers and include the following classes:

Arithmetic	(+, -, *, ÷)
Boolean	(-, ∨, ∧, ⊕, ≡)
Relational	(=, ≠, <, ≤, >, ≥)
Transfer	(←)
Concatenation	(□)

Expressions are composed of data types and data operations and can if required be followed by a modifier giving more information about the meaning of the operands or operators. Modifier consists of a data type name or an operation mode enclosed in curly brackts, for example:

A ← B + C {1's complement}

c) Instruction Formats, these are specific instances of data types and may be declared in terms of register data types and sub-fields of these registers, for instance;

Instruction Register\IR<0:11>
Operation code\OP<0:2>:= IR<0:2>
Indirect address\bit IB := IR<3>
Page 0 bit\P0 := IR<4>
Page address<0:6> := IR<5:11>

the instruction format defined by this specification is shown in figure 4.

ISP procedures take the following form:

a) The interpretation stage describes the mechanism whereby the processor fetches, decodes and executes the instructions

ISP allows concurrency of operations and the semicolon ; is used as a delimiter for lists of concurrent operations. Sequencing of operations is expressed by using the term 'next' as a delimiter for lists of sequential actions. Complex concurrent and sequential operations can be descrbed in terms of simpler activities using the operators parenthesis, next, and semicolon in a recursive manner. For example:

IR← MP[PC]	Fetch Instruction from memory
IR← MP[PC];PC←PC+1	PC incremented simultaneously with Fetch
IR← MP[PC];PC←PC+1;next INT←1	Two steps in parallel followed by third step

Thus the instruction fetch process may be expressed:

Fetch := (IR←MP[PC];PC←PC+1)

The evoking of actions can be controlled by conditional actions of the form:

Condition ⇛ action - sequence

where the condition is normally a Boolean and describes when the operation will be initiated.

b) Instruction Set definition - each instruction must be precisely defined in terms of the particular operation code the processor executes, for example the logical AND instruction may be defined as follows:

AND:=(OP=0 ⇛ AC←AC∧MP[EA])

where OP is the operation field and EA the effective address.

The ISP notation has been implemented at Carnegie Melon University primarily for use as a simulation language and in this form it is called ISPS(22). A very simplified version of an ISPS program for a processor is shown in Table 3. To create a running simulator from this description it must be compiled, translated and loaded. Simulation commences by initialising the memory and starting the ICYCLE procedure. The ISP notation and ISPS system have been used extensively by DEC in the design of the PDP11 and VAX family of computers.

3.1.1. System Design Languages. Some hardware description languages have been deve-

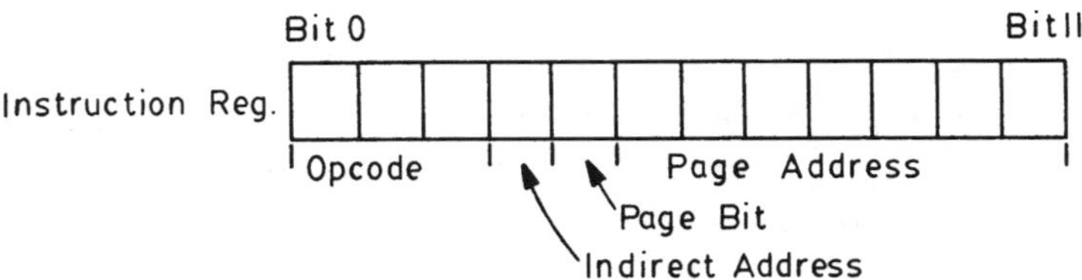

Figure 4 - Instruction Formats

TABLE 3 - ISP description of Processor

```
Processor:=
        Begin
        **Memory**
          Mp\Main Memory[0:1027]<0:15>,
        **Processor State**
        Instruction Register\IR<0:15>,
              Operation Field\OP<0:4>:=IR<0:4>,
              Indirect add Bit\IB:=IR<5>,
              Address Field\ADR<0:9>:=IR<6:15>,
        Program Counter\PC<0:15>,
        Accumulator\Acc<0:15>,
        Effective add\EA<0:9>:=
          Begin
          Decode IB ⇒
              Begin
              0:=EA←ADR
              1:=
                Begin
                IF ADR=0 ⇒EA←Mp[0]←MP[0]+1;
                IF ADR≠0 ⇒EA←Mp[ADR]
                End
              End,
          End,
        **Instruction Interpretation**
        Interpretation cycle\ICYCLE:=
          Begin
            IR←Mp[PC];
            PC←PC+1;
            IEXEC( )
            Restart ICYCLE
          End
        Instruction execution\IEXEC:=
          Begin
          Decode OP ⇒
            Begin
            0\AND:=ACC←ACC∧Mp[EA()],
            1\JMP:=PC←EA(),
            2\RTN:=Begin
                   PC←Mp[Mp[0]]Next
                   MP[0]←MP[0]-1
                   End,
                :
                :  ETC
                :
            31\
            End
          End
        End
```

loped which extend upwards from the register level and allow a partitioned system consisting of interconnected autonomous modules to be described. In the Digital Systems Design Language, DDL,[23] a system is viewed as a collection of several sub-systems or automatons each possessing "private" facilities and having access to "public" facilities communicating via common busses. In DDL a system is specified using a hierarchial block structured description, where the outermost block defines the whole system in terms of sub-system modules, global variables, input-output requirements etc., and the inner blocks specify the module in terms of state and I/O behaviour.

The description itself is in a fairly standard RTL form, for example the declaration of memory and registers:

<RE> A[10], R[21] = RL[10]oRR[9]o P o K

<ME> M[0:1023, 16]

where A is a 10-bit register with the stages numbered 1 to 10. Register R of length 21-bits is declared to consist of a left part with 10-bits, a right part with 9-bits and two individual bits P and K at the extreme right; the small circle o denotes catenation. Memory M is declared as a two-dimensional array of 1024 16-bit words. Note the use of the declaration type tags <RE> and <ME>

To enable a system level specification to be developed special operators and declarations are necessary, these are shown in Table 4. For example, since sub-system components communicate with each other via the shared bus, activity in one component could influence activity in another, consequently it is necessary to provide an activation operator of the form:

$\Rrightarrow$AVID (CSOP)

where AVID is the name of a sub-system component and CSOP a set of operations OP_i (including conditionals and transfers) which may be executed simultaneously, thus:

$CSOP = Op_1, OP_2, \ldots, OP_n$ for $n \geq 1$

For instance consider the statement

$\Rrightarrow$ACC(A=B∨D, C=E, F←G, →STATE4)

This statement indicates that signals B∨D and E are to be connected to the common bus terminals A and C (previously declared using <TE>) and register G transferred to register F. The symbol $\Rrightarrow$ACC signifies that the automaton ACC will also be affected by these signals.

Conditional statements are handled in two ways

a) $|BE|\ CSOP_1;\ CSOP_0$

this is equivalent to IF THEN ELSE statement; |BE| has value 1 if $CSOP_1$ to be executed and 0 for $CSOP_0$

b) $|BE|\ CSOP_1$

equivalent to IF THEN, $CSOP_1$ executed when $|BE|=1$

Timing control is accomplished by declaring state identifiers and the CSOP's that

TABLE 4

Declarations and Operators in the DDL Language

a) Declaration

Type	Hardware
MEmory or REgister	n - or one-dimensional arrays of bistables
TErminal	n - dimensional set of wires, terminals or buses
BOolean	logic network defined by Boolean equations
OPerator	combinational circuitry shared among facilities
ELement	Input-Output terminals of standard module
STate	defines states of an automaton
AUtomaton	defines an automation composed of FSM and facilities
SEgment	defines portion of the automaton which contains the declaration
SYstem	defines a system with K automata and the system's public facilities
IDentifier	assigns identifiers to previously defined operands
TIme	periodic clock or signal generator

b) Operators

Activation	⇛AVID (CSOP)	CSOP is a set of operations that effect automaton AVID
Connection	ID = BE	The terminals ID are connected to the network defined by Boolean expression
Transfer	ID← BE	Memory elements ID are loaded from network defined by Boolean expression
Transition type 1	→ SID	Execute a transition to state SID (in the same block)
Transition type 2	⇒SEGID(→NID,⇒RID)	Execute a transition to state NID in segment SEG and return to state RID upon execution of a return operation
Return transition	⇒	Return to the state specified by a transition type 2
IF - THEN	|BE| $CSOP_1$	If BE=1, execute $CSOP_1$
IF- THEN - ELSE	|BE| $CSOP_1$;$CSOP_0$	If BE=1, execute $CSOP_1$, if BE=0 execute $CSOP_0$

are to be performed when automaton in each of its states (finite-state machine controller). Alternatively the <Tl> declaration may be used which specifies a periodic clock generator. For example a mod 3 counter within a system may be described as follows:

```
<AU> MOD 3 : P :
<ST> S0 : G0 : → S1
     S1 : → S2
     S2 : → S0, DONE=1
```

Note the automaton waits in state S0 until signal G0 is received when the transition to S1 is effected and so on; note also that both synchronous and asynchronous machines may be defined in this way since DDL is a non-procedural language.

The main advantage of the DDL language is that it allows large digital systems to be dealt with in an organised manner. It is also possible to translate a DDL description of a system into sets of Boolean and next-state equations which describe a hardware realisation of the system, alas in conventional logic design terms(24).

A number of software implementations of DDL have been described(25)(26) in the main these have been sub-sets of the full language and used for simulation purposes.

Another multi-level design system is the language for Automated Logic and System Design, LALSD(27)(28). This system consists of three separate languages - a graphical one based on Petri nets, LALSD itself and a logic level language - reflecting the behavioural,functional and structural levels of design. Thus LALSD can support a multi-level modelling philosophy with the designer being able to specify his design at any level of detail and to decompose the system into independent subsystems. LALSD also allows parallel control operations to be specified and can be used for synchronous and asynchronous systems.

In LALSD a digital system is viewed as consisting of two parts, a control structure and a data structure comprising registers and ALU functions. The control part describes the behaviour of the system transmitting control signals to activate the data structure components (note the analogy at the lower level with FSM controllers and RTL's generally). This approach has the advantage that the control structures can be modelled using Petri nets and a high level analysis performed checking for deadlocks, determinacy etc.

Simulation packages have been implemented for LALSD at the functional level(29) and also a logic level simulator(30). Unfortunately these simulators are disparate and have quite different input language discriptors and control and output commands, thus it is very difficult to achieve a true multilevel evaluation. Moreover at the behavioural level evaluation takes place on the control structure only and a full interpreted analysis, taking into account the data structure is not possible.

The SABLE system(31) developed at Stanford University is also mutli-level in concept but does not use a directed graph approach. There are three major components - a design language for indicating behaviour called ADLIB, a structured design language (SDL) and SABLE itself which provides a structure and behaviour linking environment In SABLE digital systems are considered as being comprised of sub-system components but whose behaviour and structure, rather than separate control and data flows, are represented. ADLIB is used to describe the behaviour of each module (called comptype) using well defined input-output interfaces. The connections between the various comptypes (called nets) are described in SDL; note that the simulation system SABLE has a multi-level capability due to the inherent nature of the original specification.

Another hierarchial organised descriptive system which was originally developed to aid communication between designers is the Processor-Memory-Switch (PMS) notation[32]

The PMS system consists of a number of structural primitives connected together in such a way as to form a network of components, each performing data-processing operations on the information flow through the network. Information is assumed to occur in packets called <u>i-units</u> and is measured in bits, or equivalent units such as bytes, etc. There are seven basic primitives, each distinguished by the function it performs; they are as follows:

<u>Memory, M</u>. A read-write storage component for i-units, including an addressing scheme.

<u>Link, L</u>. A component that transfers i-units from one component to another.

<u>Control, K</u>. A component that initiates the operation of other components, analogous to the control structure of a program or a microprogram unit. All components, except for control, consist of a set of discrete operations which must be individually evoked.

<u>Switch, S</u>. This component is used to construct a link between other components and functions essentially either as a multiplexer or demultiplexer circuit.

<u>Transducer, T</u>. Used to change i-units from one form to another whilst at the same time preserving its meaning (but not necessarily its information content, that is the number of bits in the representation), for instance, parallel to serial conversion, voltage levels to magnetic flux or holes in punched paper tape,etc.

<u>Data operation, D.</u> Used to change the meaning of i-units, for example, the component would perform arithmetic functions, logical and shifting operations, etc.

<u>Processor, P</u>. A component capable of interpreting a program in order to execute a sequence of operations. It consists of a set of operations of the type described above, that is, M, L, K, S, T, and D primitives.

These components can be connected together to form a structure representing a stored-program digital computer (or any other digital system). For example, the basic configuration for a computer C is defined by:

$$C := M_p - P_c - T - X$$

where P_c represents a central processing unit (CPU) and M_p a primary memory (that is, one which is directly accessible from P_c) which holds the program. The input-output devices are represented by T which are connected to the external environment X. An alternative arrangement at a more detailed level would be

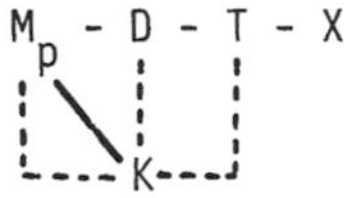

```
M  - D - T - X
 p
:\     :   :
: \    :   :
:  \   :   :
:----\K----:
```

where P_c is split into a control and arithmetic unit; the full lines represent data and the broken lines control paths. The diagram can be further expanded by associating local control with each component rather than combining all the control functions into the component K. For example, K may be decomposed into $K(M_p)$, K(P) and K(T) to represent the control of the memory, processor/data-operations, and transducer components respectively.

Using this notation computer systems can be described at various detailed levels. For instance, in the above descriptions the links were not written in as separate entities; this would only become necessary if the transmission details were relevant to system performance, etc. Note that components are themselves decomposable into other component; for example memories can be considered as a set of addressing switches and submemories, a processor may be partitioned into a data-operation component plus control, etc. Thus it will be seen that the PMS notational system embodies the principle of layering described in the last section.

As well as using component suffixes to denote particular properties (for example M_p to indicate that the function of M is that of a primary store) a detailed specification may be associated with ach component. This takes the general form

$$X(a_1:v_1;a_2:v_2;\ldots a_k:v_k)$$

where X is the component and a is an attribute having the value v. Each component parameter, that is the pair $(a_i:v_i)$ can be defined independently and thus there is no significance in the order in which they are written. The parameters may take various forms, for example, costs, memory capacities, information flow rates, power etc. There are in general a very large number of parameters that can be associated with each component; this is one of the major difficulties in specifying a viable descriptive system. The technique adopted is to abbreviate where possible, using only pertinent parameters. For example, a processor may be defined in terms of operation times, thus

P_c (operation times : add:200ns;store:200ns;multiply:1.8μs;...)

In which the times for each operation are listed independently. Alternatively, it is possible to give an abbreviated description by simply stating a range of operating times, i.e.

P_c(operation time:200ns-1.8μs)

Again, a main store may be defined as:

M(function:primary;technology:MOS;operation time:100ns;
size:4096 8;word:16 bits)

but it is also possible to convey the same information to an informed reader by the expression

M MOS(100ns;4 kB:16 bits).

The PMS notation allows complex digital computer systems to be specified at many levels, from a complete detailed description to a highly simplified schematic. Though the notation is somewhat fluid, it is sufficiently standardized to enhance the communication of ideas and systems. However, it is unsuitable in its present form for CAD purposes, since it is essentially a descriptive, rather than formal, notation which prohibits the development of analysis and synthesis procedures.

The PMS notation has been extensively used in design work at DEC and for teaching purposes. Though originally conceived as a notation for describing computer structures it has nevertheless been implemented as a language, called PMSL(33), and used as a means of describing and evaluating computer systems, in terms of performance cost and efficiency.

Though considerable effort has been expended on the development of register transfer and hardware descriptive languages generally very few have come up to the design requirements or been adopted for use in a real engineering situation. Moreover many of the RTL systems so far developed have already been outdated by the rapid progress in circuit technology. Table 5 lists and surveys some of the more important computer hardware descriptive languages.

Problem orientated programming languages when used for evaluation suffer from the inherent disadvantage that they have no formal mathematical structure. Consequently, system behaviour must be interpreted indirectly from program performance whilst operating on certain specified data types. Hardware description languages usually describe a system in terms of simulated components and their interconnection. In order to evaluate logic networks modelled in this way it is necessary to perform a physical step-by-step examination of all the relevant input-output conditions. It will be obvious that this is a time consuming process and that large amounts of storage would be required to represent the architectural model. In addition since the system is described in terms of a topological model, rather than by formal methods, the description is of limited value for general communication. Moreover since most design languages are derived from machine independent languages like ALGOL, APL, and PASCAL there are problems with hardware features such as operating speed, parallelism and asynchronism. These features are often very difficult to describe and hence the correspondance between the description and the hardware being described is often ambiguous.

3.2. Directed Graph Methods

One mathematical tool which is finding increasing application in computer systems design and analysis is graph theory(34) and some of the more successful specification systems utilise this approach. A directed graph is a mathematical model of a system showing the relationships that exist betwen members of its constituent set.

TABLE 5 - Survey of Computer Hardware Description Languages

Name	Date	Type	Use	Comments
LDT	1964	Procedural, ALGOL type blocks	Timing analysis, logic design	Sequencing given by order of statements
CDL	1965	Non-procedural ALGOL based	Simulation and logic design	Sequencing specified by conditions labels
DDL	1968	Non-procedural block structured	Simulation and logic design	System design language DDL-P subset of DDL (1979)
APL	1969	Procedural GP programming language	Description and logic design	Used in IBM ALERT system for design of logic circuits. Also the basis for AHPL
ISP	1970	Procedural, ALGOL type blocks	Description and simulation	Proposed as standard CHDL. Used to compare computer architectures.
CASSANDRE	1968	Non-procedural ALGOL based	Simulation of micro-programs	Hierarchial structured
LALSD	1971	Procedural, block structured	Modelling and logic design at all levels	System design language implemented using PL/1
CASD	1970	Procedural, based on PL/1	Simulation and logic design	System level language but never implemented, IBM feasibility study.
SABLE	1979	Procedural	Simulation	Implemented in PASCAL

The elements of the set are normally called vertices or nodes with the relationship between them being indicated by arcs or edges. An example of a directed graph is shown in Figure 5a where the set of nodes is given by

$$N = \{n_1, n_2, n_3, n_4, n_5\}$$

and the set of edges by

$$E = \{e_1, e_2, e_3, e_4, e_5, e_6\}$$

Graphs may be classified into various types according to their properties. For example a net shown in figure 5b is a directed graph consisting of a finite non-empty set of nodes and a finite set of edges. Note that a net may have parallel edges, that is two nodes connected by two different edges but both acting in the same direction. Again, a net which does not contain parallel edges but with assigned values to its edges is called a network as shown in figure 5c.

Directed graphs have been used for instance, to represent information flow in control and data structures, parallel computation schemata etc. The major advantage of using graph theory, apart from the visual convenience, is that formal methods can be used for the manipulation of graph structures represented as matrices.

A directed graph approach which has found considerable application in the description and analysis of digital systems is the Petri net[35][36]. The Petri net is an abstract, formal graph model of information flow in a system consisting of two types of node, places drawn as circles and transitions drawn as bars, connected by directed arcs. Each arc connects a place to a transition or vice versa; in the former case the place is called an input place and in the latter an output place of the transition. The places correspond to system conditions which must be satisfied in order for a transition to occur; figure 6 shows a typical Petri net. In addition to representing the static conditions of a system the dynamic behaviour may be visualised by moving markers (called tokens) from place to place round the net. It is usual to represent the presence of tokens by a black dot inside the place circle; a Petri net with tokens is called a marked net. A Petri net marking is a particular assignment of tokens to places in the net and defines a state of the system; for example, in figure 6a the marking of places B and C defines the state where the conditions B and C hold and no others.

Progress through the net from one marking to another, corresponding to state changes, is determined by the firing of transitions according to the rules;

a) a transition is enabled if all of its input places hold a token
b) any enabled transition may be fired
c) a transition is fired by transferring tokens from input places to output places; thus firing means that instantaneously the transition inputs are emptied and all of its outputs filled.

(Note that transitions cannot fire simultaneously, thus only one transition can occur at a time).

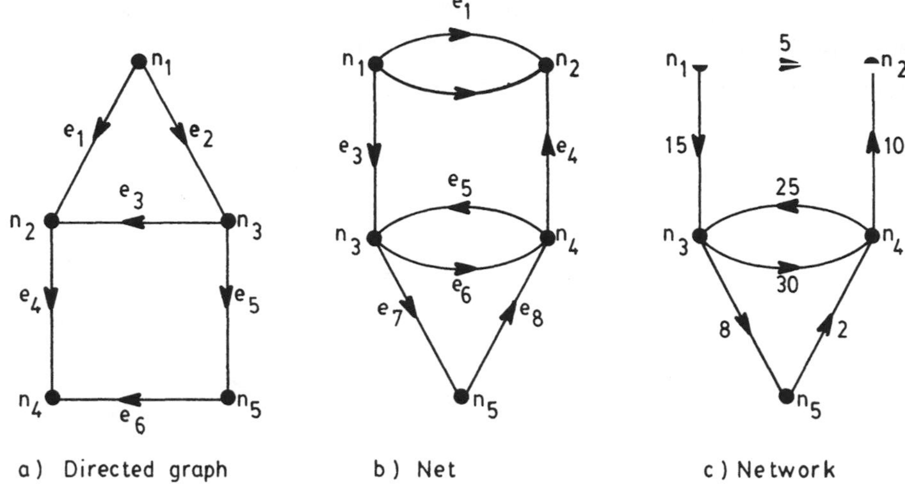

Figure 5 - Directed Graphs

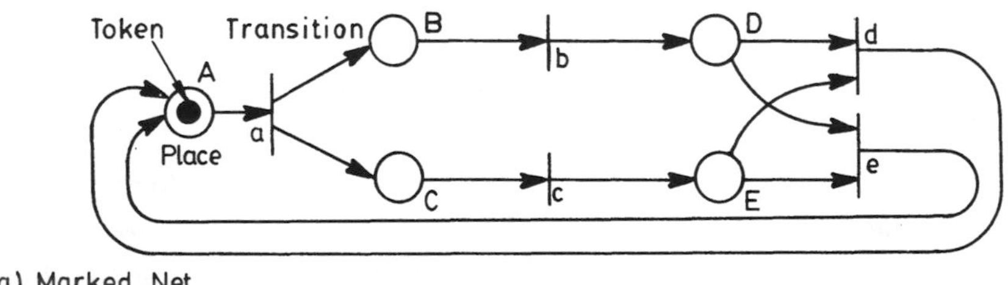

a) Marked Net

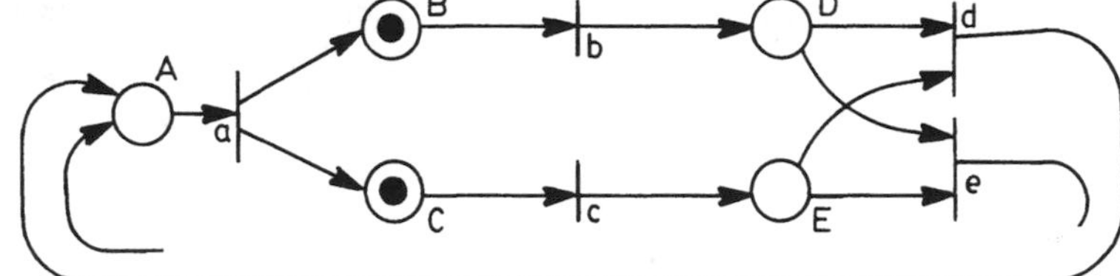

b) Net after Firing

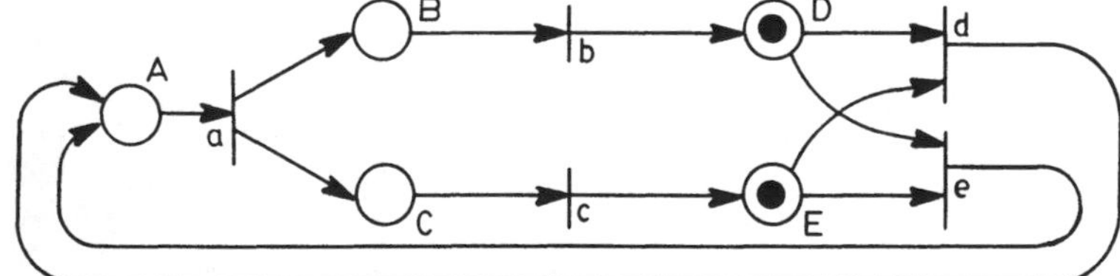

c) Conflict Situation

Figure 6 - Petri Nets

This is illustrated in figure 6, where 6a shows the original marked net and 6b the state of the net after firing transition a; note that the Petri net is able to depict concurrent operations. After two further firings the net would arrive at the marking shown in figure 6c, here the net is said to be in conflict since firing either of the transitions d or e would cause the other transition to be disabled. In general a conflict will arise when two transitions share at least one input place; Petri net models are normally constrained to be conflict free. Another limitation imposed on the model is that a place must not contain more than one token at the same time: this condition leads to a safe Petri net. This restriction is essential when the Petri net is used to represent a set of interrelated events and conditions in a practical environment. Conditions would normally be represented by places and interpreted as holding if and only if the place contains a token; to have more than one token would be irrelevant. A live Petri net is defined as one in which it is possible to fire any transition of the net by some firing sequence, irrespective of the marking that has been reached. Note that a live net would still remain live after firing. Liveness is an important property of the Petri net transitions are to be interpreted as representing processes. The liveness of a transition means that there is no way in which a sequence of process execution can cause the system to get into a state from which the given process can never again be executed. Thus the liveness property of a Petri net is directly related to the concept of deadlock.

Further sub-classes of the Petri net may be defined and of particular interest is the marked graph shown in figure 7a. A Petri net is called a marked graph if and only if each place has exactly one output transition. In this case the graph can be simplified by absorbing each place into an edge and letting the place marking be represented by a marking on the edge. A further restriction such that each transition has exactly one input and output place reduces the Petri net to a state-machine i.e. a FSM. This may be seen by simplifying the graph such that each transition is represented by a directed edge from its input place to its output place as shown in figure 7b. The net then assumes the structure of a state diagram but the edges are not labelled (but could be considered as representing the transition conditions and labelled accordingly). If one assumes an initial marking of a single token in a single place then state to state transitions will correspond to transition firings. The restricted models of Petri nets discussed above may be extended into a generalised model by allowing multiple arcs between transitions and places, thereby allowint a place to contribute (or receive) more than one token. Further extensions to the basic model such as including inhibiting arcs have also been proposed. Note that the computation difficulties involved in analysing the nets are considerably increased when one departs from the basic model.

The Petri net is considerably more powerful than the FSM model in that it can represent concurrent operations and permit indeterminate specification, hence it can provide a more faithful representation of complex system behaviour. Moreover, since

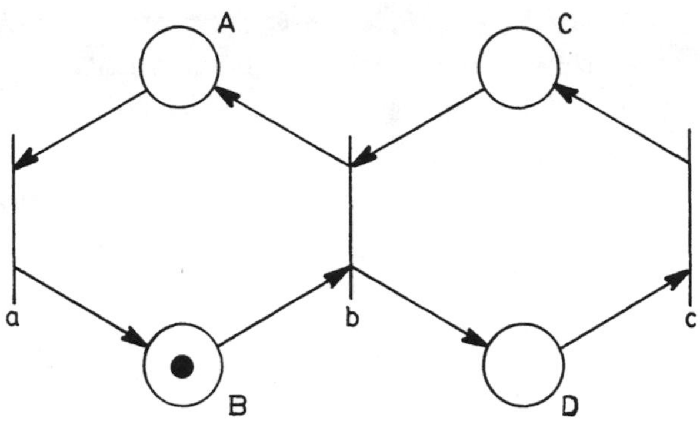

a) Marked Graph

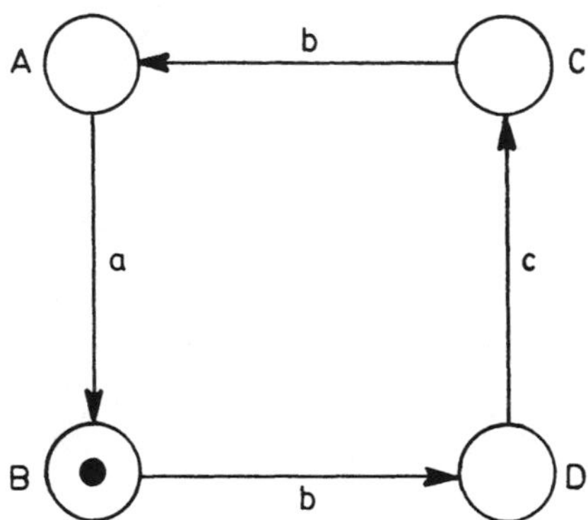

b) Equivalent State Machine

Figure 7 - Marked Graphs

Petri nets are not based on the usual concept of a central control state the nets provide a natural representation of a system with distributed control and state information. The use of FSM's to represent systems of this type would result in unmanageable large single states, being the set of all distributed states. In addition, it has been shown that any generalised extension of the Petri net is equivalent to a Turing machine, thus the modelling power of the Petri net can be considered to be slightly below that of the Turing machine.

An essential property of any model is that it must be possible by analysis to obtain precise information about its characteristics. The FSM model for example, since it has a finite number of states, can theoretically provide the answer to any question concerning its behaviour. However the Turing machine, because of its unbounded memory, is very difficult to analyse if a definite answer to a behavioural question is required. Thus we have a fundamental difficulty that the more powerful a model the more difficult it is to algorithmically determine its properties.

Petri nets have been extensively used to model and evaluate the control structures of logical systems in both software and hardware design. In addition it has been shown[(37)] that it is possible to replace the individual elements of a Petri net by hardware components, thus providing a direct realisation of the control circuits. In software design Petri nets have been used to model the properties of operating systems such as resource allocation and deadlock situations (related to the liveness of a net)[(38)]. Petri nets can also be used to model hierarchal structures, since an entire net may be replaced by a single place or transition at a higher level. Thus Petri nets can be used at all levels of design from behavioural through to structural and hence they have the advantage over most other design languages in being able to span the full range of specification and evaluation requirements.

The major advantage of the directed graph approach is that it is amenable to mathematical analysis and many authors[(38)(39)]have described algorithmic methods for their analysis. In the main the techniques apply to the control graph function only, known as an <u>uninterpreted</u> analysis, and no allowance is made for operations performed in conjunction with the data structure.

Unfortunately Petri nets are difficult to analyse and though bounded systems with a small number of variables can be effectively evaluated the computation required in the general case rapidly becomes unmanageable. One of the basic approaches to analysing Petri nets is to use the graph theoretic concept of reachability, in this case the nodes of a reachability tree of a marked net represent reachable markings of the net. However the reachability problem has been shown to be of the exponential-time type and hence computationally intractable.

Though Petri nets have many of the characteristics required for the specification and evaluation of computer systems at the behavioural level there have been very few examples of its use in a CAD scheme (it is of course used with LALSD system as previously discussed).

Project LOGOS[40][41] conceived at Case Western University was based on Petri net principles and had the objective of providing a graphical design aid which would enable complex parallel systems to be defined (on a hierarchal basis) evaluated at any level and then finally implemented in either hardware or software. The LOGOS system employed two directed graphs, one for data flow (the data-graph, DG) and one for control flow (the control-graph, CG) to define a process (called an activity). Though it was found possible to realise the control operators in the CG the problems of transforming the DG components was never fully resolved. In addition the computational problems encountered in attempting to perform an interpreted analysis (involving both CG and DG structures) of an activity was found to be extremely difficult.

A more recent development but closely related in principle to LOGOS, that of Project SARA at UCLA[42], also utilises a graph model concept to represent the system requirements at the behavioural and functional levels. The designer can interactively describe a partitioning of the required system by defining modules, module I/O sockets and module interconnections. The behaviour of the modules are then described using a Petri net like control graph and associated data graph. An interpreted analysis of the system at the abstract level, including dynamic behaviour and simulation, is said to be possible.

3.3. Finite-State Machine Techniques Finite-state machine (FSM) theory, using for example state-table representation, though theoretically capable of describing any digital system is not viable in practice owing to the considerable practical difficulties involved in expressing large variable problems and the inordinate amount of computation required to manipulate the resulting structures. This is undoubtedly true, particularly if both control and data structures are represented in the same state-table. However large systems must inevitably be partitioned by the designer into sub-system components in order to comprehend their complexity, and if the concept of separately defining data and control structures is used state-tables can still be a useful aid in design. This is borne out by the algorithmic state machine (ASM) approach to design[43] which uses a flow-chart to specify the control logic for a system, the implementation of which draws heavily on FSM theory.

The schematic components of the ASM chart are shown in figure 8; the correspondence with a state-diagram is obvious except that the chart is defined using a reduced form for the logic variables and is therefore more amenable to the designer. The ASM chart for the traffic controller described in Mead and Conway[44] is shown in figure 9.

Finite state machine techniques are still currently being used for the design of LSI/VLSI chips where a FSM, implemented in terms of a programmable logic array (PLA)

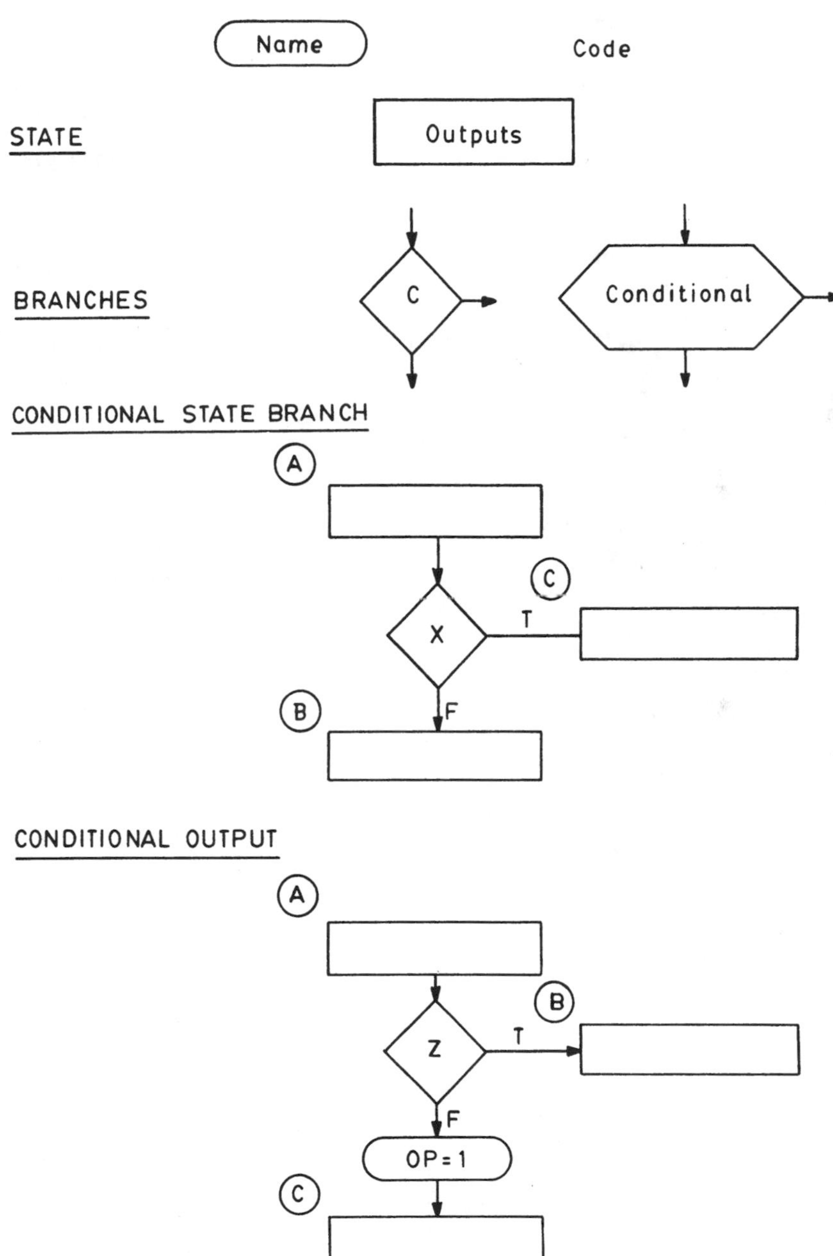

Figure 8 - Algorithmic State Machines

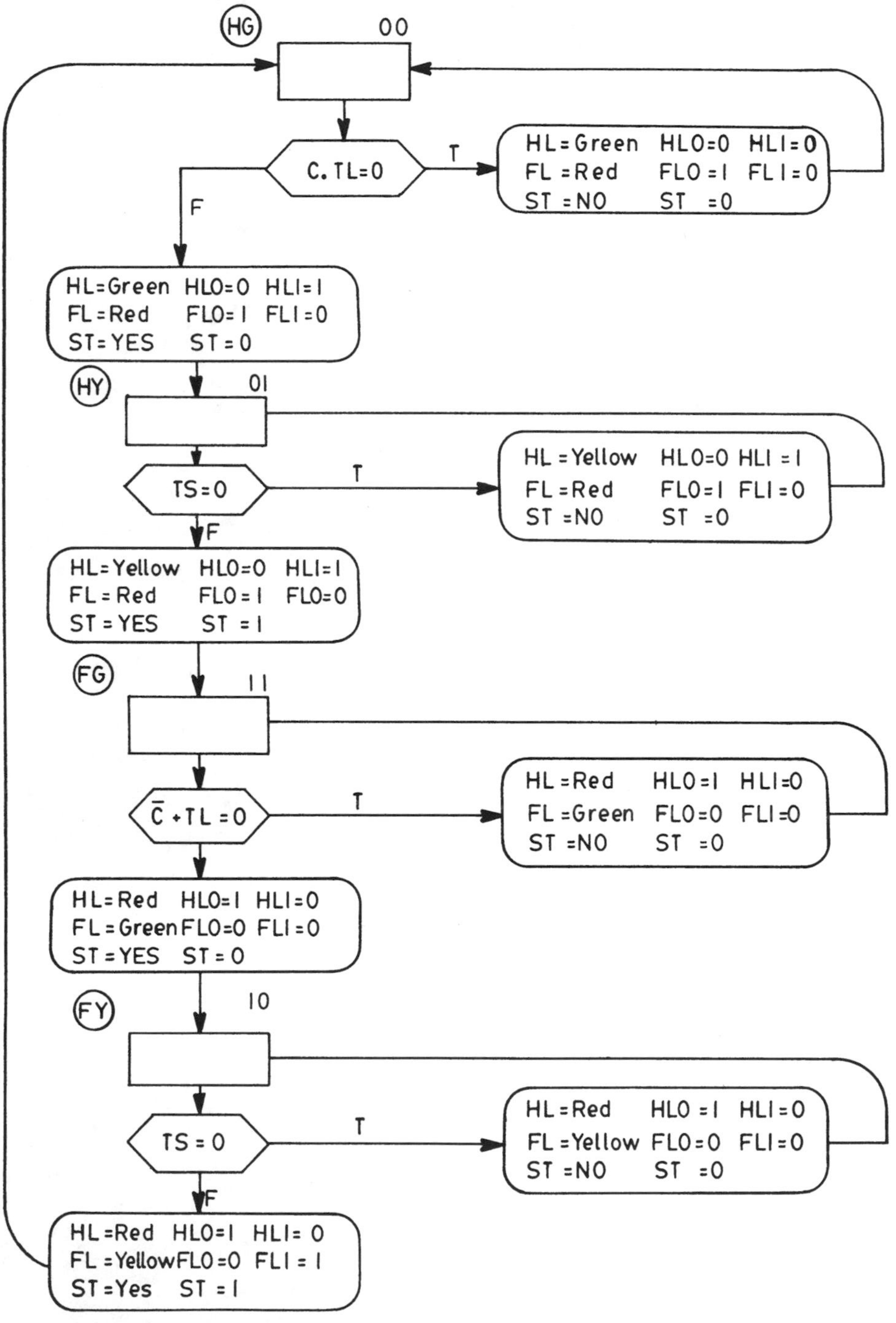

Figure 9 - ASM Chart for Traffic Light Controller

with feedback paths via shift registers, is used to control the data structures.

Finite-state machine methods, as well as having practical drawbacks, also suffer from a more fundamental disadvantage. In general the FSM accepts a serial input (or inputs) and progresses from state to state producing an output sequence (or sequences) in the process. Due to its finite memory limitation (that is, the number of internal states) the FSM is best suited to describing systems where the amount of memory required to record past events (that is the effect of earlier inputs) is both <u>small</u> and <u>finite</u>. For example, serial systems (such as pattern detectors) where the computation can proceed as a step-by-step operation on the input, and the amount of information required to be 'remembered' is very small. However some processes, such as serial multiplication, require to have <u>all</u> the input data available before the computation can proceed. Moreover large amounts of information would need to be stored during the course of the operation, (for example, the accumulation of partial sums in the case of multiplication). Thus it follows that the FSM has the inherent disadvantage that it is impossible to specify a machine which requires the manipulation of <u>arbitrarily large</u> pairs of numbers. Note also that the FSM lacks the ability to refer back to earlier inputs unless the entire input sequence is initially stored; this implies that the input sequence of interest must be of known finite length.

3.4. <u>Summary</u> There are obviously many difficult problems to be solved before a viable specification and design language for digital systems engineering can be developed. Register transfer languages would appear adequate for the design of register structured systems, but they are specifically hardware orientated, and since formal methods are not possible, evaluation must be performed using simulation techniques. Another disadvantage is that the languages tend to generate very simple constructs. This is due to the languages providing only simple elements and the users perpetuate the situation by designing at a low level. Another problem occurs in the generation and use of library routines for components used to represent complex MSI and LSI circuits and other data structures. There are two distinct cases when subsystem blocks are required:

a) to represent a component or sub-routine which will be used by the system many times over, but not actually implemented each time.

b) the insertion of a standard hardware component (analogous to a software macro) which needs to be implemented as such in various places in the system.

The major difficulty comes in isolating identical functions and, if necessary, merging them together. It is this fact which accounts for much of the redundancy encountered in RTL implementation schemes. The problem is also relevant when considering the implementation of Petri net schema, as for example in LOGOS, and generally for all systems which separate the control and data functions.

It has already been suggested that the FSM model has severe limitations when used to represent complex systems. These limitations can of course be overcome by using infinite or unbounded models such as the Turing machine or Petri net. Using this type of model the designer is unconstrained in his thinking, allowing general logical processes to be specified without reference to a particular implementation. Unfortunately the transformation from a conceptually unbounded model to a practical realisation can, and does, present serious difficulties.

Another fundamental problem is encountered in the analysis of large systems. It would appear inevitable that, if a detailed analysis of a logic algorithm is required (say in seeking the answer to a specific question) there is no other choice but to examine all possible alternatives in an iterative manner. In general, particularly if an unbounded model is adopted, it is necessary in order to determine the system operation to constrain the analysis to a restricted set of input and state conditions. This means, for example, that only particular paths through a Petri net are allowed, and the technique results in a loss of information and affects the accuracy of the model. If exact information about a system is sought the Petri net must be examined (ideally in an interpreted model) for all possible firing sequences. In general a detailed analysis of the modelled system proves to be prohibitive in computer time.

4. Simulation and Testing

Simulation is a process whereby it is possible to model, either mathematically or functionally, the behaviour of a real system; experiments can then be conducted on the model and related back to the actual system. It is important to realise that the simulated system is just a model and not necessarily an exact representation of the real physical world owing to the constraints and necessary approximations inherent in constructing the model.

In the simulation of microcomputer systems and digital systems generally the structures and processes to be modelled are so complex that formal mathematical modelling is normally impractical. Consequently functional simulation is employed. The exception to this is the use of Petri nets and other directed graph methods to model the behaviour of a system. For example though it is possible to describe the logical operation of a circuit using Boolean equations and thereby generate the input/output characteristics in the form of a truth-table no information about the performance of the implemental circuit, in terms of propagation delays, fault performance etc. can be obtained. Moreover the manipulation of Boolean equation with a large number of variables (the usual situation in practice) presents an intractable computational problem.

In functional modelling there is usually some direct correspondance between the real system and the simulated system. For example a logic circuit would be represented by a topological model with specific words in the computer memory being allocated to represent each gate and its interconnections. To evaluate a functional model it must be exercised, that is required to emulate the actions of the real system, starting from specified initial conditions and known system parameters. The information derived from observations on such a model depends on the way the experiments are run and the interpretation placed upon the results. Mathematical models on the other hand compute a result depending on initial conditions and the system parameters. Most functional models are stochastic in that the system variables cannot be previously defined and probabilistic methods must be employed; a system which has completely predictable variables, that is deterministic, is usually amenable to mathematical modelling.

The major use of simulation in digital system design is to verify and check designs, both at systems(45) and logic-gate levels(46), prior to actual manufacture. Another important use is to generate test schedules for manufacturing and operational testing procedures. Owing to the limitations mentioned earlier, and the methods used in exercising the model, simulation does not entirely eliminate the need for debugging the actual equipment, but it does considerably reduce the problems involved.

Digital systems may be simulated at basically three different levels, these are as follows:

1. Systems level. This consists at the moment of using high-level general-purpose simulation languages, such as GPSS(47) and SIMSCRIPT(48) and deals mainly with a timing analysis of the system modelled in terms of subsystem components such as arithmetic and logic units, memory modules, peripherals, etc.

2. Register-transfer level. In this case data flow at the register level is modelled,thereby enabling microprograms etc. to be evaluated. This form of language was dealt with in section 3 and would of course include APL, ISP, DDL, etc.

3. Gate or logic level. Here the actual logic gates, or modules, and their interconnections are functionally modelled in the computer. Each signal line is restricted to binary values, and time is usually quantized to gate-propagation delays.

The major benefits to be accried by using simulation techniques are savings in time and cost caused by eliminating fundamental design errors. Some of the more specific advantages of using simulation in digital systems design are as follows:

a. Operational specifications can be validated.

b. Corrections and modifications can be made during the early design stages.

c. Alternative procedures and designs may be evaluated.

d. The simulation description can serve as design documentation.

Simulation at the logic level is currently the most frequently employed technique, and has become a valuable tool for logic designers. In particular the technique is used to generate and verify fault-test procedures and to discover the presence of circuit races and hazards. It is essential, however, that the simulator should accurately model the timing of the circuit devices, to allow prediction of hazards and races, in order for it to be effective in design verification.

The major disadvantages of simulation are that it can be very time consuming, particularly if detailed results about large systems are required, and also capable of misinterpretation.

4.1 Logic level simulation The process of simulation at the logic gate level is shown in figure 10, the logic diagram is described in terms of logic modules and their interconnections using some form of problem-orientated language. This description is then compiled into a suitable data structure, such as a list or ring structure, which represents a topological network model of the logic circuit; where necessary library descriptions of logic modules are obtained from a data base. Once the model is established it must be exercised; this is done via the simulation control program which requires inputs from the user defining such parameters as initial logic states, input values and sequences, gate delays, timing steps, monitoring points, output formats, etc. Once the parameters are set the simulation may be run; note that the parameters require to be changed for each simulation run, which can be done using static or dynamic modes of operation.

The simulation process proceeds by tracing changes in logic values through the network, on a discrete-time-interval basis, to generate the signal-time behaviour of the circuit. That is, the computer program computes the output status of the logic elements at each basic machine-time interval (usually measured as a function of gate propagation delays, in the simplest case one time interval corresponding to the worst-case gate delay) and continues to advance in simulated time until the logic comes permanently to rest (a stable condition) or reaches some previously specified state. Thus, by gate-level simulation we mean the generation of a state-time map (truth or transition table) for the logic system, given the initial states and input sequences. In order to illustrate the technique let us consider a simple example which is typical of many gate-level simulators. Table 6 shows a common type of input format, using a simple logic-description language, for the half-adder circuit shown in figure 11.

A typical example of the type of output obtained after running the simulator is shown in table 7a. In this case the initial circuit conditions have been specified

Topological Description in High Level Language

Machine Description

COMPILER

Data Bank and Module Library

LOGIC FILE
Data Structure Representing the Network Model

INPUT FILE
Input Waveforms
Logic Initialization
Special Conditions
Fault - Insertion
Circuit Parameters
Delay Times
Output Formats
Monitor Points
Timing Control

Simulation Control

OUTPUT DATA
Signal Listings
Timing Diagrams
Fault Monitoring

Operator Inputs

Simulation Description

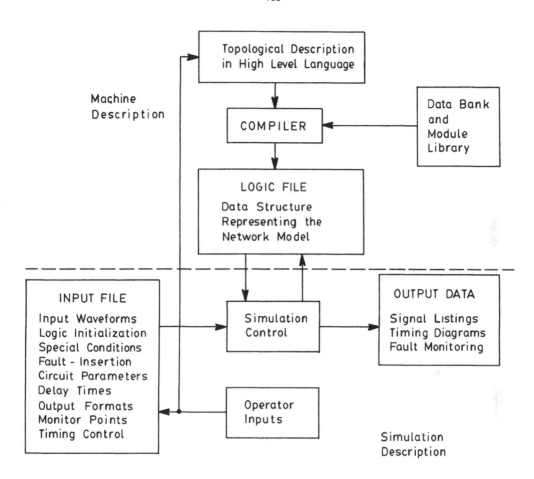

Figure 10 - Simulation System

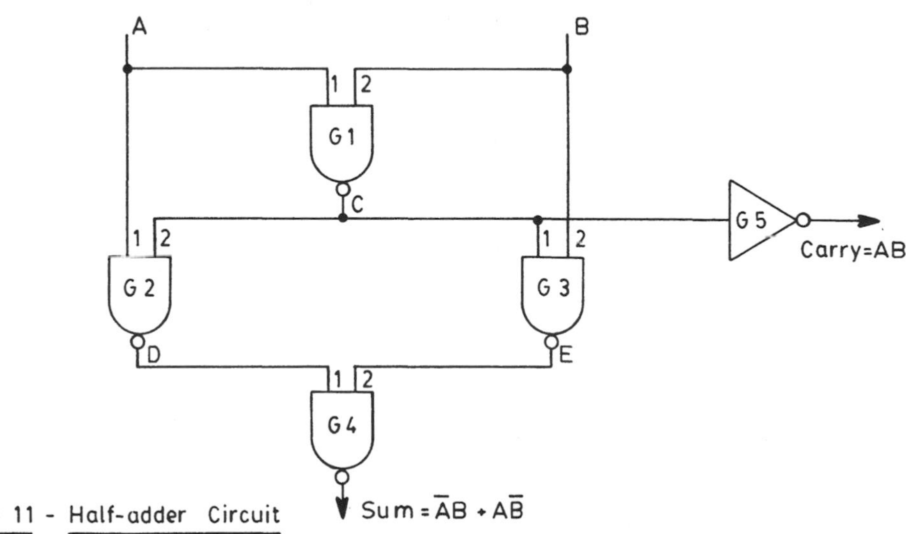

Figure 11 - Half-adder Circuit

TABLE 6

Simulator Input Description

	Code	Logic type	Input 1	Input 2	Output
1.	G1	NAND	A	B	C
2.	G2	NAND	A	C	D
3.	G3	NAND	C	B	E
4.	G4	NAND	D	E	SUM
5.	G5	INV	C		CARRY

TABLE 7

Output Timing Diagram

(a) Initial conditions A = 0 B = 0
Input A = 1 B = 0

Clock	Outputs C	D	E	SUM	CARRY
0	.1	.1	.1	0	0
1	.1	0	.1	0	0
2	.1	0	.1	.1	0
3	.1	0	.1	.1	0

(b) Initial conditions A = 0 B = 0
Input A = 1 B = 1

Clock	Outputs C	D	E	SUM	CARRY
0	.1	.1	.1	0	0
1	0	0	0	0	0
2	0	.1	.1	.1	.1
3	0	.1	.1	0	.1
4	0	1	1	0	1

as A=0, B=0 and the inputs allowed to change from AB=00→10 and 00→11. The timing has been assumed to be one gate delay per clock, that is, with the duration of the clock pulses being set equal to the propagation delay of the logic gates. In the case of the input change 00→11 a dynamic circuit hazard is indicated in the SUM output, since the output value should remain at zero during the input change. The "spike" on the SUM output is caused by the two different signal paths between the inputs A and B and the output, that is G1G2G4 and G2G4 respectively, which differ in length by one gate delay.

Note that the output routine prints the logic 1 outputs slightly displaced to the right of the logic 0 outputs, thus producing a form of waveform diagram which highlights any circuit transitions. It is of course possible to obtain more sophisticated waveform diagrams using graphics or incremental graph plotters. Other information is often required to be printed out; this could include, for example, loading (fan-out) statistics and tables showing the maximum number of gate levels a signal has to pass through for each particular clock-time.

As well as providing a descriptive language for inputing logic circuits, simulator packages must also include facilities for the user to input data and control the timing, that is to drive the simulation. (In our simple example we assumed initial values only and basic clock timing.) This is normally done by adding program instructions which are obeyed during the simulation run and operate on the circuit model.

4.1.1 Input language requirements. Input languages are normally based on a module description, with the inputs and outputs of each unit being explicitly defined. For example, the circuit elements in figure 12 could be coded using the input format

gate type/gate number:inputs;outputs

This yields the following description:

NAND/1:A,$\overline{B}$;Z1
NAND/2:$\overline{C}$,D;Z2
NOR/5:Z_1,Z_2;Z5 etc.

Note that it is essential to be able to identify uniquely each input and output of the circuit module; in some cases the gate number can be used to identify the output. This form of description is easily adapted to allow the definition of compound modules and their subsequent use in more complex circuits. Consider, for example, the D-type bistable circuit shown in figure 13; this consists of three d.c. SR bistables (latches) suitably interconnected to give the required edge-triggered characteristic. The basic SR bistable may be defined as a compound element; thus

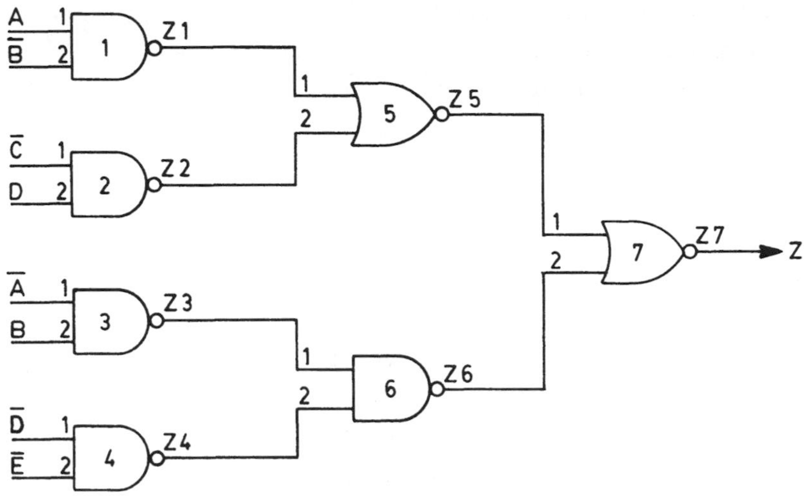

Figure 12 - Gate Description

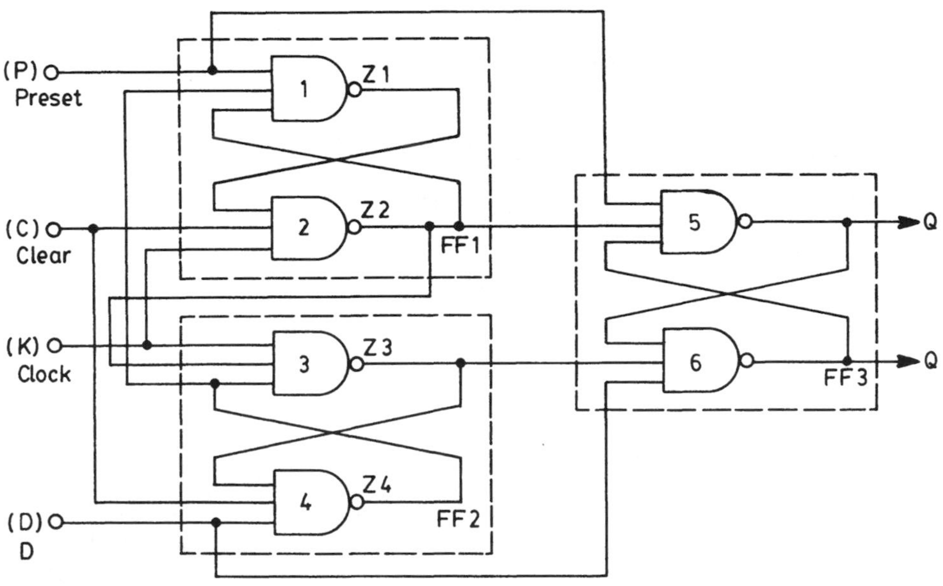

Figure 13 - D-Type Bistable Circuits

$COMP\text{-}SRFF:\bar{S}_1,\bar{S}_2,\bar{R}_1,\bar{R}_2;Q,\bar{Q}$
$NAND/1:\bar{S}_1,\bar{S}_2,\bar{Q};Q$
$NAND/2:\bar{R}_1,\bar{R}_2,Q;\bar{Q}$

The connection of the three SR bistables to form the D-type bistable may now be specified as

$SRFF/1:P,Z_4,C,K;Z_1,Z_2$

$SRFF/2:K,Z_2,D,C;Z_3,Z4$

$SRFF/3:P,Z_2,D,Z_3;Q,\bar{Q}$

Alternative forms of Boolean input, which are also used internally in the software procedures for defining compound element, are the truth table and, in the case of sequential circuits, the state table. This form of specification allows an element to be defined as a 'black box' with a given input-output transfer function. The same result can of course be achieved using a programmed macro, which may be substituted in the simulated model as and when required.

Most current simulators provide a library of simple compound elements which may be referred to directly in the input language; these could include, for example, exclusive OR gates, n-bit full adders, bistables, decoders, etc.

As well as defining circuit topology there are two other important conditions which need to be specified before the model is complete. These are the initialization of circuit nodes, such as counter and bistable outputs, and the specification of element delays.

The basic delay requirement is to be able to assign a propagation time, usually in terms of integer units of the machine clock, to each gate or compound element in the circuit (either individually or for a given module type). In the simplest case this may be done with an assignment statement of the form

<list>=<delay time>

where

<list>::=<output identifier>|<logic function>|

<output identifier>,<logic function>

which would normally be proceeded by some directive such as DELAY, for instance:

DELAY
OUT 1,OR=2

implies that all OR gates and the output function OUT 1 have a delay of 2 units.

In many cases a constant value, usually either the nominal propagation delay obtained from the manufacturer or the worst-case delay, is used. However, for some applications simple delay values of this type are insufficient to model and check out a circuit fully, for instance when checking race conditions etc., and a more sophisticated range of delay parameters must be used. In fact up to five parameters may be required as defined below:

$t_{1\to 0}$ propagation delay for 1→0 change in state

$t_{0\to 1}$ propagation delay for 0→1 change in state

t_{min} minimum time allowable between edges of input pulse that operate a device

t_{hold} minimum time input pulse must maintain its state after a clock pulse

t_{set} minimum time input pulse must maintain its state before a clock pulse

The delay parameters are shown in figure 14 for the NAND gate; note that it is assumed that, when the overlap time for the input pulses is less than t_2, the output state does not change. If t_2 < overlap time > t_1, then the output state is uncertain; in practice the parameter t_{min} is often assumed to be $t_{min}=t_1=t_2$. The parameters t_{set} and t_{hold} are only required for certain clocked devices such as bistable circuits; the very minimum delay parameters that are required in a logic simulator are $t_{0\to 1}$ and $t_{1\to 0}$. Using these parameters the assignment statement would be modified to

<List>=<$t_{1\to 0}$><$t_{0\to 1}$><t_{min}><t_{hold}><t_{set}>.

In some cases the delay times are incorporated with the element descriptions. Thus, a NAND gate might be described as

NAND-G1-$t_{1\to 0}$,$t_{0\to 1}$-IP_1,IP_2,IP_3-OUT Z1

and for an edge-triggered JK bistable:

JKFF-MEM1-$t_{1\to 0}$,$t_{0\to 1}$,t_{set},t_{hold}-J,K,CLK,C,D-Q,$\overline{Q}$

where the symbol - stands for delimiter symbols used to separate data of a different type.

In order to analyze fully circuit race conditions both the shortest and longest delay times (as stated by the manufacturer) are of concern, and in some cases a statistical distribution of the delay values is used.

The specification of initial conditions requires that the logical states of a network at the start of a simulation be defined. That is the user must be able to specify the states of any, or all, of the circuit nodes before the simulation begins. This may be done as before by using a simple assignment statement, preceded by a suitable directive; thus we have

<output variable>=<state>

where state specifies the logical state or states, usually in binary, of an output mode, for example

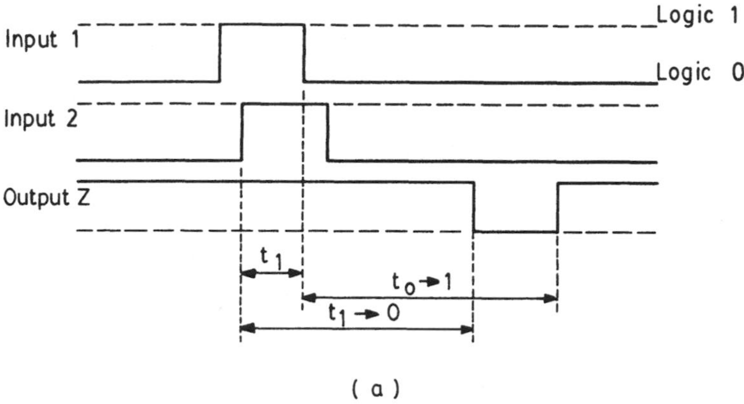

(a)

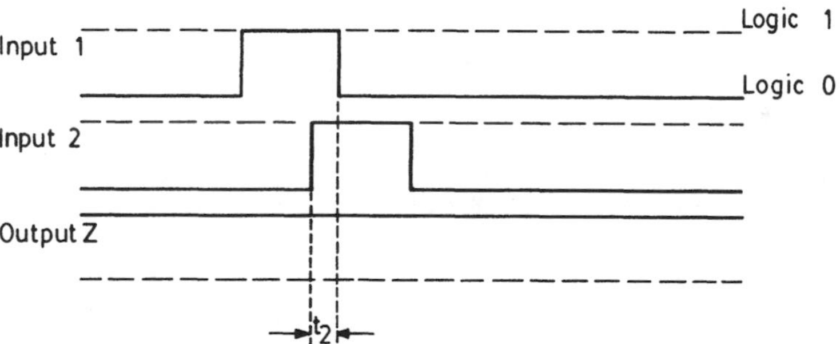

(b)

Figure 14 Delay Parameters

```
INITIAL
G1=0,G5=1,Z2=0.
```

In some simulators certain devices, such as counters and shift registers, can be set by quoting the decimal or octal equivalent of the number required to be stored. Monitor points may be specified in a similar way by using a directive to introduce a list of monitor-point statements of the form

```
<identifier>=MP<n>
```

where identifier can be any function output in the block, or a block input, and <n> is a monitor-point number within a specified range. Thus

```
MONITOR
G3=MP1;Z4=MP2;Z5=MP3.
```

4.1.2. Command Statements. In order to operate and control the simulation run a number of command codes must be provided in the language. These commands are generally concerned with the setting up of input data signals and their timing, including the provision for waveform generation, monitor points, output listings, and conditional controls. In addition basic directives such as START, FINISH, PRINT (state of monitor points), etc. are also required, including file-handling routines for large systems.

During the simulation of a network specified waveforms must be applied to the inputs. The simulator waveforms are normally read by the simulator from a compiled waveform file or inputted directly, using an interpreted mode, from user-originated declarations. Input waveforms are generally represented in idealized form, with zero rise and fall times, and specified in time order. One method of achieving this, used in the HILO system(49) is to list the new state of all those output nodes that change state at a given time using the instruction

```
@<time>:<list>
```

where <time> is an integer specifying the simulation time (in machine units) at which the list is to be evaluated, and

```
<list>:=<identifier>=<state>
```

where <identifier> is the name of the network input and <state> is its logical value, thus:

```
@0:A=0
@5:A=1
```

This mode of input can become laborious and a CHANGE statement is often employed of the form:

```
<identifier>=CHANGE@(<list of times>)
```

this statement assumes a particular starting value which must be set initially, for example,

```
@0:A=0
 A=CHANGE@(5,10,20,35)
```

The value of <time> is normally given as an integer with an upper limit determined by the characteristic of the simulator.

Instead of using complex waveform generators a simple time scale or interval may often suffice. Facilities normally exist for defining a repetitive clock of the form

OP=CLOCK($<t_1>,<t_2>,<t_3>$)

where assuming a zero start, OP goes to 1 after time t_1, stays there for a time t_2, and then goes to 0 and stays there for time t_3, the cycle repeating continuously.

Output commands are required to specify the identity and number of circuit nodes required to be monitored and their output formats. For example, it may be required to print out the state of each node and the time taken to reach that node or, alternatively, a simple truth table. A graphical output, however, is more useful, and this may be obtained in the usual way using digital plotters or outputting a page format on a line printer arranged to resemble a waveform diagram. The time scale represented may be either in the form of linear time increments or a non-linear scale where the value of monitored points are printed (together with the time) only when a change of state occurs. Table 8 shows typical output formats - note that in Table 8a the effect of a waveform diagram may be obtained by rotating the page 90^0 anticlockwise. In addition to the waveform and state print-outs fault conditions may also be indicated. For example, circuit conditions such as signals which change state together, and are thus likely to give rise to a circuit hazard, simultaneously setting and resetting of bistables, and the propagation of unacceptable narrow pulses would be indicated on the print-out. Facilities also normally exist for printing out the specified network configuration in the form of a list giving the component (or subsystem module) identity, type, input-output connections, propagation delay, and initial logical states. Commands of the type described above are normally inserted at the start of a simulation program or alternatively mixed with waveform declarations and obeyed when they occur in the program. Most simulators also include some form of editor for checking syntax and other errors (indicated to the user in the form of error messages) which can occur during program preparation.

Finally, many simulators, in particular those employed in time-shared systems, require file-handling routines. In this case special commands are provided which allow files to be created, erased, copied, dumped from, and read into main store, etc. Thus, library files, including input-output waveform data, may be created and used as input for subsequent simulator runs etc. In this way it is possible to simulate circuit blocks held on file using a library file containing waveform data as input, with the output results being stored away on an output file.

4.1.3. <u>Simulation Techniques</u> There are two basic techniques for implementing simu-

TABLE 8

Simulator Outputs

(a) Graphical Output with Non-linear Scale

Time	Z1		Z2		Z3		Z4		Z5		Z6		Output nodes
machine units	0	1	0	1	0	1	0	1	0	1	0	1	Binary output values
0		1		1		1		1		1		1	
2	1			1		1		1		1	1		
150		1		1		1		1		1		1	
160	1			1		1		1		1	1		
200	1			1	1			1	1		1		

(b) Truth-Table Output with Linear Time Scale

	Inputs		Outputs	
Time	I1	I2	Z1	Z2
0	0	0	0	0
5	0	0	0	0
10	0	1	1	0
15	0	1	1	0
20	1	1	0	1

lators, these are compiled code and table-driven.

In a compiled code simulator a set of macros are generated which perform the logic operations required by specific element types. The logic circuit to be simulated is represented in the computer as a series of interconnected macros which evaluate the logical function of the elements in the order in which they appear in the circuit (as ordered at compile time).

Using the compiled-code technique combinational circuits can be simulated in one pass through the network; sequential circuits, however, must be iterated (performing several simulations in one clock period) until a stable condition is realized. Timing is performed by using an internally generated clock and is normally synchronous, that is the gate outputs are sampled (and used as inputs) only at definite time intervals. In some cases asynchronous timing can be used: in this case the gate outputs can be applied as inputs immediately a state change occurs.

The major disadvantage of the compiled-code technique is that if any changes are required to be made to the logic configuration a new network description must be recompiled. Moreover, since all logic elements are evaluated in sequence by the program (even if a signal path is unactivated) the time required to simulate a large system can be excessive. It also follows that it is not possible to evaluate selectively parts of the network.

In the table-driven simulator a data structure is established which stores the parameters of individual logic elements in a network in a tabular form. Each table entry would comprise such data as logic function, propagation delays, output values, input sources, output destinations etc. Thus the source language statements would be translated into a data structure representing the circuit; note that the circuit topology is inherent in the data structures. During simulation the data structure is operated on by a control program which interprets the information in the lists in accordance with the simulator command statements to determine the data flow and logical values in the network. The interpreter program operates by following the linkages (pointers) from one circuit element to the next, evaluating the outputs from each element from the input-output values as it proceeds. Each logic function is evaluated by a specific subroutine which is accessed as required rather than using individual macros.

A block diagram for a table-driven simulator is shown in figure 15. The circuit could be simulated, for example, by starting with a particular gate in the element list and obtaining the inputs from the interconnection list. The output of this gate would be generated using the appropriate macro for the gate type and the result stored in the element list. The next step is to determine from the interconnection list those elements which accepts this output as their input. Once these next level gates are established other relevant inputs are obtained from the element list and the new outputs computed. Note that the simulation is driven by the data structure

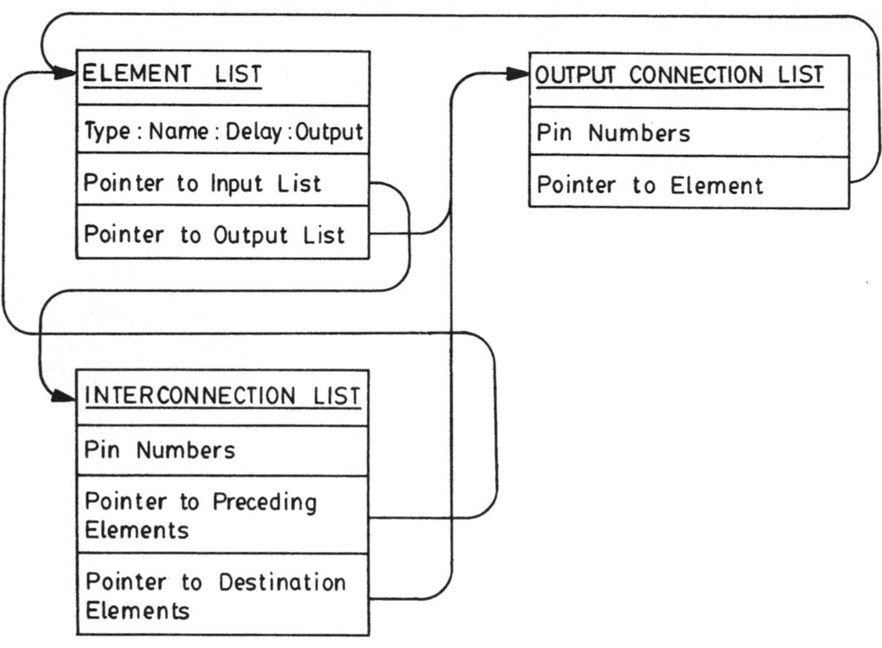

Figure 15 - Table Driven Simulator

itself; moreover particular paths are simulated through the network and as a result the process is far more efficient than simulators which need to simulate the entire circuit to find the result of an input change.

The efficiency of the simulation can be further enhanced (which is particularly necessary with LSI/VLSI) by simulating only significant events in the network. For any given input change only a small number of elements will actually change state. Thus by simulating only the behaviour of the active elements (those which change state) a considerable reduction in computation time can be achieved.

Another advantage of the table-driven simulator is that it allows easy modification to the circuit structure by simply changing the appropriate pointers in the list structure.

4.1.4. Three Value Simulation(50) The presence of hazards and races in combinational and sequential logic circuits may be detected using the concepts of ternary algebra(51). In this method a third value, X, which may assume the value of either 0 or 1, is used to represent unspecified initial conditions, unpredictable oscillations, and "don't-care" states. Basic logic gates, such as AND/OR etc., may be redefined in terms of ternary functions using the values 0, 1, and X. Table 9 gives the truth table for the functions AND, OR, and NAND; note that there are now $3^2 = 9$ possible input combinations. In general, the ternary function of a logic gate may be determined by putting the X inputs to the gate alternately at 0 and 1, and noting whether the gate output (Z) changes (Z = X) or remains at 0 or 1 (Z = 0,1).

In order to detect hazards using three-valued simulation the unknown value X is included in the primary inputs between every 0 to 1 and 1 to 0 transition. The simulation then proceeds in the normal way, except that the ternary function of the logic elements is used to generate the output values. The presence of an X in an output value indicates the presence of a hazard, which may be propagated, through the circuit, to the final output. The use of three valued simulation allows hazards to be detected which could go undetected in a two-valued simulator. It is important to realize, however, that the indicated hazard may or may not occur in the actual hardware implementation, depending on the duration of the spike and the logic delays in the circuit. This comes about because the three-valued simulator is essentially a zero unit or nominal delay simulator and takes no account of actual signal propagation times, for example rise and fall times. Most present day simulators use at least a three-valued model and in many cases a multi-valued system is employed which allows precise delay times to be used. For example if minimum or maximum delay times are used it is possible to have a six-value simulation with the values 0, 1, X, U (rising signal) D (falling signal) E (potential hazard).

4.1.5. Fault Simulation. The major objective of digital fault simulation is to generate a set of tests for a logical circuit which can be applied to the fabricated

TABLE 9

Ternary Logic Functions

Inputs		Outputs		
A	B	Z = A.B	Z = A+B	Z = $\overline{AB}$
0	0	0	0	1
0	1	0	1	1
1	0	0	1	1
1	1	1	1	0
x	0	0	x	1
0	x	0	x	1
x	1	x	1	x
1	x	x	1	x
x	x	x	x	x

design to detect if a physical defect exists in the circuit. Fault simulation can also be used to validate fault detection or diagnostic tests, create fault dictionaries, and assist in the design of diagnosable logic. Ideally the basic simulator used in the fault-simulation process should be capable of analyzing circuit races and hazards as well as performing the normal logic simulation functions.

In order to constrain the problems to a tractable form, single logical faults emanating at input-output terminals permanently stuck at either 0 or 1 are assumed (these faults are normally abbreviated to s-a-0 and s-a-1 respectively). Though it has been found that this class of fault covers a high percentage of the physical defects which occur in production boards, it should be stressed, however, that it is not inclusive. Note that the prime concern is with faults that can arise during manufacture, such as bad connections, faulty components, etc., which normally manifest themselves as logical faults; the circuit is considered to be free of design errors. Any logical network can of course be completely tested by applying all possible input combinations and comparing the output values with the correct result. This procedure becomes impossible for large networks, and consequently it is necessary to search for the minimal set of input sequences that will detect all faults.

Gate-level simulation is generally used to evolve a set of input patterns which will detect the presence of single logical faults introduced into a network. The procedure is first to simulate the fault-free circuit, and then to repeat the simulation with all possible faults inserted into the network. Comparison of the outputs obtained with the faulty and fault-free circuit yields a list of identifiable faults.

A serious disadvantage of this method is that large networks require an excessive amount of computation time. In order to ensure that all faults (s-a-0 and s-a-1 on all connections) are covered test simulations must be performed many times over, and, in the limit, all possible input combinations may be required. Consequently, most fault simulators compromise by producing an effective covering of faults (hopefully a large percentage of all possible faults)rather than the complete optimum cover. Alternatively, statistical procedures are used where the circuit is driven by random input sequences.

In order to evaluate the fault-mode characteristics of a network it is necessary to be able to introduce the effect of, say, a component failure into the circuit - this is known as fault injection(52). Using the table-driven model it is simply a case of modifying the pointers in the data structure to allow a conditional choice to be made between input and output values. In some cases a special data structure is used to contain the signal faults which must be inserted. The faulty conditions are treated as different cases of the same model, and the fault parameters can be set and reset by suitable command-language statements which operate on the data structures.

A testing sequence may be checked out by performing separate simulation runs for each possible fault; this can be a time consuming process. Current fault simulators can be classified into two main types - parallel fault simulators or deductive fault simulators both of which have considerable speed advantages over single fault simulation.

Parallel fault simulation[53] is the simulation in parallel of a number of copies of the circuit under test. One network is designated to be the correct circuit while each of the other networks represents the condition where at least one fault is present. The number of circuits that can be simulated in one pass of the simulator is normally constrained by the word length of the host computer since a fault condition is generally represented by one bit in the word. This approach was adopted for the TEGAS simulator[54] which is used fairly extensively in practice.

Deductive fault simulation[55] considers the fault-free circuit and all faults in one pass of the simulator using a fault-list. A fault-list is a list of all those simulated faults which will change the value of a gate at the present instant of simulated time. Note each gate in the network has an associated list of faults which will change as a function of simulated time thus requiring dynamic storage management.

It has been suggested that the parallel technique is more cost effective for small, highly sequential circuits or for a small number of faults. The deductive method on the other hand is more efficient for loosely sequential circuits or circuits having a large number of faults.

4.2. General Purpose Simulation Languages

General purpose simulation languages can be used for any system which changes in a descrete manner consequently they can be used for the modelling of computer systems. The internal structure of general-purpose simulators follows usual practice, and may be either event-driven, employing a list-structured data base, or interpretive systems using compiled code. Using a general-purpose simulation language it is possible to express the structure of a network, its behaviour, and the required simulation conditions; moreover, timing controls, output formats, and diagnostics are generally built into the software. In general, general-purpose simulators are used to model the overall performance of computer systems; the major objectives of these simulation studies can be categorized into five different areas[56], these are as follows.

(a) The feasibility of performing a given workload on a certain class of computer.
(b) Comparison of computer systems (and the evaluation of software systems) against a specific "benchmark" to assist in procurement decisions.
(c) Determination of processing capability for various system configurations and operating conditions.
(d) Investigation of the effect of changes in the system structure etc. during the design process.
(e) Improvement of system performance by identifying and modifying the critical

hardware/software component of a system - a process known as "tuning". Note that the system is normally simulated at the behavioural user level rather than at the lower structural or functional levels.

The most commonly used languages are SIMSCRIPT which is a FORTRAN based event driven simulator, GPSS which is an interpretive block structured language to define activities, and GASP(57) which also uses an event schedulling approach. GASP-PL/1 has been successfully employed for the simulation of microprocessors(58).

There are many problems associated with the use of general-purpose simulators. From the users point of view it is necessary to learn the syntax and semantics of the language (particularly SIMSCRIPT) as well as understanding the concept of the simulation procedures. Since the model is algorithmically based, without necessarily any exact correspondence to the actual system, the software processes must always be interpreted in terms of system behaviour. Because of this the fidelity of the simulation cannot always be assumed correct (the results must be validated in some other way), since the simulation could be invalidated by inconsistencies or ambiguities in the simulation language or its interpretation. These arguments apply of course to any simulator, but the problems are far more apparent with a general-purpose simulator since a general process is being modelled.

At a more simple, but vital, level is the amount of resources required by the simulation. This must be considered both in terms of manpower (to produce the simulation model) and the CPU time required to execute the simulation study. It is important to establish the problem areas to be studied and then "tailor" the simulation accordingly; a too ambitious simulation can easily lead to over-investment of resources.

4.3. Summary

The designer who wishes to use a simulator package is faced with a difficult choice of alternative languages. At the systems level there are several important factors to be considered. Among these are the ease of learning the language and describing the system model, the host computer, compilation and execution times, whether conversational or batch-processing mode, output facilities, storage requirements, general computing requirements, and tracing and debug facilities.

At the logic-gate level the situation is similar, and in this case the following additional factors must be taken into account.

(a) Compiled-code or table-driven (event) simulator.
(b) Time-shared terminal system or batch processing.
(c) Synchronous or asynchronous mode of logic operation.
(d) Whether all gates or only active paths are simulated.
(e) Fault simulation, including parallel or deductive simulation of several faulty machines.

(f) Two-three or multi-valued logic signals, including hazard detection.
(g) Delay facilities.
(h) Maximum number of gates that can be simulated.
(i) Hierarchical, block structured.
(j) Number of machine cycles that can be simulated in one second on the host computer.

A major consideration is that a digital logic simulator must be both accurate and cost effective in order to justify its adoption as a design tool.

5. Synthesis Tools[59]

Very few synthesis tools are available at the present time and though some register transfer languages incorporate a logic translator they rely mainly on classical switching theory, producing a realisation in terms of NAND/NOR gates. Software systems for the minimisation of multiple output combinational circuits have been reported[60][61]. These employ tabular or cubic notation to input the design specification (normally expressed in ON matrix form) and use some form of heuristic technique to obtain a near minimal (rather than optimum) solution. Unfortunately the resulting circuits are once again realised in terms of basic gates and bistables thereby limiting their usefulness for VLSI system design.

Micro-computer architectures are invariably implemented in silicon using NMOS, CMOS or I^2L technology as a LSI/VLSI circuit. Consequently synthesis tools must be capable of dealing with design at this level which invalidates much of the conventional logic design procedures.

Again at the systems level it is no longer possible to separate hardware and software techniques and it is essential that any synthesis procedure should be able to take into account the use of software as an alternative to hardware and vice-versa, in any system realisation. Thus the specific problem of logic circuit synthesis has been subsumed by the general problems of computer systems engineering. Note also that any synthesis procedure for system design presupposes the existence of some kind of behavioural specification language.

At the LSI/VLSI chip design level (that is physical design) there is another problem, that of efficiently and correctly transforming a logic or systems design into the appropriate technology for actual realisation in silicon. The logic design of MSI/-LSI circuits has proceeded along fairly conventional lines with logic circuits in terms of gates and bistables (necessitating large amounts of random logic) being translated directly into the appropriate technology. Thus classical switching theory with its formal methods of minimisation still has some relevance, for example, the cost of a MSI chip is determined by the number of pins and the surface area, thus minimising the number of input variables and gates becomes of importance. Again at the systems level using standard PLA modules (typically with 14 inputs,

96 product term and 8 outputs) there is often a requirement for multiple output minimisation in order to allow the module (if possible) to accommodate the logic function; note that there is a basic constraint imposed by the number of input terms so reducing the number of variables can in some cases determine whether or not the PLA can be used.

When designing using sub-systems modules the design goals have changed from those of classical switching theory and the emphasis is now on reducing module types and the number of interconnections between them.

With VLSI the objective of providing greater processing power on smaller surface areas invalidates almost entirely the use of classical switching theory. The area occupied on the silicon chip is more a function of the topology of circuit interconnections than the number of gates - thus "wires" are the main consideration in VLSI design. Physical characteristics such as surface area, power consumption and delay times are the new parameters of optimisation when designing logic for integrated systems, with the objective being to minimise circuit interconnections. Thus the research in logic synthesis for VLSI systems is concerned with the design of (currently the search for!) novel structures which realise the required characteristics of the digital system in terms of the physical, topological and geometrical properties of the technology.

The present approach to VLSI design is to consider a system as comprising sub-system structures such as registers, combinational logic implemented as regular structures using pass transistor networks and programmable logic arrays. The required logic processing operations would be realised as an integral part of the register to register transfer circuitry thus achieving a cascaded or pipe-line architecture; figure 16 shows such a system. The overall control of the transfer operations would be determined by a state controller realised as a FSM using PLA's and shift registers as shown in figure 17. The PLA is a basic circuit in VLSI design and is used to implement random logic in a structured manner. Since in many designs it forms a large proportion of the total system PLA minimisation and state reduction (when used as a FSM controller) is an important consideration.

The minimisation criteria in the case of an embeded PLA are primarily concerned with the overall size and shape that is the total silicon area. The factors which effect the area of the PLA are as follows:

(a) the number of product terms
(b) the number of inputs
(c) the number of outputs
(d) the number of invertor circuits
(e) logic time delay
(f) design rules for technology

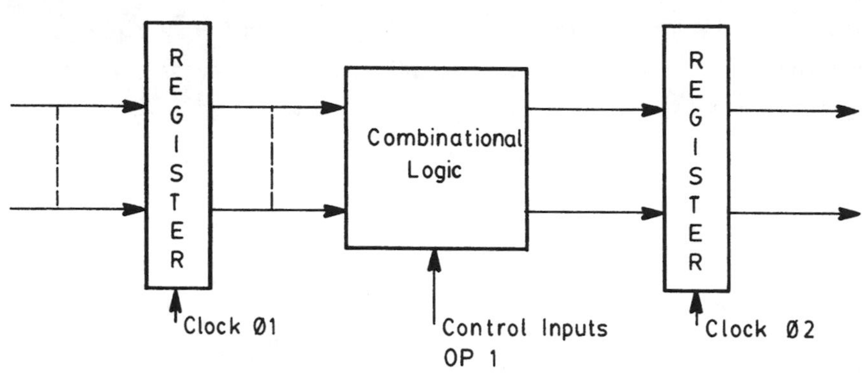

Figure 16 - Data Path Structures

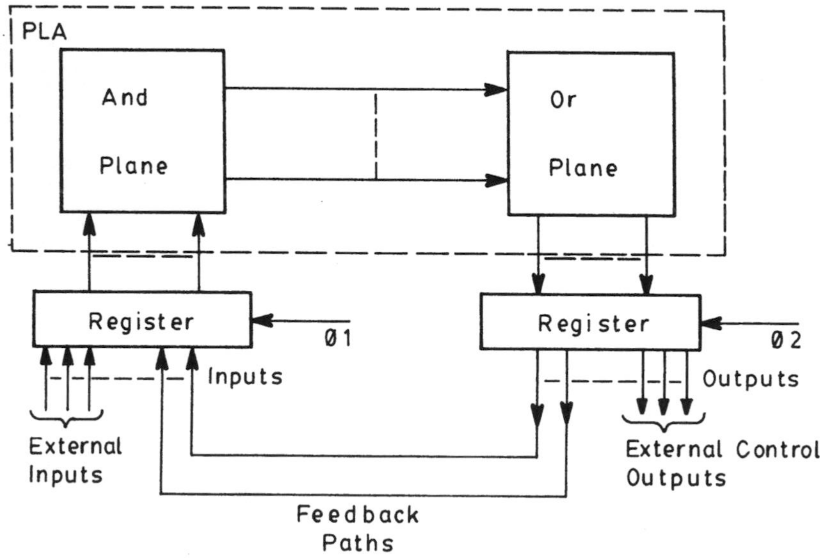

Figure 17 - Finite State Machine Controller

However the chip area is mainly determined by:
length = (Number of inputs to AND matrix) +(number of outputs) and
width = (the number of product term lines)
The number of inputs to the AND matrix is at most twice the number of input variables due to inversion.

The number of inputs and outputs would normally be determined at design time as a system requirement, hence dictating the length of the PLA. However the width of the array is dependent on the number of multiple output product terms and when used as a FSM the number of states, and to a certain extent their assignment will also effect the input and product terms. Note that the criteria for minimisation are different to those required for a PLA module.

Thus classical switching theory suitably modified can still find application in the design of VLSI chips. For example, it is possible when using PLA's to redefine the cost function used in the covering problem in multiple output minimisation to be simply the number of AND gates (product terms) required for the realisation(62). This means that the multiple output prime implicant tables can be treated as a single output table thereby considerably reducing the amount of computation. Since the minimisation problem in theory requires an exponential time solution, and because most practical PLA designs can have a large number of inputs (14-40) this is a very important consideration. Note that the minimal result obtained by this method need not be a sum of products of prime implicants. Note also that contrary to conventional gate implementation a single literal input must use an AND gate in the PLA configuration rather than be passed directly to the second level OR gates, thus the AND gate can be used to cover other terms without increasing the cost. This simplified cost function criteria can be included in any of the basic minimisation packages such as MINI, CALD etc.

When the PLA is used in a FSM configuration the machine is realised in terms of simple D-type bistables (in practice a clocked register) by extracting the excitation (application) equations. That is the next state $Y = f(x,y)$ where x is the input and y the present state. The product terms can be extracted directly from the Transition Table as shown in Table 10 for the traffic light controller of Mead and Conway.

It would of course be possible to expand the table and perform a conventional multiple output minimisation but in practice little would be gained. A better approach could be to extract monatonic next state equations (non-inverted form) to eliminate the need for invertors and hence attempt to reduce the width. Note this would involve a special state assignment which could also increase the number of state variables.

Alternatively an attempt could be made to reduce the number of states thereby reducing the number of state variables required. Unfortunately for large machines con-

TABLE 10

State-Transition Table

Input State C	TL	TS		Present State Y_0	Y_1	Next State Y_0	Y_1	Output States ST	HL0	HL1	FL0	FL1	Product Terms
0	0	0		0	0	0	0	0	0	0	1	0	$R_1 = \bar{C}\ \bar{Y}_0\bar{Y}_1$
0	0	1											$R_2 = \bar{T}L\ \bar{Y}_0\bar{Y}_1$
0	1	0	[0XX]										
0	1	1	[X0X]										
1	0	0											
1	0	1											
1	1	0	[11X]	0	0	0	1	1	0	0	1	0	$R_3 = CTL\ \bar{Y}_0\bar{Y}_1$
1	1	1											
0	0	0		0	1	0	1	0	0	1	1	0	$R_4 = \overline{TS}\ \bar{Y}_0Y_1$
0	1	0	[XX0]										
1	1	0											
1	0	0											
0	0	1		0	1	1	1	1	0	1	1	0	$R_5 = TS\ \bar{Y}_0Y_1$
0	1	1	[XX1]										
1	1	1											
1	0	1											
0	0	0		1	1	1	0	1	1	0	0	0	$R_6 = \bar{C}\ Y_0Y_1$
0	0	1											$R_7 = TL\ Y_0Y_1$
0	1	1	[0XX]										
0	1	0	[X1X]										
1	1	0											
1	1	1											
1	0	1	[10X]	1	1	1	1	0	1	0	0	0	$R_8 = C\overline{TL}\ Y_0Y_1$
1	0	0											
0	0	0		1	0	1	0	0	1	0	0	1	
0	1	0	[XX0]										$R_9 = \bar{T}S\ Y_0\bar{Y}_1$
1	1	0											
1	0	0											
0	0	1		1	0	0	0	1	1	0	0	1	
0	1	1											$R_{10} = TS\ Y_0\bar{Y}_1$
1	1	1	[XX1]										
1	0	1											

siderable reduction could be required before any real economies could be effected. This is because a reduction in state variables can only be achieved when the number of states S crosses a 2^nthreshold where n is the number of state variables. However it is possible that the availability of more dont-care conditions could effect a considerable reduction in the derivation of the product terms. It will be obvious that the problems of synthesising optimal PLA structures are far from being solved or for that matter even well specified.

A more recent approach to design aids for PLA's is the PLA generator[(63)] which enables a translation to be made from a language or ASM chart description to an actual PLA circuit description. The language may specify the function directly in terms of synchronous logic or via some higher level specification language. It is also possible to use PLA's in a hierarchial mode to overcome the problem of very large structures.

MOS technology allows the equivalent of contact circuit logic[(64)] to be implemented as pass transistor networks. Thus there is some relevance in reviving this early work and applying it directly to VLSI design. Unfortunately there is a propagation delay associated with cascaded circuits of this kind and it is necessary with NMOS technology to insert an invertor element after transmitting a signal through four pass transistor stages.

For example, the Tally circuit described in Mead and Conway can be designed directly using symmetric network theory as shown in figure 18; note the symmetric configuration is shown within dotted lines - the circuit also requires pull-up and pull-down transistors.

The same result may also be obtained, perhaps more effectively, by using iterative network design techniques. In this method a design for a basic contact cell is derived, using the concept of a transition table, and the requisite number of standard cells are cascaded to form the required circuit. Table 11 shows the transition table and associated output equations for the Tally circuit; diagrams of the basic cell and the final network are shown in figure 19 which will be seen to be identical with the earlier design.

Again contact theory can be applied to the design of sequential circuits in this case extracting the equations for a set-reset bistable and then proceding as for a relay circuit design. For example, consider the design of the Muller C-element circuit as described in Mead and Conway. This circuit is essentially a bistable element exhibiting hysteresis characteristics. The output of the element goes to one only after all of its inputs are zero. The flow-table and K-maps for the 2-input case are shown in Table 12. Expressing the set-reset bistable equations in terms of an excitation network using the characteristic equation gives:

$$Y = S + \bar{R}y = ab + (a + b)y$$

The corresponding relay network and its equivalent MOS circuit are shown in figure 20 .

TABLE 11 - Iterative Networks

Input State	Next State: External Input $X_n = 0$	Next State: External Input $X_n = 1$
A(0 out of 3)	A_+	B_+
B(1 out of 3)	B_+	C_+
C(2 out of 3)	C_+	D_+
D(3 out of 3)	D_+	D_+

$A_+ = A\bar{X}_n$

$B_+ = AX_n + B\bar{X}_n$

$C_+ = C\bar{X}_n + BX_n$

$D_+ = D + CX_n$

TABLE 12 - Muller C-Element

a) Flow Table

Y	Inputs a,b: 00	01	11	10	Output Z
0	(1)	(2)	3	(4)	0
1	1	(6)	(3)	(5)	1

b) K Maps

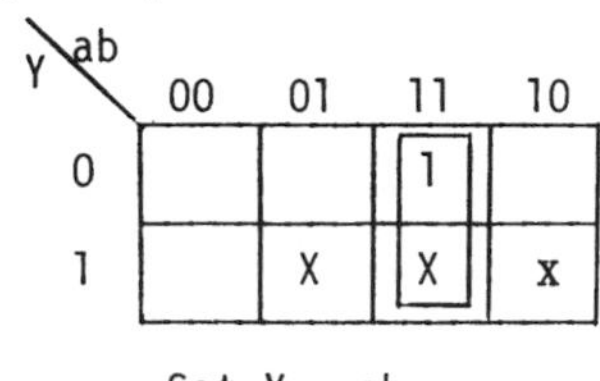

Set Y = ab

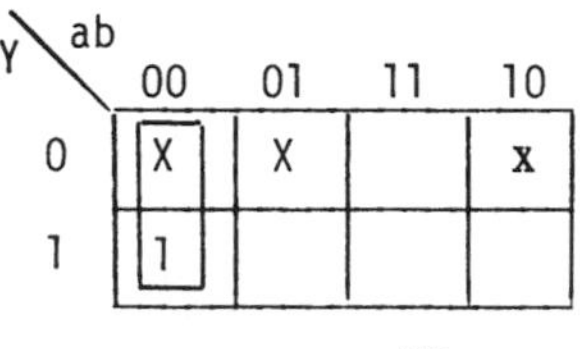

Reset Y = $\bar{a}\bar{b}$

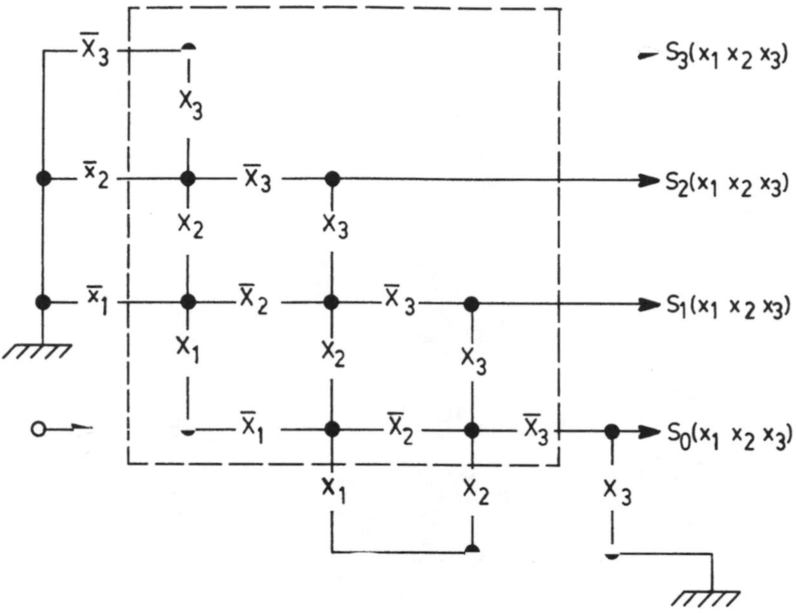

Figure 18 - Symmetric Networks

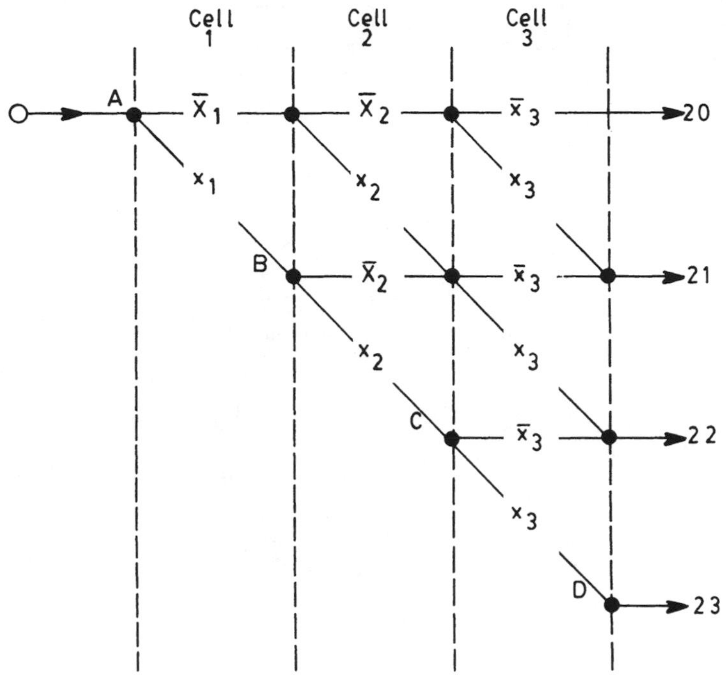

(b) Resultant tally circuit

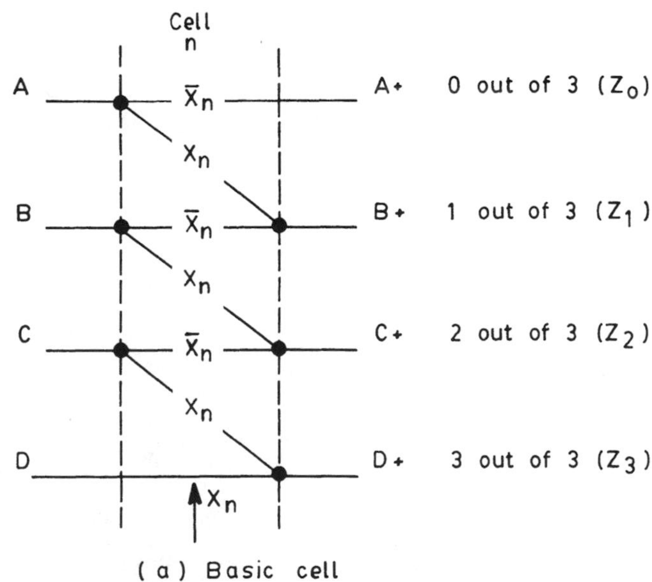

(a) Basic cell

Figure 19 - Iterative Networks

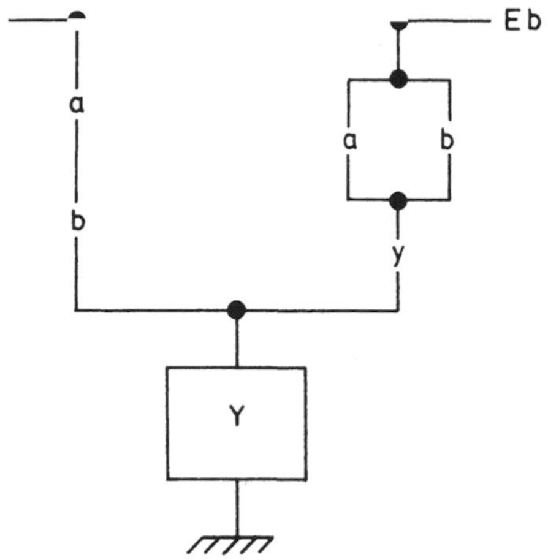

a) Relay circuit

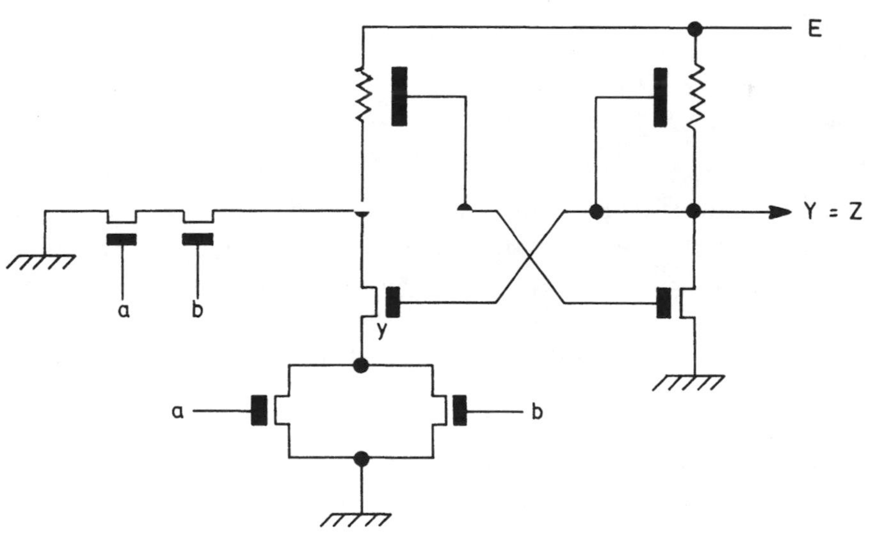

b) MOS circuit

Figure 20 - Muller C-Element

It will be apparent that contact switching theory has a useful application in VLSI design. However in order to produce a viable CAD design tool it would be essential to include the constraints imposed by the technology, propagation delays etc., as an integral part of any procedure.

Another approach to designing VLSI circuits is to use array and tree like structures to directly implement specific algorithms such as those requred for fast fourier transforms,searching, sorting etc. The character of arrays which use identical cells (in some cases programmable) arranged in a one or two-dimensional structure, makes them ideal for realisation in VLSI; some array structures are shown in figure 21. Note that this approach leads to the development of special purpose chips.

In particular the use of systolic arrays[65] which exploit pipelining and multiprocessing techniques where several data streams move at constant velocity over fixed paths in the network interacting at cells where they meet are favoured (the systems are analogous to a circulatory system where the processor pumps data in and out).

Another important area of synthesis is that of fault tolerant design[66] one method of countering the errors due to complexity is to employ the extra logic on a chip, made possible by VLSI, in some form of redundant configuration to achieve self diagnosis and fault protection.

Fault tolerant design may be employed at a variety of levels. At the systems level where replication of sub-system modules is used to increase the overall reliability, down to the use of error correcting and self-checking codes in designing logic and the automatic checking of RAM's etc. It is also important to consider the total system and include recovery and roll-back procedures in the systems and applications software.

Unfortunately no formal theory as yet exists for the design of VLSI systems. Currently the concept of structured design utilising well formed circuits like shift registers, pass transistor networks, PLA's etc. with control being executed in terms of FSM's nested together in a modular architecture is being exploited. In order to assist the logic designer to achieve a good layout both the logic and the topology of the ciruit is represented using a sticks diagram[67] which may also be labelled with relevant design rules such as the length, width and separation of connections etc. The sticks diagrams may be entered via a graphics terminal to a CAD layout package which ultimately produces the masks required for fabrication.

VLSI requires a more formal methodology for performing logic and system design at the silicon level. The concepts put forward by Mead and Conway are excellent as far as they go but still leaves far too much to the initiative and intuition of the designer. For example, synthesis tools are required for designing PLA circuits and state machines, novel logic structures which exploit the technology (such as pass-

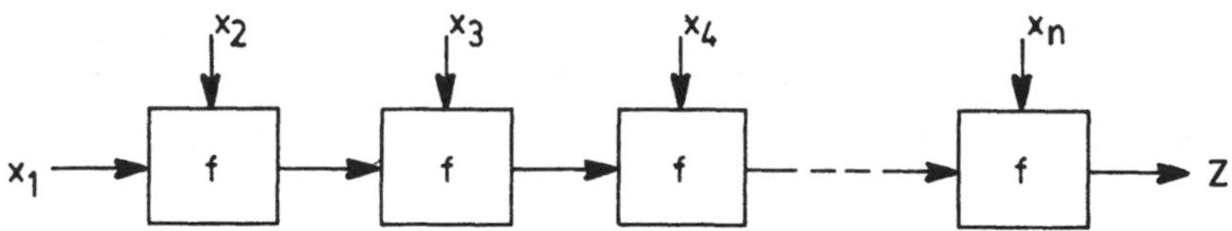

a) One-dimensional array

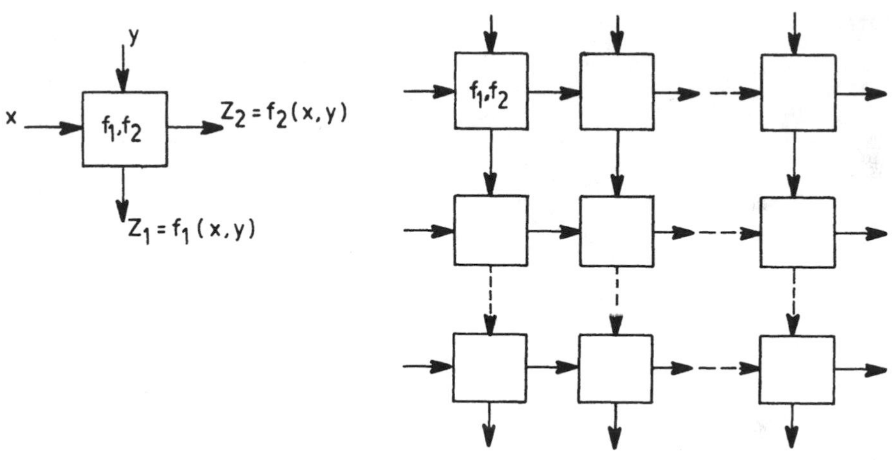

b) Two-dimensional array

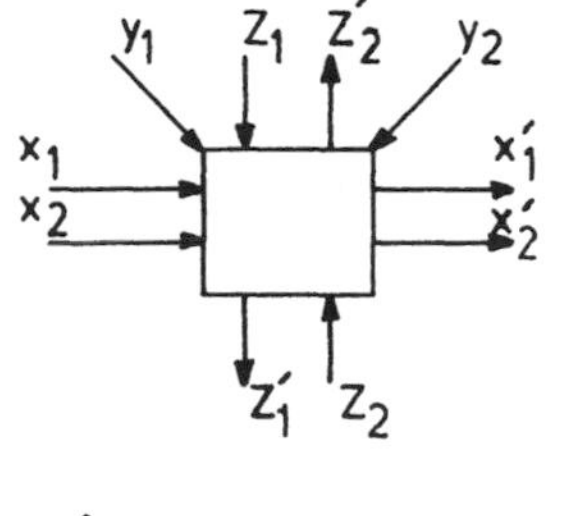

$x'_1 = x_1$

$Z'_1 = f_1(x_1, Z_1, y_1)$

$x'_2 = f_2(x_2, Z_2, y_2)$

$Z'_2 = Z_2$

y_1 y_2 are control inputs

c) Bilateral array

<u>Figure 21</u> - <u>Array Structures</u>

transistor circuits) must be developed as must hardware description languages for the design and evaluation of structured logic assemblies and design procedures for self-checking and failure-tolerant systems. In addition there are the problems of delays in VLSI circuits and the current work on self-timing systems[68] must be further extended.

It will be apparent that the entire field of synthesis is wide open and many difficult problems remain to be solved, and must be solved, if progress is to be maintained.

REFERENCES

1. P.L. Flake, G. Musgrave and I.J. White
A Digital Systems Simulator - HILO
Digital Processes I 1975 p39-53

2. A. Richard Newton
The Simulation of Large-Scale Integrated Circuits
Electronic Research Lab. University of California Berkeley
Mem. No UCB/ERL M78/52 July 1978

3. R.E. Fairley
Tutorial: Static Analysis and Dynamic Testing of Computer Software
IEEE Computer II No 4 1978 p-14-23

4. Carver Mead and Lyn Conway
Introduction to VLSI Systems
Addison-Wesley Mass. 1980

5. P. Henderson
Functional Programming - Application and Implementation
Prentice-Hall Englewood Cliffs New Jersey 1980

6. J. Holloway et. al.
The SCHEME-79 Chip
AI Memo 559 MIT AI Laboratory Jan 1980

7. T.W. Williams and K.P. Parker
Testing Logic Networks and Designing for Testability
IEEE Computer 12 No 10 1979 p 9-21

8. E.B. Eichelberger and T.W. Williams
A Logic Design Structure for LSI Testability
Journal of Design Automation and Fault Tolerant
Computing 2 No 2 1978 p 165-178

9. Special Issue Fault-Tolerant Computing
IEEE Computer 13 No 3 1980

10. A.V. Aho, J.E. Hopcroft and J.D. Ullman
The Design and Analysis of Computer Algorithms
Addison-Wesley Mass. 1974

11. R.E. Tarjan
Complexity of Combinational Algorithms
SIAM Review 20 No 3 1978 p 457-491

12. S.A. Browning
Computations on a Tree of Processors
Proc. Caltech Conf on VLSI Jan. 1979 p 453-478

13. B. Raphael
The Thinking Computer
W.H. Freeman and Co. San Francisco 1976

14. J.C. Latombe (ed)
Artificial Intelligence and Pattern Recognition in CAD
North Holland Pub. Co. Amsterdam 1978

15. D.I. Parnas
On the Criteria to be used in Decomposing Systems into Modules
Comms. ACM 15 No 12 Dec. 1972 1053-1058

16. Hardware Description Languages (Special Issue)
IEEE Computer 7 No 12 1974

17. M.R. Barbacci
A Comparison of Register Transfer Languages for Describing Computers and Digital Systems
IEEE Trans. Computers C24 p 137-150 1975

18. Y. Chu
An ALGOL-Like Computer Design Language
Comm. ACM 8 p 605-615 1965

19. M.R. Barbacci
Instruction Set Processor Specifications for Simulation, Evaluation and Synthesis
Proc. 16th Int. Design Automation Conf. San Diego 1979 p 64-72

20. M.R. Barbacci and A. Parker
Using Emulation to Verify Formal Architecture Descriptions
IEEE Computer 11 No 5 1978 p 51-56

21. C.G. Bell and A. Newell
The PMS and ISP Descriptive System for Computer Structures
AFIPS SJCC 36 1970 p 351-374

22. M.R. Barbacci
The ISPS Compiler and Simulator - Users Manual
Computer Science Dept. Tech Rept. Carnegie Melon University August 1976

23. J.R. Duley and D.L. Dietmeyer
A Digital System Design Language (DDL)
IEEE Trans Computers C17 p 850-861 1968

24. J.R. Duley and D.L. Dietmeyer
Translation of a DDL digital system specification to Boolean equations
IEEE Trans Computers C18 p 305-313 1969

25. R.L. Arndt
DDLSIM - A Digital Design Language Simulator
Proc. Nat Electronics Corp. 26 December 1970 p 116-118

26. N.E. Cory, J.R. Duley and W.M. Van Cleemput
An Introduction to the DDL-P Language
Stanford University Computer System Lab. Tech Report 163 March 1979

27. M.B. Baray and S.Y.H. Su
A Digital System Modelling Philosophy and Design Language
Proc. 8th Annual Design Automation Workshop
Atlantic City June 1971 p 1-22

28. M.B. Baray and S.Y.H. Su
LALSD - a language for Automated Logic and System Design
Proc. Int. Symp. CHDL 1975 p 30-31

29. M.B. Baray, S.Y.H. Su and R.L. Carberry
The Structure and Operation of a System Modelling Language Compatible Simulator
Proc. 8th Annual Design Automation Workshop 1971 p 23-34

30. S.Y.H. Su and G. Chinn
Expanded Logic Level Simulator
Proc. Summer Simulation Conf. San Diego 1971 p 163-180

31. D. Hill and W.M. Van Cleemput
SABLE : A tool for generating structural multilevel simulations
Proc. 16th Design Automation Conf. San Diego 1979 p 272-279

32. G.G. Bell and A. Newell
Computer Structures : Readings and Examples
McGraw Hill 1971

33. M. Knudsen
PMSL - An Interactive Language for High Level Description and Analysis of Computer Systems.
Tech Report Computer Science Department Carnegie Melon University 1972

34. P.O. Stigall and O. Tasar
A Review of Directed Graphs as Applied to Computers
IEEE Computer 7 No 10 1974 p 39-47

35. J.L. Peterson
Petri Nets
ACM Computing Surveys 9 No 3 1977 p 223-252

36. T. Agerwala
Putting Petri Nets to Work
IEEE Computer 12 No 12 1979 p 85-94

37. S.S. Patil
on Structured Digital Systems
Proc. Int. Symp. on CHDL's and their Applications New York 1975 p 1-6

38. R.M. Karp and R.E. Miller
Properties of a model for Parallel Computation: Determinacy, Termination, Queueing
J. Appl. Math. 14 1966 p 1300-1411

39. K. Lautenbach and H.A. Schmid
Use of Petri Nets for proving correctness of Concurrent Process Systems
Proc. IFIP Congress 74 1974 p 184-191

40. C.W. Rose
LOGOS and the Software Engineer
AFIPS FJCC 41 1972 p 311-323

41. C.W. Rose and M. Albarran
Modelling and Design Description of Hierarchial Hardware/Software Systems
Proc. 12th Design Automation Conf. Boston 1975 p 421-430

42. G. Estrin
A Methodology for the Design of Digital Systems - Supported by SARA at the age of one
AFIPS Conf. Proc. 47 1978 p 313-324

43. C.R. Clare
Designing Logic Systems using State Machines
McGraw Hill New York 1973

44. C. Mead and L. Conway
Introduction to VLSI Systems
Addison-Wesley Mass 1980

45. H.H. MacDougall
Computer Systems Simulation : An introduction
Computer Surveys 2 191-210 1970

46. Digital Systems Simulation - special issue
Computer 8 number 3 1975

47. R. Efron and G. Gordon
General purpose digital simulation and examples of its application
IBM Systems J 3 22-34 1964

48. F.P. Wyman
Simulation Modelling : A guide to using SIMSCRIPT
John Wiley 1970

49. P.L. Flake, G. Musgrave and I.J. White
A Digital System Simulator - HILO
Digital Processes 1 39-53 1975

50. K.A. Duke, H.D. Schnurman and T.I. Wilson
System Validation by Three Level Modelling Synthesis
IBM J. Res. Dev. 15 166-174 1971

51. B. Eichelberger
Hazard Detection in Combinational and Sequential Switching Circuits
IBM J. Res. Dev. 9 90-99 1965

52. S.A. Szygenda and E.W. Thompson
Fault injection techniques and models for logical simulation
AFIPS FJCC 41 875-884 1972

53. S.A. Szygenda and E.W. Thompson
Digital Logic Simulation in a Time Based Table Driven Environment pt. 2
Parallel Fault Simulation
Computer 8 No 3 p 38-49 1975

54. S.A. Szygenda
TEGAS2 - Anatomy of a General Purpose Test Generation and Simulation System for Digital Logic
Proc. 9th ACM IEEE Design Automation Workshop June 1972

55. H.Y. Chang and S.G. Chappell
Deductive Techniques for Simulating Logic Circuits
Computer 8 No 3 p 52-59 1975

56. T.E. Bell
Objectives and Problems in Simulating Computers
AFIPS FJCC 41 287-297 1972

57. A. Alan, B. Pritsker and R. Young
Simulation with GASP-PLI
John Wiley 1975

58. M.S. Jayakumar and T.M. McCalla
Simulation of Microprocessor Emulation using GASP-PLI
Computer 10 No 4 p 20-26 1977

59. W.M. Van Cleemput
Computer Aided Design of Digital Systems - A Bibliography Vols. I, II, III
Computer Science Press California 1978

60. D. Lewin, E. Purslow and R.G. Bennetts
Computer Assisted Logic Design - The CALD System
IEE Conf. on CAD Pub No 86 p 343-51 1972

61. S.J. Hong, R.G. Cain, and D.L. Ostapko
MINI - A Heuristic approach for Logic Minimisation
IBM J. Res. Dev. 18 p 443-458 1974

62. T. Kobylorz and A. Al-Najjar
An Examination of the Cost Function for PLA's
IEEE Trans Computers 28 p 586-590 1979

63. R. Ayres
Silicon Compilation - A Hierarchial Use of PLA's
CALTECH Conf. on VLSI Jan 1979 p 311-326

64. S.H. Caldwell
Switching Circuits and Logical Design
Wiley New York 1958

65. M.J. Foster and H.T. Kung
Design of Special Purpose VLSI chips
IEEE Computer 13 No 1 p 26-40 1980

66. Fault Tolerant Computing - special issue
IEEE Computers 13 No 3 1980

67. J.D. Williams
Sticks - A New Approach to LSI Design
MSEE Thesis Dept. of Electrical Engineering and Computer Science MIT 1977

68. C.L. Seitz
Self Timed VLSI Systems
Proc. CALTECH Conf VLSI p 345-354 1979

PROPERTIES OF INSTRUCTION SET PROCESSOR

D. ASPINALL

Department of Computation
U.M.I.S.T. Manchester

1. INTRODUCTION

The classical view of a microcomputer is that shown below of a Processor-Memory Pair. (Fig. 1).

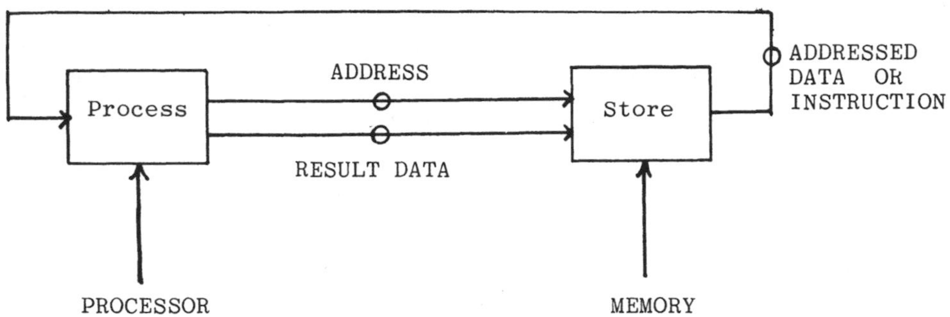

Fig. 1 : Instruction Set Processor-Memory Pair

The memory stores information to be interpreted as either instructions or data as it is processed by the Processor. In early machines there was a distinction between the memory unit which stored the instructions and that which stored the data, as shown in Fig. 2. This distinction between fixed programme and volatile data was made in the machines developed at Harvard University in the 1940's and such organisations are often termed Harvard Machines. Within the processor are two distinct processing activities : Programme Control and Compute.

The Programme Control activity is concerned with tracing the locus of control through the stored programme of instructions. It contains within it the Processor State Variable called Programme Counter (PC). It is the address of the instruction which is next to be fetched from the read only memory and obeyed in the processor. During the instruction cycle the Programme Counter variable is modified to become the address of the next instruction to be fetched and obeyed, and so on. Also, during the instruction cycle the Compute activity receives an operand, either a constant from within the instruction or a variable data word accessed from the read write memory at an address specified within the instruction. The compute activity is determined by the

Operation Code within the instruction, it may be an arithmetic or logical operation. These are performed in the processor MILL which also includes a register to hold intermediate results. This is often known as the Accumulator Register (A). Alongside this register is a second which holds the status of recent results produced in the MILL, for example "result equals zero", "carry overflow" after an addition. This register is to be termed MILL Status (MS) and together with the Accumulator and the Programme Counter makes up the Processor State Vector of the Harvard Machine. The output of the MILL Status register is processed within the MILL to produce the Condition Code which is transmitted to the Control Activity to be compared with the Qualifier from within the instruction, when choosing the method of modifying the Programme Counter variable.

The next stage in the evolution of the computer occurred at the Moore School of Electronics at Princeton University. This was to allow both the instructions and the data to reside in the same read write memory. This is an important concept since it permits a location in the memory to be altered as a Data Word and then accessed as an instruction, just as within the Turing Machine. Von Neuman was associated with the Moore School whilst this seminal step was being taken. The computer which resulted is termed the Moore-Von Neuman, or just the Von Neuman Machine, as shown in Fig. 3, and has a single primary memory, MP. The instruction cycle has two distinct phases. During the initial phase the memory is accessed for the instruction word at an address determined by the value of the Programme Counter. This value is routed to the memory by the <u>CHOOSE</u> activity. The instruction word has three main components destined for the control, compute and <u>LATCH</u> activities, as shown. The address of the data word to be accessed during the next phase of the instruction cycle is latched onto a slave register by a strobe signal. During this data phase the memory location in MP may be accessed to be read as the data word giving the variable operand to be processed in the compute activity or it may receive the result data from the output of the compute activity, depending upon the operation code.

(The STROBE and PHASE signals both originate from a central processor controller, as shown in Fig. 4. The actions of this controller will be influenced by the Instruction Type.)

The next step in the evolution of the computer occurred at the University of Manchester where it was realised that a considerable advantage could be gained by processing the address of the data word during an instruction cycle and by retaining address information within the processor as part of its state vector. Professor Tom Kilburn, who retires this year from his chair in the University, was instrumental in making this step and it is fair to call such a machine a Manchester-Kilburn machine, as shown in Fig. 4. The data address description read during the initial phase of the instruction cycle is input to the process address activity where together with the state variable stored in the B register it is used to generate the address of the data word to be accessed during the second phase of the instruction cycle.

Orthogonality

The three main components of an instruction set processor, from the programmer's viewpoint, have now been identified :

I Programme Control
State variable :- Programme Counter (PC)

II Data Computation
State variable :- Accumulator (A)
MILL Status (MS)

III Data Address Processing
State variable :- Address Register (B)

There are two sets of instructions: Assignment Statements and Programme Control Instructions. Each assignment statement implies the same basic programme control mechanism within the instruction cycle but is a pairing of the Data Computation and Data Address Processing actions. In an ideal, orthogonal, instruction set it must be possible for each and every Data Computation action to be paired with each and every Data Address Processing action. This is desirable for reliable programming and efficient automatic translation from high level language to machine code.

Though the Data Computation actions are interesting in their own right, they will not be treated further here. The Data Address Processing actions will be discussed in Section I, and the Programme Control aspects in Section II. An attempt will be made to illustrate the general principles by illustrations drawn from some 16-bit microprocessors.

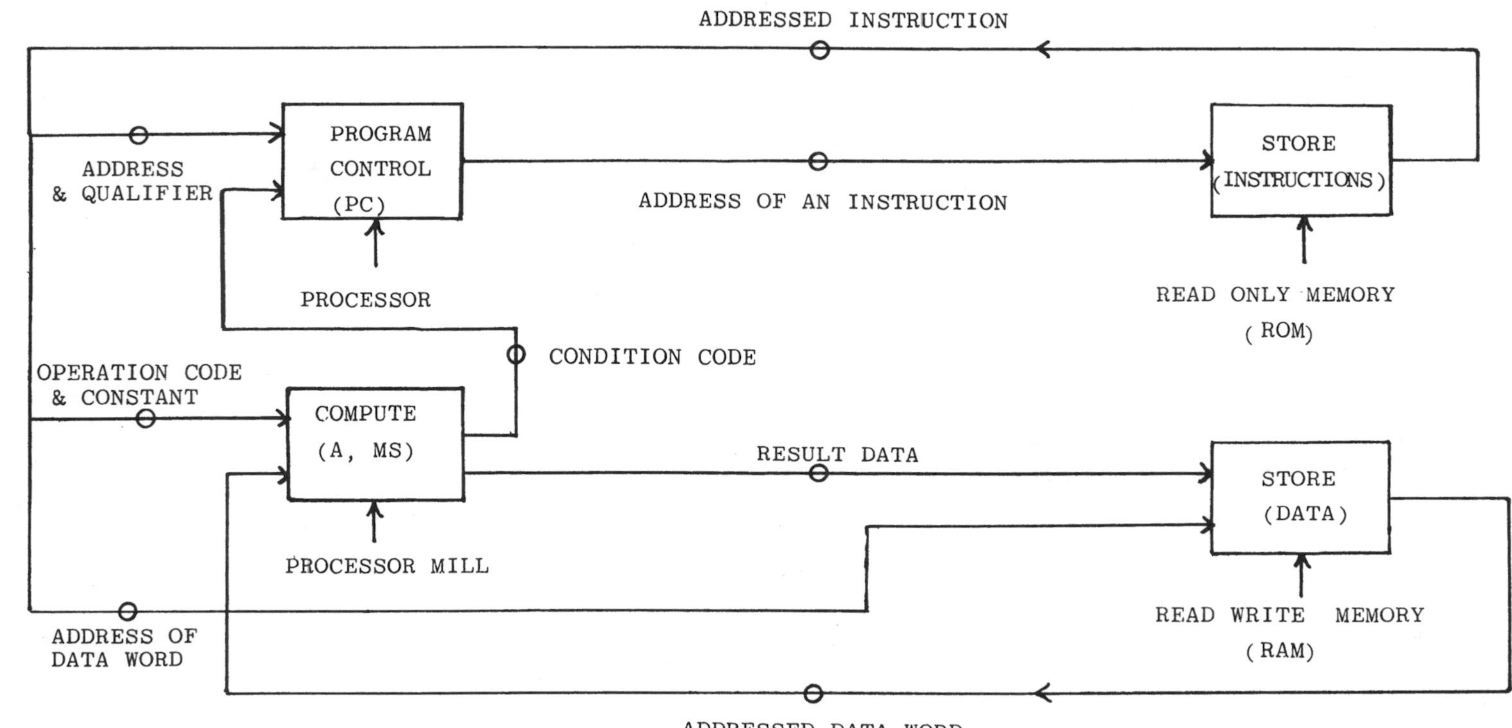

Fig. 2 : Early Computer (HARVARD)

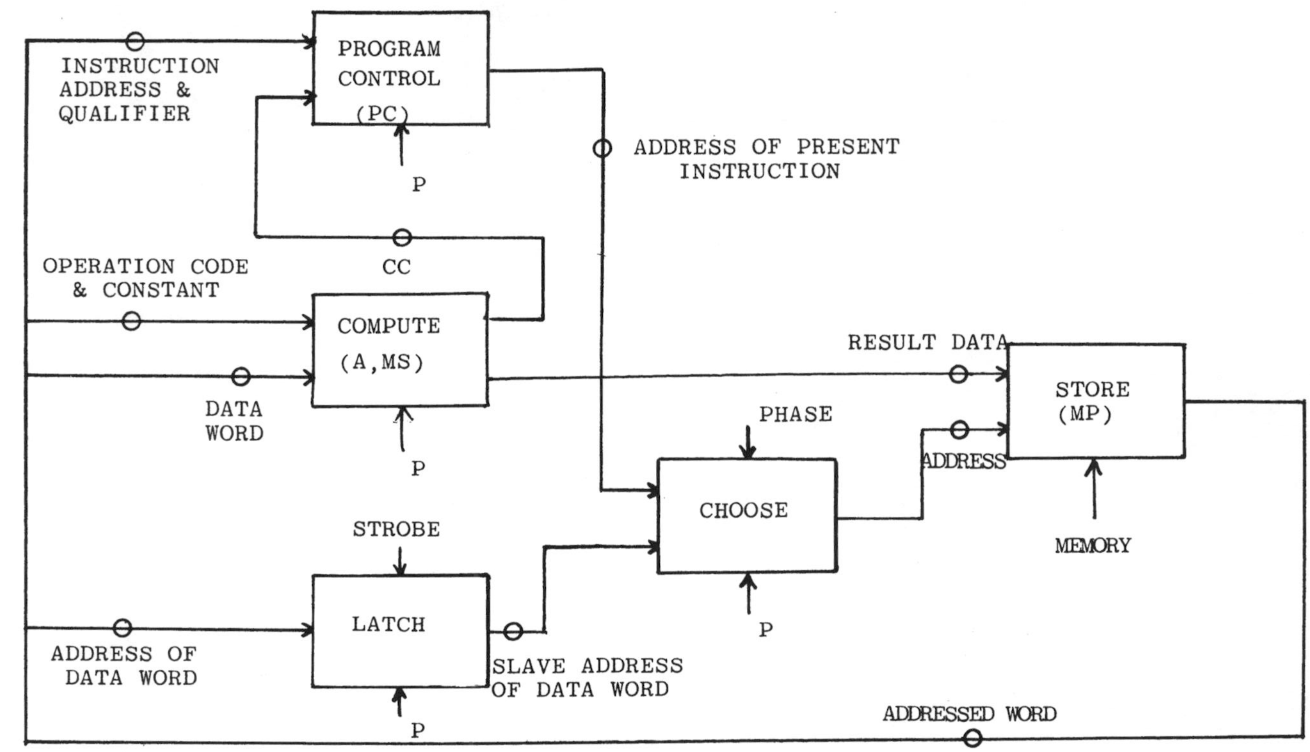

Fig. 3 : Basic Computer (Moore-Von Neuman)

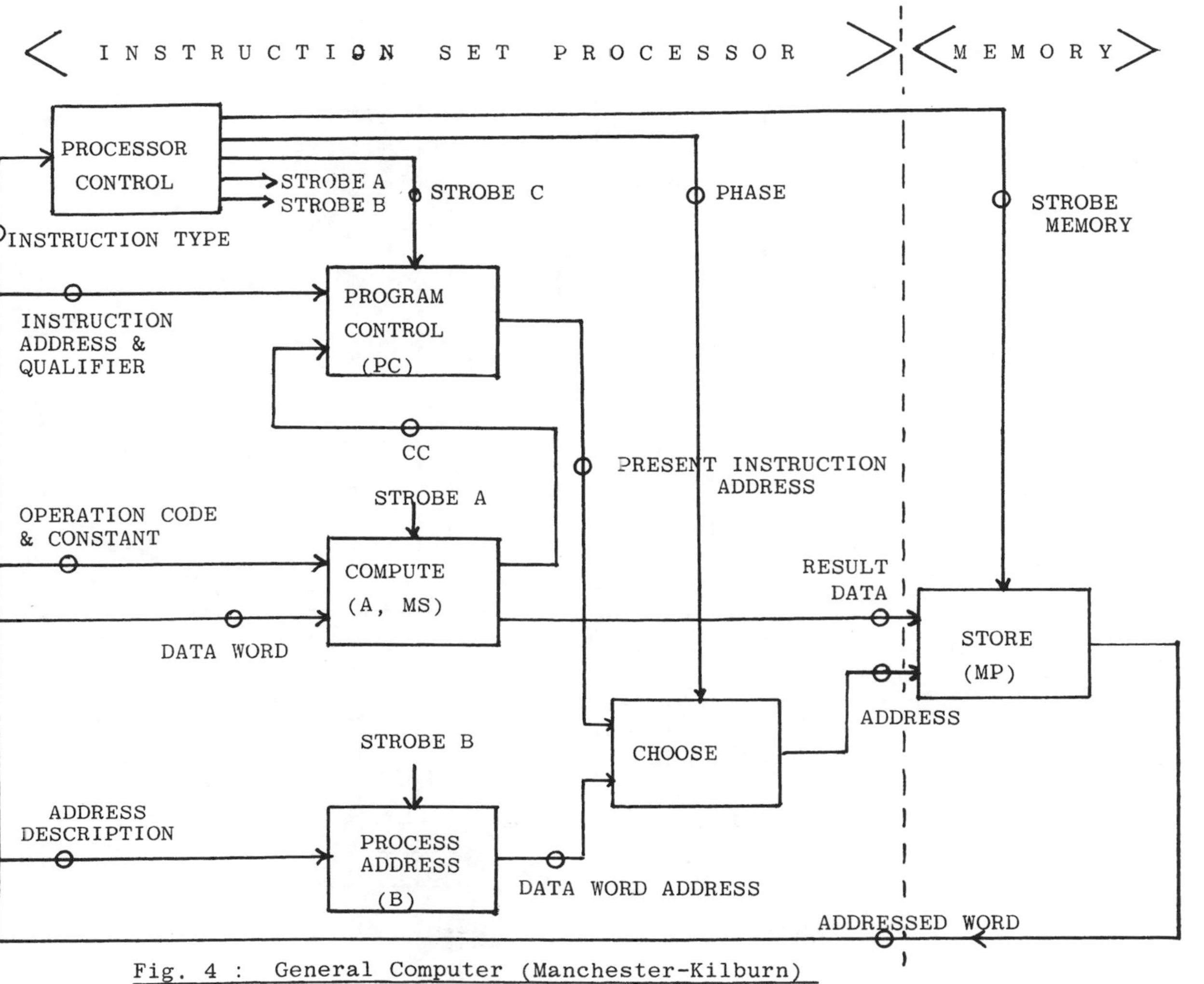

Fig. 4 : General Computer (Manchester-Kilburn)

2. INSTRUCTION SET PROCESSOR - SECTION I

Addressing of Data Words

A programmer works with the concept of an abstract machine which is capable of certain actions as described by the assignment statements which are allowed by the rules of some programming language. A statement describes how the value of a Data Word in the primary memory of the abstract machine is changed to a value given by the result of some operation involving one or more Data Words. Typical abstract machines are shown in Table 1 and are classified according to addressing scheme.

Addressing Scheme	ASSIGNMENT STATEMENT	
	Instruction	Machine Action
Three-address	Mx := My b Mz	As instruction
Two-address	Mx := My b Mx	As instruction
One-address	b Mx STORE Mx	A := A b Mx Mx := A
STACK (Zero-address)	b PUSH, Mx POP	ST := ST b STN ST := Mx M(STN) := ST

Ma\ Value of Data Word at Memory Location a
a\x\y\z\(STN)
b\ Binary Operator A\ Accumulator
ST\ Value of Data Word at Top of Stack
STN\ " " " " " Next below top of stack
(STN)\ Memory location given by STN

Table 1 : Addressing Schemes

An interesting property of a physical machine, or microprocessor, is the ease with which it may conform to a desired abstract machine. Hopefully the instruction set will provide the components which directly model the assignment statements of the abstract machine. If they do not, then one must consider the ease with which the real instruction set may be programmed to build the assignment statements of the abstract machine. As a first step it is useful to identify the natural addressing scheme of a given physical machine and then to consider the addressing modes which are provided to enable the location of the Data Word in Memory. These modes will indicate the mechanisms available to build models of other abstract addressing schemes as well as indicating the addressing power of the given physical machine.

The addressing schemes and modes of a selection of physical machines are shown in Table 2. The PDP-11 naturally appears as a two-address machine though it may also appear as a one-address machine in which the "implied" accumulator is one of a set of general registers which must be explicitly specified in the instruction. The microprocessors 68000, Z-8000 and 8086 can only appear as one-address (general register) machines.

Addressing Scheme	PDP-11	68000	8086	Z-8000
Two-Address	√	-	-	-
One-Address (General Register)	√	√	√	√
Addressing Mode				
Literal	√	√	√	√
Direct	√	√	√	√
In-direct	√	√	√	√
Auto-increment (Post)	√	√	-	-
Auto-decrement (Pre)	√	√	-	-
Register Literal	√	√	√	√
Register-Register	-	-	√	√
Reg.-Reg.-Literal	-	√	√	-
Post-Inc. Deferred	√	-	-	-
Pre-Dec. Deferred	√	-	-	-
Register-Literal Deferred	√	-	-	-
Maximum Addressable Memory Size (BYTES)	64K	16M	1M	8M

Table 2 : Physical Addressing Schemes and Modes

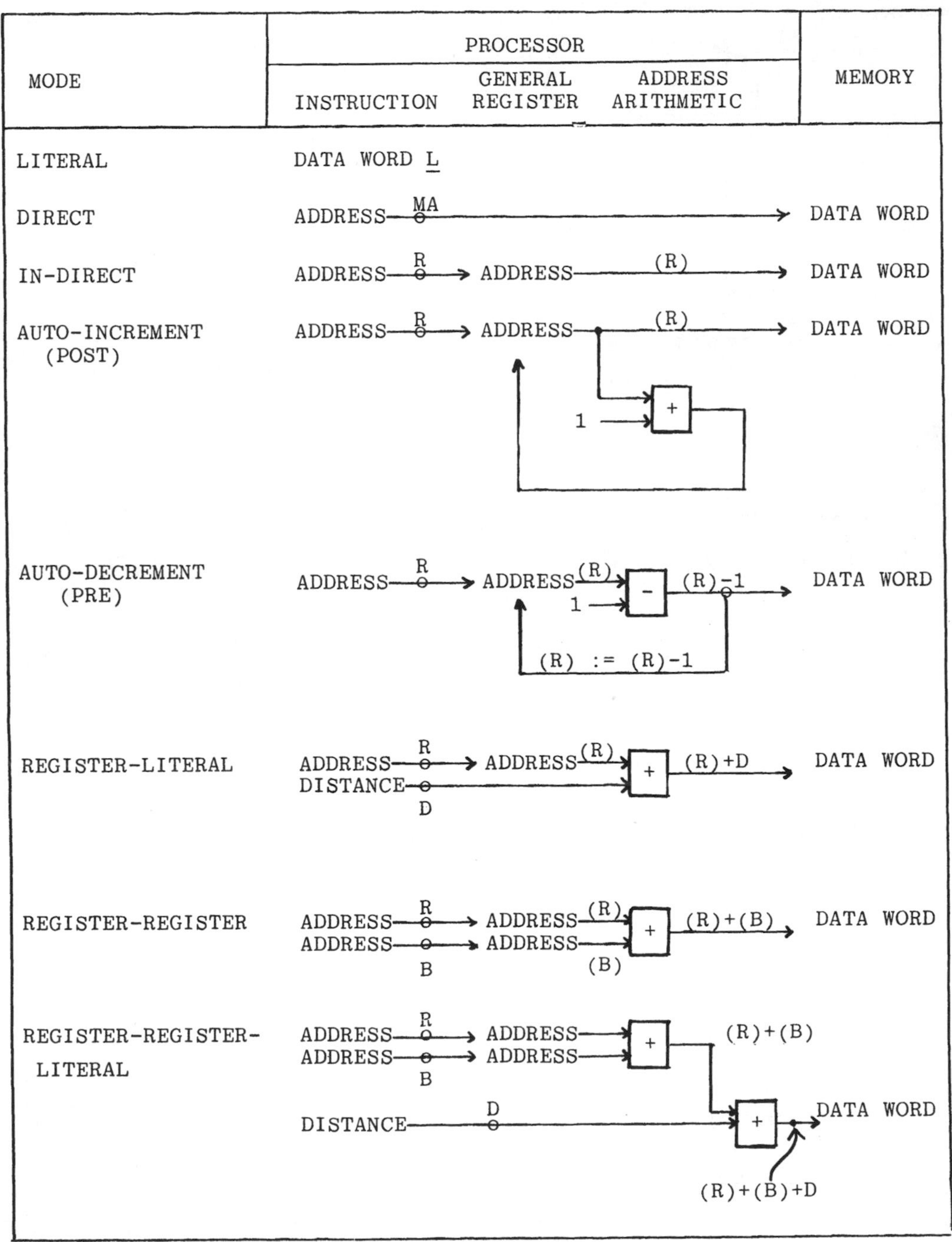

Figure 1 : Micro-Processor Addressing Modes

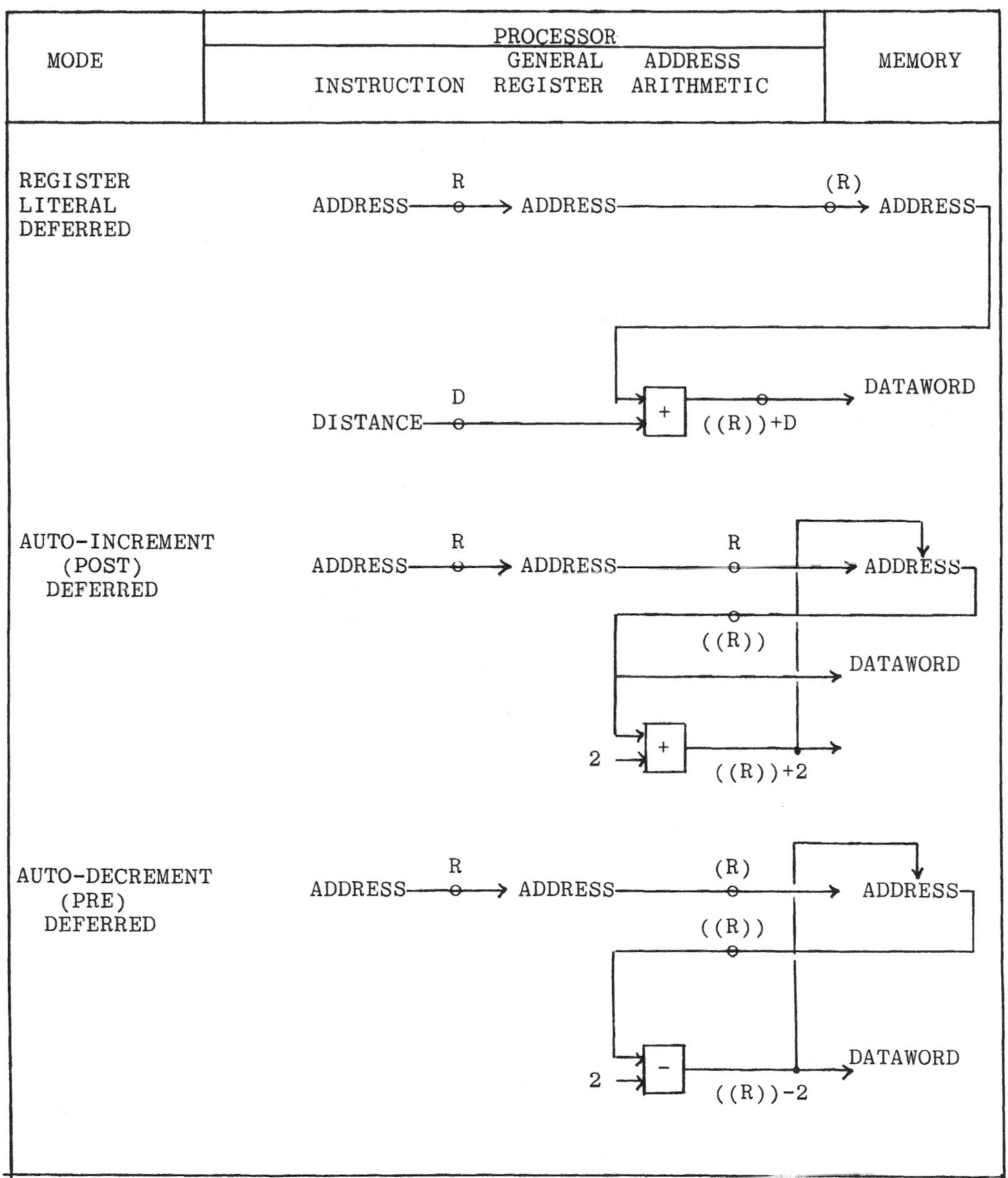

Figure 2 : PDP-11 Deferred Addressing Modes

Addressing Modes

The mode describes the way in which the Data Word description in the instruction is to be interpreted by the processor. The microprocessor addressing modes will now be described briefly with the aid of Figure 1. The deferred modes of the PDP-11 are displayed in Figure 2 which should be self explanatory.

Literal   Data Word = L

The Data Word description, L, within the instruction is interpreted as the literal value of the Data Word and is treated as an operand on the right hand side of an assignment statement. The Literal is usually to be found in the memory location IMMEDIATEly after the present instruction though in the case of the MC-68000 and Z-8000 a short literal is provided also within the 16-bit instruction.

Direct   Data Word = (MA)

The Data Word description, MA, in the instruction is interpreted as the address of a Data Word location in primary memory (may be in a General Register not shown in Fig. 1).

In-Direct   Register Value = (R)   NEXT   Data Word = ((R))

The short Data Word Description, R, in the instruction is interpreted as the address of a general register which contains the address of a Data Word location in primary memory.

Auto-Increment (POST)   Register Value = (R)
NEXT Data Word = ((R))
NEXT (R) := (R)+1

The Data Word description, R, addresses a general register. The value of the contents is first used to locate the Data Word in memory before it is incremented.

Auto-Decrement (PRE)   Register Value = (R)
NEXT (R) := (R)-1
NEXT Data Word = ((R))

The Data Word description, R, addresses a general register. The value of its contents is decremented before it is used to locate the Data Word in memory.

Register-Literal   Register value; (R)
NEXT Data Word = ((R)+D)

The Data Word description consists of two components, the register address, R, and a literal, D, which is added to the value of the selected register to form the address of the Data Word.

Register-Register General Register Value = (R)
General Register Value = (B)
NEXT Data Word = ((R) + (B))

This mode implies the use of one of the general registers, B, in a special role. The Data Description in the instruction specifies the address of a second general register. The contents of both registers are summed to form the address of the Data Word.

Register-Register-Literal General Register Value = (R)
General Register Value = (B)
NEXT Data Word =((CR) + (B) + D)

This mode employs the special B register and requires the instruction Data Word description to specify the address of the general register R and a literal D. The contents of both registers are added to the literal to form the address of the Data Word.

Modelling of Abstract Machines by Microprocessors

The summary of microprocessor addressing schemes and modes in Table 2 shows that the three microprocessors 68000, 8086 and Z-8000 naturally model a one-address (general register) machine. Furthermore each microprocessor offers a comprehensive set of addressing modes which may be employed to assess the Data Word in the primary memory. For the 68000 and 8086 microprocessors each addressing mode may be used in conjunction with each of the binary operators given below in Table 3.

Binary Operator	
Add	A := A + Ma
Subtract	A := A - Ma
Divide	A := A / Ma
Multiply	A := A * Ma
AND	A := A $\wedge$ Ma
OR	A := A $\vee$ Ma

Table 3 : Available Operations

There is good orthogonality between the operator and the addressing modes.

Other forms of the assignment statement may occur such as Ma := Ma+A. However, this type of statement in which the result of the operation is destined for a data word location in memory may not be permitted to occur for all binary operators. In order to preserve good orthogonality alternative assignment statements should not be used unless they apply to the allowed set of operations.

Three-Address Machine on One-Address Machine

The Three-Address scheme, Mx := My b Mz, may be modelled onto a one-address machine as shown :

```
e.g.  Mx := My + Mz

          LOAD My        A := My
          ADD Mz         A := A + Mz
          STORE Mx       Mx := A
```

Stack Machine on One-Address Machine

The Stack Machine must be specified in more detail before it can be modelled. It is assumed that the Stack will be built in the memory. Furthermore, the accumulator register amongst the general registers of the processor will serve as "top of stack". The "next to top of stack" will be located in the memory and pointed to by a stack pointer, SP. The stack will grow downwards from high memory address to low. The three assignment statements of the Stack Machine, as shown in Table 1, will now be encoded.

```
General Registers:
                    A    Top of Stack
                    B    Temporary Store
                    SP   Stack Pointer

Statement           b * OPERATE *
                      A := A b (SP) !  INDIRECT MODE
                      SP := SP + 1  !  Increment General Register

Statement           PUSH Mx *Push Data Word from location x onto stack*
                      SP := SP - 1  !  Decrement General Register
                      (SP) := A     !  Indirect Mode
                      A := Mx       !  Mx by any Mode

Statement           POP *Pop Word from top of stack to location given
                        by address held in next to top of stack*
                      B := (SP)     !  Move Address into General
                                        Register B
                      SP := SP + 1
                      (B) := A      !  Store A at address given by B
                      A := (SP)     !  Move new Top of Stack to A
                      SP := AP + 1  !  Increment Pointer
```

These fragments of code can be implemented on any of the physical machines listed in Table 2. However, the Auto-increment/decrement modes make it possible to reduce the number of instructions per statement. (PDP-11 & MC 68000)

```
b
  A := A b (SP)  NEXT SP := SP + 1  !  POST AUTO-INC.
PUSH Mx
  SP := SP - 1   NEXT (SP) := A     ! PRE AUTO-DEC.
  A := Mx
POP
  B := (SP)      NEXT SP := SP + 1
  (B) := A
  A := (SP)      NEXT SP := SP + 1
```

Furthermore the 8086 and Z-8000 each provide Push and Pop instructions. The 8086 uses a special stack pointer register whilst the Z-8000 allows seven out of the eight general registers to be designated as stack pointers. In each case the transfer can take place between the stack and any Data Word specified by any of the modes including register-direct. The three Stack Machine statements become :

```
b
  POP D          !  OPERAND AT NEXT TO TOP OF STACK moved
                     to General Register D
  A := A b D
PUSH Mx
  PUSH A         !  Accumulator value pushed to next to
                     top of stack
  A := Mx
POP
  POP B
  (B) := A
  POP A
```

In this encoding the addressing mode power of the stack instructions has not been exploited. Further study of all the instruction sets may produce a more efficient model of the Stack Machine in each case.

Memory Management

The size of the addressable memory for each of the processors béing considered is shown in Table 2. The microprocessors can each address a memory of at least 1 million bytes. A memory of this size needs careful management.

Segmentation

When a routine is being executed it is convenient to establish four distinct segments in the memory :

Code Segment for the instructions
Data Segment for named variables
Extra Data Segment for array variables
Stack Segment for stacks

Each segment is treated, by the programmer, as a separate abstract memory. (Shades of the Harvard Machine). The address locations within each memory (segment) range from zero to some upper limit. Ideally the programmer would wish this upper limit to be infinity but this is not practicable. In the case of the 8086 and Z-8000 the limit is 64K bytes. In other words the address word of the memory (segment) is 16 bits long. In practice it is also necessary to specify a lower limit to segment length. In the case of the 8086 this is 16 bytes whilst in the case of the Z-8000 it is 64K bytes being a fixed length physical memory segment. Within the memory (segment) the addressing modes described in Fig. 1 obtain.

Segment Location in Physical Memory

Having established the concept of separate logical memory segments it is now necessary to consider how these are to be located in the single addressable space of the physical primary memory. A typical abstract memory segment is shown below :

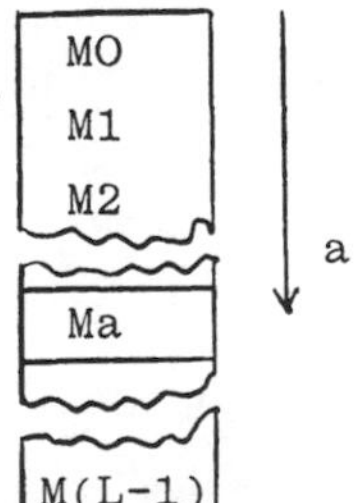

The address of memory location a is the same as its distance from the first address location.

The last word in the segment M(L-1) is at distance (L-1) from the first address location where L equals limit to segment length

This abstract segment becomes real when it is placed within physical memory as shown below :

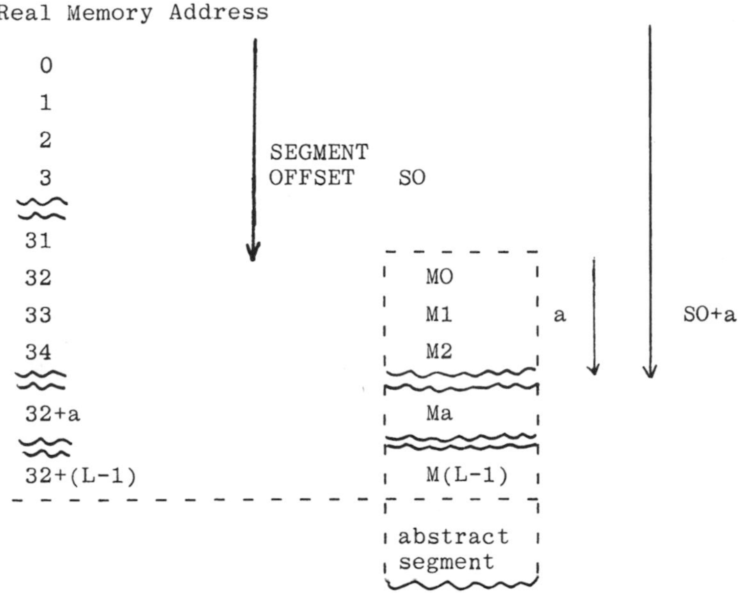

The first word of the memory segment is placed at a distance from the first word of the real memory given by the Segment OFFSET, SO. Thus if the address of a Data Word within an Abstract Segment is 'a' then its real address is 'SO+a'. This addition of segment offset to the address of the data word in memory occurs after the address mode processing as shown in Fig. 1 has occurred. The whereabouts of the value of the Segment OFFSET depends upon the specification of the physical microprocessor.

<u>8086</u>

In the case of the 8086 four 16-bit segment registers are designated to hold the OFFSET for each of four distinct segments :

CODE, DATA, STACKS and EXTRA DATA

The segment OFFSET, SO, is a word of 20 bits the four least significant bits being zero. This 20 bit word is added to the 16 bit address and generated by the address process to produce a 20 bit real address to assess a memory of 1M bytes. The segment offset has a value which is a multiple of 16, thus the minimum segment length is 16 bytes. The maximum segment length is 64K bytes given by the length of abstract memory address of 16 bits.

<u>Z-8001</u>

In the case of the Z-8001 the Segment Offset, SO, is 23 bits in length. The 16 least significant bits are zero whilst the 7 most significant bits contain a Segment Number. The segment number is contained either in a general register or within the instruction format, or in the Program Control register. The segment Offset is "added" to the 16-bit abstract address generated by the appropriate addressing mode action as shown in Table 2 and Figure 1. In effect the segment number is concatenated with the abstract address to form the real memory address. Thus the segment length is fixed at 64K bytes and there may be up to 128 segments in the addressable memory space of 8M bytes.

Three of the four general register pairs may be designated to serve the roles of Data, Extra Data and Stack Segment registers; however most instructions do not allow all the addressing modes and it is more usual to find the Segment Number contained in the instruction. (This must make it difficult to write and manage relocatable code). The ways in which the Z-8001 addressing modes relate to Segmented addressing are shown in Figure 3.

Segmented Addressing in Z-8001 (Fig. 3)

The Memory Address is generated by concatenating the 7-bit Segment Number with the abstract address generated by a process, as listed in Table 2 and described in Figure 1. The Segment Number may be contained in the instruction, SN, or in a general register addressed by the instruction (RSN). In the direct addressing mode Segment Number, SN, and the address within the segment, D, are both contained in the instruction whereas in the in-direct addressing mode both SN and D are contained in a register pair addressed by the instruction (RSN) (RD).

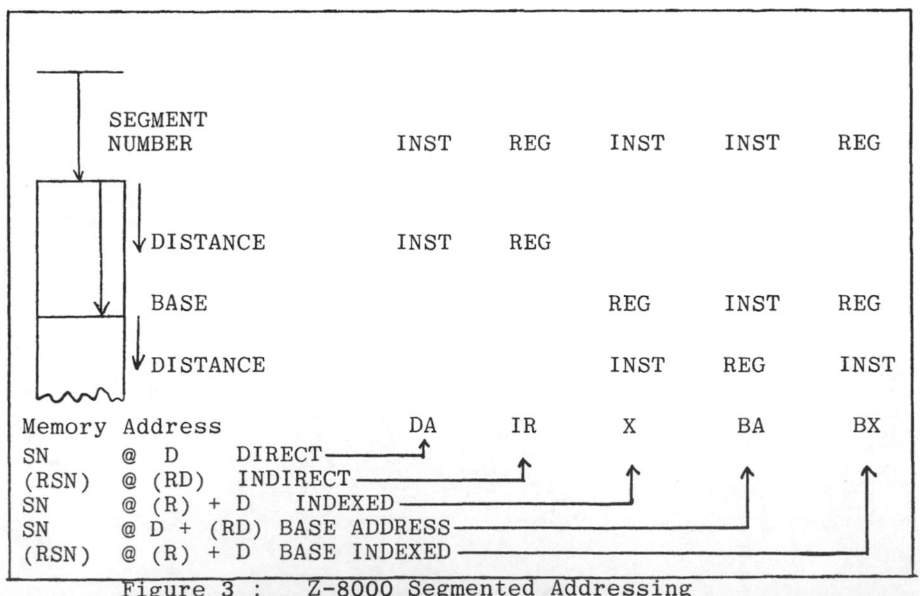

Figure 3 : Z-8000 Segmented Addressing

In both the Indexed and Base Address modes the instruction contains the Segment Number, SN. In the Base Address mode the instruction also contains the base address within the abstract memory segment whilst an addressed register contains the location with respect to this base. In the Indexed mode the instruction contains the distance from a base value located in a general register. The Base Indexed mode is similar except that the Segment Number is contained in the register pair along with the base address.

The modes Direct, Indirect and Indexed are available with all the binary operations which are listed in Table 3. They together with the Base Address and Base Indexed modes are also available with the data transfer operations such as Load.

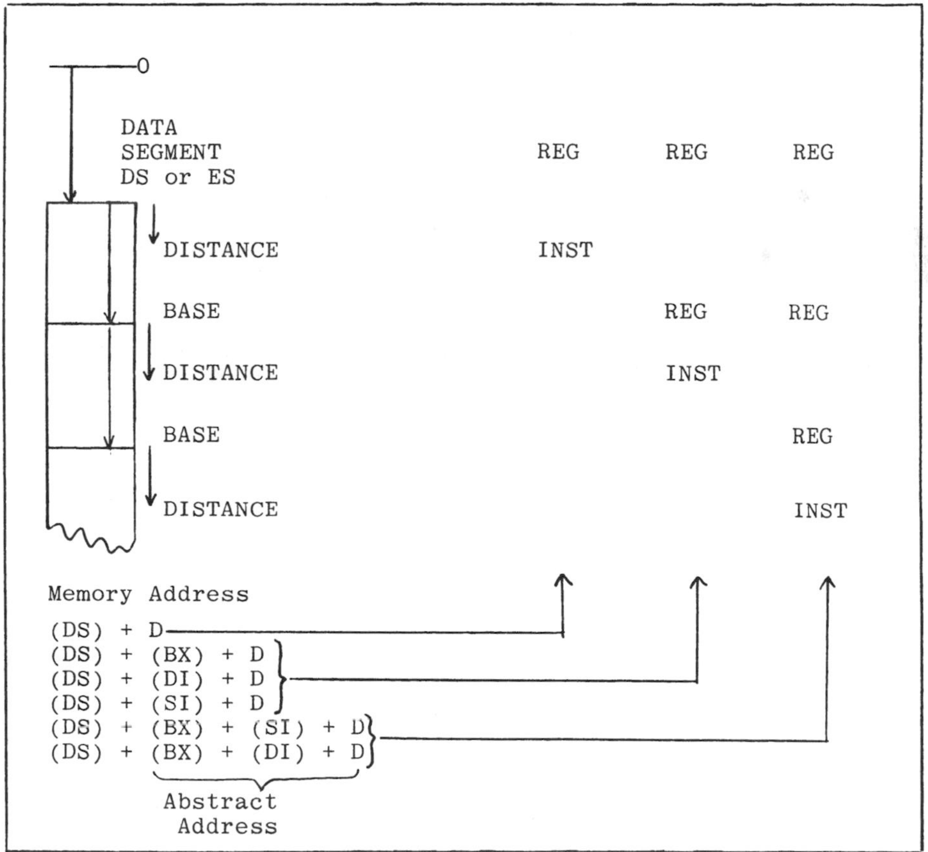

Figure 4 : 8086 Data Segment Addressing

8086 - Data Segment Addressing

The addressing with respect to the Data Segment (or Extra Segment) address of the 8086 is shown in Figure 4. The other registers of interest are as follows :

General Register File :-
BX \ Base Register
SI \ Source Index
DI \ Destination Index

These general registers together with the literal D in the instruction are used to provide the abstract address within the segment according to the addressing modes listed in Table 2 and shown in Figure 1.

8086 - Stack Segment Addressing

The addressing with respect to the Stack Segment of the 8086 is shown in Figure 5. The other registers of interest are as follows :

General Register File :
SP \ STACK POINTER
BP \ STACK BASE POINTER
SI \ Source Index
DI \ Destination Index

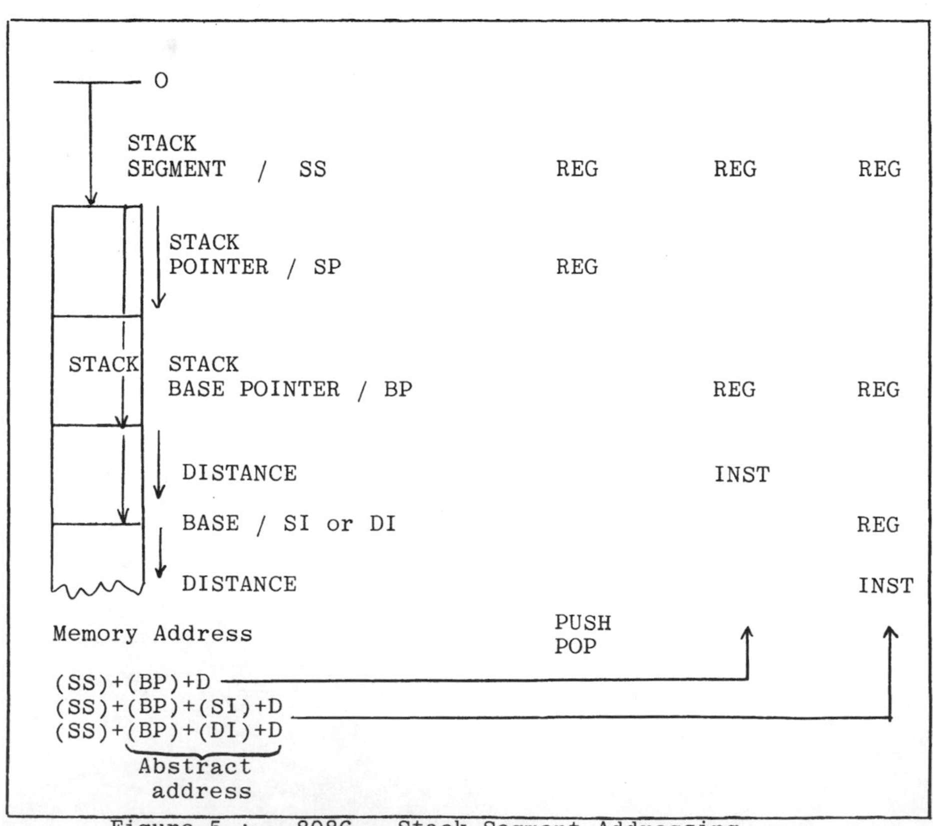

Figure 5 : 8086 - Stack Segment Addressing

The stack pointer register, SP, is Post-auto-incremented by the POP instruction and Pre-auto-decremented by the PUSH instruction. The Stack Base Pointer as well as indicating the location of the bottom of the stack provides a base address for a vector of data words. These may be accessed using the indirect addressing modes shown.

The Stack Pointer Register may only be used in conjunction with POP, PUSH and MOVE orders.

The Stack Base Pointer Register and the other Géneral Registers may be employed in the operations listed in Table 3.

Segmentation in the MC-68000

There are no explicit hardware features in the MC-68000 processor which may be directly ascribed to the management of segments. However, it does contain the following general registers of 32-bit length :

8 - Data Registers, Dn
8 - Address Registers, An (Address Register A7 used as Stack Pointer)
n = 0 - 7

The 32 bit Address Registers enable the accessing of a massive memory. In practice the number of pins provided on the package of the processor chip limit the number of address bits which may be used to 23, restricting the memory size to 16M bytes since each memory access is to a 16-bit word.

The byte address of 24 bits may be divided into a number of fields by the programmer. As a first step it may be divided into Segment Number and position within the segment.

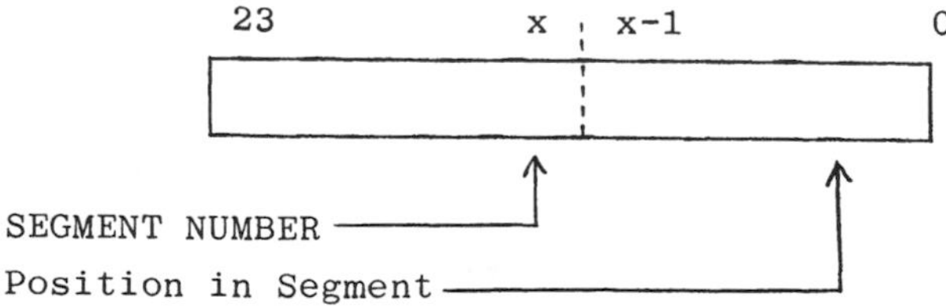

If x = 16 then 256 segments of 64K bytes.

The use of the Stack Pointer Register, R7, and a second address Register, R6, provide the capability of managing a stack segment similar to that provided in the 8086, as shown in Figure 6.

A data segment could be established by designating an address register as the Data Segment register, as shown in Figure 7.

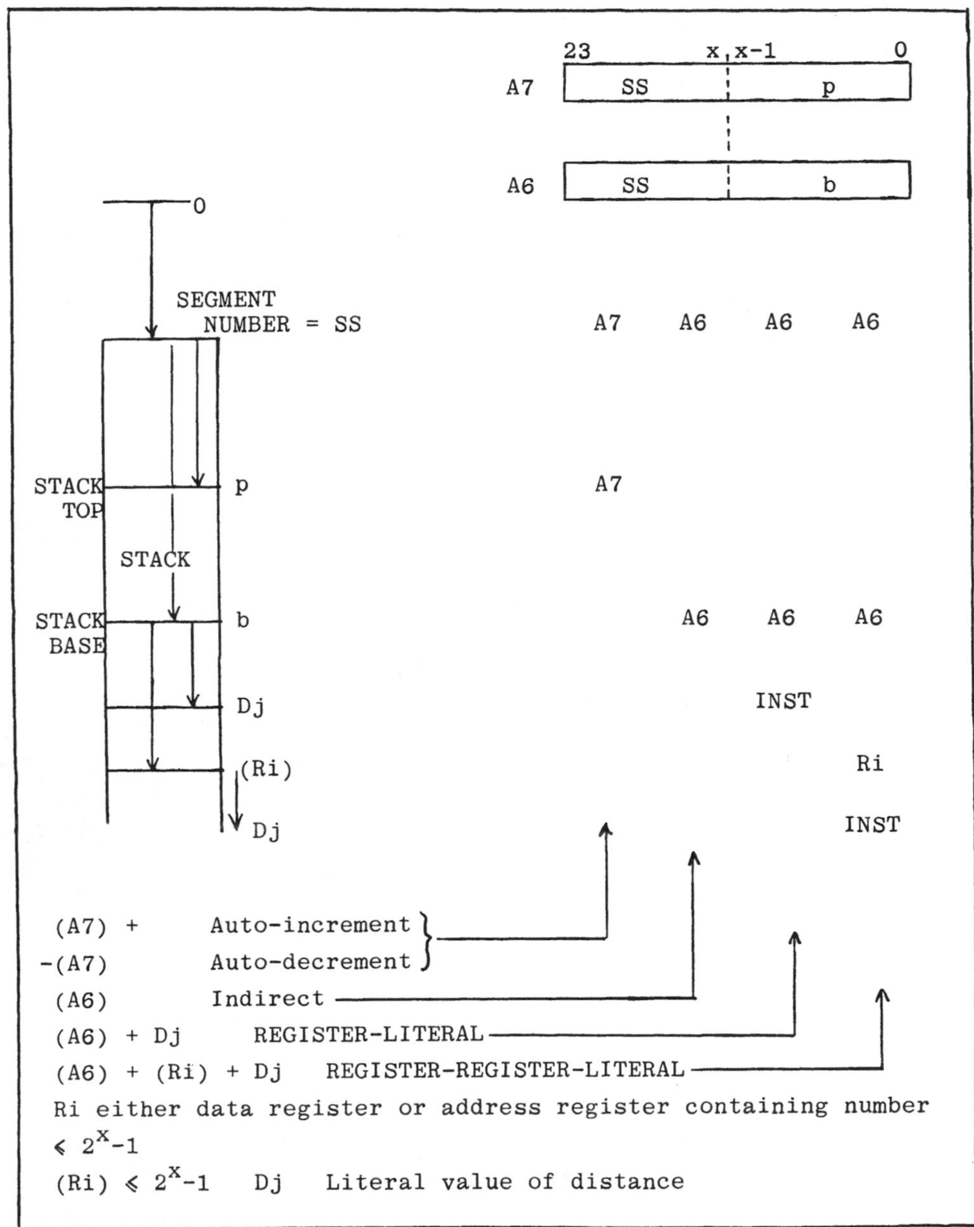

Figure 6 : Programmer defined management of stack segment in 68000

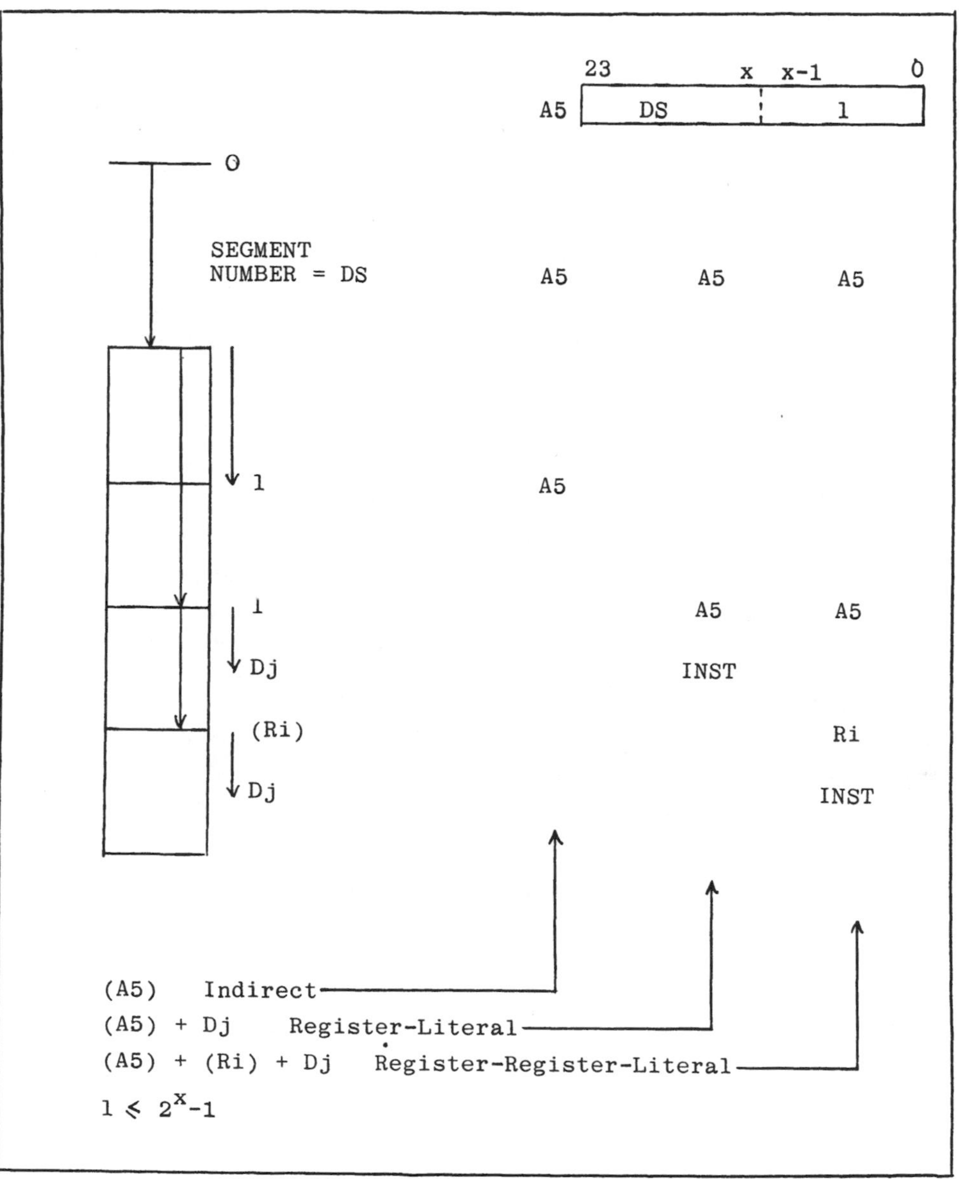

Figure 7 : Programmer defined management of Data Segment in 68000

Initial Comments on Memory Management by Microprocessors

It is possible to comment on the explicit memory management capabilities of two microprocessors, 8086 and Z-8001. The Z-8001 provides an addressable memory of 8M bytes. But this memory is segmented into 128 segments each of 64K bytes fixed length. There will be sparse use of these long segments in many applications.

The 8086 which only provides access to a memory of 1M bytes, nevertheless allows a variable segment size from 16 bytes to 64K bytes in multiples of 16 bytes. The segment length can be adjusted to match the number of data words or instructions which will reside in the segment.

The 68000 provides access to 16M bytes. The 24-bit address length in the address registers may be divided between the segment number which has a precision determined by the programmer, concatenated with the position in segment address which has a range equal to the precision of the segment address. These are automatically concatenated within the register.

The segment number of the Z-8001 can be in either a register or embedded in the instruction. If the program is to be placed in read only memory once and for all then this may not be a disadvantage, but if, as is more likely, the abstract segments will be placed in different physical memory segments at different times, this relocation will be very difficult in the case of the Z-8001, but not so difficult in the case of the 8086 which only allows the segment address to reside in a register. In the case of the 8086 the only modification on relocating a segment is to change the value in the Segment Register.

In the case of the 68000 relocation is achieved by setting the appropriate address registers.

The addressing modes of the 8086 and 68000 permit one extra level of indirection over those provided in the Z-8000. Furthermore, the Stack Base Pointer relative Data operations which they can provide are useful.

Exercise

Y := (((a-b) - (C* (D+e))) + f)

Encode the above expression for the following abstract machines.

(a) One-Address; (b) Three-address; (c) Stack

In each case estimate the length of the programme when implemented on both the Mc 68000 and Intel 8086 microprocessors.

In each case estimate the time taken for the execution of the programme on both the MC 68000 and Intel 8086.

Discuss the relative merits of the abstract machines and the real microprocessors.

REFERENCES

1. BELL, C.G. et al (editors), Computer Engineering, Digital Press, Bedford, Mass, U.S.A. 1978

2. BELL, C.G. et al, A New Architecture for Minicomputers - The DEC PDP-11, pp. 241-263, ibid.

3. MC 68000, 16-bit Microprocessor - Users Manual, Motorola Inc. 1980.

4. MCS-86, Users Manual, Intel Corp. 1979

5. AMZ 8001/2, Processor Instruction Set, AMD Inc. 1979.

3. INSTRUCTION SET PROCESSOR - SECTION II

Programme Control Instructions

The implicit programme control action within an assignment statement instruction is to increment the programme counter in readiness for the access to memory to fetch the next instruction, as shown in Fig. 1. When a selection clause is encountered an instruction is required which causes the action :

if Q then PC := PC + ℓ else PC := PC + 1

This is known as a conditional relative jump or conditional branch. The condition Q is derived from the present value of the MILL status which was last changed by a previous instruction. In the general case the exits from the conditional clause each require an unconditional jump to force the Programme Counter to the address of the next instruction following the clause. Actual programming may require only one of the exits to have the jump or even a branch instruction as shown in Fig. 1.

The repetitive clauses are as follows :

Repeat A until Q,
and While Q do A

In this case the qualifier Q is usually the value of a counter which is incremented or decremented each time the repetition occurs. The basic branch and jump orders can be used to implement a repetitive clause but the 8086 LOOP order and the Z-8000 DJNZ order both combine count and test to facilitate the control of these clauses more readily.

8086 LOOP

CX := CX - 1
if CX $\neq$ 0 then PC := PC + D else PC := PC + 1
$-128 \leq D \leq +127$

Z-8000 DJNZ

Ri := Ri - 1
if Ri $\neq$ 0 then PC := (PC + 1) - D else PC := PC + 1
$0 \leq D \leq 127$

FLOW DIAGRAM	INSTRUCTION	LOCATION
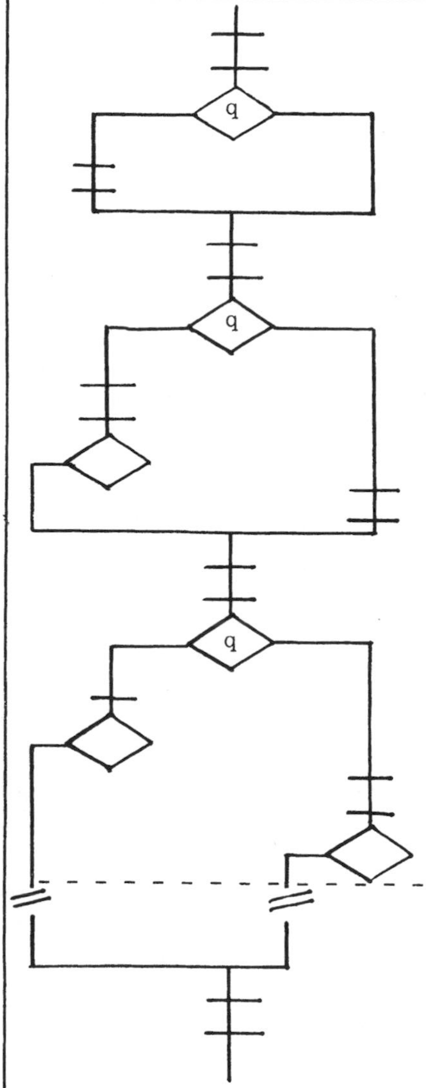	do ; PC := PC + 1	0
	do ; PC := PC + 1	1
	_if_ q=1 _then_ PC := PC + 3 _else_ PC := PC + 1	2
	do ; PC := PC + 1	3
	do ; PC := PC + 1	4
	do ; PC := PC + 1	5
	do ; PC := PC + 1	6
	_if_ q=1 _then_ PC := PC + 4 _else_ PC := PC + 1	7
	do	8
	do	9
	PC := PC+3	10
	do ; PC := PC + 1	11
	do ; PC := PC + 1	12
	do ; PC := PC + 1	13
	do ; PC := PC + 1	14
	_if_ q=1 _then_ PC := PC + 3 _else_ PC := PC + 1	15
	do ; PC := PC + 1	16
	PC := L	17
	do ; PC := PC + 1	18
	do ; PC := PC + 1	19
	PC := L	20
		. . .
	do ; PC := PC + 1	L
	do ; PC := PC + 1	L+1

Fig.1 : Selection Clause Programme Control

The MC 68000 and 8086 microprocessors each combine the counter action with a condition code derived from the MILL status.

8086 LOOP Δ

```
CX := CX - 1
if (Δ=1) & CX ≠ 0 then PC := PC + D else PC := PC + 1
-128 ≤ D & ≤ +127
```

MC 68000 DBCC

```
if CC = 1 then Dn := Dn - 1
               NEXT  if Dn ≠ 1 then PC := PC + D
          else PC := PC + 1
```

$-2^{15} \leq D \leq 2^{15} - 1$ bytes

Subroutine Entry and Exit

The instruction which causes the entry to a subroutine must contain a description of the address of the first location of the subroutine, ASR. The action includes :

```
 PC  := PC + 1          ! Increment programme counter
DUMP := PC              ! Dump contents of programme counter
 PC  := ASR             ! Load programme counter with ASR
```

On exit from the subroutine the last instruction will include :

```
 PC  := DUMP            ! Restore Return Address to PC
```

DUMP is a register which holds the address of the location of the next instruction to be obeyed in the main routine.

In order to allow the nesting of subroutines a stack of DUMP locations is arranged. The calling action becomes :

```
 PC  :=  PC + 1
 SP  := SP - 1  }
(SP) := PC      }   ! PUSH contents of PC onto Stack
 PC  := ASR
```

and the return becomes :

```
 PC  := (SP)    }   ! POP Return Address from Stack to
 SP  := SP + 1  }     PC
```

This Return Address STACK need not be the same as the Data Word STACK of the ZERO-Address machine, since it serves a different purpose. However, it is convenient to use one stack for both Return Addresses and Data Words provided that, should a subroutine use the Stack for Data Words, the Stack Pointer does point at a Return Address when the

EXIT instruction is obeyed and not at a Stacked Data Word.

The subroutine entry and exit control instructions together with the basic routine programme control instructions for the PDP-11 and three typical 16-bit microprocessors are displayed in Table 1.

	CHANGE TO PROGRAMME COUNTER	CONDITION FOR CHANGE					
		STATUS	COUNT	PDP-11	68000	8086	Z-8000
SELECTION CLAUSE	RELATIVE	✓	-	BΔ	BCC	JΔ	JRΔ
		-	-	BR	BRA	JMP*	-
	ABSOLUTE	✓	-	-	-	-	JPΔ
		-	-	JMP	JMP	JMP*	-
REPETITIVE CLAUSE	RELATIVE	-	✓	-	-	LOOP JCXZ	DJNZ
		✓	✓	-	DBCC	LOOPΔ	-
SUBROUTINE ENTRY	ABSOLUTE	-	-	JSR	JSR	CALL*	CALL
	RELATIVE	-	-	-	BSR	CALL*	CALR
SUBROUTINE EXIT	STACK	✓	-	-	-	-	RET
		-	-	RTS	RTS	RET	-

Δ :- One of several conditions of MILL Status   * Depends upon addressing mode

Table 1 : Programme Control Instructions

EXERCISE

Encode a simple repetitive clause by first not using the repetitive clause programme control instruction, and then by using those in the 8086 and 68000 instruction sets.

Comment on the benefits derived from the new instructions.

Processor Control

Trace Mode

The normal mode of operation of the processor-memory pair is for the processor to execute instruction cycles in sequence. The instruction set includes both the Assignment Statement and Programme Control types as discussed thus far. When a routine is being debugged it is often convenient to trace the action of each instruction cycle by effectively stopping after each one and scanning the registers of the processor and memory to display their contents to the programmer at a console. This mode of operation is known as the Trace Mode. It is usual to assign a bit within the State Variable of the Processor Control Unit to indicate that the Processor is in the Trace Mode. This bit also appears within the Processor Status Word alongside the MILL Status register.

Privileged Mode

Instructions must exist which enable the setting, or resetting, of the Trace Mode Bit in the processor. Such instructions must be used with great care and should not be used within a normal routine. Thus arose the concept of privileged instructions, which may only be used within system routines. In the PDP-11 and 8086 such instructions are rare and it is hoped that the normal user will not use them. In the 68000 and Z-8000 such instructions may only be executed whilst the processor is in a special privileged mode. If they are fetched during the non-privileged or normal mode, then an error will be signalled by a Trap. These last two microprocessors include a bit within the Processor Control Unit state variable to record the privileged mode. This bit also appears in the Processor Status Word.

Illegal Instruction Traps

Misuse of certain instructions is particularly serious. A good example of mischief is to divide by zero. In this case the routine cannot proceed. The error must be detected in the MILL and a Trap signal generated.

Illegal Addressing Traps

Access to code segment during the operand fetch or operand write action should not be allowed. Similar improper segment accesses can be imagined. These must be detected and cause a Trap.

Programmed Trap

The programmer may wish to insert a trace at certain positions in the routine (8086 - INT) (68000 - TRAP) or cause certain data values such as overflow to trap, (8086 - INTO) (68000 - TRAPV). In the 68000 an instruction, CHK, checks a value in a register against an addressed number. If the register is holding a negative number or a positive integer greater than the addressed number then a Trap is initiated.

Action on a TRAP

There was a time when the machine would stop, with a TRAP lamp lit, on detecting a trap condition. Nowadays it is customary for the TRAP to cause the processor to stop executing the routine, which contained the instruction which caused the TRAP, and to evoke entry to a system routine which takes the necessary action. When this system routine has finished its task then it is possible to permit the trapped routine to continue execution by fetching its next instruction. The trapped routine can only proceed in a deterministic way if the processor and memory state is not disturbed by the system routine. Since the system routine is executed on the same machine as the trapped routine, then entry to the Trap must cause an automatic saving of important sections of the Processor State Vector on a stack which must be restored before the trapped routine is allowed to continue. The two most important elements of the Processor State Vector are the Programme Counter and the Processor Status Word. The action obeys the following sequence :

```
 SP   := SP - 1  }
(SP)  := PSW     }    ! PUSH Processor Status Word
 SP   := SP - 1  }
(SP)  := PC      }    ! PUSH Return Address
 PC   := X            ! Start address of System Routine
```

The Trap signal automatically causes this sequence and the "system routine start address" is automatically generated in the processor. This address may depend upon the origin of the Trap (see Table 3). The system routine has its way with the processor-memory pair and logs the cause of the trap. Its last action will be to restore the Programme Counter and Processor Status Word by obeying a special subroutine return instruction which follows the following sequence :

```
PC  :=  (SP)    }
SP  :=  SP + 1  }    ! Restore Return Address
PSW :=  CSP     }
SP  :=  SP - 1  }    ! Restore Processor Status Word
```

Processor	Instruction
PDP-11	RTI
68000	RTE (Privileged)
8086	IRET
Z-8000	IRET (Privileged)

In the case of the PDP-11 and 8086 the stack used here is the same as that used by the normal, trapped, routine. In the 68000 and Z-8000 a special system stack is used with an implied privileged mode. This Return Address STACK need not be the same as the Data Word STACK of the ZERO-Address machine, since it serves a different purpose. However, it is convenient to use one stack for both Return Addresses and Data Words provided that, should a subroutine use the Stack for Data Words, the Stack Pointer does point at a Return Address when the EXIT instruction is obeyed and not at a stacked Data Word.

Processor State

It is possible to recapitulate the nature and form of a processor as understood from this examination of the instruction sets of some 16-bit microprocessors by listing the various state variables which exist in the processor and identifying the reason for their existence. These state variables may initially be grouped into one of the three sets of state variables given for the Manchester-Kilburn Machine, plus those for the processor control and memory management, as shown in Table 2. The set of processor state variables of a processor is known as the Processor State Vector.

Before a routine can be executed the Processor State and the Memory State must be initialised. As the routine is then executed each instruction cycle will cause unique changes to both the Processor and Memory State. When the routine has reached completion, with its output data delivered safely, then the Processor and Memory State may be cleared ready for the next routine. At all times the locus of control resides in the programme counter as determined by the routine, or its subroutines. A routine which requires a long time for its execution may suspend itself before it has reached completion. The suspension involves a dump of the Processor State and Memory State so that these may be restored when the routine is initialised the next time that it is executed. Planned or programmed suspensions may be implemented using the instructions of the type already described. Further steps need to be taken to allow an external concurrent activity to interrupt the locus of control of the sequential program, to force the suspension of the routine execution, whilst a second sequential programme is executed to service the external activity.

PROCESSOR STATE VECTOR	PDP-11		M 68000		8086		Z-8000	
	REG	PSW	REG	PSW	REG	PSW	REG	PSW
MILL								
General Registers - DATA	Rn		Dn		DX		Rn	
. Accumulator Top of Stack	Rn		Dn		AX		Rn	
. MILL Status		CC		CCR		FLAG		FLAG
. SIGN		N		N		S		S
. ZERO		Z		Z		Z		Z
. Overflow		V		V		O		P/V
. Carry								
32 bit		-		}		-		}
16 bit		C		} C		C		} C
8 bit		-		}		-		}
4 bit		-		}		A		H
. Extend		-		X		-		-
. Parity		-				P		P/V
. Decimal		-						DA
OPERAND ADDRESSING UNIT								
General Registers - ADDRESS	Rn		An		BX		Rn	
. INDEX	Rn		An		SI,DI		Rn	
. Stack Top Pointer	R6		A7		SP		R15	
. Stack Base Pointer	Rn		An		BP		Rn	
. Status		-		-		D		-
PROGRAM CONTROL UNIT								
. PROGRAMME COUNTER	R7		PC		IP		PC	
. LOOP COUNTER	Rn		Dn		CX		Rn	
MEMORY MANAGEMENT UNIT								
. CODE SEGMENT REG.	R7		PC		CS		PC	
. STACK SEGMENT REG.	R6		A7		SS		R15	
. DATA SEGMENT REG.	Rn		An		DS		Rn	
. EXTRA DATA SEGMENT REG.	Rn		An		ES		Rn	
. STATUS		-		-		-		SEG
PROCESS CONTROL UNIT								
. CONTROL STATUS								
. PRIVILEGE		-		S		-		S/N
. TRACE		T		T		T		SE
. INTERRUPT LEVEL		P_{012}		I_{012}		I		VIE NVIE

PSW := Processor Status Word

Table 2 : Processor State Vector

Processor Interruption

During the Instruction Cycle of the Instruction Set Processor immediately after the completion of an instruction execution the processor examines an input Interrupt Request Flag. If the flag is not set then the instruction cycle proceeds in the usual way. If the flag is set then an automatic entry to a system routine is invoked. The processor status word and programme counter are saved on a stack before the programme counter is set to the start address of the System Interrupt Routine. This routine services the interrupt before it returns to the interrupted routine by restoring its processor status word and programme counter from the stack.

During the early part of the System Interrupt Routine the Interrupt Request mechanism must be disenabled whilst the Interrupt Request Flag is cleared in the interrupting peripheral device by the System Interrupt Routine. The Interrupt Request Mechanism may be enabled during the Interrupt Routine to permit interruption by another device.

The episode begins by forced entry to a subroutine which, in turn, includes a special return instruction. The PDP-11 and the 8086 treat it this way. Both the 68000 and the Z-8000 use a special System Stack pointer which designates a stack in memory different to that used by normal routines. The incidence of an interrupt causes entry to a privileged mode of operation in which certain privileged instructions may be used.

Furthermore, in the case of the PDP-11 the entry to the interrupt routine includes forcing of a new value determined by the interrupt source, onto the Processor Status Word (CC and TRAP). In the case of the Z-8000 an identifier of the interrupt source is stacked on top of the Return Address.

The last action of the interrupt routine calling sequence is to force a new value, X, onto the programme counter. This value is derived from information provided by the source of the interrupt to link the interrupting device with the location of its interrupt routine in the memory. This is an interesting situation which requires one to stand back from the problem and consider the long life cycle of the instruction set processor as a commercial product.

Entry to Interrupt Routine

Each external device which is allowed to interrupt the Instruction Set Processor does so to evoke a routine to service the needs of the device. The routine and the device are inexorably linked. Each different model of a particular device will require a unique routine. For example, each model of the paper tape reader will require its own interrupt routine. Not only must a given combination of processor-memory accommodate a unique set of routines to service the peripheral devices making up the given computer system, but different processor-memory pairs include different sets of routines since each computer system is different. The interrupt routines must be placed in the memory as part of the system design. The routine for a particular device will be placed in memory at locations which are convenient for the computer system and it is not advisable to predetermine the locations to be occupied by an interrupt routine in all the computer systems which may be built. Thus the device does not know the real location of its routine in memory. What is reasonable to provide, is a directory of pointers to the interrupt routine. The directory can be at locations in the memory which are fixed for all processor-memory pairs. A location in the directory is assigned to each interrupting device in a given computer system. This location number, or vector number, is pre-set into the device as it is physically attached to the processor-memory pair.

The final action in the entry to interrupt routine sequence is thus to load the address of the first instruction of the interrupt routine into the programme counter from the directory location given by the device vector number.

Another way of looking at the actions on entry to an interrupt routine is as follows :

At a point in the instruction cycle the processor tests the interrupt flag. If not set then fetch instruction in the normal way, if set obey the instruction located in the interrupting device. This instruction is always a composite of the sequence :

```
PUSH STATUS;
CALL (X)
```

X is a literal address provided by the device and used to access memory for the address to be loaded into the programme counter.

A similar mechanism is employed when a Trap or Trace is evoked. In this case the vector number is generated within the processor. The Vector Number allocation for two microprocessors is shown in Table 3.

VECTOR NUMBER	68000	8086
0	Reset SSP	Divide by Zero
1	Reset PC	Trace
2	Bus Error	NMI (Pin 17)
3	Address Error	INT (Type 3)*
4	Illegal Instruction	INT O
5	Divide by Zero	↑ Reserved (5–31) ↓ ; ↑ INTR (Pin 18) (5–255) ↓
6	CHK	
7	TRAPV	
8	Privilege Violation	
9	Trace	
10 – 31	↑ Reserved ↓	
32 – 47	↑ TRAP ↓	↑ Available (32–255) ↓
48 – 63	↑ Reserved ↓	
64 – 255	↑ Available ↓	

* INT (TYPE 3) can specify any vector number 0 → 255.

Table 3 : TRAP and INTERRUPT VECTORS

Contention for the Processor

When a normal routine is being executed, not in trace mode and with no external devices to interrupt, then there is no contention for the processor. There is only one active locus of control, that of the routine and its subroutines. In trace mode the locus passes from the normal routine to the trace routine at the end of an instruction cycle. The entry to the trace routine must clear the Trace Mode bit in the Processor Status Word (otherwise the first instruction of the Trace routine would be traced, etc.) and it will restore its value by the return instruction, which also passes the locus of control back to the normal routine. So far there is no contention, the locus of control is determined *a priori*. Similarly if a TRAP occurs due to design or even programme error, the route taken by the locus of control is deterministic and there is no real contention for the processor since there is an implied priority assignment. Unless, that is, there are two reasons for a trap, both of which arise whilst an instruction is being obeyed. In this case an explicit priority must be applied within the processor before the next instruction is obeyed. Indeed, there may be several reasons for a trap being generated inside the processor,together with a multiplicity of external reasons due to peripheral devices which may request an interrupt. Each of these contenders must be given a priority ranking. In the case of the 68000 this is clearly set out in Table 4. This priority scheme is prewired into the processor.

Contention between External Interrupting Devices

The many external sequential devices which are concurrently active within the processor-memory pair contend for its locus of control. They will be placed in a priority ranking which reflects the crisis time of an interrupt episode and its frequency of occurrence. The priority is resolved during the following sequence of events which results in the processor entering a system interrupt routine.

1. Each interrupting device will have its own interrupt flag.
2. All interrupt flags are "OR" connected to produce a signal which is interpreted in the processor as Interrupt Request Flag.
3. Any interrupt will cause this Flag to be asserted.
4. In due time the processor will interrogate the Flag and respond across its interface to find the asserted interrupt flag of highest priority.
5. When this asserted flag has been found it will be granted permission to provide the appropriate instruction sequence (PUSH STATUS; CALL(X)) to enter the system interrupt routine.

6. Whilst this is being obeyed the Interrupt Request Flag is disenabled.

The finding of the asserted interrupt of highest priority is executed outside the processor-memory pair, typically by a "daisy chain" mechanism. This method of operation outlined above is used in principle by the four microprocessors considered. In particular, the INTR (Pin 18) interrupt input of the 8086, operates precisely in this way.

The Interrupt Request Flag being the I Flag in the Processor Status Word. The 8086 also includes a non-maskable interrupt input INT (Pin 17). This has a higher priority than INTR and cannot be disenabled. It is used for power-up and other important though infrequent events.

The PDP-11 and 68000 provide facilities which allow a device to interrupt the system interrupt routine which is servicing a device of lower priority. In each case there are, in principal, eight (4 in practice in PDP-11) levels of priority resulting in eight external "OR" gates for the device interrupt flags. These eight levels are further "OR"-ed to produce the Interrupt Request Flag. When the processor responds to an asserted Flag it first finds the interrupting level of highest priority before it signals across the interface to find the highest priority device which is interrupting on this level. This is then granted permission to force the entry to its system interrupt routine. Any further or future interrupt at or below this level will not be allowed to assert the Interrupt Request Flag, whilst any device at a higher level may assert this flag and cause its system interrupt routine to be entered. The highest level of priority is effectively non-maskable as on the INT (Pin 17) on the 8086.

The multi-level priority scheme may be added to the 8086 by using the 8259A Programmable Interrupt Controller. This manages eight levels of devices and processes their interrupts to produce a signal which is output from its pin 17 to pin 18 on the 8086, the INTR or maskable interrupt. The 8259A may be cascaded to produce up to 64 levels.

Highest Priority	-	Reset
		Bus Error
		Address Error
		Trace
		Interrupt Request
		Illegal Instruction
		Privilege Violation
		TRAP, TRAPV, CHK
		Divide by Zero
Lowest Priority	-	Normal Instruction

Table 4 : Priority Assignment within 68000

4. CONCLUSION

The structure of a microcomputer system, based on the 16-bit microprocessors which have been used to illustrate this commentary on the properties of the instruction set processor, is shown in Fig. 1. The EXECUTE activity includes the PROGRAM CONTROL, COMPUTE and PROCESS ADDRESS activities of the General Computer displayed in Fig. 4 of the introduction. The way in which these activities cooperate together to interpret the main instructions of the processor instruction set has been discussed. In particular it has been shown that a programmer may build an abstract machine, such as a stack machine, and is assisted in the use of subroutines by the automatic address operations within the instruction set. The abstract memory of such machines is mapped onto the physical memory modules with the assistance of the MANAGE activity. This activity may occur implicitly owing to the large abstract memory space provided by the processor (68000) or explicitly by the provision of segment registers. Special memory management modules (MC 6829) may also be used to manage an extended memory space.

The Real Address and Data are output from the Processor to be the Address and Write inputs of the STORE activity. They, together with the Command input and Read output signals of the STORE may be organised as a bus and routed to serve several memory modules. This common bus arrangement allows flexibility in the provision of real memory modules to act as STORE for a given microcomputer system.

The bus will also communicate with the INTERFACE activity which provides the window on the peripheral, or input/output (I/O), domain. The I/O registers visible to the programmes in the processor-memory pair will be assembled to appear within the addressable memory space, as memory mapped I/O (Ref. 1). This provides the mechanism for communication of data between the active processor and its passive peripheral registers. Active peripheral devices will produce their own interrupt signals which the INTERFACE activity will present as the External Interrupt Flag to the CONTROL activity within the Processor. This activity will respond with an External Interrupt Acknowledge command which is further processed by the INTERFACE activity to evoke the appropriate response as described in Section II. Within the Processor the EXECUTE activity may assert an Internal Interrupt Flag following a Trap or because of being in Trace Mode. The CONTROL activity orders the other actors through the various

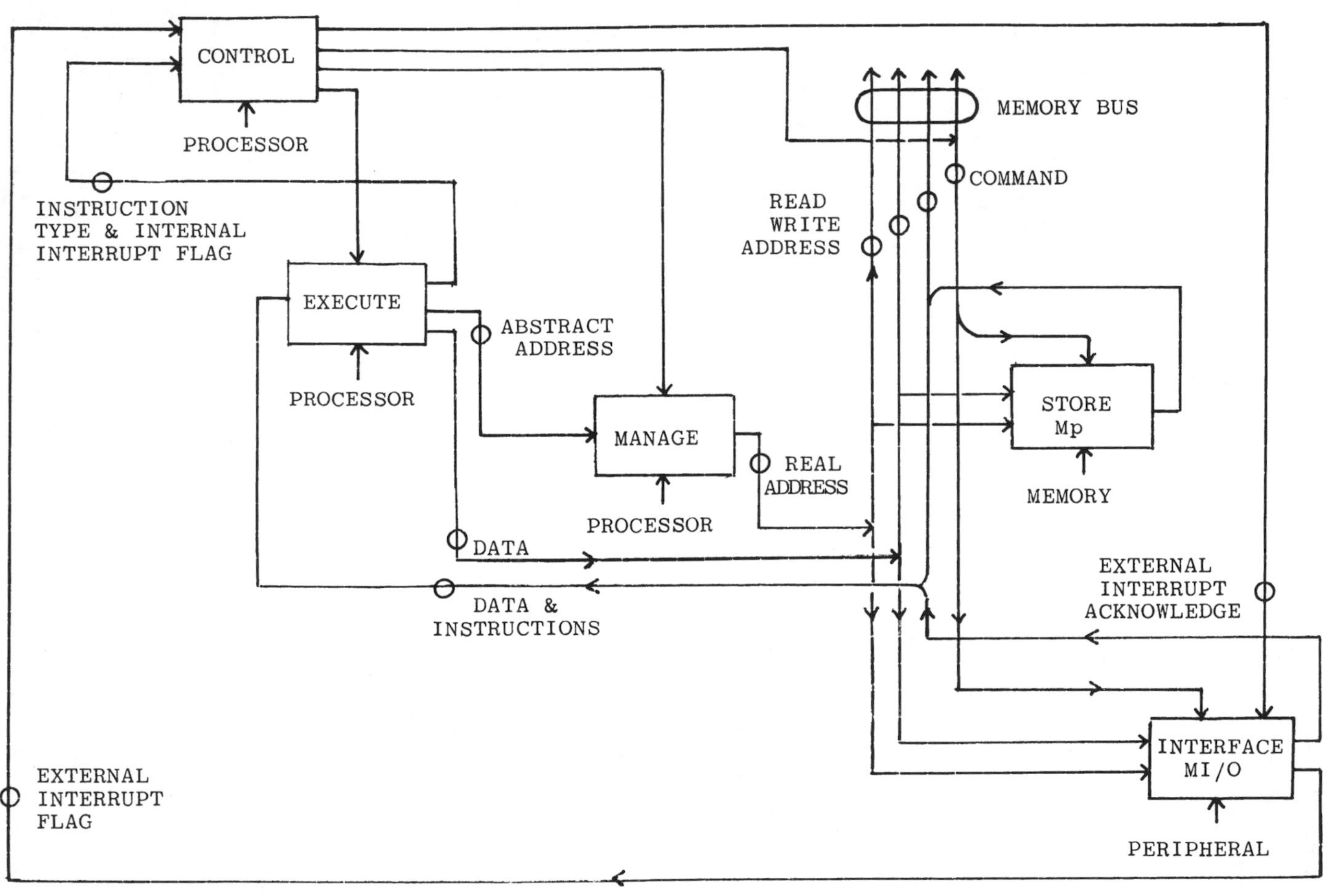

Fig. 1 Overview of Microcomputer System

phases of the instruction cycle. The rate at which they are required to act is determined by the period of the Clock, whilst the particular locus of control, through the phases of the instruction cycle, depends upon the Instruction Type and the presence of an interrupt, as shown in the flow diagram of Fig. 2.

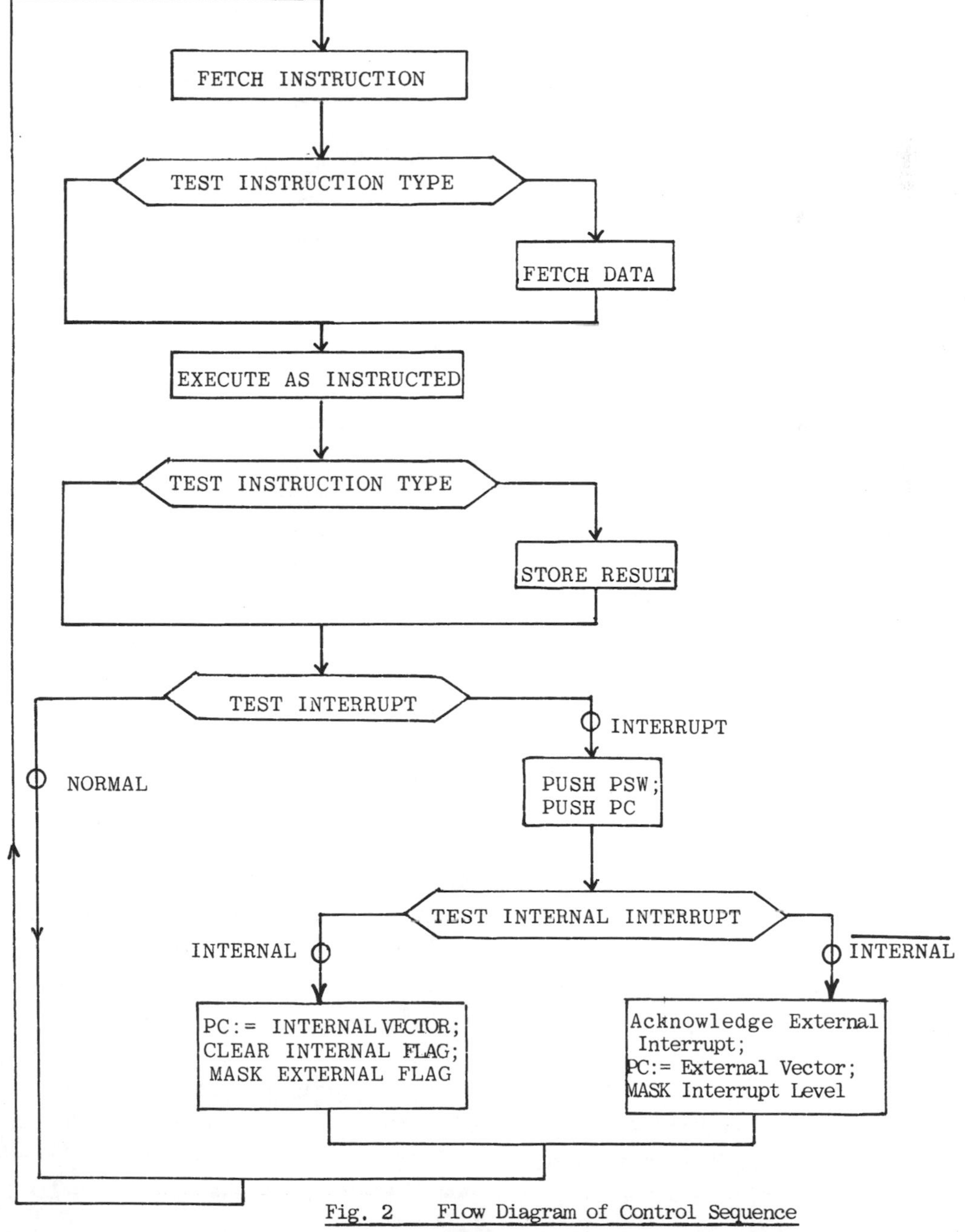

Fig. 2 Flow Diagram of Control Sequence

The Processor State Vector is contained in the three actors, CONTROL, EXECUTE and MANAGE, as shown in Table 2 of Section II. The Memory State Vector consists of Mp, being the actual memory modules attached to the Memory Bus, plus MI/O which includes the memory mapped registers of the peripheral input/output devices and their individual Interrupt Request Flags. The Processor State Vector together with the Memory State Vector constitute an individual microcomputer. Changes to these vectors occur through the execution of a programme stored in the microcomputer memory, or in the case of the MI/O vector, due to occurrences in the set of peripheral I/O devices attached directly to the Processor-Memory pair.

Concurrency

The low cost of microelectronics has made it possible to envisage systems involving more than one individual microcomputer operating concurrently, as shown in Fig. 3. (Ref. 2).

The CONTROL, EXECUTE and MANAGE activities of Fig. 1 have been combined into one activity, PROCESS, which includes the Processor State Vector, PSV. The STORE and INTERFACE actors are as in Fig. 1. The Bus and its connections are shown in a simplified form. Indeed, the Bus of the Microcomputer #1 is connected directly to that of Microcomputer #2. Each Microcomputer is comprised of a processor plus local memory and peripherals. It must be assumed that the Memory State Vector local to one microcomputer may not be read or changed by the PROCESS action of another, but only by its own processor. In other words, the (Mp, MI/O) of Microcomputer #1 does not appear in the real addressable space of any other microcomputer.

However, it is assumed that also attached to the Bus will be both Memory modules and peripheral I/O devices which may be accessed from any processor. These make up the Global State Vector. The programmer may map the abstract memory of the abstract machine onto both local and global real memories. Both local and global real peripherals may also be recognised. The program will be executed by the local processor in the normal way until there is conflict between two processors for the same real addressed word in the global memory or for the same real peripheral devices. In the case of the 8-bit microprocessors it was necessary to make special provision in external circuitry (Ref. 3). Now special instructions have been introduced into the instruction set of the processor to accommodate the sharing of global resources. Each global, or shared, resource is allocated an individual LOCK byte in the global memory. Before a process, being executed in an individual microcomputer, can have its way with a global resource it must read its LOCK

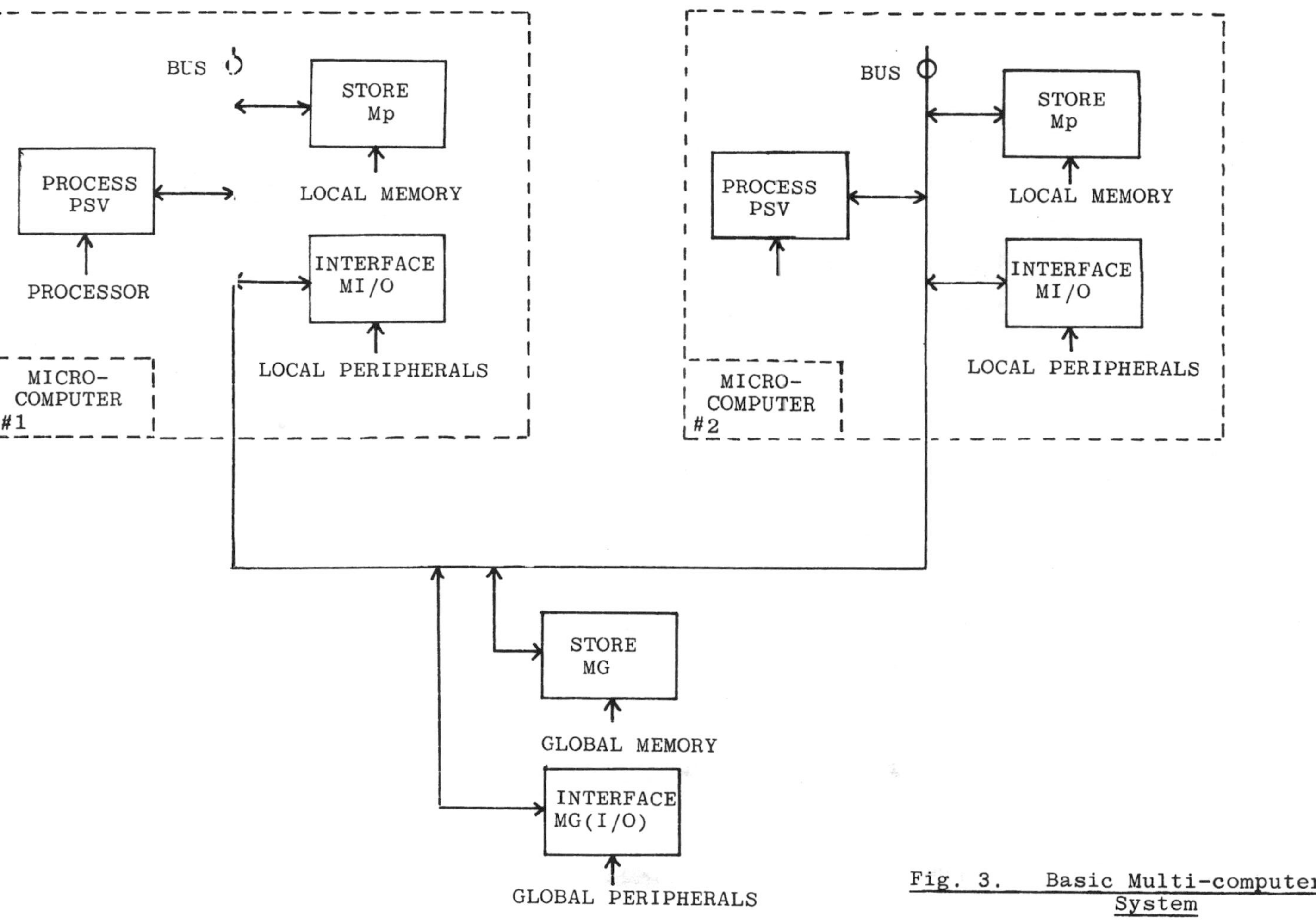

Fig. 3. Basic Multi-computer System

byte. If the LOCK is open then the resource is free in which case the process must close the LOCK by setting a particular bit in the LOCK byte in the global memory. Other processors will now be denied access to the global resource until the LOCK is opened. The action of reading a global memory, then checking the LOCK bit before writing to close the LOCK can take several instruction cycles and two or more processors may read a LOCK as open before one of them has completed the sequence to close the LOCK. Thus they all act as if they have closed the LOCK and will all try to use the resource at the same time. Confusion reigns. The 68000 avoids this by providing a special Test and Set instruction (TAS). In this sequence a byte in the global memory is accessed and read into the MILL. The memory is denied to all other accesses until the N.Z bits of the CCR have been set according to the value of the byte. The most significant bit of the byte is set to one and then returned to the memory location from whence it came. At the conclusion of this Read-Modify-Write memory sequence the global memory is released to bus accesses from any quarter.

In the 8086 a special prefix LOCK may be inserted before any instruction. LOCK denies other processors access to the bus during the execution of the associated instruction. Thus LOCK inserted before an exchange instruction can provide the Test and Set, Read-Modify-Write, facility.

Concluding Observations

The present level of microprocessor instruction set sophistication, as exemplified by the 16-bit microprocessors considered here, shows a considerable advance over that attained by the earlier 8-bit microprocessors (Ref. 2). There is a real attempt to produce an orthogonal set of assignment statements in which there is a regular matching of operator to operand addressing modes. The modes and instructions provided enable the establishment of the abstract machines suitable for the automatic translation from high level languages to the machine code. The address management facilities permit dynamic relocation of routines as the first step to an efficient operating system. Development of the interrupt and privileged mode facilities further permit the possibility of multi-programming within the one microcomputer. The special instructions to enable the test and set facility required for concurrent processor operations are the first steps to the realisation of a reliable multi-microcomputer system. Standardisation of the external bus will make it possible to achieve heterogeneous processor systems in the future (Ref. 4). As these notes are being prepared the information about the new 32-bit microprocessors is being released by the manufacturers.

At first sight these represent a further development along the route followed previously by the conventional mainframes. The aim is to produce instruction sets and architecture which improve the efficiency of the running of high level language programs and raise the reliability of distributed systems of concurrent co-operating processes (Ref. 5).

REFERENCES

1. ASPINALL, D. and DAGLESS, E.L. (1977) (editors). "Introduction to Microprocessors, Pitman, London, U.K.

2. ASPINALL, D. (1978) (editor). "The Microprocessor & its Application" Cambridge University Press, Cambridge, U.K.

3. ASPINALL, D. and DAGLESS, E.L. "Overview of a development environment", Microprocessors & Microsystems, Vol. 3. No. 7, 79, pp. 301-305.

4. Proposed Microcomputer System Bus Standard. (P.796 Bus), IEEE Computer Society Sub-committee Microcomputer System Bus Group, Oct. 1980.

5. RATTNER, J. and LATTIN, W.W. "Ada determines architecture of 32-bit microprocessor", Electronics, Vol. 4. No. 54, Feb. 1981 pp. 119-126.

CUSTOMIZED MICROCOMPUTERS

Michael J. Flynn
Department of Computer Science
Trinity College, Dublin
(on leave - Stanford University)

1.0 INTRODUCTION

Customizing the microcomputer to a particular user environment is akin to tailoring the silicon technology to this environment. The cloth - the silicon - is itself of very low cost but the tailoring technology is extremely complex and its limitations determine the extent to which the customizing works. At what point do we begin the tailoring process; with the thread, cloth or the material? The further down one goes in affecting the material the better the match between the environment and the ultimate technology; however the design costs increase at an alarming rate. The problem is multi-dimensional. Not only are we concerned with the ability of the technology to provide complex functions but also with the design process (through CAD tools) as well as the relationship between the environment and the desired design specification.

The problem of microcomputer design is largely one of design applicability in the context of design support tools (CAD). The better the tools, the lower the design costs and the more feasible a truly customized design. The purpose of this paper is to examine this problem and some possible tradeoffs. In the remainder of this section we introduce the concept of multi-staged design. In section 2 we review, for the unfamiliar reader, basic concepts in general computer design (without reference to particular microcomputer considerations). Section 3 introduces the relationship between computer architecture and computer language while section 4 considers the tradeoffs implied by the VLSI technology and some consequences for the microcomputer. Section 5 examines several "universal" computer design approaches which by-pass the applicability problem associated with customized designs. Sections 6 and 7 develop an approach to a language customized microcomputer. Finally the last two sections present available data comparing approaches.

1.1 Multi-stage Design

As observed by Dijkstra and Wirth (1), the modern programmer knows that the purpose of his programs is to take an existing machine and modify it to become some abstract machine, which suits the environmental specifications. The realization of the abstract machine involves the design of this machine and then the construction of programs which interpret the design according to the desired semantic and syntactic actions. We have two aspects of the machine: specifying the desired actions and interpreting the specifications. Moreover, there is a hierarchy of specification and interpretation of actions.

problem specifications
↓
interpreted by algorithms
↓
interpreted by high level language
↓
interpreted by a computer architecture
↓
executed

Figure 1 : Interpretation Hierarchy

As shown in figure 1 the user problem is originally stated as specifications. These specifications are interpreted by algorithms and flow-charts which define the implementation. Now a new level is introduced, since the flow-charts and algorithms must now be specified in a high level language. The high level language is interpreted by an executing machine whose specification has been interpreted on silicon. Notice that:

(i) In this hierarchy if an error or an inefficiency is introduced in an original specification, in general it cannot be recovered at a lower level. While automatic optimized program rearrangements are possible, the result must be computationally equivalent to the source. Inconsistencies may be detected but information that is either erroneous or incomplete contaminates the entire design. The incompleteness may not be fatal to the actual interpretation but may severely limit the flexibility of the interpreter.

(ii) As the original environment is more completely and narrowly specified, its applicability becomes more limited. For example, a special design for sorting exactly ten items will be significantly faster than a more general design for sorting an arbitrary number of items. Thus as the applicability decreases the performance, i.e. the efficiency of interpretation, increases but since the total design cost remains constant the cost per unit increases too.

Clearly the designer is limited not only by the above cost constraints but also the design time itself. It is entirely possible to conceive of a designer taking a specialised environment and commiting it to a custom design in silicon, i.e. a one level specification/interpretation design. But before he completes and verifies the design it is possible to have the technology changed so completely as to make his committed design inferior to a multi-staged design that shortened the design cycle and allowed the introduction of a new technology. By the same token, the availability of CAD tools may radically alter the approach to, and the extent of, customization that is possible.

The trend of technology is towards smaller feature size and increasing complexity (2). As the feature size decreases, the ensuing number of gates available per chip increases. Densities of 10^5 - 10^6 (equivalent gates) per chip either are or will be possible in the not too far distant future. This increase in available complexity opens new environments for the application of the technology. These observations have lead Fischer (2) to project the changing nature of the interface between the technology supplier and the technology user. In order to develop a custom product, the user must be in a position to specify very complex design details to the technology supplier. Fischer sees the dilemma in terms of part numbers versus complexity versus design cost in a complex system. As complexity increases the design cost increases but the use of the design decreases. The number of replicated parts is limited by the very complexity available to the designer and his desire in meeting enhanced specifications. Fischer sees at least a partial solution in what he calls "solid state programmation" - "the realisation of the specific functional process in a multi-use semiconductor integrated circuit by creating a descriptive program which is implemented in either read only memory or in an interconnection pattern".

Clearly programming/programmation is essential in dealing with complexity. The basic issue is the level at which we introduce the programmed interpretation; much depends upon both the environment and the design strategy. Certain environments may be simultaneously complex in their implementation but both constrained by algorithms and pervasive in their applicability so as to make custom designs both interesting and economically viable. Signal processing and "arithmetic chips" are potential examples of this. Generalised environments usually offer no such easy possibility for pre-packaged algorithms/architecture. In these notes we will emphasize the high level language as being the basic vehicle for defining the variability in abstract machines that are to be interpreted. Thus we assume that the environmental variability is largely determined by the variety of high level languages used to describe them. Clearly a particular environment may use only a sub-set of a language or may enhance a language in particular ways, however the same general approach to architecture design remains applicable. In this approach, the language does not necessarily determine any hardware configuration but rather given a language the various hardware - software - design effort (including CAD) compromises must be evaluated.

2.0 SOME FUNDAMENTALS

2.1 Basic Terms (3)

Throughout these notes we use a number of terms and concepts defined below for our purposes. The basic notion in any computer system is that of storage. A state is a particular configuration of collective storage (all storage) and a state transition is a change in the configuration of storage. The time required for a state transition defines a cycle. Register state transitions occur in internal cycles, whereas a memory state transition occurs in a memory cycle, i.e. the time it takes to retrieve a word from primary storage. For our purposes we will assume that the cycle is synchronous, that is it is always the same and different types of cycles are multiples of the same basic time unit. Thus the memory cycle is a multiple of the internal cycle. A command is a generic term which determines the next state given a particular state. A process is a sequence of commands and an initial state.

A machine (figure 2) is a set of commands and the collective storage which contains both the arguments and the results of the commands together with an interpretive mechanism which causes the state transitions to occur as determined by the commands. Notice that the machine includes only that storage which is identified by the set of commands. Thus any storage which is not mentioned by the commands cannot be effected by or used by the commands and is not part of the machine under this definition. Now the interpretive mechanism itself may be a machine. It may have its own set of commands, its own storage and yet another interpretive mechanism. In this case the original machine is called the image machine and its interpretive mechanism is called the host machine (figure 3).

Since the host machine has its own set of commands and its own storage, it is programmed to interpret the commands of the image machine. It actually does the execution. The program which controls this host machine is called the emulator program. The emulator is an interpreter and sometimes we use these terms synonymously. The set of all image commands represents the execution architecture of the machine. By convention the image commands are called image instructions or simply instructions and host commands are called micro-instructions or host instructions. Notice that the host storage includes all of the image storage as well as a special storage outside of the range or the domain of the image machine - the storage used to contain the emulator program. For simplicity however we will refer to that storage which is unique to the host as being the host storage. Basic to any processor is its execution architecture or simply its architecture. Once the architecture is known, the design of the processor can begin by reviewing the various

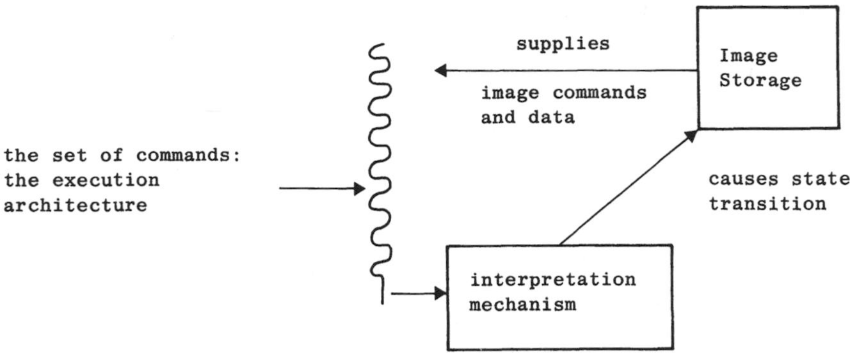

A machine: set of commands + storage
+ interpretation mechanism.

Figure 2 : A Machine Model

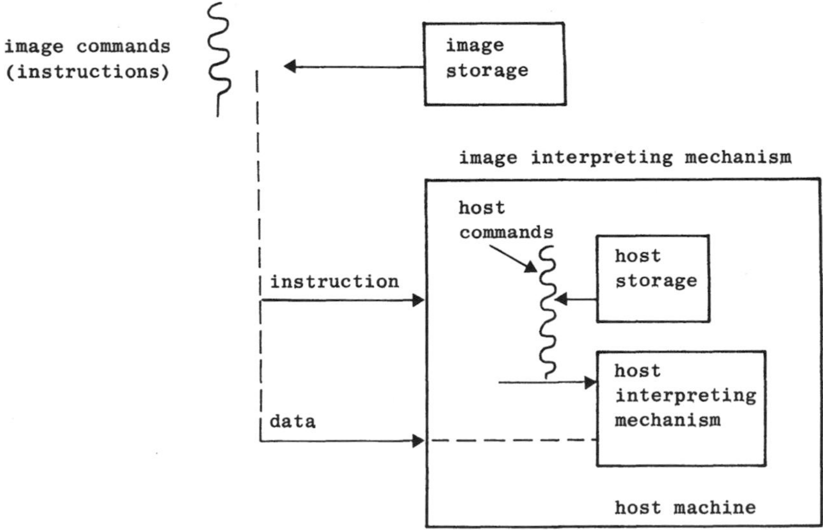

Figure 3 : Image and Host Machine

tradeoffs between computer aided design support, design effort and unit cost. But the architecture must suit the environment and environments may vary. In these notes we take the approach that architectures can be largely determined by the high level language used to specify the environment.

2.2 Microinstructions (4)

There is usually a hierarchy of image machines, the host for one image is itself an image for a sub-host. The process terminates when there is no unique host storage. At this point we have the base host machine and there is no subcycling, i.e. state transitions in storage not visible to the image. Thus, to a first approximation, a single microinstruction controls a single host state transition. In many cases, the microinstruction action appears considerably more complex. For example, the microinstruction may contain only an address of a word in another control storage which actually specifies the host control.

For the purpose of these notes we assume a fairly straight forward single level of interpretation between the image and the host. Now the image storage includes, in addition to the primary storage, named registers, i.e. registers implied by the architecture. These registers and their associated communications paths are called the data paths. Thus the mechanism includes everything except the registers, and the mechanism plus the registers are divided into three parts:

(i) The Data Paths

(ii) The Arithmetical Logic Unit (ALU)

(iii) The Control

Each register in the system can be gated to one of a number of other registers during a cycle.

Control points determine which registers (image and host) are connected to which destinations on a cycle by cycle basis. In every cycle each register position must have a defined control point value. The collection of control point values defines a control vector. Not all combinations of values in this control vector are meanful and the total number of control points are not as formidable as might first appear. Only the independent control points or ICP need to be determined each cycle by the control unit. For a typical smaller processor these might number in the range of fifty to a hundred. The output of the control unit is the sequence of microinstructions (ICP vectors) that interpret the image operation. The primary input to the control unit is the op code of the image instruction and sequence control information. For most host machines designed for the particular image ("well mapped" as discussed later), the average number of internal cycles per image instruction execution varies between five and twelve. Taking advantage of sharing, the emulator for even a relatively rich image architecture such as System 370 might not exceed 1 to 4 thousand words of microprogram storage. As shown in figure 4 sequence control is either contained in or implied by the micro-instruction.

Since many of the ICP combinations cannot be used - perhaps only a thousand out of 2^{50} - much flexibility exists with the organisation of the microinstruction. Typically groups of ICPs are encoded. A field of four bits in the microinstruction can represent sixteen combinations. If these combinations are expanded by the hardware at the output of the microprogram storage they can represent sixteen ICP configurations of arbitrary size. The "decoder" itself may be a storage which contains the ICP vectors, providing a two level control. Encoded ICPs such as the above are called <u>vertical microinstructions</u> (figure 4). Since the decoding takes additional time, we have saved space in the microprogram storage at the possible expense of increasing the cycle time. We have also limited the amount of simultaneous action that may go on. If the resources of the system are broken into many pieces, each controlled separately and by an explicit ICP vector - we have a <u>horizontal microinstruction</u>. A horizontal microinstruction allows additional concurrency and presumably fewer microinstructions per image instruction interpretation. There are also a spectrum of intermediate possibilities which allow concurrent but restricted (encoded) control over several processor resources. In all of these we are trading off among several parameters; size of the microinstruction versus number of cycles per image instruction interpretation versus duration of the cycle time.

2.3 Types of host - image correspondence (3)

An image instruction is partitioned into fields called <u>syllables</u> which must be interpreted by the host machine. Each of these syllables is to be individually decoded by the host and executed according to the semantics of the instruction. The execution of the image instruction involves a sequence of cycles usually divided into at least four phases:

(i) Instruction Fetch : Fetching the contents of the instruction counter from memory and placing it into the instruction register.

(ii) Decoding the instruction and generating the data address.

(iii) Fetching the data contents into the memory buffer register.

(iv) Executing the operation indicated by the image instructions.

Host machines vary considerably in their ability to concurrently perform the decoding and execution of syllables. Thus it is useful to classify the host machines by the amount of hardware support they provide for concurrent execution of instruction syllables (see figure 5).

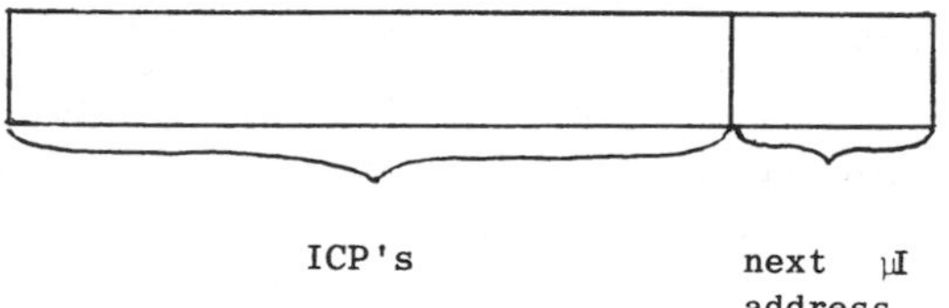

(a) simple horizontal microinstruction

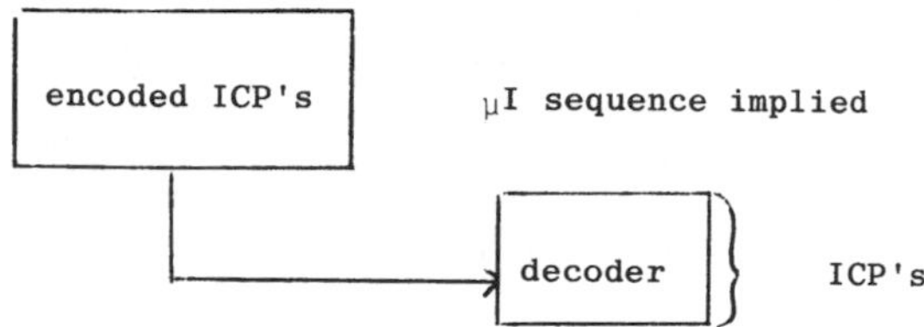

(b) simple vertical microinstruction

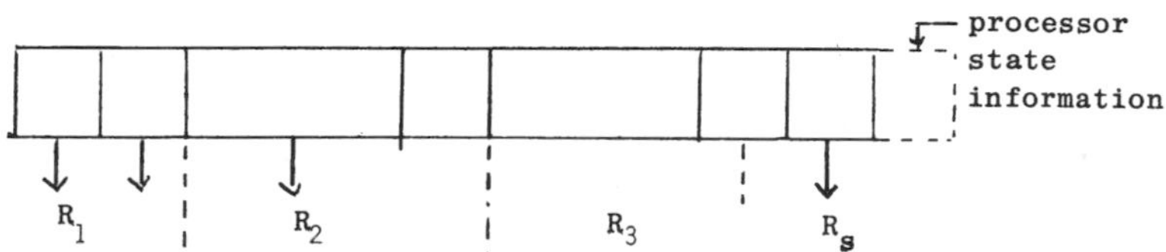

multiple resources (R) controlled by encoded fields - (Rs determines next μI)

(c) encoded horizontal microinstruction

Figure 4 : Microinstructions

(i) The partially mapped host

For a variety of reasons the host may have limited support for the image architecture. A common instance of this is a host with an eight bit ALU and eight bit supporting registers used for the interpretation of a thirty-two bit image data structure. For this type of organisation multiple interpretation cycles are required per image object. Thus instead of one memory cycle to fetch an instruction we may require four, similarly with execution and data address generation. This partially mapped host is then simply a host that requires significantly more cycles for the interpretation of an image instruction than that implied by the semantics of the image instruction itself. Partially mapped hosts may arise for reasons other than data path limitations. The universal host machine is an example. This is a host that has no a priori support for the interpretation of a particular image syllable. Each syllable of the image instruction is separately fetched from image storage, decoded and executed. Usually at least a single state transition is required for each of these actions. Figure 5 illustrates a universal host executing an image instruction.

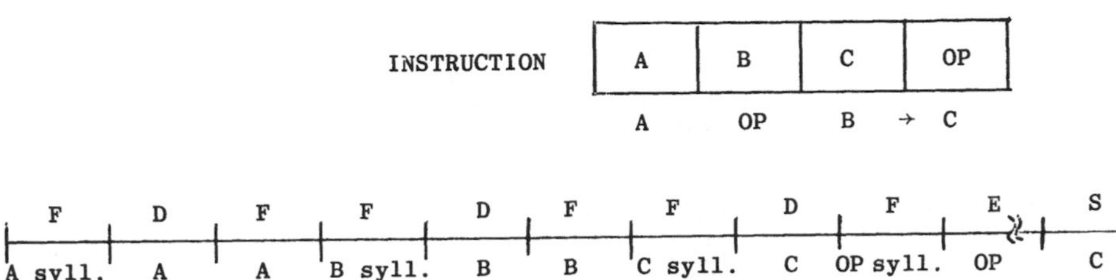

(a) Partially Mapped Host (Universal Host)

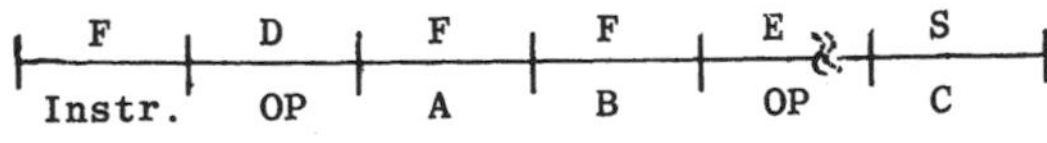

(b) Well Mapped Host Machine

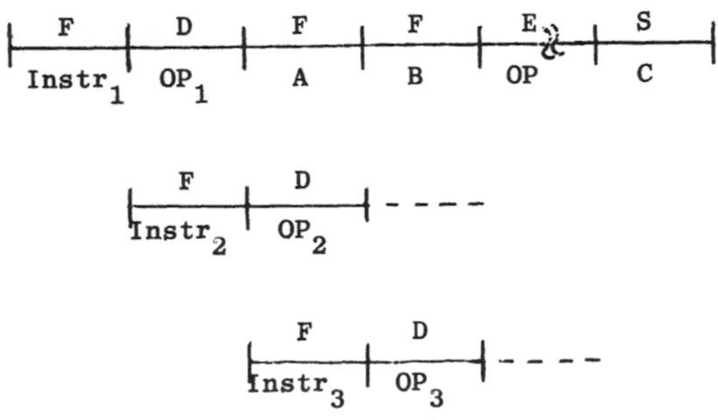

(c) Overlapped Host

F Fetch

D Decode

E Execute

S Store in

Figure 5 : Image Host Timing

(ii) The well mapped machine

This is the case where the host has full hardware support for image instruction partitioning. Thus once the instruction is decoded, the various syllables of the instruction can be executed in accordance with their semantics. The image instruction is decoded in one cycle but the syllables are executed sequentially as indicated by their semantics.

(iii) The overlapped machine

These machines have still additional hardware resources so as to permit the concurrent execution of syllables of the image instruction sequence as permitted by their semantics, i.e. the instruction dependencies must be observed. The decoding of instructions is still done sequentially but the final execution of the syllables is overlapped and the order of execution is preserved. Non-order preserving execution of instructions can also be conceived by even more formidable hosts but they lie outside the scope (at least for the near future) of the microcomputer host.

3.0 ARCHITECTURE AND LANGUAGE

The architecture, being a set of commands, describes relationships among objects - ways to transform and re-arrange data. There are several basic approaches to the design of an architecture (figure 6) largely distinguished by either:

(i) Whether the objects and relations are host oriented or language oriented. The host oriented architecture describes ALU functions operating on memory words, whereas a language oriented architecture describes relationships in much the same semantics of the high level language.

(ii) The placement of the architecture between the language and the host - the relative amount of translation versus interpretation performed specifies the level of the execution architecture. A low level architecture will be close to the microinstructions of the host. It will require extensive compilation but straightforward interpretation. A high level architecture will require simple translation and a more sophisticated interpretation process upon the part of the host.

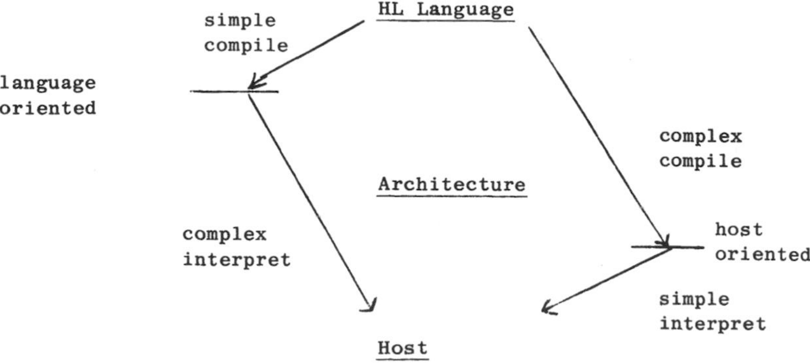

Figure 6 : Architecture Strategies

3.1 Limitations of Host Oriented Architectures

Much research has been focused on whether the best host oriented architecture is based on a stack, single accumulator, two address, or three address organization. The premise is that a single, "best" execution architecture can be uncovered by exhaustive statistical analysis of benchmark experiments. Unfortunately, slightly different assumptions lead to radically different conclusions and, in general, this type of analysis suffers without a unifying, theoretical justification. Each of the instruction organizations mentioned above, as well as heretofore untried combinations, will have some advantages in specific situations. The problem lies in using a single organization as the basis for architecture in a universal environment.

In order to quantify the degree of "overhead" forced into program representations in a universal environment, studies (6) have been made which attempt to separate instructions related directly to the original expression of an algorithm in the high level source language, and those which appear to have been introduced because of architectural constraints. For example, load or store instructions are almost always included because of requirements imposed by the execution architecture. These commands merely move items around in the image name space - which is not, in general, partitioned according to any sensible division of the space for the original high level language representation of a program. This has led to the notion of three different generic classes of instructions:

(i) Functional type

(F-type) instructions that actually operate on and transform values. It is assumed that these instructions actually correspond to operations in the higher level language representation of the program.

(ii) Memory type

(M-type) instructions that rearrange items within a memory hierarchy without changing their value.

(iii) Procedural type

(P-type) instructions (branch and compare) that alter the sequencing rule during interpretation, but do not change data values.

If we assume that only the functional instructions are absolutely necessary to a program representation and define ratios of M and P type to F type instructions we arrive at some interesting overall statistics for current machines (Table 1). From this table, it is evident that two or three memory type instructions are required for each functional instruction. Notice that the introduction of general purpose registers into the 360/370 architecture (as opposed to the single accumulator, multiple index register complement of the 7090/7094) did not reduce this ratio, but rather these extra objects created more memory type instruction overhead.

Processor	"Ideal"	7090	System 370
M-ratio	0.0	2.0	3.0
P-ratio	0.0	0.8	2.5
NF-ratio	0.0	2.8	5.5

Table 1 : Overhead Ratios

3.2 Two Phased Evaluation (5)

For our purposes, program evaluation takes place in two distinct phases. The source program written in a high level language is translated into an equivalent form during the compilation phase. The output of this form becomes a surrogate for the original source program. In the second phase this intermediate output undergoes a number of interpretations associated with the semantics of the original source representation. Thus the model consists of the following: a source language which is selected for its ability to represent the environment; a host machine - selected for its execution capabilities; a translator/compiler that takes the source program as input and produces an equivalent executable program and finally an interpreter that enables the host machine to implement state transitions as specified by the architecture and the translator.

Translation is a process of converting a program in one language into an equivalent program in another language. Compilers translate a source language into a form that can be interpreted more efficiently. They reduce complexity by binding (partially) operands to storage and operators to computational structures. Even a special case of direct interpretation of a high level language source includes compilation since the translation of a statement is still required even though this is completely internal to the interpreter. One may view this as a compilation - interpretation cycle occuring on a statement by statement basis in which the intermediate execution architecture is not visible to the user. Notice that compilation involves two quite distinct processes: optimization and translation. The distinction for us is quite important since as architects we are not particularly concerned with optimization but vitally concerned with translation. We view optimisation as a process which occurs on a source program and produces a better form of the program in the original source language. Certain forms of optimization cannot be expressed in the original language, i.e. an extended language is required. For purposes of these notes, we relegate this important problem to language designers and assume that the optimization occurs on a source to extended source basis.

The optimiser re-arranges the source program into a "best possible form", then the translator creates a surrogate form within the syntax and semantics of the execution architecture. We assume that the given HLL program is already in best possible form, it has already been optimised.

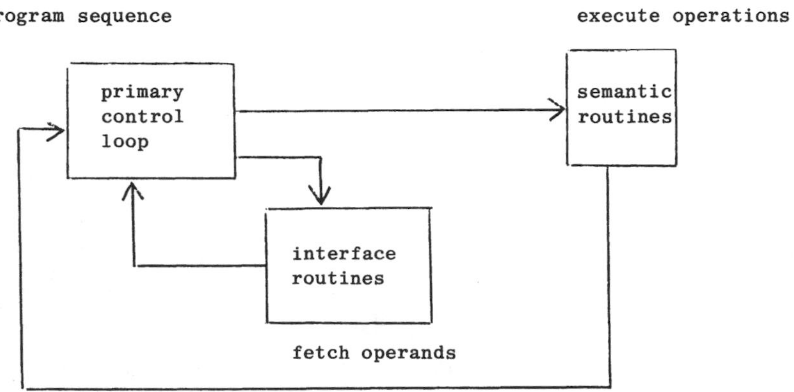

Figure 7 : Interpreter Action

The interpreter consists of a primary control loop, a set of interface routines and a set of semantic routines (figure 7). The primary control loop maintains the instruction stream and decodes the appropriate syllables that define the layout of the rest of the instruction. Control is then transferred to the appropriate interface routine when it actually parses operand references within the instruction. Interface routines are responsible for creating standard interfaces that define the location (and sometimes the value) of each operand used in the instruction. Upon emplacing the operands in a standard position, the selected interface routine returns control to a known point in the loop which then transfers control to the semantic routine that actually implements the action defined by the instruction. This completed, control returns to the top of the primary control loop and another interpretation begins.

Associated with the processes of translation and interpretation is an important property called transparency. In a transparent interpretation, state transitions in both source and object representations occur in the same order and states are preserved at the end of the state transition. No new states may be introduced in the execution architecture. Since no new data states are introduced across a source state transition there is no need to save data states if an interrupt is permitted to occur only at the end of these transitions. Also synchronisation of concurrent processes and verification of computations if valid at the source level is also valid at the object level since there is an exact correspondence of states and their order of interpretation. A similar concept of transparent interpretation can be defined to ensure that no side effects can occur in the program execution.

4.0 ARCHITECTURE AND TECHNOLOGY

Thus far we have examined architecture independent of the technology constraints and trade-offs inherent in microcomputer implementations. In this section we look at the constraints imposed.

In any practical design, we face a series of design compromises among competing goals. In the design of a microcomputer, we trade off the area available for logic on the chip versus the area required for pins and connections to the chip. We trade off speed versus power; the faster a logic element is to go the more power (and more area) it requires. Finally we trade off design costs and CAD support versus applicability of the resulting design. A tailored design may be very efficient for a particular user but implicit in the cost of the design is the requirement for a reasonable scope of applicability - a broader community of users.

4.1 The Constraints

Geography, the amount of space the microcomputer occupies, is an important design constraint. It limits the amount of logic that can be included on a chip, the number of pins - connections to the outside environment and the feasibility of achieving certain functions. Cragon (7) observes that the area requirement places "a heavy responsibility on the designer to create an architecture which uses a minimum of chip area". He cites data from T. Hasty of TI which indicates that for a NMOS process the expected manufacturing cost would be:

$$\text{Cost} = K(10^{.0368A})$$

Where A = area of the chip in mm^2

K = a constant for a given process

Because of the exponential nature of the cost area relationship, small increases in chip area can significantly decrease yields and hence increase costs - and indeed feasibility of producing a particular design.

Cragon further observes that the chip area is partitioned into CPU and memory (figure 8) as well as pins and connections to the external environment:

$$\text{Area} = (\sqrt{\text{CPU + memory}} + \text{pins})^2$$

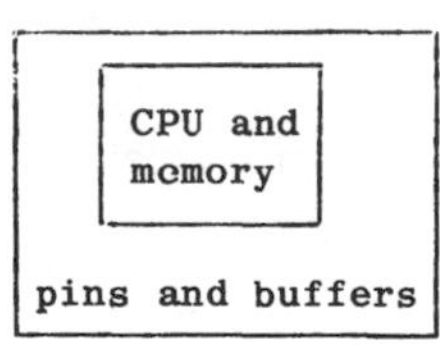

Figure 8 : Chip Area Allocation

Frequently the number of pins available are determined strictly by the parimeter available and corresponding mechanical mounting requirements. It is a difficult item to vary. If we allow ½ mm about the outer periphary of the chip for pins, buffers and connections then the area equation reduces to:

$$\text{Area} = (\sqrt{\text{CPU + memory}} + 1)^2$$

Where area is given in mm^2

Notice that the designer can trade off between memory space and CPU space. The memory factor is a summation of the image storage and the interpreter storage or host storage. Not all memory occupies the same area per bit. A single bit of register space for example occupies four times as much area as a bit of RAM which in turn occupies between four and eight times as much area as a bit of ROM. Complicating these comparisons is their non-linear nature - larger storage arrays are relatively more efficient than smaller ones.

Another fundamental consideration for the architect is the allocation of on-chip memory. Should there be an image storage or an interpretive storage on chip or should these functions be relocated to a multi chip set to implement the overall process of function? Table 2 was developed to give an indication of these trade-offs (7,8).

Let A = unit area of average MOS gate in a custom logic implementation

<u>then</u>

2A = area for custom <u>bipolar</u> gate

2A to 4A = area for <u>MOS gate</u> in <u>gate array</u>

4A = area for custom MOS register bit

A = area for custom MOS gate

$\frac{1}{4}$A = one bit of RAM memory/dynamic

$\frac{1}{16}$A = one bit of ROM memory

$\frac{1}{16}$A = one bit of PLA array (a PLA bit is defined as a minterm crossing. E.g. $\overline{A}\cdot\overline{B}\cdot C$ requires 3 PLA bits)

<u>Table 2 : Area Trade-offs</u>

Speed versus power is another important issue fundamental to the design of the micro-computer. High speed bipolar technology accommodates an internal cycle of 100 ns (register - ALU - register) but occupies perhaps four times as much area per bit as NMOS. Of course the NMOS technology supports a slower cycle time of about 200 ns. Thus higher speed technologies require more power per logic decision to achieve their speed. The power requires larger geometry device structures which in turn require that a chip be depopulated.

The regularity of the logic used to implement a particular function determines not only the area that that function can occupy but also the wireability of the function. A particular logic configuration is interconnected with support from CAD tools. The routing system may require a two to one depopulation of logic elements in order to allow sufficient space for wire and interconnection placement. Also regular arrays, i.e. logic gate arrays, are composed of universal elements. These gates have been designed to accommodate maximum fan in and fan out possibilities and other worst case situations. Because of this they will naturally require more power and hence more area than a custom implementation of the same logic function. Still the universal arrays are preferred, since CAD tools do not yet support very sophisticated and arbitrary custom designs. Regular array structures can be customised by merely changing the upper levels of metalisation on the chip leaving the basic chip intact across a wide variety of functions. The management of placement and routing of interconnections on regular arrays is possible with today's CAD systems even for rather large implementation. In order to have many of the advantages that a custom design would provide and yet retain a semblance of control over design costs, "custom macros" have been introduced by many vendors. These are customised designated functional pieces of a processor which are available for inclusion as part of a larger chip. They act in many ways as an MSI chip library in more traditional designs.

Of particular interest in a microcomputer implementation is the use of ROM and PLA type structures to implement appropriate pieces of the processor. PLAs and ROM are basically the same regular array structure used in different ways (9). They represent a regular, high density configuration of read only bits. The ROM has but one decoder taking n input address lines into 2^n arbitrary output configurations. Whereas the PLA (in usual implementation) has a decoder (a phase splitter) on each of the n input lines identifying one of 2^n possible output product configurations. These product configurations may be summed allowing the generation of arbitrary AND/OR functions logic. The advantage of the ROM is that it can generate any output function given a particular input configuration. The PLAs must generate product functions of the inputs. ROMs are particularly suited for functions where the output configurations are large and complex although being of limited number. The control function is an excellent example where a limited number of ICP configurations are required for instruction interpretation. PLAs on the other hand provide better implementations of output functions that are simple logical productions of input variables. An eight bit adder for example could be implemented with ROMs using a sixteen bit address and a sixty-five thousand entry table, each entry consisting of over eight bits. The PLA implementation for an eight bit adder can be realised with a total array requirement (10) of 3139 bits. PLAs provide the AND/OR logic function, whereas the ROMs can realise any output configuration. Both of these structures are quite amenable to sequencing control, that is they can be used as part of a sequential logic implementation; the control of the sequence largely laying within either the ROM or the PLA. In ROM this is realised simply by including the successor address in the instruction word fetched. In PLA the sequential logic is performed by registers external to the array which hold a portion of the output of a particular state. This is fed back internally to inputs of the AND array.

4.2 Some Consequences of the Technology for the Architecture

The following summarises some of the constraints (7) that the architect of the microcomputer must consider:

(i) Size. Unlike conventional architectures static program size is a significant determinate in CPU design since instruction size is reflected in larger on-chip storage requirements and larger supporting hardware. This is especially true in integrated CPU-memory chips for, as Cragen points out, each byte saved is of significant value since memory is a fixed and limited quantity on chip.

(ii) Use of ROM memory. Wherever possible ROM memory should be substituted for RAM memory since given a constant area, four times as many ROM bits can be accommodated as RAM bits.

(iii) Memory bandwidth for processing on-chip memory interaction is not a limitation. Usually on-chip memory is organised as a square array since this minimises the size of the decoder. For off-chip memory, pins/pads are the limitation and memory bandwidth plays a significant role.

(iv) CPU execution time is determined by a number of objects interpreted. Creating program representations that require interpretation of a smaller number of objects results in more efficient CPU use.

(v) Multi-programming and associated relocation requirements are not important aspects in many present microcomputer applications. Thus addressing mechanisms can be simpler than in more traditional architectural environments. Because of the advantage of ROM over RAM, the architecture should accommodate the splitting of data and instructions into different addressing environments. For many situations the entire user program can be fixed and placed in ROM. Emperical evidence suggests that at least for these fixed environments, program size dominates data size by a factor of 16 to 32 in the number of required memory words. Thus for these applications, even when the program is fully contained in ROM, the instruction area will still excede the data memory area.

(vi) Accessing the external environment. A good microcomputer architecture is organised about limited pins - ports into and out of the microcomputer. When the memory can be completely captured on-chip, the design of the chip interface is fairly simple. For most environments there will be a heavy emphasis on bit oriented I/O. This is a consequence of both the problem environments and pin limitations of the processor. When memory is off-chip, high bandwidth transfers are required through this pin limited communication facility. Multiplexing addresses and data on the same line is a common method of reducing the number of required pins. Using short addresses or multiple cycles to transmit an address is another technique. Of course the more serial and sequential one makes the access to memory, the fewer pins required but the longer the number of cycles to retrieve the desired word and hence the access time is correspondingly increased. Thus any technique that can be included in the architecture to minimise transfer protocol activity will improve overall CPU efficiency. Addressing a particular block in an external memory and moving the entire block contents into an internal memory has a number of desirable features as it shortens the size of the address and means that only one address is required per block of words rather than an address for each word.

5.0 HOSTS WITHOUT A CUSTOMIZED ARCHITECTURE

In this section we deal with the problem of applicability of customized host structures. How can the microcomputer designer create host structures without committing the design to a particular architecture and environment? We begin by discussion of the general form of host machines that are not subject to the specialised constraints of microcomputer implementation then we review some special host forms designed to cover universal environments, although in significantly different ways. The universal interpretive host machine (or UHM) is a partially mapped machine that emulates the architecture involved. Since the architecture can be varied it can be as specialised as required to realise maximum performance. Its limitation is that it takes additional cycles to interpret the unsupported image architecture. The universal executing host (UEM) on the other hand relies on compiler technology to adapt the universe of environments to the processor. The high level language (HLL) source is compiled into microcode. Both of these approaches solve the programmation problem mentioned in the initial discussion. Only one host design is required to handle multiple environments. One host requires very sophisticated compiler technology. The other one requires multiple interpreters to be written. Each has their share of "design" effort although it is in a more traditional software sense. Alternatively solid state "programmation" can be used, as for example the System 370 architecture on a gate array implementation.

5.1 Host Characteristics

In order to examine the effect of microcomputer constraints let us look at non microcomputer based host processor of reasonably modern vintage. They usually share the following characteristics:

(i) A large read write microstorage. These usually consist of bipolar technology since that technology supports the fast write function. This microstorage is at least partly used as a writable control store to contain operating system support, support for hardware diagnosis, etc. as well as to improve data access which in traditional architecture is designated as cache. The remainder of the microstorage is read only memory which supports well defined and fixed image machines. This microstorage may be pure storage and programmed logic arrays (PLAs). Since the PLA cannot be re-configured it can serve only as a replacement for the read only part of the microstorage. The use of ROM/RAM/PLA is simply a fact of technology allowing the use of regular replicated implementations.

(ii) The speed of the microstorage is at least equal to an internal cycle - a complete register, ALU to register operation. This allows fetching of a microinstruction in one cycle and its use in the next cycle. Here microinstruction accessing overlaps ALU interpretation.

(iii) Simple direct addressing and use of immediate operands in the microinstruction rather than more complex addressing requiring multi-state transitions. As a consequence, object placement in microstorage is limited - since it cannot be relocated dynamically. However the simplicity in addressing structure is a natural consequence of the single microstorage access per ALU cycle restriction

(iv) Main memory is a block oriented device for bulk storage in a multi-level storage hierarchy. Movement of environments from remote to executable levels of storage may require support ranging from simple to elaborate interpretations.

Notice that the above characteristics are generally common to recently designed host machines and derived primarily from the economics of current hardware technology.

5.2 Universal Executing Machines

Static program size is an important consideration in the universal executing machine, i.e. the compiled microcode approach. The microinstruction or host instruction must be chosen with considerable care. On the other hand, the host instruction by its nature must be fast - able to control an ALU state transition on a cycle by cycle basis. What we suggest here is a 16 bit host instruction probably with multiple formats, the basic format being the register to register instruction controlling 16 registers. The associated op code represents one of perhaps 128 ALU type operations. An alternate format is available for loading and storing the registers. The memory address is determined by the concatenation of an implied base register with the address field. Figure 9 shows the generation of a

24 bit effective address in this manner.

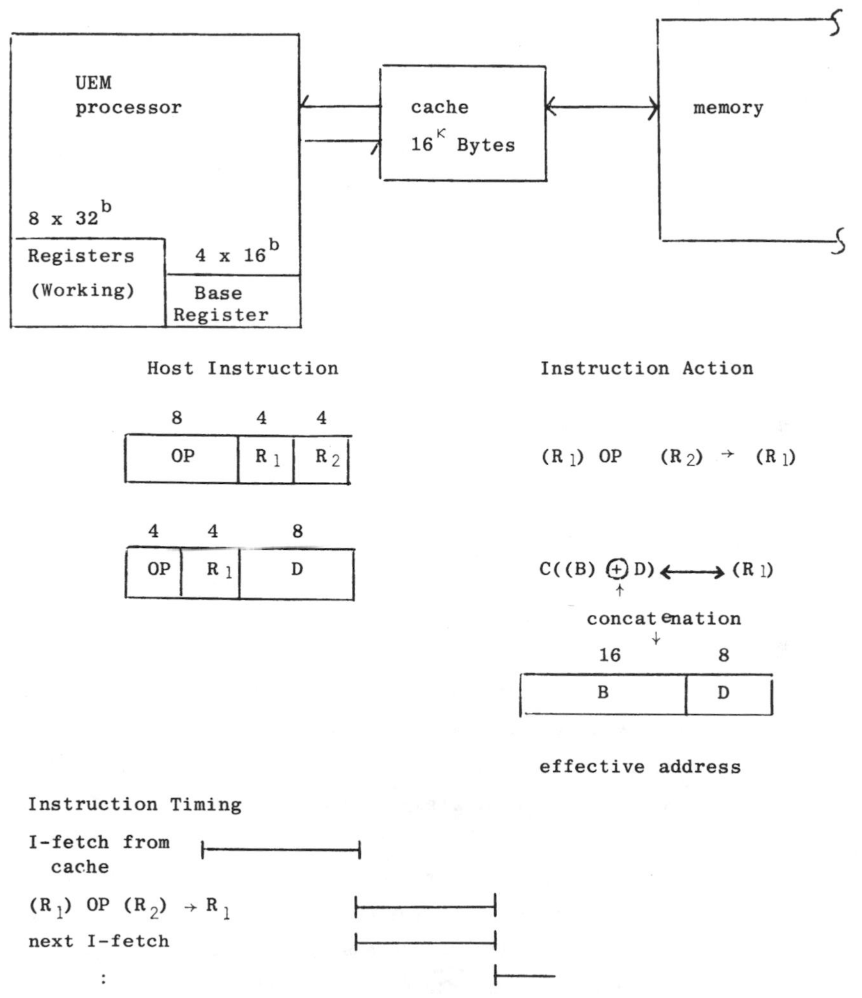

Figure 9 : The UEM

Concatenation rather than addition is chosen to ensure that instructions of both formats are able to execute in a single state transition. The host instruction timing is shown in Figure 9. The instructions are fetched from a cache into the instruction register in one state transition. The (register op register → register) operation executes in the next cycle; at the same time the next host instruction is fetched from cache. In the case of a data fetch, an extra cycle must be inserted to accommodate the fetch of data from the cache-down from the goal of an instruction executed per internal cycle. An extra cycle must also be added whenever a branch is required. Data available from conventional instruction sets suggests that branch frequency is about .3 of all instructions and a load or store register is about .4

of all instructions. Thus 70% of the instructions as executed require two cycles while the remaining 30% require one cycle. Thus we would expect an average execution rate of 1.7 cycles per host instruction. Notice that the host memory is heavily organised about the availability of data from the cache. Thus it is important that the cache be of sufficient size to ensure a reasonably good hit rate. One would expect something in excess of 16,000 KB to be available for cache in this type of organisation.

5.3 Universal Host Machine (UHM) (11)

Another approach to the problem of creating a universal structure, which by its nature allows customisation to particular environments, is to create a processor suitable for executing multiple interpreters. The interpreter then is responsible for tailoring the environment to a particular architecture. Here the static characteristics of the architecture are less important than in the UEM case. However, a UHM by its nature has no hardware available for the interpretation of any particular architecture. Thus efficient execution of an instruction set is very important. Thus the UEM is size oriented in host instruction design while the UHM is oriented towards minimising the dynamics of the instruction stream - minimising the number of microinstructions required for the interpretation of an image syllable. Our sample UHM microinstruction is very similar to our UEM. The principal differences are that its microinstruction is now a coded horizontal rather than vertical. The sample microinstruction shown in the Figure 10 is a 32 bit arrangement with three instruction fragments executing simultaneously. Fragment one is a register to register ALU operation; fragment two controls load and store from the microstorage into the registers; fragment three is a test and branch control fragment. An alternate format must also be available to provide block load and store between main memory and microstorage, to complete branch addresses and specify the upper bits of microstorage address. This provides the net effect of the cache as in the UEM case. Just as in the UEM case it is assumed that the host instruction set can be overlapped but execution of the UHM instructions may be limited by the bandwidth of the microstorage, since fragment two, when it is used in a conventional way, will require a fetch of the microstorage. Thus on all fragments requiring such a fetch, we will require two cycles for execution of the microinstruction. Similarly, while fragment three is testing a condition within the machine, a number of situations may arise where the next host instruction depends directly upon the result of this condition. For these cases an extra cycle will also be required. The net effect of this is to give a similar execution speed as the UEM - about 1.7 cycles per microinstruction. The UHM in most other ways resembles the UEM with the possible exception of its orientation towards bit string handling. One of the most frequently executed functions in an interpreter is a selection of a field in an arbitraty bit stream and the use of this field together with a base value as an effective address

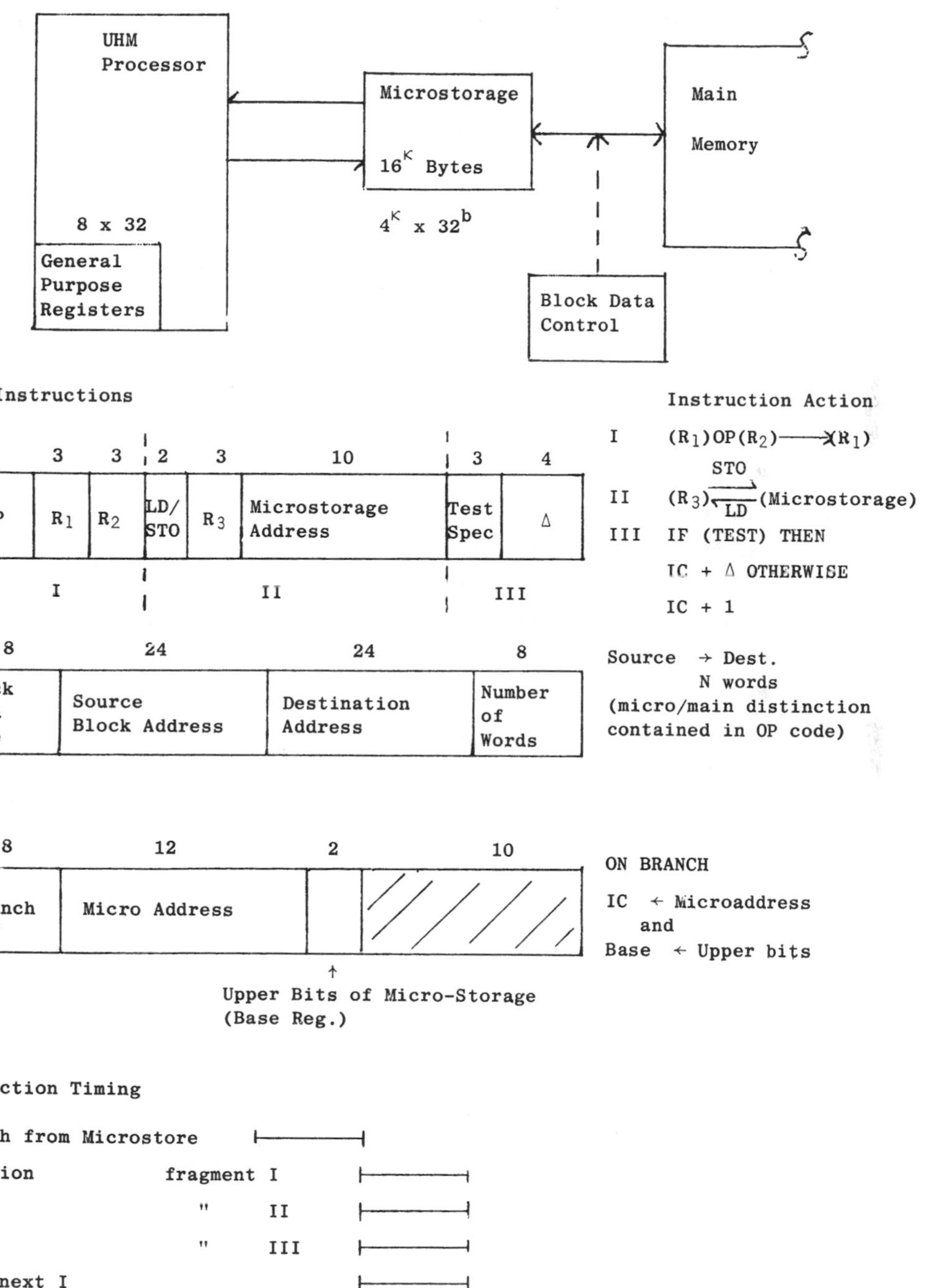

Figure 10 : The Universal Host Machine

to a table entry in the interpretive storage. This loop is a primary interpreter function and is encountered for each field in the image instruction. Thus one would expect additional ALU resources to be available to the UHM for operations such as field select, justify and add to a base value.

5.4 A Programmation of System/370 (12)

It is useful to review the results of a recent experiment performed at IBM (12) on the development of System/370 processor chip using gate array technology. The chip consists of an all bipolar gate array and uses 4,923 bipolar gates out of a possible (available) 7,640. The chip is a 49mm^2 die with 200 I/O pins. The use of a universal gate array to provide a personalisation to an architecture is an interesting contrast to the preceeding two approaches which assumed basically customised processors which would be adapted to the various environments through software. In the 370 experiment the technology itself is the flexible vehicle which is programmed to realise a particular environment. Because of the gate array approach, the designers are faced with limitations in terms of number of gates available and performance. Only the processor itself is included on the chip (Figure 11) thus the full System/370 consists of the processor chip, the control storage (ROM), a register chip and main memory.

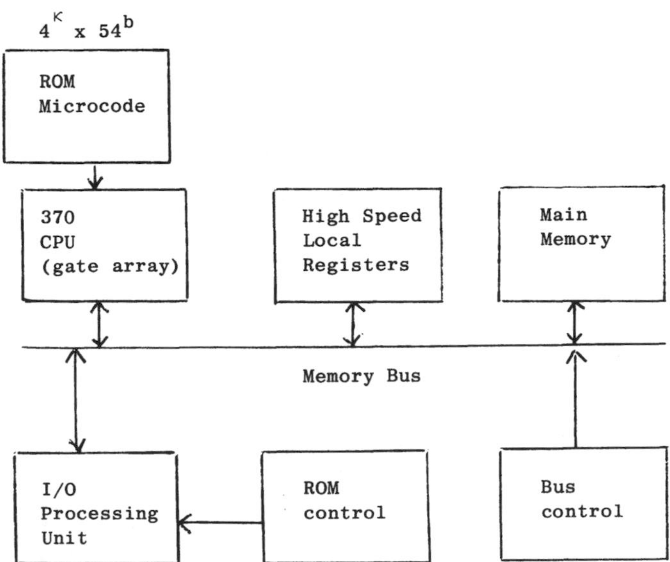

Figure 11 : The System/370 Gate Array

The implementation is area limited thus only a partially mapped host implementation is realised - with eight bit ALU execution. The address arithmetic, i.e. incrementer, is supported at a 24 bit arithmetic level. With only a partially mapped host very efficient control is required in order to achieve reasonable execution speeds. Thus a horizontal microinstruction of 54 bits is chosen. The size of the control store (ROM) is limited to about 4,000 words (the total of 250K bits). A special high speed local storage chip is used to contain all of the active 370 registers that could not fit on-chip. Total cycle time is 100ns and the weighted average of 50 cycles per instruction is achieved - an overall performance of 200,000 instructions per second. The external arrangement of the chip shows a bus orientation with bus communication used for both register and memory transfer.

Several features of the IBM technology are unusual by today's standards and deserve special mention. Three distinct levels (or planes) of metalization are used to interconnect the gates - as contrasted to the usual case of one level. Within the three levels one level is dedicated to distribution of power supply levels, another to "x-axis" communication, the final level provides "y-axis" connections. Since only a limited number of lines can run together in a channel or interstice (space between adjacent gates), congestion eventually develops. In the 370 experiment, the 4,923 gates required 10,605 interconnections; gate placement and wiring required very sophisticated CAD support to wire all but 68 connections (overflows). The overflows were then manually inserted. Note that in even the best current state of art CAD system human intervention/support is required for optimum routing. Also note that at levels above 60% of gate array usage the wiring problems limit the applicability - even with multi-level metalization.

Another comment concerns the unusually large number of chip interconnection (I/O) pins. Rather than the more conventional periphary only pin siting, IBM technology sites pins on a uniform grid across the plane of the chip carrier. This allows the relatively generous interchip pin count of 200 and thus allows the off-chip arrangement of microprogram storage and fact registers.

Perhaps the most important comment is the reminder that this experiment was just that and not a commercial product. The purpose of the experiment was to test CAD tools not to optimize chip design tradeoffs. In an experiment organized to test custom organizational arrangements a significantly different chip configuration would emerge; most probably with custom macro ALU, on chip microstorage (of smaller size) and on-chip fast registers.

6.0 CUSTOMIZED LANGUAGE ORIENTED ARCHITECTURES

In many microcomputer environments we are interested in creating architectures that support language and language fragments. The architecture issues include:

(i) Creation of ideal language oriented architectures;

(ii) measurement of these architectures compared with non-customized host oriented architectures;

(iii) the design of customized host machines.

We are trying to find the best trade-off among the design variables: design effort, performance, cost, etc. The question of cost cannot be answered here because it will depend on the tools available to the designer and the relative importance of cost and performance. So the emphasis of these notes is to present available data and evaluate the potential of a customized approach.

6.1 Measuring Ideal Architectures

Any image architecture is limited by the high level language that originally represented the program. Certain aspects of HLL program representation ultimately determine and limit image program interpretation. On quantifying these program aspects the reader should understand that there is by no means an equal weighting to the various measures. Indeed a great deal will depend upon the type of host doing the interpretation as to relative importance of a measure. These measures of architecture assume that the architecture will be a transparent representation of the HLL program and hence the HLL source was already a good representation (the best possible) of the original program architectural measures:

(i) Correspondence - Image instructions should correspond on a 1:1 basis to HLL source actions and operands.

(ii) Size - all objects of the same class (variables, operations and labels) are encoded by variable sized identifiers each of size ($\log_2$ of the number of named objects of that class in an environment or scope of definition).

(iii) Activity - the instruction set is organized to minimize the number of instructions interpreted and data items referenced. The dynamic number of instructions executed is equal to the number of HLL program actions and the number of data reference is equal to the number of HLL data objects dynamically encountered.

From the above, the ideal architecture would represent the FORTRAN statement

D = A + B * C

as two instructions: * B C

\+ A D

If there were 13 named variables and 7 unique operations occurring in the subroutine in which the above statement appeared then * and + would be coded as $\lceil \log_2 7 \rceil = 3$ bits and A, B, C and D would each be encoded as $\lceil \log_2 13 \rceil = 4$ bits and the two instructions would occupy 22 bits. Also two instructions would be executed requiring four data references.

In the next section we consider the problem of realizing ideal architectures. We call these resulting architectures Directly Executed Languages or DELs, since they are in direct correspondence with the HLL source and are in executable form.

6.2 Designing DEL Architectures (abstracted from (5))

For our purposes an image store contains both program store and data store. We will assume that the interpretive mechanism is either a well mapped host or partially mapped host. The host assumption is important since the weighting of the various aspects of the ideal architecture are different depending upon the characteristics of the interpretation mechanism. An overlapped host machine must have predictability of syllable locations in order to achieve its overlapped execution. A partially mapped machine requires none of this as it serially inspects each syllable of the instruction. Thus for the overlap machine, speed of execution will be achieved only at the expense of program size and the corollary is that program execution by a limited host offers at least a very concise program representation without further time penalty.

Storage consists of instruction environment, process environment. The instruction environment resides in host registers while the process environment resides in the microstorage along with the emulator (Figure 12). The process environment will define the logical structure of the image storage during the execution of a program. Image instructions are contained within the image program store. Instructions are partitioned into syllables each of which specifies: a format, operands, an operation, the instruction sequence.

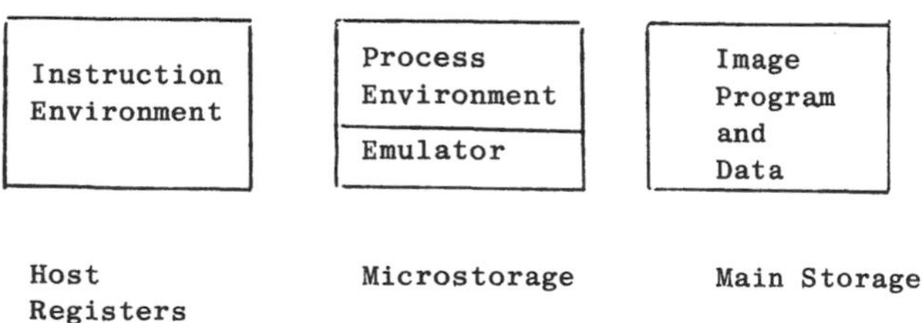

(a) Storage Assignments

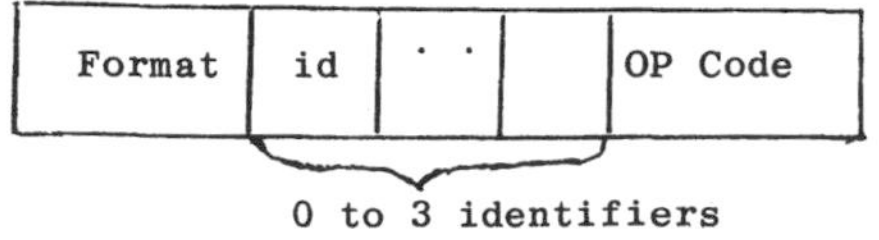

(b) DEL instruction

Figure 12 : A DEL Architecture

6.2.1 The Image Store

The goal in the design of an image storage is to provide close correspondence between the language artifacts and host capabilities. Thus the mechanism must be both flexible and yet simple in its operation.

A primary consideration in a data storage organisation is the method of binding an identifier to a value. Data is usually characterised by type, location and value where the type of the referand defines a template through which the interpreter must view the value once its location, i.e. address, has been defined. Type identification can be implemented in a number of ways (Figure 13):

(i) For simple languages with few data types, type can be associated with operation code. In this case, identifiers directly address the values.

(ii) For more complex languages a type-identification pair can be used in the program representation.

(iii) For more complex cases, descriptors are usually used. The identifier is associated with an intermediate descriptor which indicates type and location of the actual value.

Representational conciseness is an important aspect of an architectural design.

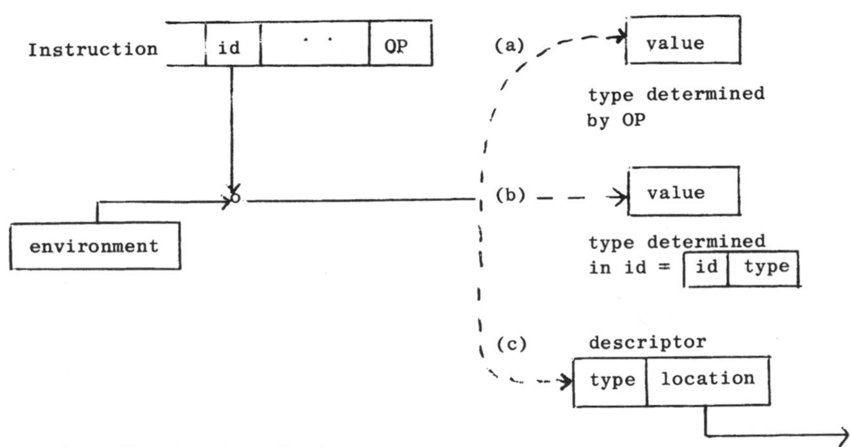

Figure 13 : DEL Data Typing

In order to achieve $\log_2$ ideal size encoding of objects a model of environment is used - due to J. Johnson (13) - which recognizes that object names have a scope of definition which Johnson calls a contour. If we take the ordered list of names used in a contour we can match a name index to each entry in the list. Thus the size of the index (or name) container is ($\log_2$ of the number of names). E.g. if a subroutine has 15 names, we use a four bit container; we can encode label in a similar way. Thus each subroutine will have its own container size for each class of object. This index is called the identifier and is uniquely associated with an environment by an environmental pointer. This pointer contains the starting point of the contour list in storage (either microstorage or main storage as determined by the implementation).

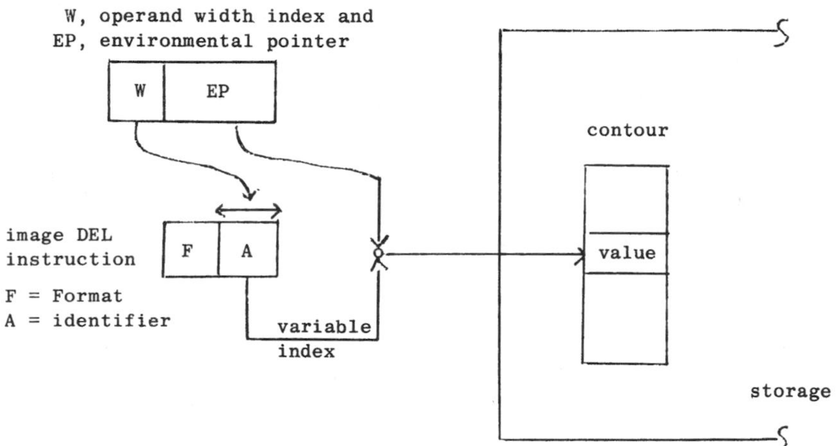

Figure 14 : DEL Variable Accessing

For operands, the interpreter recognizes from the format field, the number of names explicitly stated in the DEL instruction (Figure 14). A host register contains a width index for operand containers in the particular subroutine. The interpreter then selects the bits corresponding to this operand name. This identifier, when added to the environmental pointer for operands, forms the truc address of the value in storage. This value is then brought into one of the host registers for operation. In some cases, the value may not be present in the contour, as it must be computed or retrieved from elsewhere; an example of this is an array element. In these cases, the contour entry is typed and indicates whether the results of the storage access provide a true value or an address of the value.

We have indicated that three environmental pointers are used for the contour.

Actually, only one is required. For example, negative values for labels and positive ones for names could be indexed off the same environmental pointer.

6.2.2 The format

A format is a rule defining the instruction partition, i.e. the number and meaning of syllables in the instruction, the number of arguments and results and the association between operands and the results of the operator. The primary goal in format design is to eliminate overhead instructions especially memory movement instructions. The format is the leading syllable in the DEL instruction and the interpreter should be able to determine from it the nature and the number of syllables in the instruction. By interpreting the format syllable, the primary control loop is able to fetch the required data values from storage and place them in a standard interface - registers - for action by the semantic routine - the ALU. In order to eliminate overhead instructions, a powerful set of formats is required which provide a property we call transformational completeness. This means that we have a format available which relates the names mentioned in the instructions to temporary locations so that no redundancies are required and no additional instructions are introduced. In order to construct such a set, let us assume that we have a stack (lifo) which is part of the host storage. It is handled only by the interpreter and not by any of the image instructions (except through the format syllable). Table 3 shows a complete list of formats. The set neatly accomplishes the goal of minimising the number of identifiers and instructions. Since the format set is complete, instructions that push or pop the stack are never required since the interpreter handles this itself. Use of the top of the stack as an argument automatically pops the stack, using it as a result pushes the stack. We have assumed in the table that all operations take two operands (add, subtract, ..), lower order operations can be handled in a similar manner. Since a format is a transformation, procedural transformations, i.e. sequence operations, are truly associated with format as distinct from operation. Therefore high level language operations such as GO TO, IF and DO are encoded as specific format types rather than trailing operations. This permits the interpreter to recognise these differences and fetch label addresses rather than values in these particular cases.

6.2.3 The Control Structure

Probably more than any other area of architecture the choice of control structures depend upon the designers knowledge of or assumption about the host machine. The control structure basically determines how environments, instructions and syllables are sequenced.

Table 4

Transformationally complete formats

Format	Transformation	Number of Explicit Operand Identifiers
ABC	A op B → C	3 operands
ABB	A op B → B	2
ABA	A op B → A	2
AAA	A op A → A	1
ABT	A op B → T	2
ATB	A op T → B	2
TAB	T op A → B	2
TAA	T op A → A	1
ATA	A op T → A	1
AAT	A op A → T	1
ATT	A op T → T	1
TAT	T op A → T	1
TTA	T op T → A	1
TUA	T op U → A	1
TUT	T op U → T	0

A, B and C are any explicit operand identifiers. T is the top of a stack and U is the next element in the stack (after T)

The host memory - the physical memory - is naturally organised with fixed partitions: word and block boundaries. Thus we must be concerned with both minimising the number of partition boundaries to be crossed during interpretation and maximising the predictability of the location of the next object in the control sequence. The relative importance of these depends a good deal on the underlying host. The partially mapped host needs a good deal less predictability in the control sequence than an overlapped host.

The important host considerations are primarily associated with relative timing:

(1) The ratio of access time of microstorage to main storage.

(ii) The relative block transfer time of micro and main storage.

(iii) The proportion of time the host spends accessing data versus interpreting.

6.2.3.1 Environment Sequencing

The architectural strategy is simply to optimize about those characteristics of language and host which are present. Consider three simple cases.

Case 1 :

Identifiers point directly to values in main storage. For simple languages without data type variability and for hosts without significant access time differential between micro and main storage this is an attractive and simple approach. Environmental change is accomplished by merely changing the environment control parameter (just like the base register).

Case 2 :

Identified values are pre-loaded into microstorage. Here environments are created at either program load time for static languages or as part of the call mechanism for dynamic languages. Only named values are transferred however since structures such as arrays must remain in main storage. This is a reasonable approach for a simple source language and a host with a relatively fast microstorage.

Case 3 :

Identifiers point to descriptors residing in interpretive storage that in turn point to the values residing in main storage. Environments are represented by descriptor tables which can be interpreted according to the rules of the source language. This approach supports all familiar procedural languages with a relatively few limitations on the host.

6.2.3.2. Instruction Sequencing

While it is possible to imagine architectures with many types of instruction sequencing, most architectures will simply follow the sequencing rule employed in the language that it attempts to interpret. Tree structures, list structures and linear structures (in line) are certainly conceivable. For familiar procedural based languages the linear rule has a number of important advantages. Pointers required by tree and list structures make them less desirable because of the space these pointers occupy and the extra main store accesses needed. For most hosts it will be significantly faster to increment an instruction program counter maintained in a host register than to fetch an address from main storage. While the flexibility of the tree and list forms may be useful in the context of a particular language the predictability of the successor instruction is a significant advantage for in-line instruction sequencing.

6.2.3.3 Syllable Sequencing

A basic problem in syllable sequencing is locating a syllable with respect to a host word boundary. One could force all critical syllables, e.g. the format syllable, to lie on word boundaries obviously eliminating the problem. however this comes at the expense of program space. Certainly some hosts such as those that execute in an overlapped fashion will require such a concession from the architecture. For partially mapped and even well mapped machines careful encoding of critical syllables will both preserve concise program representation yet minimize the time lost due to fetching syllables split across word boundaries.

The technique developed by Hoevel (14) improves the effective placement of syllables by using "phantom zeros" in code assignment. Phantom zeros "fits" frequently used syllable codes into variable number of bits which complete the physical instruction word in memory. Suppose there are B bits in the next syllable to be packed into a word that has only A bits remaining where B is greater than A. Phantom zeros involves retianing the code point "all zeros" in A as an indicator that the syllable simply could not fit. But now many code points of B can fit because if the interpreter sees that the A field is anything other than zero it simply fills in the trailing bits of B with zeros. It is important to have knowledge of the frequency of occurrence of the syllable. The most frequently occurring syllable should be coded 100...0, the next most frequently, 0100...0, etc.

6.2.4 Operators

The last aspect of architecture design relates to the actual operations to be performed, the semantic routines. Since these are determined in a large measure by the HLL verb set it is a simple matter of implementation for the host designer to arrange interpretive actions in one to one correspondence with the HLL verbs. Operator identifiers may be coded in the same way as object identifiers, i.e. relative to an environmental pointer which points to a table in the microstorage which indicates the starting place of a particular semantic routine. For simple languages, i.e. with a limited operation vocabulary, even this complexity is best avoided since a fixed OP container of perhaps 5 bits can - with support from format information - distinguish among over 40 actions (5).

Certain verbs with low frequency of usage may require that their semantic routine is brought into microstorage before actual execution can begin. This might be the case in the transcendental or trigonometric routines. The result of the above design is probably best summarised by an architecture done for FORTRAN called Deltran which is illustrated in the next section.

7.0 A DEL MICROCOMPUTER

In this section we first present a DEL based host microcomputer based on architectural principles and technology constraints presented earlier. This is followed by a DEL architectural example executing on the microcomputer. The microcomputer host is hypothetical but the DEL architecture has been constructed and emulated at the Stanford Emulation Laboratory using a 32^b unbiased host (UHM) called EMMY. Performance measurements and estimates are given in the final section.

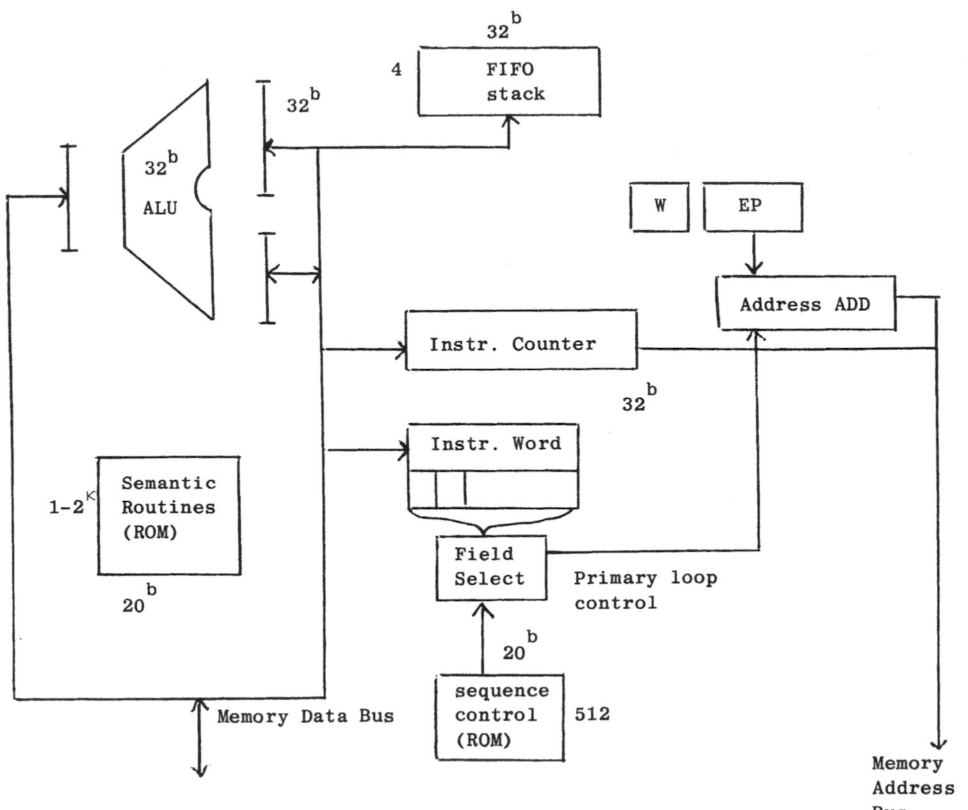

Figure 15 : A DEL Host

7.1 A Sample DEL Microcomputer

Within the limitations of area and partitioning we now derive a plausible DEL architecture for direct implementation on either a custom or technologically programmed basis. For an architecture we choose the arrangement of a format syllable followed by a variable number of object identifiers with a trailing op code. The format set includes the transformationally complete set as well as procedural actions encoded in 5 bits. Given the obvious on chip area limitations we use $\log_2$ variable encoding of identifier names. This index will be added to an environmental pointer which will identify an entry in the contour of values in the image (main) storage. We assume we are creating an architecture for a fairly simple Fortran/Pascal type language with a reasonably limited repetoire of data types (Figure 15). For simplicity we will choose a strategy of distinguishing type by the operation code in the instruction itself. This accommodates integer-floating point differentiation as well as the deferred or indirect designation. An evaluation stack of four elements is to be included on-chip. Statements consisting of more than four verbs would use more than a four level evaluation stack are detected and decomposed by the compiler into simpler statements. The instruction stream is buffered by at least a 32 bit instruction word and the ALU is buffered by an interface of a right and left source register together with the result register. This gives a total of approximately eight 32 bit registers not including an instruction word counter of 16 bits. To execute the semantic routines (interpret the ops) - which correspond to the high level language operations - control of the ALU is assumed to be a 1,000-1,200 word ROM. As most of the ROM control is strictly sequencing, since the ALU is relatively limited in its capabilities, a 16 to 20 bit ROM word entry would be sufficient. For the type of organisation proposed execution would proceed in the following way:

(i) Decode of the format.

(ii) Index to first operand.

(iii) Fetch first operand.

(iv) Index to second operand.

(v) Fetch second operand.

(vi) Transfer control to semantic routine for OP.

Assuming an average execution of about five cycles per semantic verb, ten to twelve host instructions per semantic op might be expected. To this must be added two data fetches plus one data store and one half of an instruction fetch (on average). For NMOS type logic this would account for average instruction execution in the order of one to two micro seconds per instruction.

7.2 An Example of the DELtran Architecture

In the example below we use the DELtran architecture which was designed as an execution architecture for FORTRAN II. We will present only enough details here to make the example understandable and some of the results are useful. The DELtran instruction consists of a five bit format field which encodes transformation information and the control verbs in FORTRAN. From 0 to 3 variable sized explicit operand identifiers and a trailing op operation follow the format syllable. The image module consists of a header, code body and data contour. Five host words are used as header information on module entry. Following the header and contour the code body is placed in line - actually instructions are concatenated using phantom zeros. The calling module uses three of the five words to retain its state. Thus it places the current environment pointer, instruction pointer and current instruction word in the indicated words in the header. Next the interpreter loads the new environment pointer and width index into the indicated host registers. The operator field is fixed usually at four bits depending upon the functionality of the operator. In the example, the contour is stored in the image storage where each entry is 32 bits. Label identifiers are subtracted from the environmental pointer and variable identifiers are added to the environmental pointer. For the example, a total of 7 variables are used and 4 labels. Since the variables demand a three bit container both variables and labels use this size. The width index then is set to three. The environmental pointer and width index share a common host register. Three host registers are used to provide a standard interface into the semantic routine. The primary control loop of the interpreter then, using information provided by the format field, fetches the value of each of the indicated variables into the indicated host registers. When a array element is indicated special operations are invoked, e.g. A2E and A2S. A2E takes a two dimensional array element, computes its location and places the value indicated by the identifier that follows the A2E field. Thus normally A2E would be preceded by three fields: two dimensional indices and the base field. In statement 3, the two indices are the same as indicated by the format field. Thus two identifiers precede the op code. A similar operation, A2S, computes the value of a two dimensional array element and places that value on top of the stack.

7.3 Some Comparative Data

The following is a summary comparison of various aspects of the example in the DELtran - microcomputer (as emulated at Stanford) and the corresponding System 370 representation using both optimizing (H optII) and non-optimizing compilers.

	DELtran	System 370 (optimized)	System 370 (non-opt.)
Instructions to represent	11	42	66
Static program size	147^b	1088^b	1920^b
Static program header	160^b	2032^b	2200^b
Total size	307^b	3112^b	4120^b
For one pass:			
Instruction word refr. (32^b)	6(inc return)	34	60
Data refr.	18	26	54

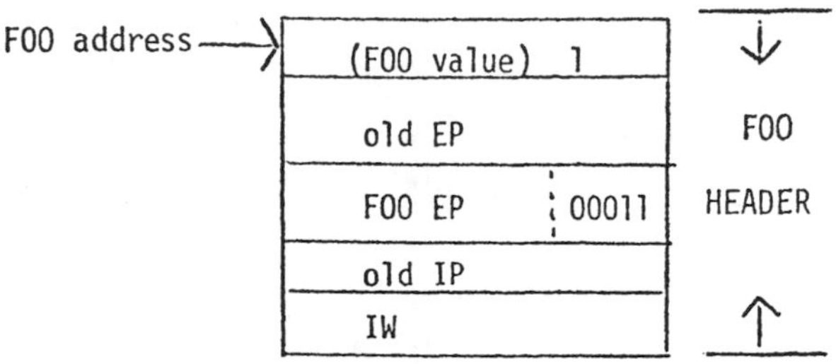

FOO address →

(FOO value) 1		↓
old EP		FOO
FOO EP	00011	HEADER
old IP		
IW		↑

```
      SUBROUTINE FOO(K)
      COMMON  B(10,10)
1     DO 4  I=1,10                 L1    MOVE <1><I>
2     K=11-I                       L2    ABC <11><I><K>ISB
3     B(K,K)=B(K,K)**B(K,I)
                                         AAB <K><B>A2E<dB>
                                         ABC <K><I><B>A2S
                                         ATA <dB>FPF
4     CONTINUE                           END1 <I><10><L2>
5     K=INT(B(10,10))-K            L5    AAB <10><B>A2S
                                         TT  FIX
                                         TAA <K> ISB
6     IF(K) 7,1,5                        IFE <K><L7>
7     RETURN                       L7    RETURN
```

A Module "FOO" and its DELtran Code

Module Layout

Size	Label	Instruction		Comment
32^b	FOO addr →	FOO value (≡1)		
32^b		Caller's EP		
32^b		FOO EP		
32^b		Caller's IP		
32^b		Caller's IW		
11^b	L1	MOVE <1><I>	.	set I=1 in word @I of the FOO data module
18^b	L2	ABC <11><I><K>ISB	.	11-I placed in K
18^b		AAB <K><B>A2E <dB>	.	B(K,K) address placed in dB in contour
20^b		ABC <K><I><B>A2S	.	B(K,I) placed on top of stack
12^b		ATA <dB>FPF	.	(B(K,K))**B(K,I) → B(K,K)
14^b		END1 <I><10><L2>	.	(I+1→I):10 less than/equal → L2 otherwise continue
17^b	L5	AAB <10><B>A2S	.	B(10,10) placed on top of stack
9^b		TT FIX	.	top of stack convert to interger
12^b		TAA <K> ISB	.	B(10,10) Integer-K → K
11^b		IFE <K><L7>	.	If K less than zero go to L7,=0→L1,+→L5
5^b	L7	RETURN	.	Return to caller

160 header (static)
+ 147 body (dynamic)
307 total

Contour Layout

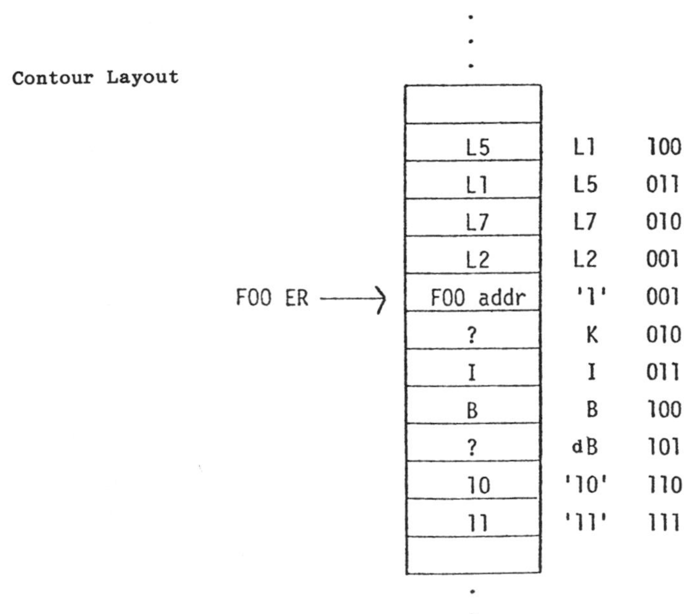

The static program size excludes the program header. In the case of System 370, the header is the subroutine prologue and epilogue. On static program size DELtran exceeds the ideal by about 50 bits - largely the format bits. Of course, the header size dominates in this small example. Memory reference activity is computed for one complete pass through the program. Instruction word references are computed as the number of 32 bit memory references required to retrieve the program.

While the example is limited, the ratio of static program size and dynamic number of instructions interpreted illustrated seem representative of more comprehensive studies (14). The DEL type architectures usually give a space and instruction execution reduction of between 3:1 and 6:1 on a variety of programs and alternative architectures studied (including Honeywell L-66, PDP-11, Burroughs FORTRAN-S).

8.0 SOME TENTATIVE CONCLUSIONS

In times of rapid change in technology it is very difficult to make a truly comparable evaluation of approaches - there are simply too many variables with an anomolous basis.

Nevertheless we attempt to summarize available data so as to draw some meaningful conclusions. The reader should understand the very limited nature of the data. Possibly the most significant variable in selecting an approach to microcomputer design is the type and degree of CAD support - and on this matter we have no specific data.

In other areas:

(1) System 370 Gate Array vs. a UHM emulation of System 370

This comparison is based on the System 370 microcomputer (12) and a UHM called EMMY built for Stanford. EMMY is an all MSI implementation; however, the data presented is derived from a gate-level simulator of an EMMY design exercise. This particular design seems comparable in approach and timing to the system 370 chip.

	System 370 chip	Comparable UHM emulating 370
Number of gates	4,923	11,000 (est.)
Cycle time	10Cns	125ns (est.)
Data paths	8^b (partially mapped)	32^b UHM
Control store	$54^b \times 4^K$ (approx) ROM	$32^b \times 4^K$ RAM
Emulator size (System 370)	NA	2,200 words
Av. cycles/image instr.	50	22

In both cases the number of gates does not include either microprogram storage or the bulk of the image registers. The estimate of 125nsec was based on T^2L schottky MSI for the UHM.

Observations :

(i) The wide microinstruction for the 370 chip is expected - a more horizontal structure is common in dedicated image biased hosts, since considerable performance can be derived.

(ii) In the UHM the microinstruction is a vertically coded horizontal as space and time are important in variable emulation.

(iii) The emulator sizes (in words) are probably comparable for a similar scope of emulation.

(iv) If the designers of the 370 chip had 11,000 gates at their disposal, they would have certainly been able to realize a well-mapped host - with about 8-10 cycles per image instruction.

(v) The 11,000 gates of the UHM would fit on the same $49mm^2$ chip as the 370 in a completely custom design. The significant trade-off is not area but design effort and CAD support.

(2) DEL's vs Conventional Architecture using UHM's

Using benchmark material and executing on EMMY, data similar to the example in the preceding section can be evaluated. The program data below is expressed as ratio of System 370 to DELtran with DELtran equal unity.

	System 370	DELtran
Static Program Size	5.3	1
Dynamic: Instructions Executed	4.6	1
Dynamic: Memory references	4.7	1
EMMY Emulator Size	2200 words	800 words
EMMY Execution time: microinstruction per image instr.	22	16

Observations :

(i) DEL's offer a significant advantage over conventional architectures in both space to represent and time to execute (on the same UHM).

(ii) DEL-type architectures are not necessarily more complex - at least when measured in terms of size of the emulator - the emulator size excludes I/O support and the DEL emulator also excludes the trig. interpretive routines

(iii) The execution time per image instruction is less in the DEL architecture since encoding possibilities are more flexible.

(3) DEL's on UHM's vs. UEM's

Data here is <u>very</u> meagre. On the basis of a small sample program (3)

	UEM	DEL on UHM
Sample Program Size	604[b]	63[b]
Execution Time (in host instructions)	{ 109	156 (including 3 multiples)
	13	60 (excluding multiples)

As discussed earlier the size (in gates) of each processor is approximately the same. The sample program included a data set of 192[b] which is the same for both approaches. This somewhat diminishes the advantage of the DEL/UHM. The execution time includes a constant 96 cycles for both approaches for multiple execution. The UEM approach would have a decided advantage without this.

Observations :

(i) An execution speed advantage of perhaps 5:1 may exist in favour of the UEM but this is diminished by the "run-on" execution of complex functions, (e.g. multiply) since this time is the same for both approaches and since even functions such as multiply may have execution time of 32 cycles even the relatively infrequent occurrence of "run-on" functions may dominate time comparisons.

(ii) A program size advantage of at least 5:1 exists in favour of the DEL UHM approach, but this may be diminished by the constant size of the data sets.

(iii) For many environments compile time is a significant proportion of the activity. For these situations, which do not achieve many program runs per compilation, the UEM is less attractive.

9.0 SOME OVERALL CONCLUSIONS

Language sensitive architectural design - whether based on UEM or DEL-UHM or well-mapped DEL on "programated" array - shows promise in being able to represent user environments more concisely and efficiently than more traditional approaches.

Rapid changes in technology obviously expand the possibilities of design approaches yet more subtle changes in relative weight of design parameters (e.g. area and pin considerations) may effect resulting design strategies in a more direct way.

Fundamental to the feasibility of <u>any</u> design approach is the ability to create, document and verify designs in a timely way. The availability of comprehensive CAD tools is a necessary condition for realizing any design. But it is even more urgent in user customized situations.

10. ACKNOWLEDGEMENTS

This work was undertaken with fellowship support from the National Board for Science and Technology - Ireland.

Much of the material (especially on DEL's) was developed jointly (5) with Lee Hoevel of IBM.

11. REFERENCES

(1) N. Wirth, Programming languages : what to demand and how to assess them; Software Engineering (Ed. R. H. Perrott) Pub. Academic Press 1978, pp 155-173.

(2) J. L. Fischer, VLSI economics and the customer interface problem; Electronics Letter (Morgan Stanley), Nov. 30, 1979.

(3) M. J. Flynn, Directions and issues in architecture and language, Computer, vol. 13, No. 10, Oct. 80, pp 5-22.

(4) H. Stone (Ed), Introduction to Computer Architecture (chap 10), pub. SRA Chicago 1980.

(5) L. Hoevel and M. Flynn, Execution Architecture: the DELtran experiment, IEEE Transactions on Computers, to be published 1981.

(6) M. J. Flynn, Trends and problems in computer organization, Proc IFIPS Congress 74, North Holland Pub. Co., 1975, pp3-10.

(7) H. G. Cragon, The elements of single chip microcomputer architecture Computer, col 13, No. 10, Oct 80, pp 24-41.

(8) R. J. Domenico, Palyn Assoc., San Jose CA., private communication, Feb. 81.

(9) H. Fleisher and L. I. Maissel, An introduction to array logic, IBM J of Res. and Dev., vol 19, March 75, pp 98-109.

(10) M. S. Schmookler, Design of large ALU's using multiple PLA macros, IBM J of Res. and Dev., vol. 24, No. 1, Jan 80, pp 2-14.

(11) M. J. Flynn, C. J. Neuhauser and R. M. McLure, EMMY - an emulation system for user microprogramming, AFIPS, vol. 44 (NCC 1975), pp 85-89.

(12) C. Davis et al, Gate array embodies System/370 processor, Electronics, Oct. 9 1980, pp 140-143 (also appears in IEEE proc. of int'l. conference on Circuits and Computers, 1980).

(13) J. B. Johnson, The contour model of block structured processes, SIGPLAN Notices, vol. 6, Feb 71, pp 52-82.

(14) L. W. Hoevel, Direct execution languages, Ph.D Thesis, Elect. Engr. Dept., Johns Hopkins University, June 78.

High Level Sequential and Concurrent Programming

R.H. Perrott
Department of Computer Science
The Queen's University
Belfast BT7 1NN

Abstract Sequential Programming

This paper examines the major developments in data structures and program constructs which have evolved in high level programming languages since the introduction of Fortran. The programming language Pascal is used to illustrate these program constructs and data structures.

The relevance of these developments to microcomputer systems is that any high level program constructs and data structures for these systems should also be independent of the hardware.

SEQUENTIAL PROGRAMMING

1. Brief History

The first high level language to gain widespread acceptance by the programming community was Fortran [2]. Fortran was introduced in 1954 by John Backus of IBM. The spread and acceptance of Fortran was not without resistance as the majority of programmers of that time used assembly languages. They had an investment in existing programs and they had to be convinced that a change was necessary or would be beneficial.

The challenge to Backus [3] and his co-workers was to develop a high level language which when translated would be comparable to hand coded programs. Backus saw the major problem as being the construction of a compiler to do the conversion efficiently rather than the design of the language. Even the name of the language Formula Translator reflects this objective.

As a result of the requirement to produce efficient code the instruction set of the machine on which the work was carried out (an IBM 704) influenced the choice of features included in Fortran. This original machine has since been superseded by several more sophisticated, powerful and efficient machines. However, many of the original Fortran features have survived and have been propagated by several Fortran standards. Other developments in the design and implementation of high level languages were taking place simultaneously, notably with Algol in the academic community and Cobol in the data processing community.

An important development towards the end of the sixties was the introduction of Pascal by N. Wirth [7]. Wirth had developed at least two other languages before beginning his work on Pascal.

The two principal aims in the development of Pascal [5] were:

(i) to make available a language suitable to teach programming as a systematic discipline based on certain fundamental concepts clearly and naturally reflected by the language;

(ii) to develop implementations of this language which were both reliable and efficient on currently available computers.

Both objectives have been achieved.

Pascal's designer benefited from the experience gained in the design, implementation and use of other languages, by being able to identify what was missing and what was necessary, and by using new techniques to produce a reliable and efficient compiler.

Initially, Pascal gained widespread acceptance as a teaching language to illustrate the concepts of structured programming but soon it was being used in other computer application areas. The use of Pascal has caused a reduction in program design and construction time, debugging, testing and maintenance effort.

It has been used in systems programming and has been extended to include parallel programming features.

Other languages have been developed or proposed since the introduction of Pascal; the majority have been influenced by Pascal's program and data structures. Recently the language ADA [1] has been designed for use by the U.S. Department of Defence on all its embedded computer systems. It has also been influenced by Pascal and includes features suitable for concurrent programming.

This brief history of programming languages illustrates how the design and implementation of programming languages became better understood as a result of research into compiler implementation techniques and how the idea of abstract programming evolved.

As a result methods for structuring the data of a problem and program constructs necessary for its manipulation could be identified and defined independent of the hardware or a compiler. These data structuring and program structuring abstractions are the subject matter of the next sections.

2. Elementary Data Structures

This section is concerned with the data which is manipulated by a program. In particular the structural relationships which exist between and within data items and how such data and relationships can be described in a programming language. The classic paper on the structuring of data is that by Hoare [4].

The concept of type is important to the description of data structures. The majority of high level languages enforce a type specification of the data items based on the following assumptions:-

(i) the type of a data item determines the range of values which it may take and the operations which may be applied to it;

(ii) a data item has a single type;

(iii) the type of a constant, variable or expression can be deduced solely from its form or context without any knowledge of the particular values it may take during execution;

(iv) each operator in the language requires operands of specified types and produces a result of a specific type;

(v) the type of a data item determines the method of its representation within the computer.

Thus by providing data types with appropriate operators, the language enables a programmer to describe the data manipulations in terms natural to the data rather than the machine representation ultimately chosen.

2.1 Unstructured types

2.1.1 Standard or primitive types

These types are the built-in types provided by the programming language. For example, in Pascal the primitive types are integer, Boolean, real and character while in Fortran the scientific nature of the language is reflected in the primitive types, namely, integer, logical, real, and complex.

2.1.2 Enumerated types

In a situation where a programmer allows a data item to take a limited range of values which does not correspond directly to any primitive type, he or she should have the ability to construct a new data type by enumerating its values. For example, in Pascal the cardinal points of a compass, may be represented by the type cardinal declared by

```
type cardinal = (north, south, east, west);
```

the actual values which variables of this type can take are listed.

The declaration of variables of this new type can then be introduced in a manner similar to the declaration of variables of a standard type. For example,

```
var compass : cardinal ; (* enumerated type *)
          i : integer ;  (* standard type *)
```

If such a user-constructed type were unavailable the primitive type integer would have to be used to represent each of the cardinal points.

The benefits of using the enumerated type is that the data can be described more appropriately and that compile-time and run-time checks can be applied to such variables. The user can then be more confident that irrelevant or meaningless values will not be assigned.

2.1.3 Subrange types

If a programmer wishes to introduce a data item which takes a range of values which is a subrange of the values of an already existing unstructured type then a subrange type may be used.

For example, a subrange type 'latitudetype' can be defined as a subrange of integer,

```
type latitudetype = 0..90 ;
```

and then instances of variables of that type declared, as follows:-

```
var lat1, lat2 : latitudetype ;
```

The variables have been declared to have the attributes of the type 'latitudetype' that is, they can assume any value in the range 0 to 90. A compiler can check that a value outside this range cannot be assigned to any of the variables when a program in which they are declared is executed.

A subrange of an enumerated type can also be defined by specifying a lower and upper value in a subrange type definition. For example,

```
type day = (sun, mon, tue, wed, thu, fri, sat) ;
 workday = mon..fri ; (* subrange type *)
var  d1 : day ;
  w1, w2 : workday ;
```

Thus a programmer is able to limit the potential range of values which a particular variable can take.

2.2 Structured types

In this section the methods for defining data items which have more than one component are considered. These are referred to as structured data types. In the last analysis these structured types must be built up from components which are unstructured types.

2.2.1 Cartesian Product

It is frequently required to represent a number of data items which are distinct in nature and perhaps in type as a composite data item. This composite data item is referred to as the cartesian product of the types of its components.

For example, to represent a location in the hemisphere we require its latitude and its longitude. Such a location can be defined as belonging to the cartesian product of two subrange types, as follows:-

```
type location = record
                    latitude : 0..90 ;
                    longitude : 0..180 ;
                end
```

where the 'latitude' and 'longitude' correspond to the fields or components of the cartesian product or record.

Variables can be declared to be of this type in the usual way, for example,

```
var london, paris : location ;
```

To select a particular field of a cartesian product a dot notation is used, for example, to select the latitude of London

```
london.latitude ;
```

and the longitude of Paris

```
paris.longitude.
```

If it is required to reference more than one field of a cartesian product then a more efficient method is to use a 'with' statement as

```
with paris do
      'statement'
```

where 'statement' manipulates the fields of the structured variable 'paris'.

2.2.2 Discriminated Union

It is sometimes useful to define the type of an object as the union of several alternative types. Such a type is referred to as a discriminated union and variables of this type may assume only one of the possible alternative types available at any time.

For example, if a data structure is required to represent one of the figures, circle, rectangle, triangle at any time then a discriminated union is the appropriate data structure. For example, a discriminated union type can be defined as follows:-

```
type figure = (circle : (radius : real) ;
            rectangle : (length, breadth : real) ;
             triangle : (base, height : integer)) ;
```

A value of type 'figure' will either be a primitive value of type real or a cartesian product value. It must be possible to distinguish to which of the alternative types any particular value of figure corresponds. Hence a tag value is required to indicate the type from which it originates, for example,

```
figure (rectangle (20.91, 16.3))
```

denotes a value from the second alternative.

A concrete representation of a discriminated union is available in Pascal and is achieved by the introduction of a 'case' clause to the record structure as follows:-

```
type formtype = (circle, rectangle, triangle) ;
     figure = record
                 case form : formtype of
                    circle : (radius : real) ;
                 rectangle : (length, breadth : real) ;
                  triangle : (base, height : integer)
              end
```

The identifier 'form' is known as the tag field and can be assigned any of the possible case limb identifiers depending upon which alternative of the discriminated union is required.

2.2.3 Array

In many programming languages such as Fortran, Algol 60, this is the only structured type available. It represents a data structure whose components are all of the same type and which can be referenced at random. It is a mapping from a domain or subscript type to some other type, the component or element type, for example,

A : array D of R ;

Each particular value x of the domain type specifies some unique element of the range type known as A of X and written as A[x]. Other examples are

```
var  punchedcard : array [1..80] of character ;
            page : array [1..40, 1..60] of character ;
```

2.2.4 Set

The set type can be used to represent a group of data items whose presence in or absence from a set rather than their actual values is important.

In mathematics the powerset of a set is all of the subsets of that set. A powerset type can be defined as a type whose values are all of the sets of values of some other type known as the base type. For example given

```
type  primarycolour = (red, yellow, blue) ;    (* base set *)
```

a powerset type colour is defined by

```
colour = set of primarycolour ;                (* powerset *)
```

Since all colours can be made up as a mixture of the two or three primary colours they can be specified as a set of the primary colours. In fact, the primary colours themselves can be specified as a set with a single member, that is, {red}, {yellow}, {blue} using the traditional method of denoting sets.

The other possible values from this particular base set are {red, yellow}, {red, blue}, {blue, yellow} and {red, yellow, blue}. The last value is referred to as the universal set. There is one other value known as the empty or null set and represented by {}.

The number of possible values in the powerset is obviously two raised to the power of the cardinality of the base type.

Sets can be efficiently represented in a computer by means of bit patterns since the presence or absence of a member is the relevant information. Not only can they be efficiently represented but they can also be efficiently manipulated.

3. Advanced Data Structures

The data structures of the last section can be easily represented and as will be shown in the next section easily manipulated. They require a fixed amount of storage which increases linearly with their definition. The number of members in each type, its cardinality, is finite, and remains fixed throughout its lifetime. This second category of data structures do not conform to these restrictions; their cardinality is potentially infinite and the amount of storage required to represent them cannot be determined until run time. The storage required may expand and/or contract during execution. Thus some method of dynamic allocation and de-allocation of storage is required.

3.1 Sequence

The most common example of an advanced data structure is the sequence. The sequence is an abstraction of a number of practical data structures such as the string, stack, queue and file. In abstract terms a sequence is defined as an arbitrary number of data items of a given type in some significant order. For example,

```
type string = sequence character ;
 polynomial = sequence coefficient ;
```

Sequences can be classified according to the role they are intended to fulfil in particular cases. For example, a stack is a sequence in which the order of manipulation of items is always last-in-first-out. A queue is a **sequence** which only permits the processing of items on a first-in-first-out basis.

There are several methods which can be used to represent a sequence. A fixed amount of storage can be allocated and the sequence is allowed to expand and contract within this limit. A more common solution is to provide a pointer data type to link together the members of the sequence and thus economise on the amount of storage required.

For example, in Pascal a programmer may define a pointer type by means of a definition of the form

```
type ptr = ↑item ;
```

where 'item' is the type of object which values of type 'ptr' may reference or to which they may point. The definition of the type 'item' must follow the definition of the pointer type 'ptr'. Variables may then be declared in the usual way by, for example,

```
var p : ptr ;
```

This declaration does not itself create an object to which 'p' points, but provides the capability of doing so. The creation of such an object is achieved by the use of the built-in procedure 'new', invoked with a pointer variable as parameter, for example, new(p). The newly created variable may subsequently be referenced by writing 'p↑'.

Once created, a dynamically allocated variable remains in existence until an indication is given that its storage is no longer required. This is achieved by a call of another built-in procedure 'dispose', as

```
dispose(p)
```

where 'p' is the pointer variable currently referencing or pointing to the variable which is no longer required.

If the data item which is being referenced is a record which has a field component which is itself a pointer type then the practical sequences referred to earlier can be easily represented. For example, a stack may be defined as follows:-

```
type pointer = ↑item ;
        item = record
                  element : datatype ;
                  next    : pointer
               end ;
var stack : pointer ;
```

and procedures 'push' and 'pop' defined to implement the only two operations permitted on an object of this type.

3.2 Recursive data structures

A recursive data structure is one which contains one or more components whose type is that of the structure itself. An example of a recursively defined data structure is a family tree. A family tree can be defined by associating with each person the family trees of all of his or her off spring. For example,

```
type family = (head : person ; sons, daughters : sequence family) ;
```

A practical requirement in the description of all finite recursive data structures is the provision of some non-recursive alternative which allows the eventual termination of the recursive development of a value. Thus each recursively defined component must be embedded within, for example, a discriminated union with a non-recursive alternative or within a sequence which is empty.

Most languages do not provide for the explicit definition of recursive data structures. However, the pointer facility can be easily used to implement a recursive data structure. For example, in Pascal

```
type family = record
                 head : person ;
                 sons, daughters, next : ↑family
              end ;
```

4. Program Statements

4.1 Composition

The assignment statement causes the value of a variable to be changed. An expression on the right hand side of the assignment operator is evaluated and its result assigned to the variable on the left. The assignment operator is denoted in Pascal by ':='. A compound statement is a group of statements syntactically enclosed in some way and usually connected with a particular action. A compound statement is used to reduce a sequence of statements to a single entity within a program. For example, in Pascal the following compound statement represents the exchange of two values between locations.

```
begin (* exchange *)
   t := x ;
   x := y ;
   y := t
end (* exchange *)
```

In this particular example the 'begin/end' pair are unnecessary.

4.2 Selection

Composition denotes how a linear sequence of statements is constructed; the simplest departure from linear program structure is one in which a selection between alternative actions is made at some point during execution. Such an action is usually indicated by means of a conditional statement which takes one of the following syntactic forms:-

```
if test then statement0
```

or

```
if test then statement1
else statement2
```

The second form represents the possibility of executing one of two mutually exclusive statements. The evaluation of the Boolean expression 'test' determines which of the statements is or is not executed.

More complex control patterns can be defined by using if statements as the statements of other if statements.

One selection pattern has been given special consideration in languages like Pascal. This is the selection of one of a set of actions according to some discrete valued expression. It is usually described as the 'case' construct and takes the following form:-

```
case selector of
   v1 : statement1 ;
   v2 : statement2 ;
      .
      .
      .
   vn : statementn ;
end
```

The variable or expression represented by 'selector' is evaluated and the result must be one of the values v1, v2, ..., vn otherwise the program will fail. If the value is 'vi' then 'statementi' will be executed after which execution continues immediately after the 'end'.

Two or more selector values may specify an identical action limb. A limb which requires no action is explicitly represented by a null or empty statement. For example,

```
      case compass of
         north : statement1 ;
  south, west : statement2 ;
          east :  ;
      end
```

4.3 Repetition

The second most important non linear control construct which is frequently required in programming is iteration. This enables the repeated application of some specified action until some termination condition is satisfied. Several forms of iteration can occur. Among these are:

(i) The iteration is to be performed a predetermined number of times.

In this case it is known in advance of the first execution of a group of statements how many times they are to be executed. The occurrence of this situation can be described by means of the Pascal 'for' statement

```
      for i := initial to final do
                 statement
or    for i := initial downto final do
                 statement
```

where 'initial' and 'final' are expressions which yield values of the same type as the control variable 'i'. The increment between these values is in steps of 1 or -1 depending on which form is chosen. However an arbitrary increment may be permitted, in some languages. The value of the control variable may not be altered within the loop. The previously defined enumerated types can be used with such a construct, for example,

```
      for compass := north to west do
              statement
```

This enables a close relationship between data and actions to be expressed.

(ii) The iteration is to be performed a variable number of times.

In this situation a statement is to be executed a number of times which depends on the computation defined by the body of the iteration. There are two recognised constructs for handling such a situation. In Pascal these are represented by a 'repeat' or 'while' construct. In the repeat statement the termination condition is tested after each iteration, if it is false the statements are executed again. This is repeated until the termination condition is true. It takes the form

```
repeat
   statement
until test
```

where 'test' is a Boolean expression.

In the while statement the termination condition is examined before the execution of the statements; the statements continue to be executed provided the condition is true. It takes the form

```
while test do
   statement.
```

Thus in the repeat statement the statements are executed at least once.

(iii) Split loop.

There is another iterative structure which is not directly catered for by the constructs given above. This arises when the termination condition is imbedded within the statement body. This structure can be represented by using either the while or repeat constructs. For example,

(a) by duplicating the first part of the statements outside the loop and moving it to the end inside the loop as

```
statement1 ;
while test do
begin
   statement2 ;
   statement1
end
```

or

(b) by testing for termination twice per iteration.

```
repeat
   statement1 ;
   if test then statement2
until not test
```

These solutions involve some overhead, in either program size or speed or both. Alternatively a GOTO statement could be used to transfer control out of the middle of an otherwise infinite loop. Several constructs such as Knuth's construct [6] have been proposed for the representation of such a construct.

4.4 Procedures and functions

The constructs introduced earlier illustrated features which are executed in a manner directly related to their textual positions within the program. Procedures and functions enable a program's action to be described by a set of components some of which are invoked or activated from within the others.

Subprograms provide a useful tool when applying the technique of stepwise refinement to the construction of a program. As the problem is broken down into smaller more manageable subproblems a stage is eventually reached where a procedure or function can be used to represent each subproblem. Each procedure or function can then be further refined using the program and data structures of the programming language.

A function subprogram is used to return as a result of its execution a single value denoted by the function's identifier. A result type is associated with a function. The function's identifier can be used in any expression where a variable of the same type as the result type can be used. The value produced by the evaluation of the function is substituted into the expression and the expression then evaluated.

A procedure is more flexible and versatile than a function in that it can return zero or more values by means of its parameter list after it has been executed. A procedure is activated by using the procedure name at the appropriate point in the program text.

The use of subprograms provides the programmer with several significant advantages in the course of program construction, namely,

(i) a means of abstraction.

Each subproblem can be expressed as an activation of a particular subprogram. The detailed text of the subprogram can be left to a later time if the programmer wishes to continue with the refinement of the rest of the program.

(ii) a means of saving code.

If a similar action is to be performed several times in a program, this can be indicated by means of a subprogram activation at appropriate points in the program text. The effect is as if the code of the subprogram is substituted at that point. This substitution is usually referred to as an application of the copy rule.

(iii) control of data access.

The data which is local to a subprogram is normally manipulated by the statements of that subprogram only. However subprograms may wish to share data. One of the ways of sharing data is by nesting subprograms. This determines the scope or the range of access of the identifiers of each subprogram.

(iv) parameterisation.

By specifying a list of parameters for a subprogram, subprograms can share data. However the main benefit of the parameterisation is to provide a substitution mechanism so that a subprogram can be executed many times with different parameter values.

Parameters can be classified into three different categories:-

(a) input parameters which contribute to but are not affected by the execution of the subprogram, most appropriate for functions;

(b) output parameters which are undefined on entry to the subprogram and assigned values by it;

(c) transput parameters which supply values and are re-assigned values during the execution of the subprogram.

By distinguishing between these different types of parameter the security of the program is improved as well as the efficiency of the implementation.

The syntax of Pascal functions and procedures have the following forms respectively,

```
function identifier (parameter list) : result type ;
   declaration part
begin
   statement part
   (* including at least one assignment to the function identifier *)
end
```

and

```
procedure identifier (parameter list) ;
   declaration part
begin
   statement part
end
```

The declaration part and the statement part are collectively referred to as a block; the block plays a crucial role in defining the scope of identifiers which are declared in a subprogram.

5. Block Structure

The application of the process of stepwise refinement will eliminate the unnecessary interaction between components. There will however remain an implicit interaction between components through the common data which they manipulate.

Block structured languages enable a programmer to eliminate the unnecessary data interaction by limiting the range over which the declaration of a variable obtains and thus the textual environment within which it can be referenced.

The identifiers which are declared in a Pascal subprogram are described as being the local identifiers of that subprogram - the scope of each identifier so declared is limited to the subprogram. If two or more subprograms use the same identifier name in the declaration part, the identifier is distinct in these subprograms and consequently could be used to represent different data types.

If several subprograms wish to share variables these can be declared to be non-local to these subprograms. For example,

```
var i : integer ;
procedure first ;
   (* data declaration and statements *)
procedure second ;
   (* data declaration and statements *)
begin
   (* statements *)
end
```

The variable 'i' has been declared non-local to these subprograms and provided 'i' does not appear in their local data declarations, any reference to 'i' within the statements of either procedure will denote the same variable 'i'.

To illustrate how blocks can be nested consider a Pascal program, it takes the form

program = program-heading ; block.

where a block consists of the label, constant and type definitions, the variable and subprogram declarations followed by the statement part. Such variables are usually referred to as global variables. The structure of a subprogram takes a similar form

procedure-declaration = procedure-heading ; block

and

function-declaration = function-heading ; block.

A Pascal program consists of a program heading followed by a block. A block can contain subprogram declarations which in turn consist of a heading followed by a block. Thus a Pascal program consists of nested blocks. The nesting of one block within another block define precisely the ways in which data can be shared or protected. In order to nest one procedure inside another the nested procedure should be defined along with the local variables of the nesting procedure. Thus the procedure which is to be nested is textually enclosed. It is defined after the local variables and before the statements of the nesting procedure. For example,

```
procedure nest ;
var straw, twigs : integer ; (* local variables of nest *)

   procedure egg ;
   var albumen, yolk : integer ; (* egg's local variables *)
   begin
      (* statements of egg *)
   end ; (* egg *)
begin
   (* statements of nest *)
end (* nest *)
```

Several subprograms can be nested at the same level by inserting their definitions in sequence.

The scope rules for identifiers can be stated as follows:-

(i) the scope of an identifier is the block in which the declaration occurs together with all of the blocks nested or enclosed by that block subject to rule (ii);

(ii) when an identifier declared in a block is re-declared in a block which is enclosed by the first then the enclosed block and all blocks enclosed by it are excluded from the scope of the identifier's declaration in the enclosing block.

The parameters of a procedure are regarded as being declared as local variables as far as their scope is concerned.

Thus the subprograms of a Pascal program can be nested in a hierarchy with several subprograms on the same level. The position of a subprogram within the hierarchy determines which subprograms it may activate, and which subprograms may activate it. In addition, the nesting of subprograms determines the identifier scope for the declaration and definition sections of a subprogram. A subprogram which is nested, has access to the variables of the subprograms within which it is nested, provided it has not used the same identifier name in its local declarations and definitions.

These identifier scope rules enable the programmer to localise names to a group of subprograms which are concerned with a particular task. The shared identifiers are localised so that the programmer has less to be concerned about when writing or modifying a program.

The amount of storage required during execution can be economised by a scheme of dynamic storage allocation and de-allocation operating on a stack basis as follows:-

(i) storage is allocated to the global variables of the program;

(ii) each block when activated is allocated storage in the next available locations; these locations are required to accommodate its local variables, a representation of its parameters and housekeeping information;

(iii) on exit from a block the storage allocated to that block is reclaimed.

Thus the locations allocated to the block being currently executed are always in the top most area of the stack. Also accessible are other non-local variables in locations below. Each variable declared in a block is created at entry to the block and is destroyed on exit from it.

6. Recursion

One facility which is provided by block structured languages is the ability of a subprogram to activate itself. This type of recursive invocation is usually referred to as self-recursion. Another possibility is mutual or cyclic recursion in which subprogram A calls a subprogram B which in turn calls subprogram A.

Such a facility can be used to describe an apparently infinite process. However a necessary property of all useful recursive definitions is that of termination. Termination occurs because of the realisation of some condition within the definition.

There are many problems which can be neatly solved by the use of a recursive process and require less effort from the programmer. Recursion is therefore a useful design tool. For example, the following procedure is intended to read a sequence of characters of arbitrary length but terminated by a character say '?' and to print out the sequence in reverse order.

```
procedure reverse ;
var ch : char ;
begin
   read(ch) ;
   if ch <> '?' then reverse ;
   write(ch)
end (* reverse *)
```

The procedure is called recursively until the terminal symbol is encountered after which the procedures complete execution on a last-called-first-to-finish basis.

Storage is automatically created and deleted and tailored to fit the size of the input sequence, without intervention or effort by the programmer. However, there are situations in which it may not be advisable to use recursion because of the overheads in time and space involved.

7. Summary

In this final section some relationships between the data structures and program constructs which were considered are identified.

(i) Cartesian product and with statement.

A cartesian product is composed of values of dissimilar type. The manipulation applied to each component is usually different.

```
data : record                      with data do
           c1 : type1 ;            begin
           c2 : type2 ;               process(c1) ;
           c3 : type3                 process(c2) ;
       end                            process(c3)
                                   end
```

(ii) Discriminated union and case statement.

The manipulation of this structure is one which selects from a range of several alternatives, one for each of the component types.

```
data : record                      with data do
           case tag of                case tag of
              tag1 : c1-field ;          tag1 : process(c1) ;
              tag2 : c2-field ;          tag2 : process(c2) ;
              tag3 : c3-field            tag3 : process(c3)
       end                            end
```

(iii) Array and bounded repetition.

The most appropriate manipulation is a bounded repetition of the processing of each element type.

```
a : array [1..n] of data type ;    for i := 1 to n do
                                      process (a[i])
```

(iv) Sequence and unbounded repetition.

For a sequence the characteristic manipulation is an unbounded repetition of a manipulation appropriate to the element type thus reflecting the unbounded nature of the sequence itself.

```
s : sequence data type ;           while S is not exhausted do
                                      process (element)
```

(v) Recursive data structure and recursive subprogram.

The most appropriate manipulation for a structure which is defined recursively is by means of the recursive procedure.

However, such close correspondence between the data structures and the program constructs are relaxed by necessity in programming languages.

8. References

1. Ada. Preliminary Reference Manual.
Sigplan Notices, 14, 6, June 1979.

2. Backus, J. et al., 1957.
The Fortran Automatic coding system in Proc. Western Joint Computer Conference, Los Angeles, 188-198.

3. Backus, J.
The History of Fortran I, II and III.
Sigplan Notices, 13, 8, August 1978, 165-180.

4. Dahl, O.-J., Dijkstra, E.W. and Hoare, C.A.R.
Structured Programming.
London & New York : Academic Press, 1972.

5. Jensen, K. and Wirth, N.
Pascal User Manual and Report.
Berlin : Springer, 1975.

6. Knuth, D.E.
Structured Programming with goto statements.
ACM Computing Surveys, 6, 4, December 1974, 261-302.

7. Wirth, N.
The programming language Pascal.
Acta Informatica, 1, 1 (1971), 35-63.

CONCURRENT PROGRAMMING : MICROCOMPUTERS

R.H. Perrott
Department of Computer Science
The Queen's University
Belfast BT7 1NN

Abstract Concurrent Programming

This paper considers the construction of algorithms in a concurrent programming environment where several microcomputers share the same memory or each microcomputer has its own local memory. Not only does a programmer require the abstractions of a sequential programming language but also a means of specifying and controlling parallel activity.

There are two major situations in which processes or tasks need to be controlled; when they are competing for a shared variable or when they are co-operating to their mutual benefit. Two major techniques have been proposed to solve these problems namely, monitors with condition variables and message passing primitives. The evolution of both techniques is examined.

Finally two concurrent programming languages, namely Pascal Plus and Ada which are based on these techniques are considered. The Bounded Buffer Problem is used to illustrate the different program design and construction methods required when using such techniques.

CONCURRENT PROGRAMMING

1. Introduction

In a sequential programming environment each time a program is submitted for execution with the same data the series of states which the machine passes through is identical and the results obtained are the same. Each instruction is executed without interference by the other instructions.

In a multiprogramming system the processing unit is switched from one program to another, causing their instructions to be interleaved at (unpredictable) points in their execution. While in a multiprocessor system more than one program can be active at the same time but each proceeds autonomously with its execution. In such systems the programs will interact and affect each other's progress.

The term process is used to describe a sequence of program instructions that can be performed in parallel with other program instructions. The point at which a processor is withdrawn from one process and given to another is dependent on the progress of the processes and the algorithm used to assign the processor(s). The simple and well-defined processor allocation strategy of a sequential system is replaced in order to achieve greater processor utilisation. The nett effect is that processes are independent and thus capable of interacting in a time-dependent manner. The series of states which the system passes through is not necessarily identical when the same batch of programs is presented with the same data for execution.

Thus in this concurrent programming environment a programmer requires not only program and data structures similar to those required in a sequential programming environment but also tools to control the interaction of the processes.

The situations in which the processes interact can be divided into two categories. The first occurs whenever processes wish to update a shared variable or a resource at the same time (or in an interleaved fashion). For example, when one process wishes to use a resource which is currently reserved by another process. A process must be able to carry out such actions without interference from the other processes; this is described as mutual exclusion. The second category occurs when processes are co-operating on some task, they must be correctly interleaved in time. For example, when one process requires a result not yet produced by another process. The processes are communicating or scheduling one another and are now aware of each other's existence and purpose; this is described as process synchronisation.

In the sequel some of the techniques which have either been proposed or used to solve these synchronisation problems are considered. The pedagogical approach as first illustrated by Dijkstra [7] is used to examine the problem of mutual exclusion and to determine the properties required of any technique. An examination of process synchronisation is then carried out.

Finally, two concurrent programming languages are considered, these languages have each chosen a different synchronisation technique, monitors and message passing respectively.

2. Mutual Exclusion

To illustrate the problem of mutual exclusion, consider a concurrent system in which it is required to keep a count of the number of completed output commands issued by all the processes. A shared variable 'count' can be used to represent this number, and inside each process the instruction 'count := count+1' should be placed after each output instruction. The inserted instructions will translate into several machine code instructions and if two processes execute these instructions simultaneously (or in an interleaved fashion) then the number of lines output by the processes may be counted incorrectly.

The instruction

```
count := count+1;
```

may translate to the following sequence of pseudo-machine instructions

```
LD   count
AD     1
STO  count
```

Thus if two processes are allowed to execute this sequence simultaneously the following interleaving of instructions may occur.

```
LD   count (* process 1 *)
LD   count (* process 2 *)
AD     1   (* process 2 *)
STO  count (* process 2 *)
AD     1   (* process 1 *)
STO  count (* process 1 *)
```

The effect of these two simultaneous increases is to increase the value of count by only one. This will occur on rare but unpredictable occasions which are unlikely to be detected by program testing. To avoid such a situation occurring requires the introduction of a critical section, i.e. a section of code which can only be executed by one process at a time which, once started, will be able to be finished without interruption. Such sections of code should be as short as possible to avoid, as far as is possible, other processes being delayed while they are being executed.

2.1 A Software Solution

An interesting question arises as to whether it is possible to protect a critical section by software, using only the assumption that individual accesses to storage locations are indivisible, that is, if several processes attempt to store or access a single value in a particular location the hardware decides arbitrarily which one succeeds first. Under this assumption a positive answer was first given for the two process case by the Dutch mathematician Dekker and for the general case of N processes by Dijkstra [6, 7].

Several attempts to achieve the mutual exclusion of two cyclic processes, each with a critical section, are now considered. Each solution is introduced to solve a defect in a preceding solution; the unsatisfactory solutions help to illustrate the pitfalls to be avoided and the criteria to be fulfilled when solving a mutual exclusion (or process synchronisation) problem.

(a) As a first attempt at achieving mutual exclusion for two concurrent processes assume that the critical sections be protected by a variable 'door' which takes the values 'open' and 'closed' only. If the value of 'door' is closed it means that one of the processes has entered its critical section; if it is open then a process can enter its critical section. A possible solution, on this basis, for the two process case could be coded as shown in Figure 1,in order to aid the clarity of the solution only the main parts of the processes is given.

```
var door : (open, closed) ;   (* shared *)
   door := open ;   (* initially the critical section is unoccupied *)

     (* process 1 *)                  (* process 2 *)
repeat until door = open ;       repeat until door = open ;
door := closed ;                 door := closed ;
   critical section 1 ;             critical section 2 ;
door := open ;                   door := open ;
```

Figure 1

The critical sections are protected by a single variable 'door'

An examination of the code of either process gives the impression that mutual exclusion is guaranteed. Unfortunately the processes communicate via the shared variable 'door' and it is possible for both processes to find the door open at the same time. Hence, in good faith, both processes will enter their critical section at the same time. Thus communication by means of a single variable is not sufficient to guarantee mutual exclusion.

(b) Now consider the use of a variable to order the processes as they try to enter their critical sections. For example consider the introduction an integer variable 'turn' which has the value 1 when process 1 is able to enter its critical section and the value 2 when process 2 is able to enter its critical section. On this basis the solution given in Figure 2 has been constructed.

```
var turn : 1..2 ;    (* shared *)
    turn := 1 ;   (* initialisation *)

   (* process 1 *)                   (* process 2 *)
repeat until turn = 1 ;          repeat until turn = 2 ;
   critical section 1  ;             critical section 2 ;
turn := 2 ;                      turn := 1 ;
```

Figure 2

Mutual Exclusion

The value of the integer 'turn' indicates which process can enter its critical section

This solution does, in fact, guarantee mutual exclusion but only by placing an unacceptably severe constraint on the two processes, namely, that in the execution of their critical sections, the processes adhere to the order 1, 2, 1, 2, ... etc. Hence, if process 1 stops or goes slower then so must process 2. This solution must therefore be rejected.

(c) This alternation of the processes can be avoided by assigning to each of the processes its own local variable which takes the values 'inside' and 'outside' only; 'inside' indicates that the process wants to enter or has entered its critical section; 'outside' indicates that the process is outside its critical section. Each process can examine its competitor's variable before entering its critical section as shown in Figure 3.

```
var process1, process2 : (inside, outside) ;
    process1 := outside ; process2 := outside ;        (* initialisation *)

   (* process1 *)                       (* process 2 *)
process1 := inside ;                 process2 := inside ;
repeat until process2 = outside ;    repeat until process1 = outside ;
   critical section 1 ;                  critical section 2 ;
process1 := outside ;                process2 := outside ;
```

Figure 3

Mutual Exclusion

Each process has its own variable which indicates if it wishes to enter or is outside its critical section

In this solution there is no shared variable and the halting of one process outside its critical section will not affect the progress of the other process. However a new difficulty arises. If both processes simultaneously make the assignments

process1 := inside ; process2 := inside

then both processes will loop indefinitely each waiting for the other process to take action.

(d) The infinite looping mentioned in the last solution arises because the processes always wait for each other to take action whenever a conflict occurs. If instead the process which detects that both processes are trying to enter their critical sections changed its value perhaps the problem could be solved. A solution with this strategy is given in Figure 4.

```
var process1, process2 : (inside, outside) ;
   process1 := outside ; process2 := outside ; (* initialisation *)
   (* process1 *)                          (* process2 *)
   repeat                                  repeat
      process1 := inside ;                    process2 := inside ;
      if process2 = inside then               if process1 = inside then
         process1 := outside ;                   process2 := outside ;
      repeat until process2 = outside         repeat until process1 = outside
   until process1 = inside ;               until process2 = inside ;
      critical section 1 ;                    critical section 2 ;
   process1 := outside ;                   process2 := outside ;
```

Figure 4

Mutual Exclusion

Each process is willing to let the other process proceed whenever a conflict occurs

Unfortunately, showing consideration towards the other process can also lead to blocking if both the processes are proceeding exactly in step. An everyday example of the occurrence of this type of situation is when two subscribers telephone each other and encounter the engaged tone. They will continue to fail to communicate if both replace their receivers and try again, after the same interval of time.

(e) Dekker was the first to present a correct solution which avoided the earlier difficulties. His solution is essentially a combination of the two previous proposals, i.e. each process has its own value to indicate if it wishes to enter its critical section and, whenever both processes try to do so simultaneously, an integer variable is used to resolve the conflict. The solution is given in Figure 5.

```
var process1, process2 : (inside, outside) ;
   turn : 1..2 ;
   process1 := outside ; process2 := outside ;          (* initialisation *)
   turn := 1 ;

   (* process 1 *)                              (* process 2 *)
process1 := inside ;                        process2 := inside ;
if process2 = inside then                   if process1 = inside then
begin                                       begin
   if turn = 2 then                            if turn = 1 then
   begin                                       begin
      process1 := outside ;                       process2 := outside ;
      repeat until turn = 1 ;                     repeat until turn = 2 ;
      process1 := inside                          process2 := inside
   end ;                                       end ;
   repeat until process2 = outside             repeat until process1 = outside
end ;                                       end ;
   critical section 1 ;                        critical section 2 ;
turn := 2 ; process1 := outside ;           turn := 1 ; process2 := outside ;
```

Figure 5

Mutual Exclusion

Dekker's solution for two processes

As before, in this solution, a process operates only on its own process variable and inspects the other process's variable if its own is set to 'inside'. It will only enter its critical section provided the other process is outside its critical section. The integer 'turn' is used to resolve conflicts by enabling the process which has its process number currently assigned to 'turn' to enter its critical section (after the other process has given up its attempt to enter). On exit it changes the value of 'turn' and the other process can now enter its critical section. Hence blocking cannot occur. Whenever a conflict does occur it is resolved in a finite time.

Dijkstra [6] considered the more general problem of providing mutual exclusion for N cyclic processes, each with a critical section. As in the two processes case, each process has its own variable to indicate that it wishes to enter its critical section and an integer variable 'turn' is used to ensure that only one process does.

The provision of mutual exclusion using this method is cumbersome and impractical. However, the development of the solution does illustrate the conditions which are required by any technique which claims to guarantee mutual exclusion, namely:

(i) at any moment there can be at most one process inside a critical section;

(ii) the stopping of one process outside its critical section does not affect the other processes;

(iii) no assumptions can be made about the relative speeds of the processes;

(iv) processes about to enter a critical section should not block each other indefinitely.

A detailed examination of the software solution has enabled a fuller understanding of the mutual exclusion problem from a theoretical point of view. The following sections consider more practical methods which have either been proposed or used.

2.2 Disabling Interrupts

Historically, the first solution to the mutual exclusion problem was achieved by hardware. The hardware, by means of an interrupt, was used to indicate when an entry to a critical section was being attempted by a process. When only one processor is being used the only possible cause of interleaving sequences of instructions from different processes is therefore an interrupt. Hence, if on each occasion that a process wishes to enter a critical section it disables further interrupts and, on exit, allows interrupts, then the mutual exclusion of the various competing processes can be guaranteed.

If there is more than one processor, the hardware must ensure that only one processor can disable interrupts at any time; otherwise mutual exclusion will not be guaranteed. Hence the interrupts are always handled by the same processor and no interleaving of the critical sections can occur.

The advantage of such a technique is the simplicity and the efficiency of its implementation; the critical sections are catered for without complex coding.

However the ability to disable (and allow) interrupts is spread throughout the system and must be programmed very carefully. Also the disabling of interrupts is not selective, i.e. large and probably important parts of the system are prohibited from general use and this can cause other processes to be delayed, especially if the critical sections are long.

2.3 The Exchange Instruction

The earlier software solution assumed only the indivisibility of single store accesses. However, if two particular operations could be performed without interruption, such as exchanging the value of a location with (say) a local register of a process then mutual exclusion can be programmed much more easily. For this purpose a global variable 'exclusion' is initially set to a unit value. Before entering a critical section a process must acquire the unit value stored in 'exclusion' and set the value of 'exclusion' to zero in a single indivisible operation. At the end of the critical section, the process returns the unit value to 'exclusion'. Since there is only one unit value in the system at most one process can acquire it at any time. If, however, a prócess is unable to enter its critical section it must loop continually, this is called the busy form of waiting; when the exclusion is released one and only one of the looping processes must proceed. This method of solution is illustrated in Figure 6.

```
var exclusion : 0..1 ;    (* shared *)
   exclusion := 1 ;    (* initialisation *)
           (* process x *)
var   local : 0..1 ;
      local := 0 ;
      while local = 0 do exchange (local, exclusion) ;
         critical section x ;
      exclusion := 1 ;

where          exchange (local, exclusion) ;
               begin
                  local := exclusion ;    (* indivisible *)
                  exclusion := 0          (* operation *)
               end ;
```

Figure 6

Mutual exclusion using the exchange instruction

This technique may be acceptable if there is little demand for the resource and if the critical sections are short, i.e. the amount of busy waiting is not a substantial overhead.

2.4 Binary Semaphores

A common characteristic of the previous techniques is that if a process is trying to enter its critical section and it is unable to do so it will waste processing power.

It is preferable that a process which is unable to enter its critical section goes to sleep and is woken up whenever the access to its critical section becomes possible.

On the basis of this idea Dijkstra [7] introduced the Boolean or binary semaphore; this is an integer variable taking only the values 0 or 1. Only two operations are permitted on a semaphore (other than initialisation).

(i) a P operation which causes the value to be decreased by 1 (provided it is not already zero)

(ii) a V operation which causes the value to be increased by 1 (provided it is not already 1).

Every critical section now has a semaphore associated with it (initially 1) and a process wishing to enter its critical section performs a P operation; the process is allowed to do so only if the decremented semaphore has the value zero. Otherwise the process goes to sleep and its processor can be redeployed.

On exit from a critical section the process performs a V operation which causes the value of the semaphore to be increased by 1; if there are any sleeping processes one of them is allowed to proceed.

Hence a process remains blocked until another process indicates that it is now safe for it to continue.

The operations P and V are indivisible and only one process can execute a P or V operation at any time on a given semaphore. Hence mutual exclusion can be obtained by merely bracketing the critical sections by the primitives P and V on the chosen semaphore as shown in Figure 7.

```
var mutex : semaphore ;
   mutex := 1 ;   (* initialisation *)

   (* process x *)
   P(mutex) ;
      critical section x ;
   V(mutex) ;
```

Figure 7

Mutual exclusion using a binary semaphore

Now a process waits if it is unable to enter a critical section and its processor can be more profitably employed.

The primitive operations on semaphores can be implemented in hardware, but normally are implemented by software under the protection of disabled interrupts. A queueing technique is used to avoid the busy form of waiting with the insertion and removal of processes being performed under disabled interrupts. For example, if 'mutex' is a binary semaphore then the P and V operations have the following effect:-

```
P(mutex) ≡ if mutex > 0 then mutex := mutex - 1
                        else 'wait on the queue associated with mutex' ;

V(mutex) ≡ mutex := mutex + 1 ;
           if queue ≠ empty then
           begin
              mutex := mutex - 1 ;
              'remove a process from the queue and execute it'
           end.
```

Semaphores are logically complete but often lead to complex constructions which are difficult to comprehend and sensitive to minor changes. The disadvantages however lie in the need for careful programming. For example if a P primitive is written instead of a **V** primitive then the processes are blocked indefinitely.

2.5 Simple Critical Regions

To help alleviate the coding problems of the correct use of semaphores it is possible to employ a high-level language construct which will be translated by a compiler into one of the former techniques described above. Such a language construct, as suggested by Hoare [10] is the <u>simple critical region</u>

<u>with</u> R <u>do</u> S ;

which permits the critical statements S to operate on the shared variable R.

The notation removes the necessity of writing P and V around the set of critical statements S, and removes the burden of checking that the entry and exit to critical sections are properly complemented, and in the correct order. Furthermore, the compiler checks that shared variables are used only inside critical regions and the updating of shared variables is thus protected. The programming effort and the likelihood of error is therefore reduced.

The implementation of critical regions is relatively straightforward if there is a hardware **or** software semaphore available. The declaration of a shared variable causes a binary semaphore to be created and each critical section is preceded by a P, and followed by a V operation.

2.6 Monitors

Another approach to the mutual exclusion problem is to gather together the shared variables and the operations which can be performed on this data into a single construct; such a construct is called a <u>monitor</u> or secretary (Brinch Hánsen [3]; Dijkstra [8]; Hoare [11]). The monitor therefore collects all the critical sections into a single structure and only one process can have access to this structure at any time. The critical sections are removed from the bodies of the processes and become procedures or functions of a monitor. Whenever a process wishes to enter its critical section it invokes the appropriate procedure of the monitor; only one process can succeed in entering the monitor at any time and any subsequent calls of monitor procedures must wait until the monitor becomes free.

The language construct takes the form

```
monitor monitorname ;
... declaration of local data ... ;
    procedure procname (parameter list) ;
       begin ... procedure body ... end ;
    ... declaration of other local procedures ... ;
begin
... initialisation of local data ...
end ;
```

The monitor procedures should not access any non-local variables other than those local to the monitor in which they are declared and these non-local variables should be inaccessible from outside the monitor. If these restrictions are imposed it is possible to guarantee mutual exclusion.

On declaration the monitor initialises its local data and all subsequent calls use the values of the local variables obtained on completion of the previous call. To invoke a monitor procedure the monitorname and the required procedure and its parameters are specified as follows

monitorname.procname (actual parameters).

3. Process Synchronisation

The previous techniques can be used to organise processes whenever they are competing for the use of some shared resource or variable. Now we consider situations where the processes wish to co-operate with each other and are therefore to some extent aware of each other's purpose. In such circumstances they are still competing to gain entry to a critical section, but once this has been achieved their actions within the critical section may make a condition true which previously had caused another process to be delayed. Hence some method is required to enable a process to indicate that a particular event has occurred (or to wait until a particular event has occurred). The emphasis is now on finding ways of ensuring that processes co-operate with each other to their mutual benefit, i.e. process synchronisation.

3.1 General Semaphores

Dijkstra introduced the general semaphore which can be used for process synchronisation. This is an integer variable taking only non-negative values, and the only operations which can be applied to it are the P and V primitive operations. If the semaphore is zero a process attempting a P operation is suspended and waits for another process to perform a V operation. The essential difference between the general and the binary semaphores is that it is possible for several processes to perform a P operation on the general semaphore and continue execution. In fact the effect of a general semaphore can be achieved by using two binary semaphores and a variable, as shown in Figure 8.

```
var mutex, delay : semaphore ;    (* binary semaphore *)
     n : semaphore ;    (* general semaphore *)
    mutex := 1 ;    delay := 0 ;
    n := general semaphore value ;    (* initialisation *)

    P(n) ≡ P(mutex) ;
           n := n - 1 ;
           if n <= -1 then
           begin
              V(mutex) ;    P(delay)
           end else
               V(mutex) ;

    V(n) ≡ P(mutex) ;
           n := n + 1 ;
           if n <= 0 then V(delay) ;
           V(mutex) ;
```

Figure 8

A general semaphore expressed in terms of binary semaphores

To illustrate the use of general semaphores, consider the situation where several processes (producers) wish to communicate a series of items to other processes (the consumers). This can be achieved by means of a buffer of finite capacity into which the producers deposit these items and from which the consumers remove items when ready. The processes must be synchronised in such a way that the producers will not produce when the buffer is full and the consumers will not consume when the buffer is empty. This is known as the bounded buffer problem.

The necessary process synchronisation can be achieved by using general semaphores to represent the possible waiting conditions, namely, a full or an empty buffer. If a general semaphore 'full' is used to represent the number of full buffer elements then a consumer should be delayed when the value of 'full' is zero. Thus, if a producer performs a V operation on 'full' after it has placed an item in the buffer and a consumer performs a P operation before removing an item then the consumers will be delayed whenever the buffer is empty. In a similar fashion a second general semaphore 'empty' can be used to delay producers when necessary. A signal must be given by a consumer process when it is safe for a delayed producer to continue and vice versa. To avoid the overwriting or skipping of any of the items in the buffer these operations must be performed in a mutually exclusive fashion. Consequently a binary semaphore 'mutex' has been introduced as shown in Figure 9.

```
var buffer : array [0..n-1] of message ;    (* shared *)
    insert, remove : 0..n-1 ;
    full, empty : semaphore ;    (* general semaphore *)
    mutex : semaphore ;          (* binary semaphore *)

    insert := 0 ; remove := 0 ; (* initialisation *)
    empty := n ; full := 0 ; mutex := 1 ;
```

```
  (* inside a producer *)                 (* inside a consumer *)
item : message ;                        item : message ;
P(empty) ;                              P(full) ;
P(mutex) ;                              P(mutex) ;
  buffer [insert] := item ;               item := buffer [remove] ;
  insert := (insert+1) mod n ;            remove := (remove+1) mod n ;
V(mutex) ;                              V(mutex) ;
V(full) ;                               V(empty) ;
```

Figure 9

The bounded buffer problem using general semaphores

In general, if a process wishes to wait until a certain condition holds, a semaphore must be associated with this waiting condition and any process which might make this condition true must take the responsibility for performing a V operation on it. Therefore the programmer must build into each process an awareness of the requirements of the other processes. Because of this awareness, even more care is necessary when coding synchronisation problems using semaphores.

If several consumers are waiting they will eventually be scheduled in a neutral manner as the result of V operations after new items are produced. In many cases, however, a more complicated or partisan scheduling algorithm is required, for example, in cases where all of the consumers are not identical. This can be regarded as a disadvantage of using general semaphores for process synchronisation.

3.2 Conditional Critical Regions

To avoid the programming difficulties associated with general semaphores, Hoare [10] introduced the high-level language construct, the conditional critical region

```
with R when B do S ;
```

where B is a Boolean expression and S a critical section operating on the shared variable R. It specifies that the critical section S is to be executed only when the condition B holds; when a process is delayed the mutual exclusion of the critical section is released. Brinch Hansen [1, 2] proposed a generalised construct

```
with R do
begin
   statement1 ;
   await B ;
   statement2
end ;
```

where the 'await' statement is allowed anywhere within the critical section. In this instance, a process can, for example, indicate in 'statement1' a request for a resource and then wait until the resource becomes available.

The conditional critical region is a more natural construct when a process wishes to wait until a certain condition is satisfied, as is illustrated by the solution of the bounded buffer problem in Figure 10.

```
var r : record
          buffer : array [0..n-1] of message ;
          pointer : 0..n-1 ;
          count : 0..n    (* number of items in the buffer *)
        end ;
     r.pointer := 0 ; r.count := 0 ;   (* initialisation *)
```

```
(* inside a producer *)

with r
   when count < n do
   begin
      buffer [(pointer+count) mod n] := item ;
      count := count+1
   end
```

```
(* inside a consumer *)

with r
   when count > 0 do
   begin
      item := buffer [pointer] ;
      pointer := (pointer+1) mod n ;
      count := count-1
   end ;
```

Figure 10

The bounded buffer problem using
conditional critical regions

The implementation of a conditional critical region is possible if the compiler associates a binary semaphore with the resource R. A process first performs a P operation before testing its condition B. If the condition B is false the process joins a queue of processes waiting for the resource and releases exclusion. If, however, the condition B is true the critical section is executed without releasing exclusion. On completion of the critical section the queue of waiting processes must be examined in case any of the conditions has become true. One of the waiting processes whose condition is now satisfied enters the critical section; if none of the waiting processes is able to continue a new request for the critical section can be considered. It is possible, therefore, for a process whose condition B is not immediately satisfied to evaluate its condition B several times before entering its critical section. Brinch Hansen [3] has called this the controlled amount of busy waiting because the retesting is done only occasionally whenever some other process has completed a critical section with respect to the same resource.

If this construction is used with arbitrarily complex conditions it is possible for processes to remain unaware of the synchronisation problems. However in the case of a heavy demand on a resource it is probably necessary to restrict the condition to a simple boolean expression to limit the cost of re-evaluating the conditions.

3.3 Condition variables

Earlier we examined Hoare's monitor as a means of providing mutual exclusion. Hoare also proposed a new data type, the condition variable, which could only be declared within a monitor. This data type is provided for use on occasions when a process wishes to delay itself or re-awaken a previously delayed process.

Condition variables are used to identify queues of waiting processes which are manipulated by the operations 'wait' and 'signal', as follows:

condition variable.signal

and condition variable.wait.

The wait operation deactivates a process and appends it to a queue associated with the specified condition variable; a wait operation automatically releases the exclusion which would otherwise prevent other processes entering the monitor. The signal operation causes the resumption of the first process on a queue associated with the condition variable; if there are no processes waiting the signal operation has no effect. The process which performs a signal operation and causes a delayed process to be resumed is suspended until this process exits the monitor or performs a wait operation.

This form of enforced politeness is necessary in case the condition for resuming a delayed process is subsequently changed by the signalling process or another process intervening. The exclusion is 'passed' from the signalling process to the newly woken process, and the signalling process regains the exclusion and continues execution only when the newly woken process exits the monitor or waits again.

Hence by specifically detailing the conditions under which the processes may be delayed and resumed the scheduling of the processes can be more explicitly handled than with conditional critical regions, i.e. no repeated evaluations are required and each condition variable queue is served on a first come first served basis whenever a signal operation is applied to that condition variable.

To illustrate the properties of the monitor the earlier technique of semaphores is implemented in Figure 11.

```
monitor semaphore ;
var mutex : 0..1 ;
    positive : condition ;
   procedure P ;
   begin
      if mutex = 0 then positive.wait ;
      mutex := mutex - 1
   end ;     (* P *)
   procedure V ;
   begin
      mutex := mutex + 1 ;
      positive.signal
   end ;    (* V *)
begin
   mutex := 1   (* initialisation *)
end ;

(* process 1 *)                      (* process 2 *)
semaphore.P ;                        semaphore.P ;
   critical section 1 ;                 critical section 2 ;
semaphore.V ;                        semaphore.V ;
```

Figure 11

A binary semaphore expressed by means of a monitor

This illustrates a monitor 'semaphore' with two procedures P and V. If a process, after calling the P procedure, finds the value of the semaphore to be zero then it joins the queue associated with the condition variable 'positive'. It will remain there until some other process calls the V procedure, increases **'mutex'** and then signals the first process on the queue 'positive'. As with the semaphore solution previously presented, each critical section must be bracketed by calls to the monitor procedures P and V.

There are situations, however, when first come first served scheduling is inadequate, and to give closer control over the scheduling it is possible, when performing a wait operation, to specify a priority for the process, this takes the form

condition variable.wait(p) ;

where p is an integer. The queue of delayed processes will then be sequenced in order of increasing p and a signal operation activates the highest priority process, i.e. no explicit queue scanning is necessary.

Hence the monitor construct:

(a) combines the requirements of mutual exclusion and process synchronisation;

(b) provides a systematic method of isolating synchronisation problems, i.e. processes no longer need to share data explicitly; instead shared data is gathered together and accessed within the monitor;

(c) provides a systematic method of solving a synchronisation problem, i.e. list the conditions and consider the problem sequentially;

(d) complex process interactions are specifically ordered within the monitor and thus easier to understand.

4. Message Passing Primitives

Message passing primitives, like the previous constructs, were introduced to avoid the problems associated with low level synchronisation primitives. As the name implies the processes pass messages between each other when they wish to communicate. A signal can be thought of as a message with no content which enables processes to be synchronised. The origin of message passing synchronisation techniques is attributed to the work of Conway [5] on coroutines.

Recently two languages CSP [12] and DP [4] have been proposed which provide the programmer with synchronisation primitives based on passing messages. These languages have, in turn, influenced the design of the language Ada.

4.1 Coroutines

In most programming languages when a procedure A calls another procedure B to perform a particular task, the procedure B is regarded as a slave procedure. However, there are many situations in which the relationship would be better expressed in terms of two procedures operating at the same level. To represent this situation Conway introduced the coroutine. This is a block the execution of whose text is not completed before returning control to the calling block and whose execution can be resumed later. In this way both the synchronisation of the procedures and the transmission of any data is combined. This relationship can be easily extended to a system consisting of a set of coroutines.

In a two coroutine system control (and, if necessary, data) is passed back and forth as each is executed. Thus neither coroutine is a slave to the other. This introduces a symmetry into the calling procedure/called procedure structure. For example, a two player game such as chess can be more appropriately represented as a pair coroutines rather than as two player procedures under the control of a third procedure, which would be the case in Pascal. Each coroutine can store its data local to itself rather than non locally as in the procedural representation.

A primitive such as

resume(player)

is required to transfer control to the named **coroutine** which then resumes execution at the point where control was previously relinquished. Another primitive 'detach' is required to return control to the point at which the coroutine was activated. The 'detach' primitive may also play a role in the initialisation of the local data of a coroutine.

For example, the structure of a chess player coroutine could be defined as

```
coroutine player1 ;
begin
   initialise local variables ;
   detach ;    (* return to activating routine *)
   while true do
   begin
      make a move ;
      if game won then
      begin print message ; detach end
      else resume(player 2)    (* call other player *)
   end
end (* player 1 *)
```

When the coroutines are **declared** their local variables are initialised and control is returned to the activating block by executing the 'detach' primitive. When activated again, the coroutines will resume after the (first) 'detach' statement. Subsequently control is passed back and forth between the players by means of the 'resume' primitive.

The parallel activity associated with this particular example is more appropriately described as quasi-parallelism since only one of the processes is active in real time at any moment. However it does provide the basis of the message passing techniques of the next sections.

4.2 Communicating Sequential Processes

Communicating Sequential Processes (CSP) is a language proposed by Hoare [12]. One of the main features of CSP is Dijkstra's guarded commands [9]. Guarded commands are used to express non-deterministic behaviour of processes, in response to, for example, unpredictably ordered external events.

A guarded command consists of a guard, which is a boolean expression followed by a list of statements; the statements may only be executed if the guard is true. Alternative and repetitive constructs may be expressed using guarded command sets. In either case a list of statements belonging to a true guard will be arbitrarily selected for execution from among those whose guards are true.

The alternative and repetitive constructs take the following forms:

```
[guard1 → command1          *[guard1 → command1
□guard2 → command2            □guard2 → command2
□guard3 → command3            □ - - -
□ - - -                       ]
]
```

where □ is used to separate guarded commands and * indicates repetition, 'guardn' is a boolean expression and 'commandn' is a statement or guarded list of the language. For example,

```
[x >= y → m := x
□y >= x → m := y
]
```

If both guards are true either assignment command will be executed. If none are true the process will abort. In a repetitive construct as many iterations as possible are performed, that is, until all the guards are false.

Processes communicate by means of input and output commands. A process 'sender' outputs or sends information to a process 'receiver' by executing a command of the form

receiver! link(values)

and the process 'receiver' inputs or receives information by executing a command of the form

sender? link(variables).

Each process must name the process with which it wishes to communicate. Thus there is a symmetry in the synchronisation relationship. Both the 'link' and the value and the variable lists must correspond if communication is to succeed. The synchronisation of the two processes is known as a rendezvous; they come together, exchange the information and then proceed on their separate ways in parallel. No buffer is required to hold the message as it is passed directly.

Whichever process encounters the input or output statement first will wait for the other process to reach a corresponding output or input statement in which the waiting process is named and then they both execute their communication statement.

To illustrate some of the features of CSP consider the implementation of a general semaphore 'sem' shared among 100 processes.

A process may increment the semaphore by means of a command of the form sem!V(), and decrement the semaphore by sem!P(). In either case no parameters are required. The latter command must not take place if the value of the semaphore is not positive.

The semaphore can be described as follows:-

```
sem :: value : integer ; value := 0 ;    (* initialisation *)
     * [(i : 1..100) X(i) ? V( ) → value := value + 1
       □(i : 1..100) value > 0 ; X(i) ? P( ) → value := value - 1
       ]
```

where (i : 1..100) X(i) ? V( ) → value := value + 1

```
stands for          X(1) ? V( ) → value := value + 1
                   □X(2) ? V( ) → value := value + 1
                   □ - - - -                      etc.
```

On each iteration either a V( ) signal or a P( ) signal from one of the processes is accepted. The second alternative cannot be chosen if the first part of the guard is false, that is if value is less than or equal to zero.

The semaphore will terminate whenever all 100 processes have terminated.

4.3 Distributed Processes

The second language based on message passing primitives was proposed by Brinch Hansen [4] and is known as Distributed Processes (DP). Communication between processes is achieved by one process calling a procedure defined in the process with which it wishes to communicate. The parameter list of this procedure is used as a channel for the transfer of data between the processes.

One process 'sender' would execute a command of the form

<u>call</u> receiver.link (values, variables)

where the process 'receiver' contains a procedure declaration of the form

<u>procedure</u> link (value parameters# result parameters)
    (* body of link *)

The value parameters carry information from the process 'sender' to the process 'receiver', the result parameters carry information back.

A process which calls a procedure of another procedure is delayed until the requested execution of the procedure is completed.

A major difference between this mechanism and the CSP communication mechanism is that the process defining a procedure need not identify processes which call it. Thus there is an asymmetric relationship between the called and the calling processes.

It is argued that this structure is useful in programming a service task, particularly a library task, which may not or cannot know the identity of its users. If it is necessary to distinguish between callers this requirement must be catered for explicitly.

Non-determinism has been introduced to the language by means of guarded commands in the 'if' and 'do' statements. Special 'when' and 'cycle' statements are used to express waiting. The 'when' statement takes the form

<u>when</u> guard1 : command1 | guard2 : command2 - - - <u>end</u>

and means wait until one of the conditions is true and execute the corresponding statement. The 'cycle' statement means endless repetition of a 'when' statement. If several guards are true within either statement then it is unpredictable which one will be selected.

A general semaphore can be implemented as a process semaphore which defines P and V operations as follows:

```
process semaphore ; value : int (* integer *)
   proc V ; value := value + 1
   proc P when value > 0 ; value := value - 1 end
   value := 0    (* initialisation *)
```

The initialisation statement is executed first after which the process waits for requests from other processes to use its procedures, by invocations of the form

<u>call</u> semaphore.P or <u>call</u> semaphore.V

If the process 'semaphore' is to be used by a 100 processes this fact is not apparent in its definition since the identity of a calling process is not required, as was the case in CSP.

5. Concurrent Programming Languages

In this section two concurrent programming languages, namely Ada [13] and Pascal-plus [14] are considered. These languages are based on the synchronisation techniques of message passing and monitors with condition variables respectively. Only the concurrent facilities of each language are described and these are then illustrated by means of the bounded buffer problem. The solutions illustrate the main considerations which must be addressed in a parallel programming environment as well as enabling a comparison of the two languages to be made.

5.1 Pascal-plus

Pascal-plus, as its name implies, is an extension of Pascal. The extensions are of three types:-

(i) the envelope structure which is an aid to program modularisation and data abstraction;

(ii) the process, monitor and condition structures which provide a means of representing parallel processes and controlling any subsequent interaction;

(iii) a simulation monitor, which provides pseudo-time control facilities for parallel programs.

Only the features listed in (ii) will be examined. These features are essentially a realisation of the monitor and condition structures described previously.

Processes are used to identify independent action which may take place in parallel. After a process has been defined, instances of it can be declared. Once activated the processes proceed conceptually in parallel.

A process is defined as a block with a suitable heading which may include parameters. For example,

```
process producer ;
   - local data  definitions and declarations -
begin
   - statements of producer -
end (* producer *)
instance
   beel, bee2 : producer ;
```

The last statement activates two processes which may subsequently run in parallel. The monitor construct can be used to ensure that shared data is protected when processes wish to interact with each other. The shared data can only be accessed and updated by a single process at a time by means of the procedures of the monitor.

If a process enters a monitor it may have to be suspended pending the action of another process; this is achieved by means of condition queues. The user can declare these queues in the form

```
instance empty : condition ;
```

To suspend itself on a condition queue a process performs a wait operation expressed as

```
empty.wait
```

and the mutual exclusion of the monitor is released.

To release a process from a queue another process performs a signal operation indicating to the signalled process that the reason for its delay no longer holds. This operation is expressed as

```
empty.signal.
```

When a process signals, it immediately passes control to the process at the head of the condition queue. The signalling process is delayed until the awoken process releases the exclusion of the monitor; a signal operation has no effect if no process is waiting.

To give closer control over the scheduling of the processes a 'pwait' primitive may be used which specifies a priority in the form of a non negative integer parameter,

```
empty.pwait(i)
```

The processes are then queued in the order of decreasing priority. The length of a queue can be obtained using the instruction

```
empty.length
```

if there are processes waiting. The priority of the first process can be determined

```
empty.priority.
```

A solution to the bounded buffer problem is now given. The structure of the monitor which protects the buffer takes the following form.

```
type message = 'definition' ;

monitor boundedbuffer ;

var buffer : array [0..(n-1)] of message ;
    pointer : 0..n-1 ;
    count : 0..n ; (* number of items in buffer *)
instance empty, full : condition ;

procedure * deposit (item : message) ;
begin
   if count = n then full.wait ;
   buffer [(pointer + count) mod n] := item ;
   count := count + 1 ;
   empty.signal
end ; (* deposit *)

procedure * remove (var item : message) ;
begin
   if count = 0 then empty.wait ;
   item := buffer [pointer] ;
   count := count - 1 ;
   pointer := (pointer + 1) mod n ;
   full.signal
end ; (* remove *)

begin
   count := 0 ; pointer := 0
end (* bounded buffer *)
```

The procedures 'deposit' and 'remove' are starred indicating that they may be called from outside the monitor. The value of the variable 'count' determines whether a process should or should not be delayed.

An instance of this monitor can then be declared and the starred produces called as shown below.

```
instance buffer1 : boundedbuffer ;
process producer ;
var item : message ;
begin
   repeat
      'produce item'
      buffer1.deposit (item) ;
   until finished ;
end ; (* producer *)

process consumer ;
var item : message ;
begin
   repeat
      buffer1.remove (item) ;
      'consume item'
   until finished
end ; (* consumer *)

instance
      p : array [1..x] of producer ;
      c : array [1..y] of consumer ;
   (* x producers and y consumers are activated *)

begin
end.
```

Figure 12

A bounded buffer solution using monitors

5.2 Ada

The programming language Ada was commissioned by the U.S. Department of Defense specifically for their embedded computer systems. All four of the potential language designs were based on Pascal.

The major features of the language are

(i) strong typing enabling more errors to be detected at compile time;

(ii) mechanisms for encapsulation and separate compilation;

(iii) exception handling to give the user control of error recovery;

(iv) data abstraction, private data types and representation specifications which separate the abstract properties of data from its physical realisation;

(v) generic units, the ability to parameterise units over appropriate data types;

(vi) tasking, the program units for concurrent programming.

It is the last topic which will be considered in more detail.

In Ada 'task' rather than 'process' is used to indicate a sequence of actions which are conceptually executed in parallel with other actions.

The definition of a task consists of two parts, its specification and its body. The specification part may contain type, subprogram and entry specifications (see later); the task body contains the sequence of statements to be executed when the task is initiated. For example, -- indicates a comment in Ada,

```
    task      producer is
       -- specification
    end ;
    task body producer is
       -- body
    end producer ;
 begin -- active here
 end ;
```

The task automatically becomes active, its body is executed, when the 'begin' statement is reached. The task terminates normally by reaching the final end. The procedure in which the task is declared cannot be left until all tasks in that procedure have terminated.

Several tasks with similar characteristics can be declared such as

beel, bee2 : producer.

The language does not specify the order in which the tasks are activated.

The communication method used in Ada closely resembles that of Distributed Processes; one task calls a procedure defined in another task and the parameter list is used to provide for the transfer of data.

The task specification section is used to declare the procedures which other tasks can call. For this reason they are referred to as entry procedures. For example, the specification of a task 'bounded buffer' is described by

```
task boundedbuffer is
   entry deposit (item : in message) ;
   entry remove (item : out message) ;
end ;
```

indicating that it will accept calls to the procedures 'deposit' and 'remove' from other tasks. In the body of the task 'bounded buffer' more details of the entry procedures must be given in the following form:-

```
accept deposit (item : in message) do
   - - - - -
end ;
   - - - - -
accept remove (item : out message) do
   - - - - -
end ;
```

To use any of the entry procedures another task must make a call of the form

boundedbuffer.deposit (item) ;

Whichever task reaches its communication statement first, that is, the accept or call statement, waits for the other task. At the rendezvous the parameters are transferred and the body of the accept statement executed. The calling task is held up and can only proceed when the execution of the accept statement has been completed. The two tasks then proceed independently. Thus the synchronisation of the tasks is implicit.

As in DP the synchronisation is asymmetric, the called task is named by the caller but not vice versa. Associated with each entry there is a single queue of waiting tasks which are processed on a first come first served basis.

Non determinism has been introduced by means of the select statement. The select statement enables a choice among several entry calls to be specified. For example,

```
select
   accept deposit (item : in message) do
   - - -
   end ;
or
   accept remove (item : out message) do
   - - -
   end ;
end select ;
```

If neither of the entry procedures has been called the task waits; if one of them has been called it is executed; if both have been called then either one is selected and executed.

A conditional execution of a select alternative can be introduced by means of a 'when' statement, this is equivalent to a guarded command. For example,

```
when count < n =>
   accept deposit (item : in message) do
   - - -
   end ;
```

will ensure that the value of 'count' is less than n before the accept statement is activated. A solution for the bounded buffer problem is now given in Figure 13.

```
task boundedbuffer is
   entry deposit (item : in message) ;
   entry remove (item : out message) ;
end boundedbuffer ;
task body boundedbuffer is

   buffer : array (0..n-1) of message ;
   pointer : integer range 0..n-1 := 0 ; - - initially 0
   count : integer range 0..n := 0 ; - - initially 0

begin
   loop
      select
         when count < n =>
            accept deposit (item : in message) do
               buffer ((pointer + count) mod n) := item ;
            end ;
            count := count + 1 ;

      or

         when count > 0 =>
            accept remove (item : out message) do
               item := buffer (pointer) ;
            end ;
            pointer := (pointer + 1) mod n ;
            count := count - 1 ;
      end select ;
   end loop ;
end boundedbuffer ;
```

The producer and consumer tasks can be defined as follows:-

```
task producer is
end ;

task body producer is
   item : message ;
begin
   loop
      - - produce an item
      boundedbuffer.deposit (item) ;
   end loop
end producer ;
task consumer is
end ;
task body consumer is
   item : message ;
begin
   loop
      boundedbuffer.remove (item) ;
      - - process item
   end loop ;
end consumer ;
```

Figure 13

A bounded buffer solution based on message passing

The 'accept' statements are the critical sections and the calling task is delayed while an accept statement is executed. However the updating of the variables 'pointer' and 'count' is not part of the critical sections which was the case in the monitor solution.

The Pascal-Plus and Ada solutions to the bounded buffer problem illustrate the essential differences between these two synchronisation methods. In Ada the transfer of data is direct and synchronised while in Pascal-Plus it is through a passive abstract data structure. These two different communication techniques require different program design methods.

In Ada the buffer is represented as a task with the synchronisation specified in terms of entry, select and accept operators while in Pascal-Plus the condition, wait and signal are used to control the buffer. In both cases the buffer is accessed in a mutually exclusive manner. In Ada the tidying-up operations, for example, the adjustment of the value of the variable 'count' can be performed without delaying the calling process.

6. Summary

In a concurrent programming environment a programmer requires not only program and data structures to represent those parts of the program which can conceptually proceed in parallel but also a means of controlling the interaction of such parts. The need to control such interaction arises when information is to be exchanged or the progress of one process depends on another.

The first major step forward in this area was the introduction of the semaphore to regulate the parallel activity. However semaphores can lead to programs which are difficult to write and understand and which are sensitive to minor change. To avoid such difficulties critical regions and conditional critical regions were introduced. These, in turn, evolved into the monitor with condition variables. Such a structure gathers together the critical sections and the operations upon the critical sections into one structure. The monitor is best suited to a configuration in which the processors share a common memory.

A second approach to the synchronisation of processes is that of message passing. In this approach the processes rendezvous to exchange information and then continue their activity in parallel and independently. Such a technique is best suited to a system in which each processor has its own local memory.

Acknowledgement

I would like to express my thanks to Maurice Clint for his criticisms and suggestions on an earlier draft of this material.

7. References

1. Brinch Hansen, P. (1972a).
   A comparison of two synchronising concepts.
   Acta Informatica 1. 190-199.

2. Brinch Hansen, P. (1972b).
   Structured multiprogramming.
   Comm. ACM. 15, 574-578.

3. Brinch Hansen, P. (1973).
   Operating Systems Principles.
   Prentice-Hall, Englewood Cliffs, New Jersey.

4. Brinch Hansen, P. (1978).
   Distributed Processes.
   Comm. ACM. 21, 11, 934-940.

5. Conway, M.E. (1963).
   Design of a separate transition-diagram compiler.
   Comm. ACM. 6, 7, 396-408.

6. Dijkstra, E.W. (1965).
Solution of a problem in concurrent programming control.
Comm. ACM. 8, 569.

7. Dijkstra, E.W. (1968).
Co-operating Sequential Processes.
in Programming Languages. (F. Genuys, ed.), 43-112.
Academic Press, London and New York.

8. Dijkstra, E.W. (1972).
Hierarchical Ordering of Sequential Processes.
in Operating Systems Techniques. (C.A.R. Hoare and R.H. Perrott, eds.)
72-9 , Academic Press, London and New York.

9. Dijkstra, E.W. (1975).
Guarded commands, non-determinacy, and formal deriviation of problems.
Comm. ACM. 18, 8, 453-457.

10. Hoare, C.A.R. (1972).
Towards a theory of parallel programming.
in Operating Systems Techniques. (C.A.R. Hoare and R.H. Perrott, eds.)
6I-7 , Academic Press, London and New York.

11. Hoare, C.A.R. (1974).
Monitors : An operating system structuring concept.
Comm. ACM. 17, 10, 549-557.

12. Hoare, C.A.R. (1978).
Communicating sequential processes.
Comm. ACM. 21, 8, 666-677.

13. Ichbiah, J.D. et al. (1979).
Preliminary ADA Reference Manual.
Sigplan Notices, 14, 6.

14. Welsh, J. and Bustard, D.W. (1979).
Pascal-Plus - Another Language for Modular Multi-programming.
Software - Practice and Experience, 9, 947-957.

MICROCOMPUTER OPERATING SYSTEMS

N R Harris, Department of Computer Science, Trinity College, University of Dublin, Dublin 2.

The purpose of these lectures is to introduce some of the fundamental concepts of operating systems and to show their relation to one another. With the advent of relatively cheap processing power and memory some of the premises on which operating systems were designed are no longer true, hence the important areas for future operating systems for microcomputers are indicated.

Operating systems are introduced with a discussion of an early spooling operating system and a multi access system. This is followed by a discussion of the components of operating systems. The impact of distributed systems on operating system design is left to the distributed systems lectures [3].

1. INTRODUCTION

In the 1950's many computers were used in a stand alone manner [1]. Users booked the computer for a period of time, loaded in their program and tested it. When the program failed they made changes to the program, usually in memory, and proceeded to execute their program again. After many iterations of this procedure the user handed over the computer to the next user and went off to reflect on the success of his debugging session. The user then returned the next day (or night) to continue his debugging. Only one user had access to the computer at a time hence using the system very inefficiently. Also the user worked with a bare machine and wrote all his own software. This led to inefficient use of the user's time and the re-invention of the wheel by many users. The first piece of system software was the subroutine library. This allowed users to share common routines hence increasing their productivity. The inefficient use of computer hardware was partly overcome by the use of a basic operating system. User jobs were batched in a card reader and were read into memory and executed. The usual output was a listing of the program and results if any, together with a complete listing of the contents of memory if the program halted. The user then spent many hours studying the memory listing trying to work out why the program failed. Then operating systems were developed for large systems in order to use them more effectively. These were batch oriented with the input read from punched cards and output printed on a line printer. Online spooling operating systems which provided more efficient use of the CPU followed and finally multi-access time sharing operating systems arrived. The premise on which these operating systems were based was that the CPU was expensive and hence must be kept busy. First of all input/output to slow devices like card readers and line printers was replaced by input/output to disks. Also efforts were made to execute a number of jobs concurrently so when the CPU was not executing one job it could pass on to another job and hence keep itself busy. Many useful principles can be learned by studying operating systems for large machines and many of these principles may be applied directly to micro computer operating systems.

Operating systems for micro computers have evolved along the same lines as the large systems. Initially micro computers are used, and many still are, in a stand alone mode. Operating systems have developed from simple single user systems to multi-access time sharing systems and are just as complex as their large parents. While many of the components of large operating systems apply directly to micro computers the relative importance of the components is different. There is not so much need to use processors efficiently because they are cheap and often many processors may be used instead of the normal one processor system. In contrast memory is still relatively expensive and users normally desire more than is available hence memory must be managed efficiently. Disk storage may be the most expensive part of a micro computer system and the tendency is towards sharing this storage. The development in micro computer operating systems is towards the operating system being distributed, towards the use of many CPUs working together and towards the use of local networks. Hence the development in micro computer operating systems is the coherent use of multiple CPUs and the controlled sharing of data.

This paper concentrates on the components of operating systems and highlights the areas which are important for micro computers. Distributed systems are discussed in later lectures [3].

2. SPOOLING OPERATING SYSTEM

An insight into the structure and components of a simple operating system may be obtained by considering a spooling operating system. It was a very familiar operating system in the 1960's . It processed a batch of jobs from an input device, usually a card reader, and produced output on a line printer. Each job, including its' data, is submitted on punched cards and is preceeded by appropriate control cards. The jobs are read from the card reader and stored in an input queue on disk. They are then selected from this input queue and executed one at a time by the processor. All input for a job comes from the input queue and all output from the job goes to the output queue on disk. The output for all the jobs is held on the output queue on disk and it is selected, one at a time, for printing on the line printer. A hardware configuration to support this operating system is shown in figure 1.

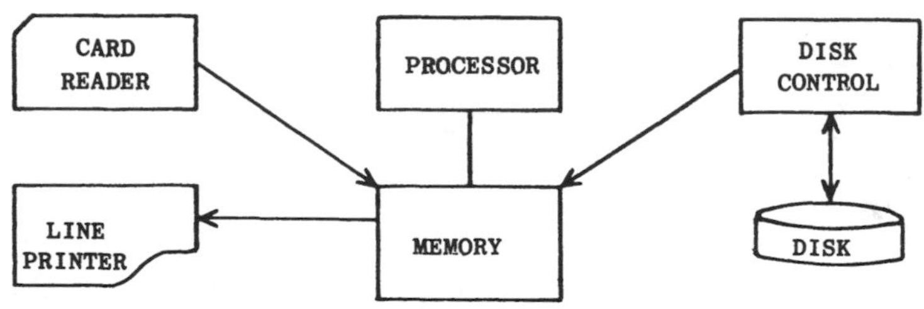

Figure 1.

The operating system is structured to consist of three almost independent parts. The first part reads the input jobs from the card reader and stores them on the input queue. This is called input spooling. The second part chooses a job from the input queue and supervises its' execution by the processor. This is called the job supervisor part. The final part chooses the output of a job from the output queue and lists it on the line printer and this is called the output spooler. The execution of the parts may overlap in time so that the input spooler is reading in a job while another job is executing, and at the same time the output of another job is being listed on the line printer. These parts of the operating system are called processes and when their execution is overlapped they are called concurrent processes. Concurrent processes are achieved by the processor executing one process for a short period of time, usually until the process requests input/output and then the processor executes another process and continues to switch from one process to another. This gives the impression of concurrent processes all executing at the same time. A basic piece of software called a kernel or nucleus provides the facilities for switching the processor from one process to another and for the support of concurrent processes. The processes are executed almost independently of one another. The only restrictions are that a job must be read into the input queue before it is executed. Likewise the job must be executed and have its output on the output queue before the output is listed on the line printer. The precedence constraints of the input spooler (IS), job supervisor (JS) and output spooler (OS), while running a number of jobs, are shown in figure 2.

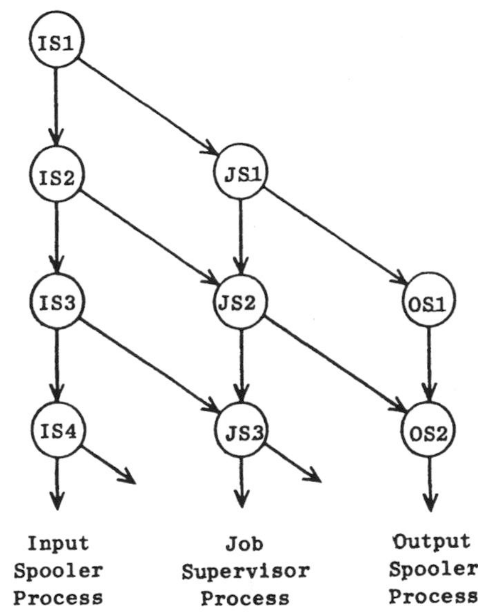

Figure 2.

The vertical arrows show the sequence of reading, execution, and listing of the jobs by the input spooler, job supervisor and output spooler respectively. The diagonal arrows show the interaction (synchronisation) of the input spooler with the job supervisor and also the job supervisor with the output spooler.

A more detailed examination of the operating system reveals six processes. These are:

Input spooler

This process drives the card reader. It takes characters from the card reader and packs them into physical records. The physical records are written to the disk to form files on the input queue.

Job scheduler

This process chooses which job on the input queue to run next. The options available are first come first served or more likely a priority scheme. The priority may be based on the estimate of CPU time for the job, the number of output lines, the amount of money he is paying in order to obtain a quick turnaround etc.

Job supervisor

This process is in charge of running the user job. It decodes the job control cards and calls any assemblers, compilers or loaders required by the execution of the job.

Output scheduler

This process is very similar to the job scheduler. It chooses which job to print from all the jobs on the output queue. Again the algorithm used may be a first come first served one or more likely is based on priority. Again the priority depends on the number of lines to be printed - short jobs have higher priority, the length of time spent in the queue, the rate paid for running the job etc.

Output spooler

This process controls the line printer. It receives data from the output files associated with the job and prints it on the line printer. It extracts characters from the physical records and prints them as characters on the line printer.

Disk manager

This process controls the disk and does all of the input/output of physical records to and from the disk. It maintains a queue of buffers waiting to be read/written to the disk and may contain an algorithm for optimising the seek time for the disk. This process has the greatest amount of interaction with the other processes. It provides data for the user program and for the output spooler and it receives data from the input spooler and the user program.

As mentioned previously the processes run almost independently and only have to synchronise with each other. This means that they must at some time wait on synchronisation signals from other processes. The job scheduler must wait for a signal from the input spooler indicating that a job is in the input queue ready to be run. Likewise the input spooler must wait for the card reader to provide data for the input spooler. In the same manner the job supervisor must wait for the job scheduler, the output scheduler must wait for the job supervisor and the output spooler must wait for the output scheduler. In addition the input and output spoolers, which are performing input/output to physical devices, must wait for that input/output to complete. This is indicated by a hardware signal called an interrupt.

When the processes are not in the wait state then one of them is running on the processor and the other processes are in a queue waiting for the processor. A simple state transition diagram for the processes is given in figure 3.

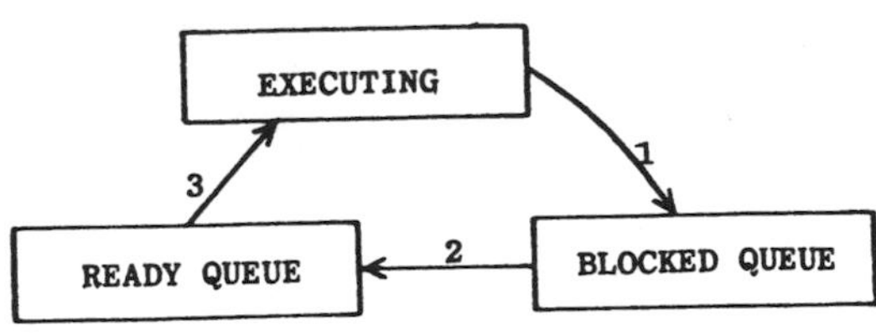

Figure 3.

The state transition number 1 is performed when the process performs an input/output operation or if the process performs a wait on a signal from another process. The state transition number 2 is performed when an input/output is complete as signalled by a hardware signal (interrupt) from the card reader or line printer, or when a process, which is in a blocked state, receives a signal from another process. The processes which are ready to run are kept in a ready queue. The next process to run is chosen by the process scheduler. The algorithm used by the process scheduler may be a simple round robin (first come first served) or an algorithm based on priority. The highest priority process is the disk manager as it is servicing the fastest device and is also performing input/output for the input spooler, user program and the output spooler. A diagram showing the data flow and synchronisation between processes is shown in figure 4.

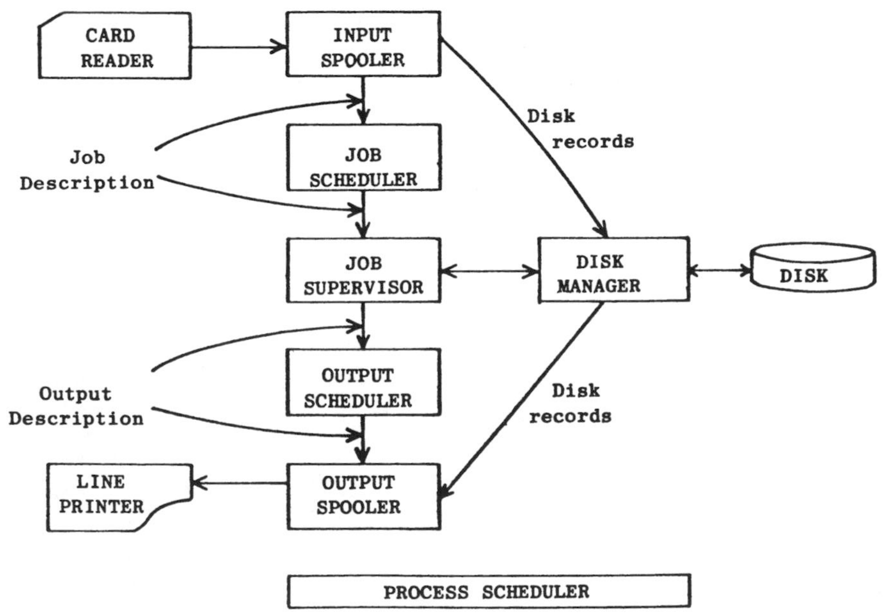

Figure 4.

As shown in the figure a small amount of data is passed between the processes. This is either a job description giving the files required in the job, or an output description consisting of the files required for the output of the job. The files on the disk are organised in fixed size blocks or sectors of say 512 bytes and hence the disk manager works in terms of blocks of this size. All the buffers in the disk manager and in the input and output spoolers are the same fixed size. Hence the spoolers must build up character streams into fixed size buffers and pass them to the disk manager. Likewise a user program may request characters and hence has interface routines for packing and unpacking characters from blocks.

The online spooling operating system was designed to make efficient use of the CPU. It reduced the time that the CPU was waiting for input/output by making the user program perform all input/output to disk. Input from the card reader and output to the line printer is performed in parallel with user program execution. Card readers have been replaced by terminals, especially in microcomputer systems, and hence online spooling is not very evident in microcomputer operating systems but they invariably contain output spoolers. Some of the concepts available in microcomputer operating systems have been introduced by studying an online spooling system e.g. concurrent processes and synchronisation between processes. Also the ideas of job scheduler and output scheduler have been introduced along with the notion of sharing the processor alternately among many processes by means of a process scheduler. The notion of files organised as many disk blocks along with buffering of data has also been introduced. To introduce some more fundamental concepts we look at multiaccess systems in the next section.

3. MULTI ACCESS SYSTEMS

Multi access systems are characterised by the fact that many terminals are connected to the computer system and the users may interact with the system. From the user point of view it seems that he is the only one with access to the system. In fact the computer is time shared between the users and the resources of the system e.g. the processor, memory, disks, etc., are shared between the users. In the simple spooling system described above only one user job runs at a time, and it runs to completion before the job scheduler choses another job to run. Normally in a multi access system a number of user jobs are executing concurrently in memory and the processor is switched from one job to the next quite frequently. Even the user jobs on disk are swapped with those in memory so that all jobs are progressed and hence no users suffer great delays. These systems provide interactive editing of programs which are held on disk. The execution of the user programs are performed either by:

Batch mode

The user submits his program to be run and it is put into a queue just like the input of the spooling system. The job is then run from the batch queue, requesting all its input from the input queue and outputting all its output to an output queue. When the program is finished execution the user inspects his output file and the error file if any. The user then edits his program and resubmits it to the batch queue for execution. This cycle continues until the program is correct.

Interactive mode

the user interacts with his running program providing input from the terminal and obtaining output at the terminal. He may also interact with the running program by setting breakpoints in his program. When the program reaches a breakpoint the execution stops and the user may inspect the values of variables in the program and change these values if required. In this way the user may debug his program in an interactive manner.

Real time mode

A special case of an interactive system is a real time system. The system is connected to and monitoring the operation of a piece of equipment or controlling an engineering plant in real time. The main characteristic of this system is that it works in real time and must perform operations in a specified amount of time. It receives inputs from the plant and performs some calculations on these input values and then produces outputs to control the plant. The inputs arrive in any sequence and the system must be so designed to give a response in less than a specified time. The consequence of not meeting this specified time is that the control of the system does not meet its design criteria possibly with disastrous results.

In the interactive mode the only consequence of bad response from the system is that the user will become annoyed but normally with no disastrous consequences.

The emphasis with multi access systems is on executing more than one job at a time and attempting to satisfy as many users or requests as possible. In this context satisfy means giving an acceptable response to human users sitting at terminals, or in real time systems it means being able to service and respond to interrupts fast enough to maintain the stability of the system being controlled. Hence jobs are loaded into memory and executed concurrently (multiprogrammed) and during execution are swapped out to disk to allow other user jobs into memory. When their turn for execution comes round again they are brought back into memory and continued at the point where they left off. The components of this operating system are shown in figure 5.

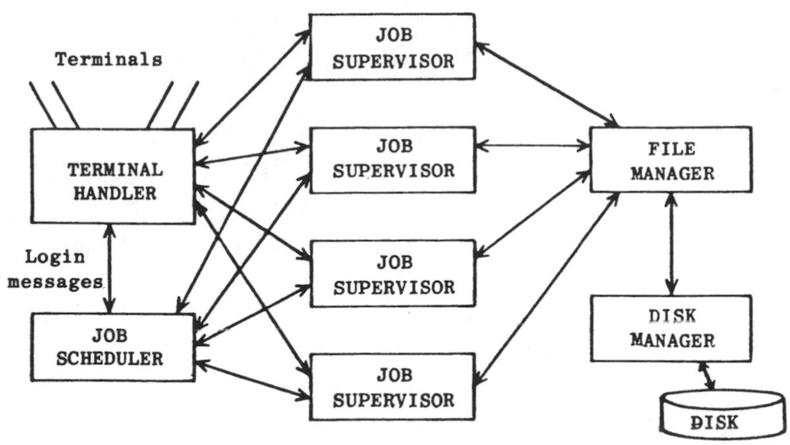

Figure 5.

In the system shown four user jobs are executing with a job supervisor controlling each one. The main difference from the spooling system is the multiple job supervisor. The job scheduler or the job initiator handles the login commands of the user and verifies his authority to use the system. Then a job supervisor is set up to control the execution of the user job. If the system has a batch stream in the background then there is a batch job supervisor which takes its input from and writes its output to the disk. The batch stream is the same as the batch stream in the spooling system. Previously we loosely talked about files on the disk, now a file manager is introduced into the system. The disk manager still works with fixed size blocks of data and does the buffering and management of the queues of blocks being transferred to and from the disk. The file manager allows users to refer to files by character string names and uses a directory to translate these names to an internal file identifier. It also maintains control over the access to files by the owner and other users.

The jobs in memory are multiprogrammed and they receive the processor alternatively according to some scheduling algorithm. This scheduling is performed by the process scheduler. A process gives up the processor when it performs an input/output or when it performs a wait for a signal from another process. This is called non preemptive scheduling. With a compute bound process this may be quite a long time and other users would be locked out, consequently receiving no response from their jobs. Hence preemptive scheduling is introduced where a process is given a maximum time slice. If it has not given up the processor before the expiry of the time slice then the processor is passed to another process. This implies the existence of a clock which interrupts after a given time quantum and allows the process scheduler to re schedule. In this manner response to the user is kept at an acceptable level.

It is usually not possible to keep all of the user jobs in memory at the same time and hence they are periodically swapped out to disk. When they are swapped out they release almost all their resources. Then the job scheduler picks one of the swapped out jobs and brings it back into memory. It is then given its turn to use the processor by the process scheduler. A user must be able to continue doing input/output to his job even when the job is swapped out to disk. Hence the operating system must buffer this input/output. The minimum size of this input/output is a line length but may be larger.

Another important consideration in the design of operating systems is memory protection. Even in the simple spooling system where only one user job and the operating system modules are in memory there is need to protect the operating system from the user job. If the user job makes an addressing error, like addressing an array with an invalid subscript, then the operating system may be overwritten unless there is memory protection. Even more so in a multiaccess system where there are a number of user jobs in memory at the same time. Then the user jobs must be protected from one another as well as protecting the operating system from all of the users. One method of memory protection is to have a protection field, say four bits, on each block of memory and to have a protection key in the program status word (PSW) in the processor. If the protection key in the PSW does not match the protection field of the block of memory being accessed then there is a memory protection interrupt. A user program executing in a number of memory blocks has the same value ,eg 5, in all the protection fields of those memory blocks. When the operating system starts the program executing it loads the key ,eg 5, into the PSW register of the processor. Hence when the program accesses its own memory blocks the key matches but when it accesses outside its own memory blocks there is a mismatch and a memory protection interrupt occurs. A key of zero used by the operating system allows it to access all of the memory blocks. Setting the protection fields and manipulating the PSW register is done by privileged instructions executed by the operating system and hence can not be manipulated by the user program. A variation of this protection scheme is a protection register with a bit representing each memory block. If the bit is set then the program may access that block, otherwise it may not. On every context switch to another user program this register is loaded by the operating system giving the memory blocks the user program may access without causing a protection fault. Again the protection register may only be loaded by the operating system.

A more common memory protection scheme is provided by a base and limit register pair. Every address accessed by the processor is tested against the limit register and, if greater, a memory protection interrupt occurs. At the same time the address is added to the address in the base register to give the actual memory address (figure 6).

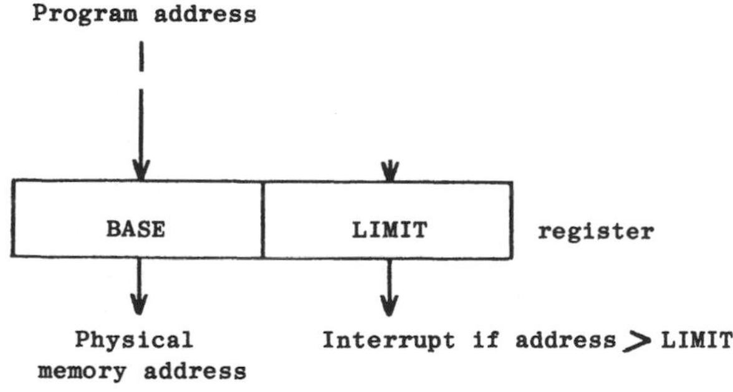

Figure 6.

On every memory access the processor performs an addition and a comparison with the base and limit register. If the address is greater than the limit a memory protection interrupt occurs showing that the program has accessed outside its memory address space. This scheme requires the processor to do an addition for every memory access but outweighs this disadvantage by providing a very easy method of program relocation. This is very important where the operating system must swap user jobs in and out of memory during their execution. When a job is swapped in to a memory location the operating system only has to set the base register pointing to that location. No changes are required to the addresses in the program.

Multi-access systems are esentially the same both for the microcomputer and the large computer. The main difference is the emphasis attached to the various components of the system. Process scheduling is not as important because efficient use of the processor is not crucial. In contrast, memory protection is equally important and has resulted in micro computer manufacturers producing chips which provide memory protection. Our overview of an operating system is now complete and in the remaining sections we discuss the topics in more detail and will comment on their importance to microcomputer operating systems.

4. INTERPROCESS COMMUNICATION

An operating system may be subdivided into components in order to understand what is normally a very large piece of software. In this way it is possible to study each component as an almost independent piece of software. Each component executes sequentially but they overlap their execution hence giving a system consisting of concurrent processes. This division of the system into processes also gives an easier understanding of the concurrent operation in terms of sequential processes interacting with one another. This interaction between processes is called interprocess communication, IPC. The language facilities provided for this are discussed in [2].

The main methods of interprocess communication are mailboxes, pipes, monitors and messages. The VAX 11/780 VMS operating system uses mailboxes for communication between processes [4]. Similarly the UNIX operating system [5,6] uses a structure called a pipe for the same purpose. A pipe is similar to a file and is referenced by a file pointer. One process writes to a pipe and another process reads from a pipe. Reading from an empty pipe causes the process to block.

The two most common forms of interprocess communication are the monitor, also called interface procedure or interface module, and message passing. Pilot [7] is a single user operating system designed and implemented for a very powerful personal computer. The scheme adopted for process communication is the monitor. This mechanism depends on the use of shared memory by the co-operating processes. The kernel of the operating system for the Manchester University MU5 computer [8], consists of a number of processes. These processes interact with one another by means of interface procedures (monitors). In contrast the whole operating system is constructed of processes and these interact by means of message passing. Other examples of operating systems based on message passing are RC 4000 [9,10], THOTH [11,12] and DEMOS [13].

The main variations in the message passing schemes is whether they have variable or fixed sized messages, whether the data in the message is typed or untyped, whether the send and receive are synchronous or asynchronous and also how the movement of large amounts of data from one process to another is achieved. Other considerations are the number of messages a process may send without receiving a reply and whether the control of this is on a basis local to a process or on a basis which is global to the operating system. Another consideration is how to send a message to a process which is swapped out to disk. The remarks here are restricted to the simplest message based operating system Thoth[11,12].

Messages are fixed length and consist of eight words (16 bytes). A process sends a message by

```
id = .Send (msg,id)
```

The contents of the message are sent to the process specified by id and the sending process blocks until it receives a reply. Hence the message system is synchronous and only needs one buffer per process. The receiving process uses

```
id = .Receive (msg)
```

and blocks if necessary to receive the message. The command to send a reply is

```
.Reply (msg,id)
```

which sends an eight word reply to the specified process, providing it is waiting for a reply, from the receiving process. The sending process is readied on receiving a reply and the replying process does not block. The interprocess communication is shown in figure 7.

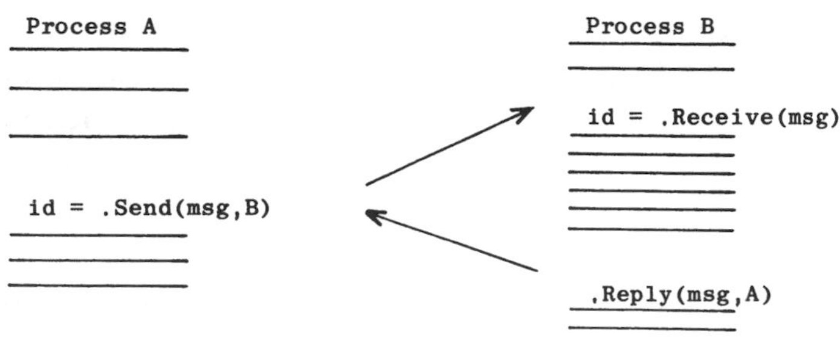

Figure 7.

The id's of the sending and replying processes are given as the returned values for the above primitives. Receiving from a non existent process results in an undefined message and a reply to a non existent process is a null operation. Instead of replying to a sending process the receiving process may forward a message to another process with the statement

```
.Forward (msg, fromid, toid)
```

and the transfer of large quantities of data may be performed with the statement

```
.Transfer (dest-id,src-id,dest,src,size)
```

These primitives are used for synchronizing processes and have been successfully used in this real time operating system.

A conceptual view of an operating system as a number of processes is shown in figure 8.

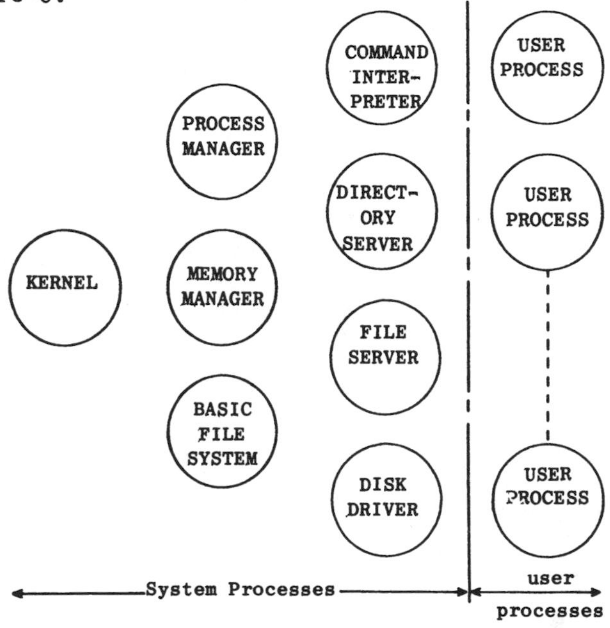

Figure 8.

Initially large operating systems were written as a monolithic unit and were extremely difficult to understand and maintain. To overcome this problem later operating systems were structured as processes with communication between them. This gave a better structure to the system and the communication between the processes was relatively straightforward. Microcomputer operating systems are tending towards distribution with processes running on different processors [3] hence interprocess communication is becoming much more important. Old operating systems were characterised by their type of memory management, for example, variable partition, segmented paged etc. Future microcomputer operating systems will be known as message based or monitor based which tells what interprocess communication is used. The design and implementation of the IPC, on which the efficiency of the operating system depends, will largely determine the success of the operating system.

5. PROCESS SCHEDULING

An operating system consists of both system processes and user processes. All of the processes must be given some processor time and this is the function of the process scheduler which is resident in the kernel. The simplest possible algorithm for process scheduling is round robin where all processes have equal priority and, providing they are ready to run, they take it in turn to use the processor. The ready processes are kept in a ready queue and the processes waiting on an input/output to complete or waiting on an event are kept in a blocked queue.

It is more usual to have a priority associated with processes. In this manner the process with the highest priority which is ready to run is given the processor. Lower priority processes are only given the processor if the higher priority processes are blocked or waiting. The system processes are given the highest priority and the user processes the lowest priority and hence the user processes only run when no system processes are ready. There are many algorithms for process scheduling . Discussion of them is outside the scope of this paper.

As mentioned previously user processes may be swapped out to disk and hence only a subset of the user processes may be in the schedule mix at any one time. The concept of swapping processes is usually associated with the particular memory management used and hence it is under the control of the process manager and the memory manager.

Many textbooks on operating systems have given prominence to queueing models and scheduling. For microcomputers process scheduling is still important but is not a central part of the operating system and normally a simple priority based scheduler is sufficient. In future operating systems scheduling will not receive the prominence that it has received in the past.

6. MEMORY MANAGEMENT.

6.1 SEGMENTATION

Base and limit registers were discussed in relation to memory protection. In addition to giving memory protection they have an added benefit in providing easy relocation of programs. This facility of base and limit registers underlies many of the memory management schemes. A segmented memory management scheme is shown in figure 9.
A job is loaded into memory and the base register is loaded with the starting address of the job and the limit register is assigned the size of the segment. During the execution of the job the base and

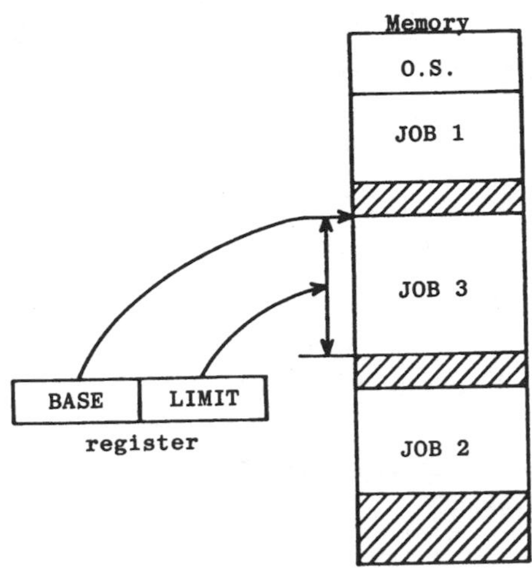

Figure 9.

limit register provide both the relocation of addresses and the memory protection required. On a program switch from one job to another the base and limit register are reloaded for the new job hence giving relocation and memory protection for that job. This scheme is easily generalised to multiple base and limit registers allowing jobs to be divided up into a number of segments each with their own base and limit register. The segments of the job may then be located anywhere in memory not necessarily in contiguous memory locations.

The addresses in a job (virtual addresses) are broken up into the segment numbers (eg. three bits) and the displacement within the segment. The segment number is used to address into the bank of hardware base and limit registers and the displacement is used to add to the base address (figure 10).

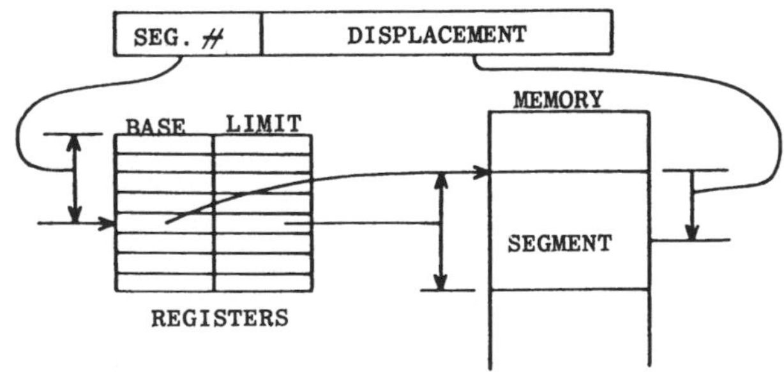

Figure 10.

The address translation is performed by the processor on each address which is accessed by the processor and hence the base and limit registers are hardware registers used exclusively for this address translation. These registers are also called segmentation registers. Associated with each process is a segment table and on a context switch to the process the contents of the segment table is loaded into the segment registers.

In a multi access time sharing system memory space can be used more efficiently by the sharing of compilers, editors etc. by different users. The code must be re entrant and seperatě from the data area of the program. Segmentation facilitates this by jobs sharing code segments and retaining their own data segments.

Memory management in the above scheme is achieved by keeping track of memory used by the segments or more importantly keeping track of the free areas of memory (holes). When a segment area is freed then it is added to the list of holes and if it joins a piece of memory which is already a hole the two are coalesced together to form a larger hole. Then the allocation of memory to a segment is achieved by choosing a hole of memory large enough for the segment and allocating the memory to the segment and putting the piece of memory left over in the list of holes. One method of keeping the list of holes in memory is in address order where the holes with the lowest addresses are first in the linked list. An allocation algorithm to go with this order is the "first fit" where the first hole in the list large enough for the segment is chosen. A second method is to keep the list in increasing size of holes regardless of the addresses of the holes. An allocation algorithm which goes with this scheme is the "best fit" one. Again the first hole large enough, which is the one most closely fitting the segment, is the one chosen.

6.2 PAGING

While the concept of segmentation allows programmers to subdivide their programs into logical units, the actual implementation and management of a segmented memory is difficult. Memory becomes very fragmented with holes of varying sizes and the mangement and allocation of the holes is complex. This problem of memory fragmentation may be overcome by using paging. The memory is divided into fixed size blocks or page frames usually 1K, 2K or 4K in size. The job's address space is also divided into fixed size units called pages. In a manner very similar to the segmentation already discussed, the logical address space of the job is mapped into the physical address space of the system by means of a page map or page table (figure 11).

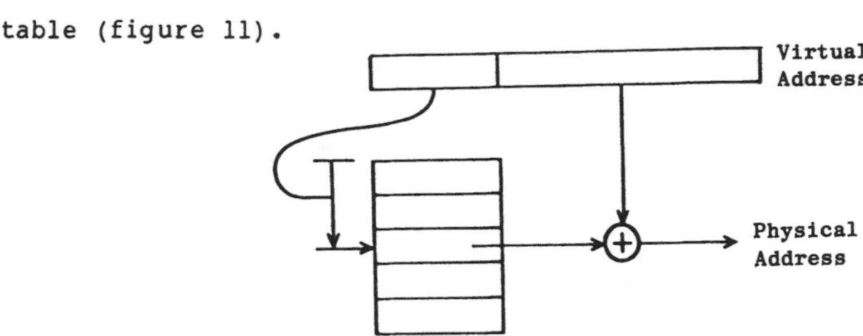

Figure 11.

The pages of the job's address space are located anywhere in physical memory and the address translation is done by means of the page table for every memory reference. The addresses in a job are always mapped into physical addresses and are referred to as virtual addresses. The management of memory using this scheme is much easier than with segmentation. The blocks are fixed in size and hence the scheme is oriented towards the operating system.

In the above translation scheme two interesting alternatives exist

1) virtual address < physical address

This scheme has been used on many processors as a means of increasing the physical size of memory without changing the logical address size within the programs eg the logical address size may be sixteen bits and the physical address size say eighteen or twenty bits.

2) virtual address > physical address

When the virtual address is greater than the physical address the programmer may address memory which is physically not available in the system and because of this it is referred to as virtual memory. Because the virtual memory is larger than the physical memory it is not possible for all of it to be in memory at the same time. Hence entries in the page map often refer to pages held on disk. When these pages are referenced during the address translation the processor is interrupted (page fault) and the page on disk is brought into memory. When the process is restarted the reference is made again and this time the reference is successful. This is known as demand paging and is the method used to implement virtual memory.

6.3 SEGMENTATION and PAGING

By using both segmentation and paging the programmer can enjoy the benefit of a segmented address space and the operating system can eliminate the memory fragmentation problem. The programmer can share segments in the normal way while the paging is invisible to him, and the operating system uses the paging to manage the memory. The tables required for segmentation and paging of a number of processes are shown in figure 12.

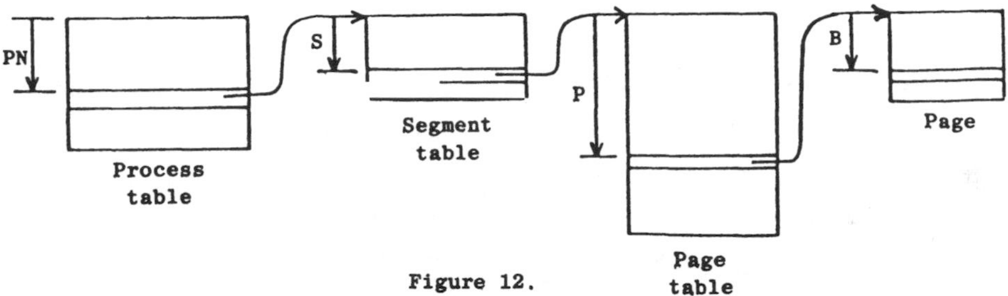

Figure 12.

The tables consist of the process table which includes an entry for each of the processes in the system. The entry in the process table points to the segment table for that process. The segment table contains an entry for each of the segments in the process and each entry points to the page table for that segment. Likewise the page table contains an entry for each page in the segment and gives the addresses of all of the pages in the segment. When the processor is executing a process it holds the base address of the the segment table in a register. Hence a virtual address which consists of a segment number, page number and byte number in the page (figure 13)

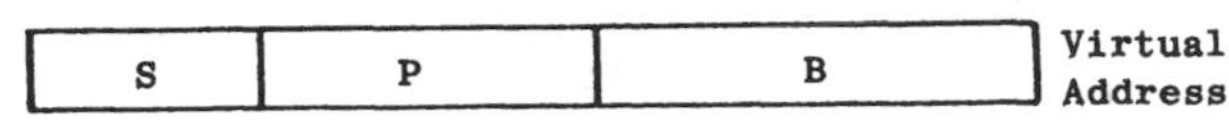

Figure 13

is translated to a physical address by indexing into the segment table and the page table by using S and P respectively. This gives the address of the page in memory which is concatenated with the byte number to give the complete physical address. This address translation requires three memory references in order to make one memory access. Hence the address translation is always supported by a hardware address translation buffer (current page registers, hardware page table) to speed up this address translation. Usually there are only eight or sixteen of these registers to do the address translation. They contain the segment number and page number of the virtual address and also the real address of the page in memory. The registers which are content addressable or associative registers are searched in parallel on address translation. If a match is made the physical address is obtained and a reference is made to the operand in memory. If a match is not made then providing the page is in memory, the hardware loads the registers from the tables in memory and again the address translation is completed. However if the page is not in memory then a page fault interrupt occurs and the operating system brings the page into memory.

The arrival of large memory chips (64K and 256K bits) is on the horizon and the days of microcomputers with memories in the megabyte range are not too far distant. Even so the cost of memory is still a large part of the total cost of a microcomputer system. Also the demand for memory seems to increase along with the supply so much so that the demand always is greater than the supply. Even for single user micro computer systems there is a need for memory management and it will continue to play an important part in micro computer operating systems. The 16 bit microcomputer manufacturers are producing chips which provide the facilities of memory protection and form the basis for memory management software.

An alternative method [14,15] which is attractive for micro computers is to store a subset of the segment and page tables in high speed memory and to index into them by hardware during address translation (figure 14).

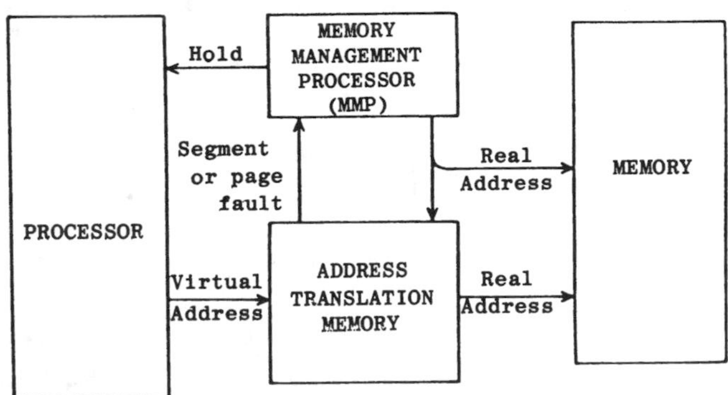

Figure 14.

If the address translation memory contains the information for the address mapping then the real address is sent to physical memory. Otherwise if there is a segment or page fault a memory management support processor (MMP) is interrupted. The MMP asserts the hold line of the main processor while it updates the address translation memory from main memory. When the updating is complete the address translation is completed as before. If the page table or the page is not in real memory then the MMP executes a page fault interrupt routine and brings the page table or page into main memory. Again when the address translation is complete the main processor continues. The address translation memory is made up of a small number of high speed chips and associated logic and is shown in figure 15.

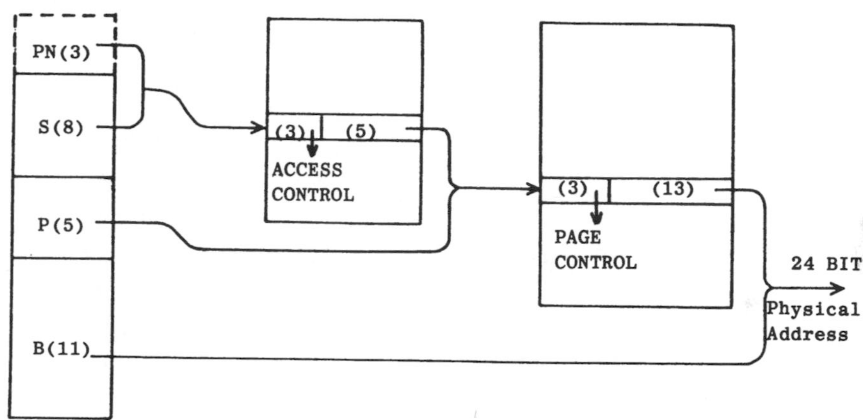

Figure 15.

In this layout the virtual address is broken up into eight bits for a segment number, five bits for a page number and eleven bits for a page. This gives two hundred and fifty six segments of thirty two pages each of size 2K. The address translation memory accomodates eight active processes each with their complete segment map in fast memory. The page map contains thirty two page tables belonging to processes currently active. On address translation the index into the segment map is always possible because the complete map is held for the process. The access control specifies whether the segment is valid and if its associated page table is in the page map. The page control in the page map tells whether the page is valid or not.

The advantage of this scheme is that it may be constructed from standard components with the support of a memory management processor. It also performs its address translation without any additions or comparisons hence making it pretty fast.

6.4 PERFORMANCE of PAGING SYSTEMS

No discussion of paging is complete without talking about performance of paging in a virtual memory environment. As the level of multi-programming is increased the CPU utilisation increases. Above a certain level of multiprogramming the CPU utilisation falls off dramatically because the number of pages in memory per process is too small. Hence the system spends most of its time waiting for pages to be transferred from disk to memory. A diagram showing the number of instructions executed by a process per page fault is shown in figure 16.

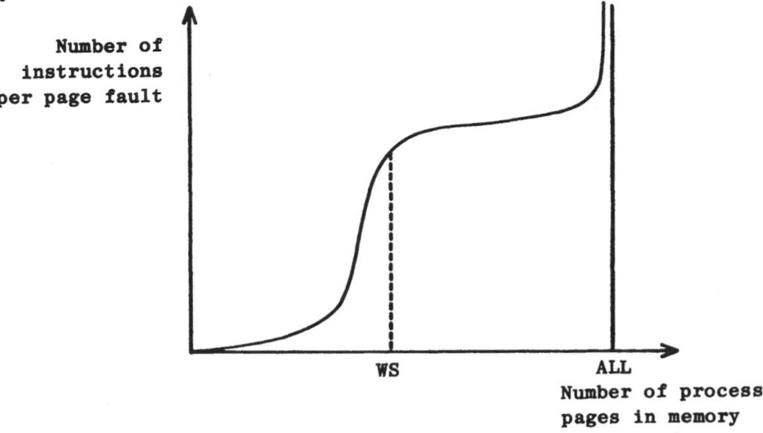

Figure 16.

If none of the pages belonging to a process are in memory then a page fault occurs immediately. As the number of pages in memory increases the number of instructions executed per page fault increases steeply and then levels off. When all of the pages are in memory the process executes indefinitely without any page faults. The number of pages marked WS in figure 16 is called the working set of the process [16]. It is the minimum number of pages required in memory to keep the page fault rate at an acceptable level. A decrease in the number of pages in memory increases the page fault rate while an increase in the number of pages in memory doesn't significantly decrease the page fault rate. A graph showing processor utilisation (figure 17) demonstrates the effect of trying to multiprogram too many jobs.

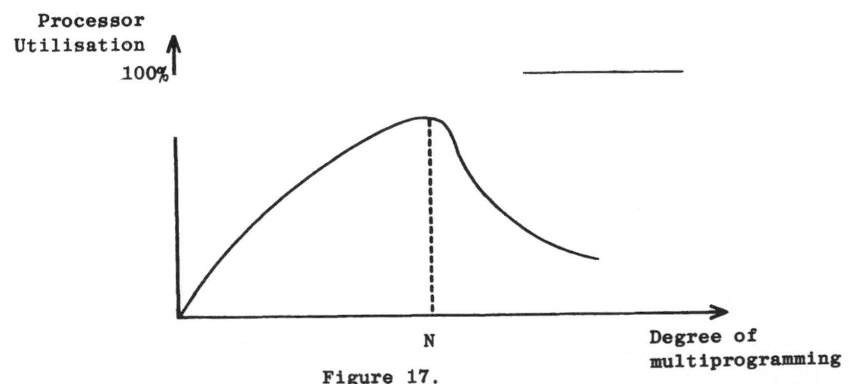

Figure 17.

At the point N the processor utilisation is at its maximum because the working sets of all the processes are in memory. Above this point the working sets of the processes are not in memory and on a page fault the page brought into memory replaces a page in the working set of another process. Hence that process when it runs again most probably will cause a page fault due to the fact that its page has been removed from memory. Very soon a phenomenon known as thrashing sets in and the processor utilisation rapidily degrades.

6.5 MEMORY MANAGEMENT in PILOT

Pilot is an operating system for a high performance personal computer [7]. The system is structured so that all computations run in the same address space. This homogeneous address space is structured into contiguous runs of pages called spaces. The structuring is done both by the operating system and by the client software. The difference between spaces and segments is that the spaces may be subdivided into subspaces and further subdivided as required. At the lowest level are pages. The swapping entity is a space and not a page and the swapping is performed when a page of a mapped space is referenced and it is not in memory. The minimum amount swapped is the smallest space containing the page. This seems to give greater control over the swapping of pages. A client program may optimise its swapping behaviour by subdividing its mapped spaces into subspaces whose access patterns are known to be strongly correlated. Because it is a single user system a user program may give hints to the operating system to help it optimise the swapping of spaces. A "space activate" statement gives a hint to the operating system that it should swap in this space because the program will reference it in the near future. By the time the program references this space the operating system may already have the space in memory hence eliminating the page replacement time. Likewise a "space deactivate" gives a hint to the operating system that this space may be swapped out of memory hence making room for other active spaces.

7. FILE SYSTEMS

7.1 FILES

One of the most important parts of present day operating systems is the file system. It is almost impossible to use any interactive system without using the file system many times. Normally a user logs on to a computer system by giving his name and password and and the system assigns him his current working directory and an internal user identification (UID). The UID controls the access of the user to files within the system and gives the user owner priviliges to his own files. Users refer to files by character string names and a directory is required to translate these external names to internal file identifiers (FID).

The UNIX [5,6] operating system, which is now available on many micro computer systems, has a simple file system which is worth considering. A disk consists of a very large number of fixed size blocks often called sectors with a usual size of 512 bytes. A file consists of a sequence of blocks spread randomly over the disk. The free or unallocated blocks are kept in a free list. Blocks are allocated from and returned to this free list. Some of the sectors on the disk may be unuseable and these are kept in a permanent file. This file instead of containing data just contains bad sectors. The logical order of the blocks in a file is contained in the header for the file. The addresses of the first ten blocks of the file are kept in the header (figure 18) and the eleventh address points to a block giving the addresses of the next one hundred and twenty eight blocks of the file. This is called a singly indirect block. The twelvth and thirteenth addresses point to doubly and triply indirect blocks respectively. The triple indirect blocks are omitted from the figure.

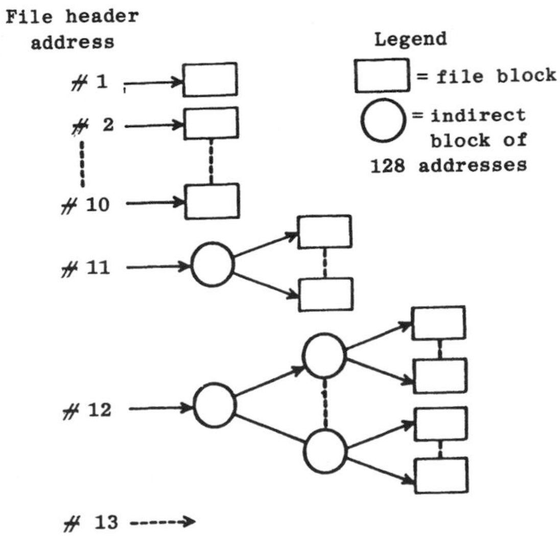

Figure 18.

The addresses of the blocks of a small file are obtained directly through the file header and for a larger file they are obtained indirectly through a block of addresses. This structure can accomodate extremely large files greater than any presently available disk pack.

The file header also contains fields for the owner of the file, protection, file type, time of creation, time of last modification, the number of times the file appears in a directory and other associated information.

7.2 DIRECTORIES

A directory is used for mapping external file names into internal file identifiers. In UNIX the directory structure is a rooted tree with the actual files appearing as the leaves of the tree structure. A section of a directory structure is shown in figure 19. The internal nodes of the directory are implemented as files called directory files.

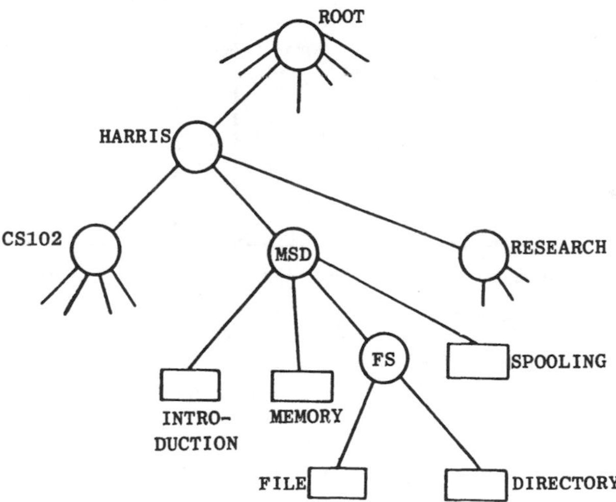

Figure 19.

The entries in the directory files are a list of external file names and their associated file identifiers. These entries may be the names of other file directories or the names of ordinary files. Searching the directory structure for the file called "MEMORY" is performed by specifying the pathname "/HARRIS/MSD/MEMORY". The initial "/" means to start at the root of the directory structure and the other strings separated by "/" are the names of directory files or the final ordinary file. A user may set the current working directory to "/HARRIS/MSD" and the pathnames to files which do not begin with "/" start at this point in the directory structure. Hence the pathname "MEMORY" accesses the memory file from the current working directory and the pathname "FS/DIRECTORY" also uses the current working directory.

7.3 STABLE STORAGE

One of the most important properties of a file system is that it is robust and can survive a system crash or bad sectors on a disk. The Alto [17] file system is considered to see how this is implemented. The basic idea is to distribute the structural information for the file system and to maintain redundant information. Hence if a disk crashes it is possible to restructure the file system with a minimum loss of data. Each page in the Alto file system (figure 2∅) consists of a header field, a label record and the data record.

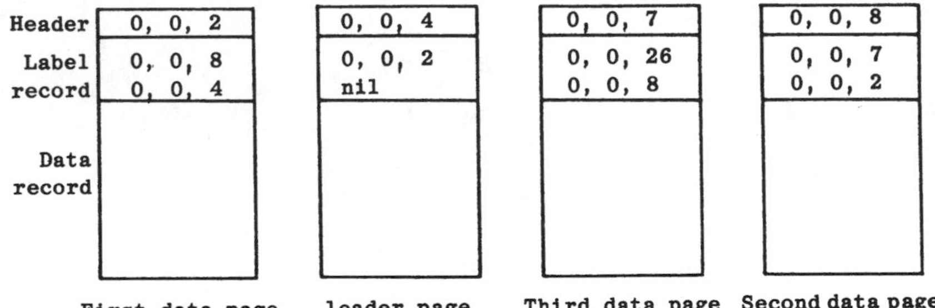

Figure 20.

The label record contains the file identifier, the block number of the file, the number of bytes in this page as well as the pointers to the previous and next blocks in the file. Block zero of this file contains all the header information including the owner of the file, time of last modification etc. The header block plus the label records of the other blocks in the file comprise the basic system data structure for the file. Access to the file may be achieved by this information alone. This distributed data structure is supplemented by redundant information called hints which, although not neccessary, improve the performance of the file system. Hence a directory is maintained with the locations of the headers of the file and the locations of the blocks in the file. The hints are used to locate the block but before the block is read or written this information is checked against the label information contained in the block. If the hints are found to be erroneous they are reconstructed from the distributed structural information in the file. There is a second level of software checking in addition to the one just described. A disk operation is invoked with a command block which specifies a disk address, a buffer address in main memory and the transfer operation to be performed. Because file system damage may be caused by errant software specifying an invalid command block the command block must also contain a seal (like a password) which must be correct for the disk controller to act. Hence if the controller is activated on a block of memory, which is not a valid disk control block, the access will be aborted due to an improper seal.

Failures due to improper functioning of the cylinder head and sector seeking mechanism are caught by comparing the disk address being sought with the address of the sector found. If the addresses do not correspond then a hardware fault is generated.

A recent proposal for stable storage [18] is to build a stable disk page from two normal disk pages. To write a page of stable storage requires the writing of two copies where the second copy is not written until the first copy has been safely completed. The pages of a pair are allocated on the disk far away from one another so that a single head crash on the disk will not destroy both copies.

If a failure should occur during the logical write, the pair of pages forming the single stable page will be in one of the following states

1) both pages have the same valid data
2) both pages have valid data, but they are not the same
3) one of the pages is detectably bad.

During crash recovery each pair of pages in stable storage is read and the two are made to be the same. In case 2 the first page is written into the second to make a correct stable page. In case 3 the data in the good page is written into the other page.

Reading a stable page involves reading one of its copies. If it is detectably bad then the other page is read instead. Stable storage is only required for important data on the disk such as intentions lists, pointers to files, disk allocation etc. Other file information is kept in single copies.

Another important property of file systems is that a sequence of reads and writes to a file are performed as an indivisible atomic operation. Either they are all performed or none are performed. Such an action sequence is called a transaction and is started by an open transaction and finished by a close transaction [18,19]. The method by which this is performed is discussed in the distributed systems lectures.

7.4 SUMMARY

The need for a file system does not depend on whether the processor is a mainframe or a microcomputer. It is still one of the most important parts of the operating system. The file sizes may be much smaller and the media used may be slower but the concepts remain the same. The directions are towards stable storage and atomic actions to increase the reliability of the data in the system. There is also a move towards distributed file systems [3].

8. SINGLE USER OPERATING SYSTEMS

The earliest operating systems were the batch stream operating systems processing a single user job at a time. These were followed by the multiprogrammed batch stream systems and now the present day multi access time sharing operating systems. Now the cycle is being completed again with the single user operating system for a personal computer. One of the earliest examples was OS6 [20] written mainly in BCPL which provided the concept of stream input output. Pilot [7] is a more recent example written in the high level language MESA and only supporting the same language. There is an extremely close coupling between Pilot and the MESA language and it is possible to think of PILOT as the run time structure of MESA. Pilot provides interfaces through which client programs in MESA may gain access to Pilot services. Each interface defines a group of related types, operations and error signals. Interfaces are provided for the file system, virtual memory etc.

The protection mechanism provided is interesting in that it relies on the strong type checking of the MESA language. A client's program and the interfaces used are type checked and because it is a single user system this protection is sufficient. The protection can be visualised as that provided if the operating system and the client program were compiled as a single unit in a language like Pascal.

The Modula language[21,22] which is discussed in later lectures provides similar facilities for the implementation of this type of operating system and its' protection mechanism.

REFERENCES

1 Rosen, R.F., "Supervisory and Monitor Systems". Computing Surveys Vol 1, Number 1 (March 1969).

2 Perrott, R.H., "High Level Sequential and Concurrent Programming" Springer-Verlag Lecture notes in Computer Science (this publication)

3 Popek, G., "Distributed Systems of Microprocessors". Springer-Verlag Lecture notes in Computer Science (this publication)

4 Levy, H.M. and Eckhouse, R.H., "Computer Programming and Architecture: The VAX-11". Digital Press (1980).

5 Ritchie, D.M., and Thompson, K., "The Unix Time-Sharing System". CACM Vol 17 Number 7 (July 1974).

6 The Bell System Technical Journal. Vol 57 Part II (July/August 1978).

7 Redell, D., et al., "Pilot: An Operating System for a Personal Computer". CACM Vol 23 Number 2 (Feb 1980)

8 Frank, G.R., and Theaker, C.J., "The Design of the MUSS Operating System". Software Practice and Experience Vol 9 (1979).

9 Brinch Hansen, P., "The Nucleus of a Multiprogramming System". CACM Vol 13 Number 4 (April 1970)

10 Brinch Hansen, P., "A Case Study: RC 4000, Operating System Principles". Prentice Hall (1973).

11 Cheriton, D.R., et al., "Thoth, a Portable Real-Time Operating System". CACM Vol 22 Number 2 (Feb 1979).

12 Cheriton, D.R., "Multi-Process structuring and the Thoth Operating System". PHD Thesis, Department of Computer Science, University of British Columbia. (March 1979).

13 Baskett, F., Howard, J.H., and Montague, J.T., "Task Communication in DEMOS". Sixth ACM Symposium on Operating System Principles, (Nov 1977).

14 Johansson, L.A., "Virtual Memory Management for Micro Computers in Real-Time Applications". Euromicro Vol 5 Number 4 (July 1979).

15 Baskett, F., "Pascal and Virtual Memory in a Z8ØØØ or MC 68ØØØ Based Design Station". COMPCOM Spring (198Ø).

16 Thacker,C.P. et al "Alto: A personal computer" Xerox Palo Alto Research Center CSL 79-11 (Aug !979)

17 Denning, P.J., "virtual memory". Computing Survey Vol 2 Number 3 (197Ø).

18 Sturgis, H., Mitchell, J. and Israel, J., "Issues in the Design and Use of a Distributed File System". ACM Operating Systems Review, Vol 14 Number 3 (July 198Ø).

19 Paxton, W.H., "A Client-Based Transaction System to Maintain Data Integrity". Seventh Symposium on Operating Systems Principles (ACM - SIGOPS) (Dec 1979).

2Ø Stoy, J.E., and Strachey, C., "OS6 - An Experimental Operating System for a Small Computer". Computer Journal, Vol 15 Numbers 2 and 3 (1972).

21 Wirth, N. "Modula-2" ETH Technical Report No.36 (Mar 198Ø).

22 Wirth, N. "Lilith: A Personal Computer for the Software Engineer" Springer-Verlag Lecture notes in Computer Science (this publication)

Notes on Distributed Systems of Microprocessors*

Gerald J. Popek
University of California at Los Angeles

INTRODUCTION

The power and utility of microprocessor based computing is increasingly appearing in the form of multiple microprocessor based systems, either tightly or loosely coupled; or as small processors in support of large ones. In these notes, we outline many of the major issues which are often faced in building distributed computing systems, giving references to sources which examine those issues in greater depth. We also examine a number of the issues for which deeper discussions are not generally available.

1. Motivations for Distributed Computing

Here, we briefly review in general the practical motivations for distributed computing.

1.1. Reduced Communications Costs.

Many are familiar with the rapidly decreasing cost and significantly increasing power of small processors and computer configurations based on them. The costs of communications over any appreciable distance (greater, say, than an internal machine bus) have also been dropping, although not at so great a rate. The decrease in communications costs makes distributed computing quite feasible; the significant and increasing disparity between computing and communications costs raises the motivation for placing intelligence (and storage) close to the point of use, each such node still coordinated with the others. In this way, the amount of data that must be shipped over the lines can be reduced, or batched at lower cost in larger units or at low rate times of day.

This view depends crucially on a basic assumption of locality of reference of the data stored in the distributed computing system. Fortunately, most applications exhibit a high degree of locality. Distributed computing thus has a significant and increasing economic incentive.

*This research was supported in part by ARPA Research Contract DSS MDA-903-77-C--0211.

1.2. Reliability and Availability

Distributed, interacting machines offer the potential for greatly increased reliability and availability of specific functions. This increase is accomplished in two major ways. First, a large system can be partitioned into many smaller components, each one of which posesses considerable local autonomy - the ability to do much of its assigned work without interacting with other parts of the system. This functional decomposition is illustrated by many examples; a large inventory system with a local computer at each storage site, responsible for that given warehouse, that updates the company master file once a day is an obvious one. In this case, any local warehouse can go forward with its local activity even though other warehouses may be temporarily inoperative, or even if the master machine is unavailable because of communications or other failures. Second, redundancy can be used, at many levels in the system, so that a failure of part of the system providing a critical function is masked by another part that can also supply that function. Replicated hardware, duplicate storage of data, multiple communication paths through a network, are all examples.

Often both techniques are employed. In a modern hospital, there is generally a central machine for data processing, with separate machines, sometimes replicated, in the intensive care ward. Intensive care operation continues while the main machine is down for maintenance. (Of course, the separate machines were present for other reasons as well.)

These mechanisms of functional decomposition and redundancy apply at many levels in a system, from memory chips, to file header information, to duplicate databases, to entire machines. Often the techniques are incompletely employed. Rather than duplicating storage, error correcting codes are used. Rather than duplicating the file system structure, file membership is indicated by links among the pages as well as inverted indexes. If one structure is destroyed, it can be reconstructed (laboriously) from the other.

It should be clear that without care, distributed systems contain the potential for considerably reduced reliability and availability as well. If multiple machines and communications lines must operate successfully for a given function to occur, then the reliability with which that function can be delivered is the product of the reliability measures of each of the components. This issue is quite a bit more subtle than one might imagine, especially where software algorithms are involved. The designers of the flight control computer system for the American space shuttle Columbia learned this lesson to their chagrin, as a quadruplicated machine delayed first launch due to a single initialization error. Nevertheless, the technical cost of considerably increased system reliability need not be dramatic if currently understood techniques are carefully applied. A later section of these notes examines these issues in more detail.

1.3. Speed and Cost of Computing Power

It has been often observed that, in the commercial marketplace, it is frequently possible to obtain x units of computing power more cheaply in n small units of power x/n, rather than in the form of one larger unit of power x. While part of this phenomenon is no doubt due to commercial pricing policies rather than any intrinsic technical reason, it is also true that the internal structure of small machines is far simpler than large ones. Small machines also generally do not include high cost components to support large I/O bandwidths with general purpose channels, or other such facilities which are essential to the operation of the large mainframe. Software is generally far simpler, in part because of less function, but also because the limits on resources led to additional care in design. On the other hand, the cost of interconnecting the small machines is often ignored.

Said differently, the observed cost differential seems to result in part from market based pricing policies, in part from intrinsic differences in complexity, and in part from the lack of supporting function found in small machines. Nevertheless, if a given problem can be effectively partitioned into parts that map well to a collection of small machines, then there is the resulting opportunity to obtain considerably better price/performance than on a single larger machine.

A related issue is the opportunity for the use of the high degree of parallelism presented by the collection of small machines. Once again, the significance of this observation depends on the degree to which the given problem can be partitioned. Some stylized partitioning is quite common, as illustrated by the use of microprocessor based terminals, storage controllers, communications front ends, and the like. Occasional partitioning of the main computational function is also found, for example in array processors. Distributed data management is another often cited potential application for parallel processing.

We will not consider specialized distributed intelligence as represented by device controllers, terminal microprocessors (at least those which are not user programmable) and the like in our view of distributed systems, instead focussing only on those systems with multiple main machines operating with considerable general functionality.

1.4. Local Autonomy

A number of people have observed that distributed computing more naturally fits the desires of components of a large organization of people than a single centralized computing resource. When a given subdivision has its own machine, it is able to exercise substantial control over such issues as: scheduling of maintenance, introduction of new software releases, acquisition of new resources, and operating costs. The question of costs may benefit from some explanation. Individual subdivisions are often charged for their proportional use of the central facility. Other than by varying use, there is often little the subdivision can do to manage such cost components as equipment choice, personnel, maintenance policy, etc. The computing center is not under their control. These legitimate issues are what is meant by the desire for local autonomy.

Another aspect of this issue, that also increases the trend to larger numbers of smaller machines, is the manner by which purchasing decisions are typically made. [Saltzer78] In general, the larger the cost, the higher in an organization approval must be obtained, and the longer it takes to do so. Therefore, smaller machines can be more easily and more rapidly purchased. The advent of 16 bit and 32 bit microprocessors, together with such powerful storage technology as Winchester disks, permits significant computing to be done in these inexpensive local installations.

The costs of decentralized computing can be nontrivial however. Each such machine has the potential to require significant, technically competent, support; an unsatisfactory situation for many potential customers. Hence small machine developers must make much more significant efforts to permit operation and maintenance of their systems by computer-unskilled personnel than those manufacturers of large mainframes.

Once many of these small machines have been installed, one also rapidly discovers that there frequently is a need to exchange information among the machines, and cooperate in certain activities. Some form of distributed system is the result, and the compatibility problems can be fierce. Of course, care on the part of the organization, with early establishment of interface, equipment, and software standards can minimize such costs while still permitting a significant degree of local autonomy. Communication and management of "turf" problems among groups to avoid redundant effort is an issue that must be effectively faced.

2. Differences Between Distributed and Centralized Systems

The introduction of a distributed computing environment changes the systems problems in a number of intrinsic ways, that are discussed below.

2.1. Errors and Failures

In a distributed environment, it is typical to make two important, related assumptions about expected failures. First, the communications lines which connect the computing nodes are usually assumed to have error and failure rates that are far higher than the nodes in the network. Furthermore, the failure modes are varied and asymmetric; i.e. a full duplex line may fail or be noisy in one direction with higher probability than the other. (Note that this assumption is often not made in a local network, which is generally assumed to be quite reliable.) Second, partial computations are a fact of life. In a centralized system, it is common to assume that when there is a failure of the system, the result is termination of all activity. It is not generally expected, for example, that of a set of cooperating jobs, some fail while others continue unaffected. In a distributed system however, it is quite possible, and expected, that one or several nodes involved in a given function may crash or be disconnected from the rest. Further, since the timing characteristics of a distributed computation differ from that same software organized as multiple tasks on a single machine, and differ from invocation to invocation, additional errors may appear as the environment changes.

Said differently, the frequency and nature of errors in a distributed system require one to keep in mind a much richer failure model when building software than in the case of a centralized system. It is not that these more varied errors necessarily can't occur in a single machine, but that their likelihood is low enough that they are generally ignored.

It is therefore necessary to pay significantly more attention to error and failure management, both in the structure of the system and application software, as well as in the detailed recovery algorithms. Not to do so can easily lead to software whose algorithm for normal conditions is correct, but which is essentially unusable.

2.2. Heterogeneity

Support of n significantly different versions of something is often considerably more costly than one expects because of the need to maintain compatibility among all of the versions, thereby necessitating conversion tools as well as serious management problems in attempts to legislate standard interfaces. Distributed systems can easily provide the "insurmountable opportunity" of heterogeneity at many levels of the overall system. At the hardware level, processors in the network may be different. If they are the same, the amount of memory available and the nature of peripherals may differ widely. The machines may be interconnected in a number of different ways, sometimes using public common carrier links, necessitating support of a number of different communication protocols. If existing systems are being connected, the operating systems may not be the same. If different organizations control the various systems, then the application software, and the formats of data in files, documents, etc. generally will not match. This tower of Babel, unless controlled, can easily lead to failure, as given functions must be built and tested multiple times, with each version continually maintained. Compatibility of interfaces becomes a major problem.

In a different vein, even when there is considerable heterogeneity, the method by which access is obtained to a remote resource is generally quite different from, and more complex than, the method for a corresponding local resource. For example, one opens a local file, but may have to execute a multistep file transfer protocol to access a remote file. Rarely are tools provided to easily effect intermachine optimization steps (such as file location control), even though single machine tools (such as extent based file systems, or multiple access methods and index management) are common.

The net result of these observations is that the cost and difficulty of developing distributed system software can easily be considerably greater than building the analagous software for a centralized environment. The concept of network transparency is a powerful idea to control this complexity and cost of distributed system software, and will be discussed later.

3. Bandwidth and Delay Issues

Much of the experience in network systems has grown out of geographically distributed networks. These environments are generally characterized as thin wire connections. That is, the bandwidth of the communications medium was typically far less than the internal bandwidth of the nodes connected to the network. For example the lines composing the Arpanet are 50Kbit/sec., while the bus bandwidth of even so small a machine as a PDP-11 is 1.5 Megabytes/sec. or more. Bandwidth ratios of more than a small fraction of 1% are very rare. Further, the delays of the thin wire media are far greater than internal communcation delays. Several tenths of a second are often required to get a message from one host in the Arpanet to another one across the United States. By comparison, bus delays in the hundreds of nanoseconds are typical.

A dramatically different network environment is presented by the proliferation of local network technology and its use. The Ethernet, for example, supports a 1.2 Megabyte/sec. transfer rate, with delays typically in the millisecond range. The bandwidth compares with the internal Vax-11/780 bus of 13 Megabytes/sec. or the Tandem bus of 14 Megabytes/sec. Here we see a ratio of network to node bandwidth of 5-8%; a far greater capacity than thin wire systems. While the network delays are still significant compared to bus delays, another comparison is useful; the time needed to get a disk transfer started. A figure of merit would suggest that tens of milliseconds are required. Thus the local network would typically pose no significant additional delay even if one wished to support paging across the network, and a 10 megabit Ethernet has the raw capacity to transfer 800 1K byte pages per second. By comparison to long haul networks, this is a thick wire environment.

To paraphrase R. Hamming, a difference in quantity of an order of magnitude leads to an essential difference in quality. Because local networks provide a qualitatively different environment, one is led to reevaluate the way that software uses and controls the available resources. In our discussions here, we will pay particular attention to microprocessor operation in a local network environment, both because of its significant technical implications, and because of the importance of such local net based applications of small computers as office automation.

A SURVEY OF DISTRIBUTED SYSTEMS ISSUES

The major part of the remaining discussion will be devoted to a set of issues which, while present in centralized systems, take on a considerably different and more important character in distributed systems, especially those composed of a substantial number of small machines. Transparency and autonomy will be discussed first. Reliable operation in a distributed environment is examined next. Then multiple copy support methods are outlined. In the section following these, a case study of a distributed system designed to address many of the problems raised in this report is given.

4. Network Transparency

As real distributed systems come into existence, an unpleasant truth has been learned; the development of software for distributed systems, and for true distributed applications, is often far harder to design, implement, debug, and maintain than the analogous software written for a centralized system. The reasons - the errors/failures problem and issues of heterogeneity have already been mentioned.

Some of these problems need not be intrinsic to the application view of distributed systems, however. It may be perfectly reasonable to open a file in precisely the same manner independent of whether the file is local or remote; i.e. issue the same system call, with parameters in the same order, etc. That is, the syntax and semantics of services should not be affected by whether or not a given function involves local or remote support. This concept of hiding the existence of the network, at least so far as the nature of interfaces is concerned, can greatly ease software development.*

An appealing solution to this increasingly serious problem is to develop a network operating system that supports a high degree of network transparency; all resources are accessed in the same manner independent of their location. If open (file-name) is used to access local files, it also is used to access remote files. That is, the network becomes "invisible", in a similar manner to the way that virtual memory hides secondary store. Of course, one still needs some way to control resource location for optimization purposes, but that control should be separated from the syntax and semantics of the system calls used to access the resources. Ideally then, one would like the graceful behavior of an integrated storage system for the entire network while still retaining the many advantages of the distributed system architecture. That is, the existence of the network should not concern the user or application programs in the way that resources are accessed. If such a goal could be achieved, its advantages include the following.

1. Easier software development. Since there is only one way to access resources, and the details of moving data across the network are built in, individual software packages do not require special purpose software for this purpose. Functions are location independent.

2. Incremental Change Supported. Changes made below the level of the network wide storage system are not visible to application software. Therefore, changes in resources can be made easily.

3. Potential for Increased Reliability. Local networks, with a fair level of redundancy of resources (both hardware and stored data), possess considerable potential for reliable, available operation. However, if this potential is to be realized, it must be possible to easily substitute various resources for one another (including processors, copies of files and programs, etc.). A uniform interface which hides

* At the local network installed at UCLA, the first version of network software made the network appear like another Arpanet, in which the details of the network are visible to application programs. The construction of a network wide printer daemon required over 20 processes and several thousand lines of code beyond the spooler function itself, to deal with error conditions, size problems, and asychronous events. Once a network transparent system was installed, virtually all of this mechanism vanished.

the binding of those resources to programs would seem to be necessary if the higher reliability goal is to be realized.

4. Simpler User Model. By taking care of the details of managing the network, the user sees a conceptually simpler storage facility, composed merely of files, without machine boundaries, replicated copies, etc. The same is true for other user visible resources. Therefore, when moving from a simple machine to multisite operation, the user view is not needlessly disturbed.

There are a number of aspects to network transparency. First is the manner in which objects and resources are named. Clearly, each object (such as a file) must have a globally unique name from the application point of view. In particular, the meaning of a name, i.e. the object with which it is associated, should not depend on the site in the network from which it is issued. This characteristic is called name transparency. Without it, moving or distibuting software in the network can be very painful, since the effect of the program changes with the move.

Second, is the location of the resource encoded in the name? This is often the approach taken in early systems; the site name would be prepended to the existing file name to provide uniqueness. However, this choice has the unfortunate effect of making it quite difficult to move a file. The reason is that it is common to embed file names in programs. Moving a file implies changing its name, making previously correct software no longer operational. The challenge, of course, is to provide location transparency in an efficient way, without significant system overhead to find the node(s) storing the file. Some additional mechanism is necessary, since location would no longer be discernible from inspection of the name of the object.

Semantic consistency is a third, important issue. By this we mean that system services, support libraries, commonly used application programs, and the like have the same effect independent of the site on which they are executed. This property is obviously essential if one is to be able to move program execution and data storage sites; a critical facility for the sake of reliability and availability methods. However, it is also very important from the viewpoint of managing software maintenance. If multiple versions of software are needed to avoid subtle differences in environments, the maintenance problem grows significantly.

Actually, this environment consistency problem is an old one. People commonly complain that it is not possible to directly transport software even between two identical hardware environments, because of local changes to the operating systems, because of differences in location or naming of libraries and other application services, or even because of differences between the versions of software currently installed. While this compatibility issue is serious enough among unconnected installations, it is far worse in a distributed system, where a much more intimate mode of cooperation among sites is the rule.

Unfortunately, this issue of semantic consistency conflicts with goals of local autonomy, because it constrains the conditions under which individual sites install new software and customize existing facilities. Methods by which this conflict can be reduced are outlined below.

4.1. Naming

How resources are named in a distributed system is an issue central to the system's design. There are a number of relevant considerations. What is the relation between naming and addressing? Will names be location transparent? How is mapping done? Can names be invalidated? If so, how? How is caching and rebinding done? How reliable is the mechanism in the face of failures? How well does it perform?

Lindsay's [Lindsay80] list of naming requirements are as follows:

1. The same name can be employed by different users to refer to different objects.

2. Different names can be used by different users to get to the same object.

3. A name instance may be resolved differently a different times. (Consider testing, for example.

4. Global name resolution information is not required at any one site.

5. Names may be context independent.

6. Names may be context dependent.

7. An object's representation may migrate without changing names.

While all of these issues are important, it is best to first develop a network wide, uniform naming mechanism, upon which some of the more sophisticated functions suggested above can be built.

It is also worthwhile to distinguish between a name and an address. An address indicates <u>where</u> the named item can be found, while a name is a label for the object with other properties. It is often quite useful to avoid encoding any location information in a name, especially user sensible ones, so that objects may be moved without impact. There are also distinctions between user sensible names and internal system names. System names need also to be unique, but may, for example, encode location information. If that information is treated as a guess, optimizing the location mapping operation, then when the object is moved, some additional work is done to find it. Alternately, it may be possible to invalidate all internal names for an object before it is moved.

4.2. Implementation Issues

While there is considerable agreement on the goal of network transparency, there is far less consensus on how to achieve it. One of the obvious questions is at what level in the system software the network should be hidden. There are several choices. Early efforts toward transparency, seen in systems such as the National Software Works [Hollar81] and RSEXEC, placed an additional layer of software between the existing operating systems and the application programs. Whenever a service request was made, this layer intercepted the call, decided where it was to be serviced, and translated it into a form suitable for the destination system. This approach preserved the existing system software untouched, but was terribly inefficient. A much more promising method, used in LOCUS and discussed later, builds network support deep in the internals of the operating system nucleus. This avoids multiple mappings and conversions and permits significant performance optimization, but requires integration into the operating systems themselves.

A second issue concerns the fact that, while network transparency is very valuable, it cannot be achieved totally. There are a number of situations where compromise is essential. One of the most obvious occurs in the file system where there are heterogeneous hardware facilities in the network. In this case one needs different compiled versions of a given program. Under normal circumstances, whenever a user or another program issues the name of the given program, the system should automatically pick the right one (as a function of the intended hardware execution environment). That is, the interpretation of a given name should differ, depending on the environment. One name should be bindable to multiple (executable) files. Unfortunately, there are other times at which each of these binary files should be accessible as distinct, unique objects, named in the usual global way. This is needed to replace the version or move it.

There are other examples as well. It is useful for many system initialization files to have a generic name, but exist in particularized form for each of the sites. Some systems put scratch files in the general file system catelogs; it is much more efficient to have local scratch file space, each one known by the same name or access path. A globally unique solution implies overhead that is unnecessary, and of little use.

The suitable approach to network transparency also depends on the thickness of the wire. While demand faulting for resources may be quite reasonable in a thick wire local network, it is an unsuitable strategy in a thin wire environment. There, needed resources must in general be gathered before needed, to avoid serious delays.

4.3. Separation of Function from Optimization Control

In systems without network transparency, the statement of algorithms, i.e. the programs, by necessity must encode current resource allocations. The most obvious example is a file system that uses the name of the site as part of the network file name. As a result, there is little to be gained from separating optimization commands from the rest of the program. Hence, the program often contains in it procedural statements to move resources around. Since the new location of a resource affects how it is accessed, the rest of the program depends on the successful effect of these preparatory steps. Indeed, in many programs, one would have a difficult time distinguishing among those steps in a program that are there only as optimization commands.

We argue that a better design separates the steps required to accomplish the algorithm from those directed to the system to better arrange resources needed by the algorithm. This view applies in a centralized system as well. In the case of a file system with inverted indexes, its application would demand that the manner in which a record with certain field values is requested is the same whether or not applicable indexes exist; the system intersects indexes, performs sequential searches, etc., as appropriate, rather than having the program changed to take advantage of a newly installed index.

To follow this approach requires two significant steps. First, a system interface is needed that hides the optimization relevant structure of the system; e.g. the indexes in the preceding example, and network transparency in the distributed system. Second, a separate set of directives (i.e. another interface) is needed by which application software can inform the system of its optimization desires.

The important aspect of the optimization directive "language" is that the correct operation of the algorithm must not depend on the directives. If, for example, the system chose to totally ignore the optimization directives, or worse, do something different, the algorithm should run successfully, if more slowly. We are not suggesting so uncooperative a system; rather the point is the recommended degree of de-coupling. The advantages which result if this path is followed include the general gains of network transparency, as well as the elimination of a class of software failures that would otherwise occur if the optimization directive cannot be followed by the system. An example would be a file transfer to move a file from an archive server in the local network to the local machine before a program to use that file were started; but the local disk overflows.

The cost of this separation is the need to carefully develop the design which supports it.

4.4. Local Autonomy Impacts on Transparency

Many people have realized that an important aspect of distributed systems, despite the implied intimacy of cooperation, is the ability for different ogranizational entities whose computers are part of the distributed system to nevertheless retain a significant level of control over their resources. While network transparency is necessary, there must still be means by which local control is retained. Local autonomy appears to have several components; a) resource control, b) administrative tools, and c) version issues. Below we discuss each one.

The resource control question is the easiest to deal with. The issue is how to permit users, application programs, and individual systems to make suitable resource optimization decisions and implement them in the face of network transparency. This clearly requires system mechanisms that make it possible to determine where a resource, such as a file, is located, as well as to instruct the system where to put a given resource. Providing such facilities is easy. The trick is doing so without violating transparency. Local autonomy with respect to resource control still makes sense if most machines are under a simple administrative umbrella, as a component of the defensive systems design that increases overall reliability.

The set of administrative tools needed to manage a distributed system of loosely cooperating machines is considerably greater than a single centralized system. This occurs for several reasons. One is that there is no single point where the overall performance of the system can be observed. It is quite possible that the local machine is performing quite well, while because of errors in the network protocols or failures elsewhere in the network, significant parts of the distributed system are seriously degraded. This "partial performance failure", while also possible in a central system (when deadlock occurs, for example) has greater potential in the distributed environment. Therefore, additional tools are needed, first to be able to determine the state of the overall distributed system, and then to be able to make alterations in the behavior of both local and remote sites.

There are several practical methods of version control that minimize loss of local autonomy. For example, the binding methods used in Multics, Unix, and other systems permit the institution of special software without it being generally visible. Most installations already install new software in a way that requires special action to access it; the default is the standard. Similar methods help in the distributed enviroment.

These issues point out that network transparency is a concept that can be profitably applied in degrees rather than merely absolutely. (We of course recommend a considerable degree.)

5. Problem Oriented Protocols

It is often argued that network software should be structured into a number of layers , each one implementing a protocol or function using the characteristics of the lower layer. In this way, it is argued, the difficulties of building complex network software are eased; each layer hides more and more of the network complexities and provides additional function. Thus layers of "abstract networks" are constructed. More recently, however, it has been observed that layers of protocol generally lead to layers of performance cost. (See for example, [Kleinrock75]). In the case of local networks, it is common to observe a cost of up to 5,000 instructions being executed to move a small collection of data from one user program out to the network.[Lampson79]

In a local network, the approach of layered protocols may be wrong, at least as it has been applied in long haul nets. Functionally, the various layers were typically dealing with issues such as error handling, congestion, flow control, name management, etc. In our case, these functions are not very useful, especially given that they have significant cost. The observed error rate on local networks is very low, although certainly not zero. Congestion is generally not a problem; the token ring in use at UCLA [Farber74][Clark78] uses a circulating token, supported by hardware, to control access to the transmission medium. The Ethernet [Xerox80] has an analogous mechanism. The Cambridge ring uses a version of TDMA. Much flow control in a distributed system may often be a natural consequence of the nature of higher level activity, since many incoming messages to a site result from explicit requests made by that site. Some additional flow control is needed, since a storage site can in principle be swamped by write requests from using sites which have open files supported by the given storage site. Name management largely must be done at a high level within distributed systems, so that any nontrivial lower level mechanism within the network layer would largely be ignored.

In fact, despite its limitations, Saltzer's "end-to-end" argument applies very strongly [Saltzer80a]. Summarized very quickly, Saltzer points out that much of the error handling that is done at low levels in computer networks is redone at higher levels. This is because low level handling cannot mask or provide recovery from higher level faults.

6. Atomic and Reliable Operation

Techniques for providing reliable operation of computing systems generally fall into a few groups: a) redundancy, b) correctness, and c) fast recovery. By redundancy, we mean not only that major parts of the system such as machines or data storage have been replicated, but also, in an information theory sense, that consistency checks can be made among various data structures and other dynamic state information in the overall system. These permit detection of difficulties, and in some cases the ability to repair errors by reconstructing the correct value of the damaged item from others. Redundancy is the quality which permits a system to detect an error in the first place; there is no way for the machine to deduce difficulty except by comparing some part of its internal state with another part. Hence redundancy is essential for error detection. It is also necessary if significant steps are to be taken to recover from the problems; by casting aside or repairing the broken part of the system.

These observations apply equally well to the hardware or software portions of a system. However, we will concentrate on software related issues here.

By correctness, we refer to efforts to assure that the algorithms of the system, be they implemented in hardware or software, contain no logical errors; that they concretely express precisely what was desired. Software experience indicates that this worthy goal is never attained in practice in large systems, but incremental efforts in that direction are helpful and to be lauded.

By fast recovery we refer to a system which, once an error has been found, can take suitable corrective action rapidly to come to a consistent enough state that permits continued operation of most services. Wide variation is seen in this area. Some databases require an entire reload after many classes of failures, while other systems make use of available redundancy to quickly find and repair the difficulty, having a structure that blocked much propagation of the effects of the error. In the American flight to the moon, the large computer systems were set up so that, in the case of software failure, the entire operating system and support programs could be restarted in a few seconds by a core image reload.

The partitioning of system state to prevent propagation of the effects of failures is quite important in the design of a distributed system. Otherwise, one can easily be faced with the spector of the reliability of the result being the product of the reliabilities of the individual nodes.

Distributed computer systems, especially those composed of small machines, tend naturally to be configured with considerable redundancy. Not only are there multiple copies of complete hardware nodes, but the necessity for local storage and copies of system software and data, as well as the desire to store user data close to the point of use, lead to considerable redundancy at various software levels as well. These observations appear particularly apt for small machines, since one tends to use more of them than large mainframes. If properly designed and managed, distributed computer systems have considerable potential for highly reliable, available operation. The problem, of course, is how to realize that potential at reasonable cost. While there is by no means a suitably complete set of concepts for reliable software systems design, a number of principles are now well understood, and these will be outlined below. Spefifically, we refer to transaction management, multiple copy support, and atomicity. We will also illustrate in the case study what little is understood about defensive structure; the case where each node does not entirely trust other members of the network and each machine tries to isolate itself from failures of others. This is an especially serious problem in an integrated distributed system, and when goals such as network transparency are being pursued, care is needed to avoid the obvious possibility of one machine 's failure crashing the entire network of computers.

6.1. Transactions

While in principle it would be possible to keep track of the interactions of all processes in the distributed system, and restore the system to a consistent state if failures occur, this is not practical. However, if one introduces a temporary boundary around a group of processes, then this group can be monitored and supported. The typical approach is to mark the beginning and end of monitored computation. Communication between the processes being monitored and the outside world is ignored by the monitoring mechanism. The activity of this group of processes is called a <u>transaction</u>, and the property of transactions which it is possible to provide is that they are <u>atomic</u>. Transactions actually were motivated by synchronizations issues, but they are a very important concept for reliability and recovery as well.

6.2. Atomic Transactions

One of the significant issues raised over the last several years is how to guarantee that a computer operation, composed of several distinct actions, either all occurs, or doesn't occur at all. This issue is quite important, as it prevents a system from being in an inconsistent state after a failure. To illustrate the problem, consider an operation to transfer money from one account to another by a credit followed by a withdrawal. A crash after the first operation but before the second has the obvious effect unless precautions are taken. Surely one wants money to be conserved in such a system. Solutions for single machine systems involve replicated writes of information in stylized ways. In the distributed environment, more is needed. In both cases, the methods will depend on idempotent operations. These are ones that can be repeated multiple times with the effect being the same as if they were executed once. Both the single machine and the distributed cases are discussed below.

6.3. Single Machine Atomic Transactions

The usual assumption is that when a failure occurs on a single machine, it is catastrophic, in the sense that the system stops operation; i.e. crashes. There are other types of failures of course; however this is the "error model" which is most often assumed when concerned with atomic transactions. Many people also assume that any I/O in progress at the time of the crash is already atomic; i.e. either the entire write takes place successfully, or no part of the intended destination has been altered. This assumption in fact is sometimes not true. Some devices' failure mode gives no assurance about the state of the last transfer. In these cases, a technique called stable storage is required. It will be discussed later.

The goal then is to assure that a series of actions ordered by an application or system program either all happen or none happen. To accomplish this goal, it is typically the programmer's responsibility to bracket the series of "atomic" actions by a BeginTransaction and EndTransaction. Then it is the system's responsibility to assure that, in the event of a crash, all transactions for which the EndTransaction had been reached are permanently recorded in non-volatile media, while all evidence of partially completed "transactions" have been removed as part of system recovery. A transaction then is an "atomic" collection of operations.*

The issue then is how to realize atomic transactions in the face of failures, while still maintaining suitable system performance. All currently used or proposed techniques depend on duplicate writes of each update, although clever batching can be used to reduce overhead. The best known technique is the use of an update log, called the undo log. The system automatically precedes every actual data update by an entry to the log that contains at least the identifier of the object being updated and the old value. Care must be taken to "force out" (i.e. write to non volatile storage) the log entry before the actual data update is done to the

*The concept of transaction also plays an important role in synchronization. Most systems also assure that all the operations of a transaction see the same version of the shared collection of data in the system, whether it is a file system, database, or other data collection.

permanent storage medium. In this way, if a system crash occurs while there are partially completed transactions in progress, the system restart procedure can use the entries in the log to undo those actions which had occurred. Then the system's operation can be continued by reinitiating those undone transactions.

Now in order to permit proper recovery, it is necessary for additional records to be written in the log. In particular, BeginTransaction and EndTransaction records, complete with a unique transaction id are required. Further, the transaction id is included in every data record previously mentioned. Also, it is necessary for all data updates to be forced out to the storage medium before the EndTransaction record is written to the log. Otherwise, these updates might be lost if a crash occurred immediately after the EndTransaction log write.

The recovery process consists of reading the log in the forward direction to determine which transactions were started but did not complete, and then "playing" the log in reverse, replacing actual data values in secondary store with their old values, for each record in the log marked with the id of an incomplete transaction. By running in reverse, i.e. processing the newest log entry first and the oldest last, it is possible for the log records to be generated in a simple way, by just taking the data value read in for update, even though it might previously have been updated in the given transaction.

It is worth understanding, in the light of this outline, when a transaction is actually completed. It is when the Endtransaction record is written to the log. This is called the <u>commit point</u> of the transaction. Any crash before this point will result in the effects of the transaction being undone; a crash after this point leads to recovery action that guarantees completion of the transaction, even in the face of the optimizations discussed below. More detailed discussions of this commit protocol may be found in [Gray79] or [Lindsay80].

6.3.1. Commit Optimizations

Clearly the support of atomic transactions is accompanied by potentially substantial I/O costs, as well as limits in the order by which I/O activity can be scheduled. However, a number of optimizations may be employed to reduce this cost. They are generally found in large systems, but are also important for small systems where the relative costs of I/O are still large (i.e. I/O is slow).

The first optimization is motivated by the desire to avoid having to force out all data updates before the EndTransaction record is written to the log. This is especially important in applications where data is often reused from transaction to transaction. To obtain this freedom, <u>redo log entries</u> are kept as part of the recovery log. That is, for each data update, the log entry contains the new value of the data item, in addition to the old value and the transaction id. Now it is merely required that each log record be actually written before the corresponding data update, and that all log records for a given transaction be written before the EndTransaction record. Then, even though some actual data updates may not have been written before the transaction to which they belong completed and a crash occurred, the new-value entries in the log can be used to redo them.

Support for a redo log is actually somewhat more complex than indicated here if one wishes to avoid redoing all values of updates of completed transactions that appear in the log. That is, the log must give some indication of which updates may have to be redone. There are a number of ways to provide this information; interested readers are referred to [Lindsay80].

A second, obvious optimization is to batch log records, actually outputting several of them in a single I/O. Care is required to still assure that the writing of the actual data records must not precede the log writes.

There are other approaches to support of atomic transactions on single site systems, using <u>intentions</u> <u>lists</u>. See Lampson [Lampson76]. There, the new value of the data is not written on top of the old, but written to a previously unused position in permanent storage. The act of committing is composed of changing the data structures which indicate which data items belong to the active version of the data collection. While this approach often integrates more easily into existing systems, it has the disadvantage that any physical layout of the data is altered by the substitution of a different physical copy of the new version into the logical structure. For example, if page i of a file is updated, a new free page is allocated, the new value of the page is written there, and a copy of the data structure indicating which pages belong to the file is created. The commit act consists of making that new data structure be the real one, usually by just replacing a directory entry that used to point to the old. If the old page had been physically near the file pages to which it was logically adjacent, that relationship could have been easily altered by this approach. The undo-redo log described earlier does not have this problem, since the original copy is retained in altered form.

The amount of I/O required by each method in the normal case is also different, but somewhat difficult to compare. The log at first glance requires two I/Os per actual data write, since the actual data write is still done, and a log record must also be written. The intentions list seems to require only one plus some small increment, since the new value is written, and subsequently a data structure change makes it current and releases the old. However, since log records can be batched, the actual number of writes is again one plus some increment. A careful analysis is needed to evaluate these tradeoffs, since the expected size of the update, the degree of inter-transaction locality, and existing software structure are all relevant.

The log based mechanism is also oriented to operate at either the physical or logical level. That is, the entries in the log may either be copies of the physical disk blocks which have been altered, or the specific logical records that were actually updated. The intentions list approach on the other hand has been thought through only for a physical level implementation. If it were to be used at the logical level, careful structuring of the supporting data structures would be required. In the remainder of this report, we will assume that the logging mechanism is being employed.

6.4. Atomic Transactions in a Distributed Environment

The goal of supporting atomicity in a distributed system is complicated by the fact that, without imposing additional structure, there is no single action which can cause multiple sites to perform their commits, at least in a way that works in the face of individual site failures as well as failures and errors in the network. In fact however, it _is_ possible by employing a stylized coordination strategy among the participating machines. The rules for message exchange among a collection of sites and the corresponding actions at each site to implement a distributed atomic transaction mechanism are quite subtle and merit careful attention. The basic idea behind a distributed commit mechanism is outlined below.

The best known distributed commit protocol is known as the _two phase commit_ [Grey78][Lampson76], and in its most straightforward form involves a single site as coordinator. It requires four messages in the normal case between the coordinator and each other participant. First, the coordinator asks each participant to _prepare-to-commit_. Each participant takes appropriate action at its local site (to be discussed below) and responds _prepared_. The coordinator takes local action of its own and then issues the _commit_ command to each site. Each site does so, and confirms that it has done so with a _commit-acknowledge_. The coordinator records when it has received all these replies.

We will assume that each site is maintaining a log, similar to that discussed in the earlier section on single site commit. When the _prepare-to-commit_ is received at each site however, a new log record type, PrepareCommit, is written to the log. This record includes the transaction id, and is just like EndTransaction in its requirements about other transaction related writes and log records having been forced out.

When the coordinator receives all the prepared replies, it writes a local CommitTransaction record, which contains the transaction id, to its log. This is the actual commit point of the distributed transaction. After the coordinator receives all the final commit-acknowledge replies, it records a local EndTransaction in its log.

To understand the significance of this protocol, let us consider the effects of various failures along the way. If any site fails before returning prepared the coordinator declares the transaction aborted, and notifies all sites. Since none of them have an EndTransaction record in their logs, they can each abort their part of the transaction. Once the coordinator has committed, the transaction is guaranteed to (eventually) be completed. It is true that the coordinator may crash at any time after itself committing, but before the remaining message exchanges are completed. However, it can determine that upon restart by examining its own log. It can then reinitiate the last message exchange between itself and each site.*

It is also possible for any of the other sites to have failed after sending off the prepared reply. When such a site restarts, it must contact the coordinators for all transactions for which there is a PrepareCommit in its own log but no EndTransaction to find out whether to commit or abort that transaction. The coordinator must remember the outcome of all such transactions.

Before going further, the reader should convince himself that this distributed commit protocol successfully operates as advertized. Once that is done, there are a number of useful remarks that can be made.

6.4.1. Observations on Distributed Commit

All distributed commit protocols known, including the two phase commit describe here, conflict to some degree with full local autonomy. In the protocol outlined above, any site can abort the transaction at any time it wishes, except during the period after it has acted on the prepare-to-commit message. From that point on, its actions on the given tranaction are completely under control of the coordinator. In particular, any resource locking done as part of this transaction at the local site must remain reserved until either a commit message is received, or the site is instructed to abort. If the coordinator should crash during this period, participating sites could wait a long time.

*This is a reasonable step to take because this message exchange is idempotent. Thus, even though it is not possible for the coordinator to know exactly how far along in the protocol it was, that indeterminacy doesn't matter.

This vulnerable period can be reduced when there are a number of sites involved in the transaction by notifying each site of the identities of all the other sites involved. Then if the coordinator crashes during the commit protocol, all the other sites can compare notes to see if all of them had acknowledged the prepare-to-commit messages with prepared replies, and if any of them got a commit message. If not all replies were issued, then the transaction can be aborted. If any site received a commit message, the rest can go ahead with their local commits as well. Hence the vulnerable period has been reduced to the time between the last prepared message is received by the coordinator to the time the first commit is issued. This is a short exposure.

Taking action when the coordinator fails is actually more complex than it seems because of the possible errors and asymmetric delays which can occur in the transmission media. For example, certain sites may decide that the coordinator has crashed, even though others believe it is still functioning. The coordinator may be getting the mesages sent by the other sites in a timely way, even though the replies to some of those sites are delayed. The outline of distributed commit protocols here has tacitly assumed that the underlying transmission media were reliable and without serious delays. Additional mechanims are needed to cope with these unfortunately real problems. They are common to most long haul networks. They are not expected in local area networks.

6.4.2. Distributed Commit Optimizations

When the cost or delay in sending messages is high, the two phase commit can be quite expensive or slow. However, it is possible to greatly reduce these costs, at the expense of increasing the activity required at each site, and further reducing the local autonomy of individual sites. Individual improvements were pointed out by a number of people, but most of them were first organized in a coherent way by Gray. [Gray80] They can be motivated intuitively by understanding the purpose of each of the two phase commit messages.

First, consider the last message, the commit-acknowledge. It permitted the coordinator, after receiving all of them, to write an EndTransaction to its local log. The purpose of this entry is essentially to allow the coordinator to forget all entries in the log pertaining to this transaction. Without it, the coordinator must remember whether he committed or aborted, since he doesn't know whether all of the other sites succeeded in their own local commits. Indeed, he doesn't even know whether his earlier commit command was even received. Since each site had the resources involved reserved, the system can work without this last message, for when someone else attempts to use those resources the site involved can query the coordinator to find out what happened.

The requirement for long term memory at the coordinator site can be limited by having all sites occasionally "batch" a reply to many completed commits to the coordinator. In this way, we have a commit protocol with essentially three messages per site per transaction.

Further optimization can be obtained by examining the role played by the first two messages, prepare-to-commit and prepared. Until the prepare-to-commit is received at a site, that site is fully able to unilaterally abort the current transaction, since when the request to commit is received, it can refuse. By acknowledging the request to commit, two things at the data site happen. First, the site prepares to commit by making sure that all of the transaction's relevant information has been logged or otherwise safely written. Second, the site gives up its local autonomy with respect to this transaction by replying that it is prepared to commit, and will await the decision of the coordinator whether or not to do so.

Preceding this message exchange, there presumably had been some messages and computation taking place in support of the transaction's work itself.

If one were willing to give up the ability to unilaterally abort a partially completed transaction, then the two messages needed to prepare to commit could be dropped. That is, whenever an update request is received at a site, it must be immediately logged so that a commit is possible. This method seems to work only if a "linear commit" policy is being followed. In such a case, rather than having a fixed coordinator, who broadcasts to all other participants, one assumes that there is no parallelism in the transaction. Instead the coordination site is the only one involved in actual computation, and it can move from site to site.

In this way, one may have a one message commit protocol, through loss of local autonomy, increased storage at the coordinator site, and additional log activity at the data sites (since logging must be immediate, not batched).

6.5. Related Issues

There are a number of issues related to distributed commit that should not be forgotten. Some of these are outlined below.

6.5.1. Sharing and Logical vs. Physical Writes

In the preceding discussions about the use of logs or intentions lists for the recording of ongoing updates, it was implicitly assumed that the object being logged was a physical one; a page or disk track for example, even though the update may have been to a field, record, character, or other logical level object. If a given logical level object crosses physical object boundaries, then both physical objects are simply recorded. While this approach is fairly straightforward, a problem occurs if there is concurrent access by different users. Consider what happens if program A updates item 1 on a given page. This causes the new and old versions of the page to be logged. Program B then updates item 2 on the same page. The new and (not so) old versions of the page are again logged. Suppose program B then completes and A subsequently aborts. The item 2 update will have been lost since the abort of program A caused the old version of the page to be restored!

There are two straightforward solutions to this problem. One is to lock the physical objects that contain the logical object being updated. These locks are strictly local, and are in addition to any other synchronization controls. They solve the problem, at the expense of creating potential deadlocks which were not present before, since these locks interact with any other resource control mechanims in the system. Another method is to do logging at the logical level. That is, the new and old values put in the log are the actual logical objects updated. Then any use of the log does not affect other objects contained in the same physical object. Of course, if two concurrent transactions have updated the same logical object there is potential trouble, but virtually any synchronization policy prohibits this case anyway. However, in many environments, logical level logging leads to considerably more I/O traffic unless batching of log entries is done.

In the distributed case, concurrency does not create any additional serious problems.

6.5.2. Information Hiding Structures and Distributed Commit

The commit protocols outlined here require the coordinator to interact with each site where any update activity on bahalf of the transaction is taking place. This structure is inappropriate when one is composing software from already developed and debugged routines. It would be most desirable if a distributed operation, supported by a commit protocol such as those described here, could be invoked as a subroutine of another operation, itself distributed, which had no knowledge of how the subroutine were implemented, not even being concerned, for example, whether the subroutine involved distributed operation or not.

Fortunately, it appears that the commit methods do operate quite nicely in this fashion. When the subroutine coordinator site receives a prepare-to-commit, for example, he sends a similar message to all of his sites, awaits the prepared reply, and the returns one of his own. The remainder of the commit protocol seems to operate just as straightforwardly.

6.5.3. Stable Storage

Earlier, the typically assumed failure modes of secondary storage were briefly outlined. There it was said that one often assumes that the last write to non-volatile storage maintained integrity; i.e. either it occurred correctly in its entirety, or it didn't happen at all. In those cases where this assumption cannot be made, the commit protocols we have outlined here require additional mechanism. We will obtain the desired property of storage, which is called stable storage, by double writes and error detection methods. Any data block that needs to be stored stably can be stored in the following way. Prepare a version of the block which, upon examination, reveals whether the block is valid or not. A good checksum appended to the block will suffice. Write the block, including checksum and block id, to a reserved location on the non-volatile store in a single I/O. Then write it again to the intended destination. If there is a crash the recovery software examines the reserved location. If there is a valid block there, the block is copied to its intended location. A quick analysis shows that this procedure provides the functional equivalent of correct writes during crash (so long as, whatever the device does, it is done to the intended location!)

The intentions list method requires stable storage for at least the last write of the data structure header which installs the new data structure, causing the commit. Otherwise a failure at that point could cause the entire object to be lost. The logging method does not seem to have this problem. If a crash occurs while writing a log record, no update could have been done to the corresponding actual data value. The only exception is if the log is being blocked, several records per block, so that the write of a new record actually causes the write of a block that contains several previously written records.

7. Multiple Copy Support

With multiple sites in a distributed network, there are several motivations for maintaining several copies of data. The first concerns response, especially in a slow network. If there is a copy of the data "near" the requesting site, the delay in getting it may be considerably reduced, at least for read access. The second motivation is one of reliability and availability. If the network or a storage site is unavailable, the data may still be obtained if it has been stored redundantly at some site which is accessible.

The primary problem with supporting multiple copies of data concern update; how is it to be done in a way that does not seriously impact system performance while at the same time maintaining a single logical version of the data throughout the network. Clearly some synchronization protocol is required.

In principle, one could use the distributed commit protocols described earlier. That is, any operation intended to modify a replicated data item could be thought of as a transaction involving several objects; the copies themselves. However, this approach is really not satisfactory. The goal in the case of multiple copy support involves more than mutual consistency. In particular, one wishes to permit access to a copy of the data even if the network has been partitioned and there is other activity possible elsewhere in the network, where a copy of the data may be stored. The commit protocols previously discussed would not permit the transaction to go forward; one of the sites needed would not be available, and so the transaction would be aborted. The methods proposed to deal with multiple copy support are as follows.

1. Voting. In voting-based systems such as proposed by Thomas [Thomsas78] and Menasce, Popek, and Muntz [MPM77], mutual consistency is guaranteed at the expense of availability. Users desiring to modify a data object must lock it by obtaining majority assent in a vote. Since there can be at most one partition containing a majority of the sites, any file will be accessible in at most one partition. Unfortunately, it is possible that there will be no partition which contains a majority of the sites, so in this case no updates could occur anywhere. Weighted voting schemes do not correct this limitation.

2. Tokens. Here it is assumed that each data object has a token associated with it, which permits it bearer to modify the object. Obtaining the token is another issue, reducible more or less to locking. In this model only sites in the partition containing the token are permitted to modify the object, so using tokens is less restrictive than using voting. However, the problem of recreating lost tokens is a serious one.

3. Primary sites. Originally discussed by Alsberg & Day [Alsberg76], this approach suggests that a single site be appointed responsible for a file's activities. Upon partitioning (possibly involving a primary site crash) either: a) a backup site is elected as the new primary and consistency becomes a possible problem (the proposed approach), or else b) the file becomes inaccessible in all but the primary site partition.

4. Reliable networks and Optimism. Communications in the SDD-1 system are based on the use of a "reliable network" [Hammer78], which guarantees the eventual delivery of all messages even if partitioning occurs. This delivery depends on "spoolers" which save messages to be transmitted following a break in communications. No guarantee of post-partition consistency exists; as with the primary site model, assuming consistent data afterwards is "optimistic" [Kung79] in the sense that it may work out, but quite possibly the work done in different partitions will have to

be undone or coalesced somehow by users.

5. Media Transporting. In this approach, employed at Xerox PARC and other installations where very intelligent terminals are linked via a network, files are not stored redundantly but are kept on removable storage media which can be carried around during prolonged partitions. Thus availability and consistency are simultaneously achieved, but they are not achieved automatically. This approach is clearly only useful for local networks with compatible portable storage media at each site.

6. Hot Shadows. A common, simple method to provide high reliability, replicated storage is arrange two identical storage mediums connected to a given system. Each write is then done twice by the system; first to one store, and then to the other. In this way one is protected against media failure. To obtain additional protection, from processor or system software errors, it is necessary to replicate much more of the configuration, connect input lines to both replicated systems, and have them compute in parallel. In this case, it is common for only one of the systems to be "on line", i.e. to have its outputs actually used by other machines. Typically, there is a connection between the duplexed systems which both are required to periodically service; a watchdog counter is common. If the hot shadow system (the one not on line) detects malfunction of the other, it can cause itself to be switched on line and the other cut off. This switchover causes virtually no loss of data on the output lines.

7. Version Vectors. At UCLA, a straightforward method was developed which permits update to copies of data in different partitions, and correctly detects conflicts at merge time [Parker81]. The method labels each copy of the data with a version vector that has as many elements as there are copies of the data, each element corresponding to a given site. Whenever a site updates a copy, the corresponding element of the vector is incremented. At merge time, if one version vector dominates the other (i.e. each of its elements is pairwise greater or equal to the other) then there is no conflict. Otherwise there is.

Once conflict is detected, automatic reconciliation is possible if the semantics of the updates which have taken place are straighforward enough. A surprising number of cases are, including system structures such as file directories and user mailboxes, as well as applications such as funds transfer and reservations systems [Faissol81].

8. Synchronization

Synchronization issues are different in a distributed environment than in a single machine environment. While the user visible functionality which is desired is similar, one often expects additional sharing, and therefore greater needs. This hypothesis is motivated by the observation that often, users share a single machine because of the desire to share the cost of the machine rather than to share information. Despite the development of low cost computing, this factor is still real. In a distributed environment, the connections among the machines were presumably constructed to share information. Certainly computer networks are often used to provide remote access to a computing resource not available at the local site. The Arpanet is used mostly in this manner. In the environment of small machines, this motivation is considerably less, since the remote resource is not very different from the local one. Therefore the sharing motivation is expected to dominate.

A much more apparent, and less hypothetical reason for the difference in synchronization issues concerns the nature of the underlying hardware environment. In a single machine environment, typified by shared memory among processes (even if it is only the supervisor's data space), the cost of setting or checking a lock can easily be reduced to a few hundred instructions if desired. This amounts to a few hundred microseconds. In a distributed environment, even a local network, the cost is far greater. Any distributed synchronization method involves messages. The fastest message over a local network from one operating system to another (which involves preparing the message, executing device driver code, etc. on both the sending and receiving machine) requires several milliseconds; at least an order of magnitude more per message. Further, many synchronization protocols require more than one message to accomplish their work.

For these reasons, it is necessary to carefully examine the actual synchronization needs and select an appropriate solution. There are two major classes of synchronization techniques proposed for distributed environments; locking and timestamps. There are numerous versions of each. For an in depth review and analysis of the various choices, see Bernstein and Goodman [Bernstein80]. Most real systems use some form of locking, however.

9. Deadlock in Distributed Systems

The problem of deadlock in a centralized system is well recognized and has been extensively studied. Readers are referred to Holt [Holt72] for a review of the issue. In a distributed system, the problem is altered by two considerations. First, the resource dependency cycle may cross multiple machine boundaries, making any deadlock detection (or avoidance) algorithm a distributed application. Second, to the degree that local autonomy is a significant consideration, it may not be feasible to legislate certain simple solutions.

The problem then becomes how to efficiently detect deadlock in a distributed environment. Numbers of proposals have been made to search for cycles in parallel, to use a hierarchical organization, etc. See for example [Menasce80]. Gray [Gray81] has observed that, in the distributed database arena, virtually all observed distributed deadlocks have been cycles of length two, suggesting that very simple, inexpensive methods may be used to catch virtually all deadlocks in most cases, with a more extensive fallback mechanism to be run less frequently. It is also the usual experience that, in a well designed system, deadlocks are rare in the first place. For these reasons, we do not pursue these issues further here.

THE LOCUS CASE STUDY

10. Introduction

LOCUS is an integrated distributed system whose goals include a) making the development of distributed applications no more difficult than single machine programming, and b) realizing the potential that distributed systems with redundancy have for highly reliable, available operation. The system is application code compatible with the Unix operating system, and runs on DEC PDP-11s, models 44, 45, and 70, connected by a 10 megabit ring network. A prototype is operational at UCLA.

10.1. System Design Assumptions and Goals

Most existing distributed systems were constructed by making relatively minor modifications to adapt single machine systems to permit them to interact with other copies of themselves, or even with other systems. The basic structure and operational philosophy of those systems were invariably preserved. Our goal was to understand, given the freedom to start largely anew, what the structure of a distributed system ought to be. One fundamental assumption we made concerned the interconnection network; it was of high bandwidth, low delay, with a low error rate - so called "thick wire" networks, represented by such examples as the Ethernet. Broadcast capability was not assumed. We explicitly ruled out Arpanet or Telenet style networks because of their limited bandwidth and significant delay. Satellite based networks were not explicitly addressed because of their significant delay.

General applications were to be supported, with focus on "computer utility" functions and data management. High reliability/availability was essential, and ease of programming very important. We were willing to insist that all sites in the network run a given system, but the sites should be able to vary widely in power and storage capacity. At the outset, good performance was considered to be an important measure of success.

10.2. LOCUS Overview

LOCUS is a distributed operating system whose architecture strongly addresses the issues of network transparency, reliability and availability, and performance that drove the design. The machines in a LOCUS net cooperate to give all users the illusion of operating on a single machine; the network is essentially invisible. Nevertheless, each machine is a complete system and can operate gracefully alone. Data storage is designed to be automatically replicated to the degree indicated by associated reliability profiles. Graceful operation in the face of network partitions, as well as nodal failures, is supported. It is expected that these characteristics are suitable for the support of a wide variety of applications, including general distributed computing, office automation, and database management.

Here, we discuss the major issues that influenced the design, suggest the effects that those issues had, and comment on the current state of the LOCUS implementation.

11. General System Architecture

The structure of LOCUS has been designed to directly address issues of transparency and reliability. From an implementation point of view, the major components of LOCUS, in terms of size, design subtlety, and overall risk (with respect to proving the feasibility of the general approach) are its naming mechanism, as supported by the network wide file system, and the accompanying resource synchronization design.

11.1. Global Names

In developing a naming mechanism for a distributed system, one faces a number of issues. What is the nature of user sensible, global names? What are the system internal global names? How, and when, is mapping between the two done? How and when are names of either sort allocated and invalidated? Should there be multiple levels of naming? The design choices made in LOCUS, and the basic reasons, are outlined below.

There are two significant levels of abstraction in the LOCUS file system, which serves as the heart of the naming mechanism. The user and application program view of object names in LOCUS is analogous to a single, centralized Unix environment; virtually all objects appear with globally unique names in a single, uniform, hierarchical name space. Each object is known by its path name in a tree[1], with each element of the path being a character string. Any user and/or program can set its working directory appropriately to avoid having to employ the longer path names that this large hierarchy may imply. No notion of object location appears in the path name, so that an object can easily be moved without changing its visible name.

Low level names in LOCUS are also globally unique. The name space is organized around the concept of file groups.[2] As in Unix, each file group (of which there may be many on a single standard Unix system) is composed of a section of a mass store, and divided into two parts; a small set of file descriptors which serve as a simple low level "directory", and a large number of standard sized data blocks. A file descriptor (inode) contains pointers to the data blocks which compose that file. Data blocks can be used as indirect pointer blocks for large files. Under these conditions, a low level file name is a <file group number, file descriptor number>.[3]

LOCUS uses the same method, although since a file group can be replicated, one speaks of a logical file group number. There is an additional map from logical to physical file group number; this is a one to many map.[4] Files may be replicated only at sites which store the containing file group. However, it is not necessary to replicate a given file at all such sites. Thus the amount of storage allocated to the physical versions of a file group can differ, since each can be incomplete. When a file is not stored at a physical file group, the file descriptor there is not kept current.

The application visible naming hierarchy is implemented by having certain low level files serve as high level directories. An entry in such a directory contains an element of a path name and the index of the file descriptor corresponding to the next directory or data file in the path.

The collection of file groups therefore represent a set of naming trees; these are patched together to form the single, network wide naming tree by system code and a network wide mount table.

Creating a file requires allocating a file descriptor, so race conditions could lead to the same file descriptor being allocated to different files. Therefore,

1 There are a few exceptions to the tree structure, provided by Unix links.
2 The term file group in this paper corresponds directly to the Unix term file system.
3 Devices also appear in the file system as leaves in the name structure.
4 It is implemented as an extension to mounting a file group.

some control is needed. One solution would be not to use the descriptor number as part of the name; rather have some unique id as the name, and store it in the descriptor as well as in the higher level directory entry that pointed at the descriptor. The descriptor number would be treated only as a guess and the ids would be compared at each access attempt. No particular method to manage file deletion and subsequent reuse of file descriptors is then needed, assuming that ids are never reused.

However, in LOCUS, this approach would have meant changing the contents of higher level directories, which are application code visible in Unix. Therefore, we chose to retain the file descriptor number as part of the name. To avoid allocation races, the file descriptor space for each file group is logically partitioned; each storage site for a file group may allocate descriptors only from its own part. Deletion of a file requires interaction among all storage sites for a given file before the descriptor may actually be reused.

Given the high and low level name space, the next issue concerns the map between the two. In LOCUS, conversion to low level name is done as soon as possible; then only low level names are passed within the system. In this way, one avoids remapping names. This philosophy could have been carried even further; one could have found the disk address of a page, and used that as a component of the 'name' to be passed. We did not do this for two reasons. First, since a given file may not be stored at all storage sites for that file group, address information might not be available, and so another mechanism would be needed anyway. Second, we wanted each storage site to be able to provide some significant degree of internal system data structure consistency by itself. For example, while a using site updating a file can cause the contents of that file to be inappropriately altered at the storage site, it cannot damage other files stored at the storage site (an action which would be possible if physical page addresses were being used.)

11.2. Synchronization

Storage may be replicated, and there are multiple users, so the problem of synchronization of access to logical files and their physical counterparts must be addressed if a consistent file system is to be presented to users. Standard Unix is quite bereft of such controls, so these represent an addition to the user and program interface.*

*The introduction of synchronization control is also a minor source of incompatibility for occasional existing programs.

11.2.1. Synchronization Policy in LOCUS

A synchronization policy more sophisticated than simple "multiple readers, single writers" is necessary, for two principal reasons. First, in a modern operating system environment, more functionality is appropriate. For example, when one process forks another, it is best for the newly created process to inherit and retain the access rights held by the parent, since in most cases the family of processes are cooperating on the same task. They can coordinate among themselves if intrafamily synchronization is needed.

Another example results from the hierarchical file system. Whenever a file is opened through the use of a full path name, it is necessary to open for read all the directory files in the path. One expects high traffic of this sort in an environment with many users. Shared read locks would suffice, if it were not for the fact that any file creation or rename implies a write lock to the containing directory. While these locks would be of short duration, the potential performance impact of temporarily blocking all file opens in the network that contain that directory in their path name is significant.

The LOCUS solution is a new access type, nolock read. When a file is opened for nolock read, there is essentially no synchronization with other activity on the file. The only guarantee is that a single operating system read call will return with a consistent set of bits, i.e. from one version of a (possibly dynamically changing) file.* Directory entries and the system software that accesses them have suitable characteristics to be accessed in this way (although convincing oneself of this fact is not easy). A higher overhead alternative would have been to implement record locks in the file system.

The second reason for a sophisticated synchronization policy is Unix compatibility. Since standard Unix has few restrictions, normal program behavior sometimes would be blocked by a straightforward policy.

11.2.2. Synchronization Mechanism in LOCUS

Many techniques have been proposed for the synchronization mechanisms in distributed systems [Bernstein80]. After careful analysis, we chose a centralized synchronization protocol with distributed recovery. For a given file group, one site is designated as the Current Synchronization Site (CSS) This site is responsible for coordinating access to the files contained in the associated file group. That is,

*So long as the read did not cross a block boundary.

all open calls involve a message to the CSS (except for nolock reads). In this way it is possible for the CSS to assure that a requester gets the latest version of a file. However, it is not necessary for the CSS to be the site from which data access is obtained. Any site which has a copy of the file can support this open request; that is, a particular Storage Site (SS) is designated to support an open request at the time of the open. A fairly general synchronization policy can be supported, since the synchronizing point is centralized for any given decision.

An outline of how an actual file operation is handled may serve to clarify the interaction of synchronization and file system structure. Suppose an open request is made for file /A/B/C. The file descriptor for A is found by examining the (already) open root directory. Suppose the file descriptor indicates remote storage. A message is sent by low level network code to the CSS requesting to open file <g#,f#>, the two part low level name corresponding to A. The CSS selects a storage site and sends two messages, one to the storage site and one to the using site. The using site installs the appropriate file descriptor in its internal table (just as if the file were local) and sends a message to the SS requesting the first block. Processing at the using site now continues as if the directory had been local; i.e. the directory page(s) are searched for the desired entry. When found, the low level name is used to open the next directory in the path. Eventually, data blocks are obtained.

The mechanism used in LOCUS is quite different than primary copy strategies, [Alsberg78] since all physical copies of a logical file may be used, even for update. In this way, optimization that takes into account the location of resources can be done.

12. Reliability

Reliability and availability represent a whole other aspect of distributed systems which has had considerable impact on LOCUS. Four major classes of steps have been taken to achieve the potential for very high reliability and availability present in distributed systems with redundancy.

First, an important aspect of reliable operation is the ability to substitute alternate versions of resources when the original is found to be flawed. In order to make the act of substitution as straightforward as possible, it is desirable for the interfaces to the resource versions to look identical to the user of those resources. While this observation may seem obvious, especially at the hardware level, it also applies at various levels in software, and is another powerful justification for network transparency. In LOCUS, copies of a file can be substituted for one another with no visibility to application code.

From another point of view, once network transparency is present, one has the opportunity to enhance system reliability by substituting software as well as hardware resources when errors are detected. In LOCUS, considerable advantage is taken of this approach. Since the file system supports automatic replication of files transparently to application code, it is possible for graceful operation in the face of network partition to take place. If the resources for an operation are available in a given partition, then the operation may proceed, even if some of those are data resources replicated in other partitions. A partition merge procedure detects any inconsistencies which may result from this philosophy, and for those objects whose semantics the system understands (like file directories, mailboxes, and the like), automatic reconciliation is done. See the next section.

Recovery from partitioned operation is done hierarchically, in that first lower level software attempts to merge a file; if it cannot, then the problem is reported to the next level up, eventually to the user (owner) of the file.

Second, the concept of committing [Lampson76] [Gray78] a file is supported in LOCUS. For a given file, one can be assured that either all the updates are done, or none of them are done. Commit normally occurs automatically at file close time if the file had been open for write, but application software may request commits at any time during the period when a file is open. To do a commit, first the current storage site permanently records the changed file. Then the CSS and user code are notified of successful commit, and user execution may go on. From this point on, the new version of the file is propagated in parallel to other storage sites.

Third, even though a very high level of network transparency is present in the syntax and semantics of the system interface, each site is still largely autonomous. When, for example, a site is disconnected from the network, it can still go forward with work local to it. This goal has had significant architectural impact, which is discussed in section 6.2.

Fourth, the interaction among machines is strongly stylized to promote "arms length" cooperation. The nature of the low level interfaces and protocols among the machines permits each machine to perform a fair amount of defensive consistency checking of system information. As much as feasible, maintenance of internal consistency at any given site does not depend on the correct behavior of other sites. (There are, of course, limits to how well this goal can be achieved.) Each site is master of its own resources, so it can prevent flooding from the network.

13. Recovery

Given that a data resource can be replicated, a policy issue arises. When the network is partitioned and a copy of that resource is found in more than one partition, can the resource be modified in the various partitions? It was felt important for the sake of availability that such updates be permitted. Of course, this freedom can easily lead to consistency conflicts at partition merge time. However, our view is that such conflicts are likely to be rare, since actual sharing in computer utilities is known to be relatively low.

Further, we developed a simple, elegant algorithm using version vectors to detect conflicts if they have occurred. See [Parker80].

Most significant, for those data items whose update and use semantics are simple and well understood, it may be quite possible to reconcile the conflicting versions automatically, in a manner that does not have a "domino effect"; i.e. such a reconciliation does not require any actions to data items that were updated during partitioned operation as a function of the item(s) being reconciled.

Good examples of data types whose operations permit automatic reconciliation are file directories and user mailboxes. The operations which apply to these data types are basically simple: <u>add</u> and <u>remove</u>. The reconciled version is the union of the several versions, less those items which have been removed.* There are of course situations where the system does not understand the semantics of the object in conflict. The LOCUS philosophy is to report the conflict to the next level of software, in case resolution can be done there. An example of this case might be data management software. Eventually, the conflict is reported to the user. It is surprising how many applications have straightforward enough semantics that nearly full operation can be permitted during partitioned operation while still allowing automated reconciliation at merge time. See [Rudisin81] for a more extensive discussion of recovery in LOCUS. See [Faissol81] for discussion of partitioned operation in applications such as banking and airlines reservations.

When a partition actually occurs, it may be necessary to establish new CSSs for various file groups. Selection of a CSS is done by a simple protocol that deals with the race conditions which may occur as sites are failing and returning to operation. Once a CSS is established, it must acquire knowledge about the file

*The situation for directories is somewhat more complex, since it is possible to have a <u>name</u> conflict; when two different files of the same name are created in two different partitions. LOCUS detects such conflicts and reports them to the users.

group from the other storage sites for that group which remain accessible.

14. Performance and its Impact on Software Architecture

"In software, virtually anything is possible; however, few things are feasible." [Cheatham71] While the goals outlined in the preceding sections may be attainable in principle, the more difficult goal is to meet all of the above while still maintaining good performance within the framework of a well structured system without a great deal of code. A considerable amount of the LOCUS design was tempered by the desire to maintain high performance. Perhaps the most significant design decisions in this respect are:

a) specialized "problem oriented protocols",

b) integrated rather than partitioned function,

c) a lightweight process mechanism inside the operating system kernel,

d) special handling for local operation.

Below, we discuss each of these in turn.

14.1. Problem Oriented Protocols

The problem oriented protocol arguement presented earlier seems to apply quite directly to LOCUS. The ring hardware automatically provides congestion control. Naming is done by the operating system file mechanism already outlined. The error situation is especially significant. In the design of LOCUS, we found it necessary to deal with a significant collection of error events within the operating system; managing the impact of remote sites failing, synchronization difficulties, etc. Many types of low level errors therefore are also detected by the mechanisms that we needed to build anyway; hence the (expensive) low level supports were dropped. Notice that this principle cannot be followed blithefully. There are certain low level events that cannot be detected at a higher level. These must be addressed in the basic network protocols. So, for example, we support automatic retransmission, as well as certain forms of redundancy in data transmission.

All of these observations lead one to develop specialized _problem oriented protocols_ for the problem at hand. That is what occurred in LOCUS. For example, when a user wishes to read a page of a file, the _only_ message that is sent from the using site to the storage site is a _read_ message request. A _read_ is one of the primitive, lowest level message types. There is no connection management, no acknowledgement overhead, etc. The only software ack in this case is the delivery of the requested page. (The hardware does provide a low level acknowledgement.)

Our experience with these lean, problem oriented protocols has been excellent. The effect on system performance has been dramatic.

14.2. Functional Partitioning

It has become common in some local network developments to rely heavily on the idea of "servers", where a particular machine is given a single role, such as file storage, name lookup, authentication or computation. [Swinehart79] [Rashid80] [Needham 80] We call this approach the server model of distributed systems. Thus one speaks of "file servers", "authentication servers", etc. However, to follow this approach purely is inadvisable, for several reasons. First, it means that the reliability/availability of an operation which depends on multiple servers is the product of the reliability of all the machines and network links involved. The server design insures that, for many operations of interest, there will be a number of machines whose involvement is essential.

Second, because certain operations involve multiple servers, it is necessary for multiple machine boundaries to be crossed in the midst of performing the operation. Even though the cost of network use has been minimized in LOCUS as discussed above, it is still far from free; the cost of a remote procedure call or message is still far greater than a local procedure call. One wants a design where there is freedom to configure functions on a single machine when the situation warrants. Otherwise serious performance costs may result, even though the original designers believed their functional decomposition was excellent.

Third, since it is unreasonable to follow the server machine philosophy strictly, one is led to multiple implementations of similar functions; to avoid serious performance costs, a local cache of information otherwise supplied by a server is usually provided for at least some server functions. The common example is file storage. Even though there may be several file servers on the network, each machine typically has its own local file system. It would be desirable to avoid these additional implementations if possible.

An alternative to the server model is to design each machine's software as a complete facility, with a general file system, name interpretation mechanism, etc. Each machine in the local network would run the same software, so that there would be only one implementation. Of course, the system would be highly configurable, so that adaptation to the nature of the supporting hardware as well as the characteristics of use could be made. We call this view the integrated model of distributed systems. LOCUS takes this approach.

It should be noted that an integrated architecture can be easily made to largely look like a server oriented system if suitable configuration flexibility has been provided. For example, if there were significant cost or performance advantages to be gained by having most files stored at a few sites, no software changes would be necessary to LOCUS. In fact, one of the planned configurations for LOCUS includes workstation-like machines with no local file storage at all.

14.3. Lightweight Processes

To maximize LOCUS performance, we wished at any given site to be able to serve a network request without the usual overhead of scheduling and invoking an application level process. Hence, implementing much of LOCUS as user processes was not acceptable. Further, the services that a given machine must provide to remote requesters is quite stylized in LOCUS; they correspond to the specific message types in the low level protocols. Hence implementation in the nucleus of LOCUS was indicated. We took this view even though it could have been quite convenient to implement network service in user processes.

The solution chosen was to build a fast but limited process facility called server processes. These are processes which have no non-privileged address space at all. All their code and stack are resident in the operating system nucleus. Any of their globals are part of the operating system nucleus' permanent storage. Server processes also can call internal system subroutines directly. As a result of this organization, the body of server processes is quite small; the largest one contains several hundred lines of C code (not counting the subroutine calls to already existing system functions). As network requests arrive, they are placed in a system queue, and when a server process finishes an operation, it looks in the queue for more work to do. Each server process serially serves a request. The system is statically configured with some number of these processes at system initialization time.

These lightweight processes permit efficient serving of network requests (therefore keeping protocol support cost low) while at the same time avoiding implementation of another structuring facility besides processes. In retrospect, this was an excellent early design decision, both because of the structuring simplicity which resulted, and because of the contribution to performance.

14.4. Local Operation

The site at which the file access is made, the Using Site (US), may or may not be the same as the CSS or SS. In fact, any combination of these roles are possible, or all may be played by different sites.

When multiple roles are being played by a single site, it is important to avoid much of the mechanism needed to support full, distributed operation. These optimizations are supported in LOCUS. For example if, for a given file open, CSS = SS = US, then this fact is detected immediatcly and virtually all the network support overhead is avoided. The cost of this approach is some additional complexity in protocols and system nucleus code.

The system design is intended to support machines of heterogeneous power interacting in an efficient way; large mainframes and small personal computers sharing a replicated file system, for example. Therefore, when a file is updated, it is not desirable for the requesting site to wait until copies of the update have propagated to all sites storing copies of the file, even if a commit operation is desired. The design choice made in LOCUS is for updated pages to be posted, as they are produced, at the storage site providing the service. When the file is closed, the disk image at the storage site is updated and the using site program now continues. Copies of the file are propagated to all other storage sites for that file in a demand paging manner.* In this way, it is straightforward for a system with no local file storage to participate in a LOCUS network.

14.5. Performance Results

To satisfactorily evaluate the performance of a network transparent system such as LOCUS, one would like answers to at least the following questions. First, when all the resources involved in an operation are local, what is the cost of that operation, especially compared to the corresponding system that does not provide for network operation, either in its design or implementation? This is often a difficult comparison to make. It is not sufficient just to "turn off" the network support code in LOCUS, as the existence of that code altered the very structure of the system in ways that wouldn't happen otherwise. Fortunately, in our case, we could compare local operation under LOCUS with the corresponding situation under standard

*While this method avoids useless waiting at the using site, it does raise the possibility that a new copy of the file is successfully created and then immediately made unavailable by a crash or partition. In fact, this is just one of the many race conditions which can occur. They are all handled by the version management algorithm described in [Parker80].

Unix. LOCUS local operation can be thought of as the "null distributed call".

The performance of remote behavior is also of paramount importance, since after all, it is distributed operation that largely motivated the LOCUS architecture.

Three initial experiments are reported here:

i) reading one file page,

ii) writing one file page, and

iii) sequentially reading a 600 block file.

Each experiment was run on:

a) standard Version 7 Unix,

b) local LOCUS (i.e. the program and data both resided at the same machine),

c) distributed LOCUS (i.e. the data resided on the machine used in cases a and b, but the program ran on another machine.)

For the first two experiments, the quantity reported is system time - the amount of cpu time consumed in servicing the request. For distributed LOCUS, the quantity given is the sum of the system time at the using site and the storage site. In the third experiment, total elapsed time is reported.

A great deal of care was taken to assure comparability of results; the same data blocks were read, numbers of buffers were comparable, the same disk was employed, etc. The tests were repeated multiple times. The values reported are means, but the standard deviations were very small. The machines on which these measurements were run are DEC PDP-11/45s, with an average time of greater than 2 microseconds per instruction. The disk used is capable of delivering one data page per 15 milliseconds if there is no head movement.

System Time Measurements
(one data-page access - results in milliseconds)

System	Read	Write
Unix	6.07	4.28
Local LOCUS	6.15	4.27
Dist. LOCUS	14.27	7.50

The distributed LOCUS results are further decomposed into the load at the using site and the storage site. These results are as follows.

Distributed LOCUS System Loads

Test	Using Site	Storage Site
Read Page	6.30	7.97
Write Page	4.27	3.23

The sequential activity results are as follows.

Elapsed Time Measurements
(600 block sequential read)

System	Time (seconds)	Milliseconds/page
Unix	9.40	15.6
Local LOCUS	9.15	15.25
Dist. LOCUS	10.31	17.18

15. Interpretation of Results

In our view, these results strongly support the argument for network transparency. Local operation for the cases measured is clearly comparable to a system without such a facility. There is more system overhead for remote operation, but this is not surprising. Two network interface devices are involved in every remote access in addition to the one storage device. For a read, there are two messages involved, the request and the data-reply; hence a total of four additional I/Os must occur beyond the single disk I/O that was always present. That additional cost is about 4000 instructions in LOCUS (8 milliseconds, 2 instructions/millisecond). In the absence of special hardware or microcode to support network I/O, we consider this result quite reasonable.

It is especially encouraging that for operations which can take advantage of the involvement of multiple processors, the speed of remote transparent access is indeed comparable to local access. Sequential processing is one such example, since prefetching of data, both from the disk and across the network, is supported in

LOCUS. Here, access in all cases is running at the maximum limit of the storage medium. No significant delay is imposed by the network transparent system.

Most important however, one should compare the performance of a distributed system such as LOCUS, where the network support is integrated deep into the software system architecture, with alternate ways of gaining access to remote resources. The traditional means of layering software on top of centralized systems leads to dramatically greater overhead. Before the development of LOCUS, Arpanet protocols were run on on the same network hardware connecting the PDP-11s. Throughput was not even within an order of magnitude of the results reported here.

Several caveats are in order however as these results are examined. First, at the time these measurements were made, replicated storage had not yet been implemented. Hence no conclusions in that respect can be made. Second, because of the lack of available network interconnection hardware, only a small network configuration is available for study, and so only light loading occurs. On the other hand, since most computer utility experience shows limited concurrent sharing, we expect little synchronization interference when the network is significantly larger and more users are supported.

LOCUS also requires more memory to operate than standard Unix for comparable performance. This fact occurs for two principal reasons. First, there is more code in the LOCUS nucleus than in the Unix kernel, in part because of low level network support and synchronization mechanisms, because of more sophisticated buffer management, and also because of all the server process code. Second, LOCUS data structures are generally larger than the corresponding structures in Unix. For example, a LOCUS file descriptor has additional fields for a version vector, site information, and (when at a storage site) a bit map marking which sites are currently being served (i.e. have this file open). For the configuration at UCLA, Unix requires 41K bytes code and 44K bytes data. The equivalent LOCUS system (with the same number of buffers, etc.) would require 53K bytes code and 51K bytes data.

LOCUS also contains considerable additional code to handle recovery, but this code is run as a conventional user process, and therefore is not locked down.

The two most significant specific conclusions we draw from our LOCUS experience are:

1. High performance network transparency in a local network is feasible.

2. Network transparency in a local network possesses so many advantages that a choice not to adopt it ought to be very carefully justified.

We have not gained enough experience with the effects of the integrated vs. server model to make a strong statement. Nothing we have seen so far shakes our confidence in the integrated model however.

In general, our experience suggests that the system architectures suitable for local networks differ markedly from those for significantly lower bandwidth, higher delay environments. Remaining with the more traditional structures misses significant opportunities.

CONCLUSIONS

As small machines proliferate and more and more information is kept in digital form, the desire to share that information will correspondingly increase. This desire, together with the architectural plans of many office automation vendors to provide their products in the form of multiple machines networked together, insures that distributed systems will become increasingly important. While compatibility with the past has been a terrible sword hanging over the heads of major mainframe manufacturers, it may be an even more binding force in some respects in the distributed system market, especially those segments where multiple vendors are involved. It is often more difficult to motivate and coordinate change in a marketplace than within a single, albeit large, company.

Therefore, proper consideration of the kind of issues raised in this discussion is all the more important.

BIBLIOGRAPHY

Alsberg, P. A., Day, J. D., A Principle for Resilient Sharing of Distributed Resources, Second International Conference on Software Engineering, San Francisco, California, October 13-15, 1976, pp. 562-570. <primary copy reference>

Bernstein, P., and N. Goodman, Fundamental Algorithms for Concurrency Control in Distributed Database Systems, Technical Report CCA-80-05, Computer Corporation of America, February 1980.

Cheatham, T., Private communication 1971.

Clark, D., K. Pogran, and D. Reed, An Introduction to Local Area Networks, Proceedings of the IEEE, Vol. 66, No. 11, November, 1978, pp. 1497-1517.

Faissol, S., Availability and Reliability Issues in Distributed Databases, Ph.D.

Dissertation, Computer Science Department, University of California, Los Angeles, 1981 (forthcoming).

Gray, J., Minimizing the Number of Messages in Commit Protocols, position paper for ACM Workshop on Fundamental Issues in Distributed Computing, Fallbrook, California, December 15-17, 1980.

Gray, J., Notes on Database Operating Systems, in Operating Systems: An Advanced Course, Vol 60 of Lecture Notes in Computer Science, Springer-Verlag, (1978), pp. 393-481.

Hammer, M. and D. Shipman, An Overview of Reliability Mechanism for a Distributed Data Base System, Spring Compcon 78, February 28 - March 3, 1978, pp. 63-65.

Holler, E., The National Software Works, in Lecture Notes in Computer Science: Distributed Systems, B. Lampson, ed., Springer-Verlag, NY, 1981, pp.421-445.

Holt, R.C., Some Deadlock Properties of Computer Systems, ACM Computing Surveys, Vol. 4, No. 3, September 1972, pp. 179-196.

Kleinrock, L., Opderbeck, H., Throughput in the Arpanet - Protocols and Measurement Fourth Data Communications Symposium, Quebec City, Canada, October 7-9, 1975, pp. 6-1 to 6-11.

Kung, H.T. and J.R. Robinson, On Optimistic Methods for Concurrency Control, proc., 5th VLDB Conference, October 1979, Rio de Janeiro.

Lampson, B., and H. Sturgis, Crash Recovery in a Distributed Data Storage System, working paper, Xerox PARC, Nov 1976.

Lampson, B., Private Communication, 1979.

Lindsay, B., et al, Notes on Distributed Databases, IBM Research Report, San Jose Laboratory, 1979.

Menasce, D.A. and R.R. Muntz, Locking and Deadlock Detection in Distributed Databases, IEEE Transactions on Software Engineering.

Mockapetris, P. V., Lyle, M.R., Farber, D.J., On the Design of Local Network Interfaces, Proceedings of IFIP Congress '77, Toronto, August 8-12, 1977, pp. 427-430.

Parker, S., G. Popek, et. al., Detection of Mutual Inconsistency of Distributed Systems, accepted for publication in IEE Transactions on Software Engineering.

Rashid, R., and P. Hibbard, Research into loosely-coupled Distributed Systems at CMU, Notes from IEE Workshop on Fundamental Issues in Distributed Systems, Pala Mesa, Ca., Dec 15-17, 1980.

Rudisin, G., Reliability and Recovery Methods for Partitioned, Distributed File Systems, Ph.D., Dissertation, Computer Science Department, University of California, Los Angeles, 1981 (forthcoming).

Saltzer, J., Research Problems of Decentralized Systems with largely Autonomous Nodes, in Operating Systems: An Advanced Course, Vol 60 of Lecture Notes in Computer Science, Springer-Verlag, (1978), pp. 583-591.

Saltzer, J., D. Reed, and D. Clark, End-to-End Arguments in System Design, Notes from IEEE Workshop on Fundamental Issues in Distributed Systems, Pala Mesa, Ca., Dec 15-17, 1980.

Swinehart, D., G. McDaniel, D. Boggs, WFS: A Simple Shared File System for a Distributed Environment, Proceedings of the Seventh Symposium on Operating Systems Principles, Dec 10-12, 1979, Asilomar, Ca. pp 9-17.

Thomas, R.F., A Solution to the Concurrency Control Problem for Multiple Copy Data Bases, Proc. Spring Compcon, Feb 28 - Mar 3, 1978, pp. 56-62.

Wilkes, M., and R. Needham, The Cambridge Model Distributed System, Notes from IEEE Workshop on Fundamental Issues in Distributed Systems, Pala Mesa, Ca., Dec 15-17, 1980.

Xerox, The Ethernet: A Local Area Network - Data Link Layer and Physical Layer Specifications, Version 1.0, Sept 30, 1980. Available from Digital Equipment Corporation, Maynard, Massachusetts; Intel Corporation, Santa Clara, California; Xerox Corporation, Stamford, Connecticut.

Lilith: A Personal Computer for the Software Engineer

N.Wirth

Federal Institute of Technology (ETH), Zurich

Abstract

The personal work station offers significant advantages over the large-scale, central computing facility accessed via a terminal. Among them are availability, reliability, simplicity of operation, and a high bandwidth to the user. Modern technology allows to build systems for high-level language programming with significant computing power for a reasonable price.

At the Institut fur Informatik of ETH we have designed and built such a personal computer tailored to the language Modula-2. This paper is a report on this project which encompasses language design, development of a compiler and a single-user operating system, design of an architecture suitable for compiling and yielding a high density of code, and the development and construction of the hardware. 20 Lilith computers are now in use at ETH.

A principal theme is that the requirements of software engineering influence the design of the language, and that its facilities are reflected by the architecture of the computer and the structure of the hardware. The module structure is used to exemplify this theme. That the hardware should be designed according to the programming language, instead of vice-versa, is particularly relevant in view of the trend towards VLSI technology.

1. Introduction

Software Engineering builds upon two pillars: methods and tools. Their interrelation is strong. In order to apply new methods effectively, we need the appropriate tools. In order to build supporting tools, we must master powerful methods. Much effort has been spent on improving our methods, particularly in programming, and many discussions and conferences have been devoted to the subject of furthering the state of the art by applying more effective methods. This includes a tendency towards the highly mathematical treatment of programming, the postulation of high-level languages for programming large systems, the method of structured programming, and the managerial aspects of organizing the work of programmers' teams.

All of these areas are important; they form the part of a whole. But perhaps none is as important as the adequate training of the individual team number into a habit of systematic thinking. No team can be successful without all its members being trained to regard programming as a highly logical and mathematical activity. And the success of a mathematical treatment rests largely on the use of an adequate notation, i.e. programming "language". The designer of algorithms might be content with the adequate notation and regard it as his only tool needed. However, our subject at large is not the design of algorithms or programs, but the design of machines. We must regard programming as designing machinery, for programs turn "raw hardware" into that machinery which fulfils the specified task.

Obviously a good notation must therefore be supported by an excellent implementation, just as a good mathematical framework for program design must be supported by an appropriate notation. Moving one step further, the notation's implementation must be supported by an appropriate computer system. The measure of its quality not only includes aspects of computing power, cost-effectiveness, and software support (the so-called programming environment), but also a simplicity and perspicuity of the entire system, a convenience to use the system, a high degree of availability, and - on the more technical side - a high bandwidth of information transfer between computer and programmer. The latter aspects point in the direction of a personal work station in contrast to the remote, time-shared, large-scale computing facility.

Fortunately, modern semiconductor technology has made it possible to implement a modern programming language with excellent support facilities on relatively small computers that are very inexpensive compared to conventional large computing installations. The fact that the mechanisms for sharing a computer - and in particular that for protecting the users from the mistakes of others - can be discarded, reduces a system's complexity drastically, and thereby improves both its reliability and perspicuity. The possibility to implement modern, high-level languages on relatively small non-shared computers was perhaps the most significant "discovery" during the last five years. A personal computer, programmable in such a language, constitutes, in my opinion, a necessary tool for the creative software engineer of the future.

2. Project history and overview

The decision to design and build a personal computer as motivated above was made in the fall of 1977, after the author had learned to appreciate the advantages of working with an Alto computer [1]. The project included the following principal parts [2]:

- design of the programming language Modula-2.
- implementation of a multipass compiler suitable for relatively small computers.
- development of a basic, single-user operating system, including a file system and a linking loader.
- design and implementation of a modern, flexible text editor taking full advantage of the computer's capabilities.
- implementation of a set of basic utility programs for file directory inspection, copying, renaming, deleting, and listing files.
- programming and implementing an appropriate set of library modules for file handling, access to peripheral devices - in particular the display - and storage management.
- designing a suitable machine architecture as ideal interface between compiler and hardware, and programming this architecture in microcode.
- design of the hardware capable of efficiently interpreting the microcode and supporting the desirable peripheral devices.
- building two prototypes of the designed hardware, and modifying them according to insight gained from the concurrent development of hard- and software.
- building a series of 20 computers, debugging and testing them.
- writing documentation and user manuals.

The language Modula-2 - the notation in which this system presents itself to the software engineer - was designed as a general system programming language [3]. The guiding principle was that this language would be the only language available on the computer. Especially, no assembler would be available, and hence, the language should be suitable for both high-level programming in a machine-independent manner and low-level programming of machine-particular aspects, such as device handling and storage allocation. In fact, the entire operating system, the compiler, the utility programs, and the library modules are programmed exclusively in Modula-2.

The compiler is subdivided into four parts. Each part processes the output of its predecessor in sequential fashion and is therefore called a pass. The first pass performs lexical and syntactic analysis, and it collects identifiers, allocating them in a table. The second pass processes declarations, generating the so-called symbol tables that are accessed in the third pass to perform the type consistency checking in expressions and statements. The fourth pass generates code. Its output is called M-code.

The operating system is conceived according to the concept of an "open" system [4]. It is divided into three principal parts, namely the linking loader, the file system, and routines for keyboard input and text output on the display. The file system maps abstract files (sequences of words or characters) onto disk pages and provides the necessary basic routines for creating, naming, writing, reading, positioning, and deleting files. Both, loader and file system present themselves to the Modula-2 programmer as modules (packages) whose routines can be imported into any program. Whenever a program terminates, the basic operating system activates the command interpreter which requests the file name of the next program to be loaded and initiated.

The computer as "seen by the compiler" is implemented as a microprogrammed interpreter of the M-code. The M-code is designed with the principal goals of obtaining a high density of code and of making the process of its generation relatively systematic and straight-forward. Although space is definitely the scarcer resource than time, a high density of code is desirable not only in the interest of saving memory space, but also for reducing the frequency of instruction fetches. A comparison between two different, but strongly related compilers revealed that M-code is shorter than code for the PDP-11 by a factor of almost 4. This surprising figure is clear evidence of the inappropriate structure of "conventional" computer instruction sets, including those of most modern microprocessors that were still designed with the human assembly language coder in mind.

The actual hardware consists of a central processing unit based on an Am2901 bit-slice unit, a multi-port memory with 128K words of 16 bits, a micro-code memory of 2K instructions implemented with PROMs, a controller each for the display, the disk, and a local network, and interfaces for the keyboard, a cursor tracking device called the mouse, and a V-24 (RS-232) serial line interface. The central processor operates at a basic clock cycle of 150 ns, the time required to interpret a micro-instruction. The most frequently occuring M-code instructions correspond to about 5 micro-instructions on the average.

The display is based on the raster scan technique using 594 lines of 768 dots each. Each of the 456'192 dots is represented in main memory by one bit. If the entire screen is fully used, its bitmap occupies 28'512 words, i.e. 22% of memory. The representation of each dot (picture element) in program accessible main memory makes the display equally suitable for text, technical diagrams, and graphics in general. In the case of text, each character is generated by copying the character's bitmap into the appropriate place of the entire screen's bitmap. This is done by software, supported by appropriate microcoded routines, corresponding to special M-code instructions. This solution, in contrast to hardware character generators, offers the possibility to vary the characters' size, thickness (boldface), inclination (italics) and even style. In short, different fonts can be displayed. This feature, which is particularly attractive for text processing, requires a substantial amount of computing power to be available in short bursts. The writing of a full screen, i.e. conversion of characters from ASCII code to correctly positioned bitmaps, takes about 1/4 second. Using a small font, a full screen may display up to 10'000 characters.

The disk used in this personal computer is a Honeywell-Bull D-120 cartridge disk with a capacity of 10 MBytes and a potential transfer rate of 720 kB/s, which results in an actual rate of 60 kB/s for reading or writing of sequential files. Disk sectors, each containing 256 Bytes, are allocated in multiples of 8 on the same track. Allocation is entirely dynamic, and hence no storage contraction processes are needed to retrieve "holes". The use of exchangeable cartridge disks in contrast to sealed (Winchester) disks has been considered as essential in order that a work station may be used by different people at different times without reliance on the existence of a network and a central file store.

The mouse is a device that transmits signals to the computer which represent the mouse's movements on the table. These movements are translated (again by software) into a cursor displayed on the screen. The accuracy of position is as high as the resolution of the screen, because the feedback from cursor to mouse travels via the user's eye and hand. The mouse also contains three pushbuttons (keys) which are convenient for giving commands while positioning the mouse.

The various principal parts of the projects were undertaken more or less concurrently. The team consisted of 8 (part time) people in the average (not counting the production of 20 machines), and was small enough to require neither management staff nor methods. The hardware was designed and built by three engineers (including the author), two computer scientists built the compiler, one the operating system, one implemented the microcode and most of the editor. The software effort was based on the use of a PDP-11/40 computer (with a 28K store) and was initiated with the development of a compiler for Modula-2 generating code for the PDP-11 itself. This "preliminary" compiler development constituted a significant part of the entire software effort, and resulted in a valuable software tool that had recently been released for distribution. It also made the development of the Lilith software quite independent from the progress of the hardware. Both the Modula-2 compiler for M-code, the operating system, and even the highly display-oriented editor were developed on the PDP-11, and the subsequent transport to the Lilith computer proved to be quite unproblematic due to programming in Modula-2. In fact, the untested compiler was transported and debugged (at least to an acceptable degree) in a few days only.

Whereas the software development could profit from our previous experience in designing compilers and programming in general, such was not the case in the hardware sector, as our institute had neither hardware expertise nor facilities. To gain experience and develop such facilities was, however, a prime challenge, and this project offered a welcome opportunity.

From the start it was planned to base the Lilith computer on the 2901 bit-slice processor, because one-chip processors available in 1977 did not offer the computing speed required for the efficient handling of the planned bitmap operations. This decision proved to be a good one. After 15 months of development, a first prototype was operational (without disk), proved to be too unreliable for extensive use, but confirmed the sensibility of the overall design. An additional year was needed to produce two identical prototypes which served to test the software that had been developed in the meantime. In the spring of 1980, a team was formed at the Department of Electrical Engineering of Brigham Young University in Provo, Utah, to build a series of 20 Lilith computers. This goal was achieved within 8 months by three graduating engineers and with the aid of student employees during the summer months. The cost per unit, not counting the development of the prototypes nor of organizing the production effort, but including labor and parts, in particular the 10MB disk, was about SFr 20'000.

In the meantime, a few important application programs were written at ETH, including a text editor, an editor for drawing circuit diagrams, and a window handler module. Some sample pictures illustrating their use are shown in Fig 1. They are printed with the same resolution as seen on the screen.

3. Modules and interfaces in Modula-2

Perhaps the most important criterion of a language for programming large systems is how well it supports program modularization. The earliest facilities introduced for effective program decomposition was the concept of locality, i.e. the restriction of the validity of names (identifiers) to well-delineated parts of the program, such as a block or a procedure. This concept was introduced by Algol 60 and adopted in Algol 68, PL/I, and Pascal, among others. The range of validity is called a name's scope. Scopes can be nested, and the rule is that names valid in the scope's environment are also valid inside it, whereas names declared within the scope are invisible outside. This rule immediately suggests a connection between the range of visibility (scope) of a name within the program text, and the time of existence of the object associated with the name: as soon as control enters the scope (procedure, block), the object must be created (e.g. storage must be allocated to a variable), and as soon as it leaves the scope, the object can be deleted, for it will no longer be visible. In spite of the tremendous value of this locality concept, there are two reasons why it is inadequate for large programs.

- there is a need to hide objects, i.e. to retain them while they are invisible. This calls for a separation of visibility and existence: visiblity as a property of names, existence as a property of objects.
- there is a need for closer control of visibility, i.e. for selection of particular names to be visible or invisible, in contrast to the "inheritance" of the total environment into a local scope.

In Modula-2, we have therefore added the structure of a module to the structure of the procedure. Both structures appear syntactically as almost identical, but are governed by different rules about visibility of local names and existence of the associated objects:

P1. An object declared local to a procedure exists only as long as the procedure remains activated.
M1. An object local to a module exists as long as the enclosing procedure remains activated.
P2. A name local to a procedure is invisible outside the text of that procedure, one visible in the environment is also visible inside the procedure.
M2. A name local to a module is visible inside the module, and outside too, if it appears in the so-called export list in the module heading. A name visible in a module's environment is visible inside that module only if it appears in its so-called import list.

From these rules, we can draw the following conclusion: A module itself has no "existence", since its local objects inherit their lifetime from the module's environment (procedure). Hence, the module is a purely syntactic structure acting like a wall enclosing its local objects and controlling their visibility by means of export and import lists. Modules therefore need not be instantiated; there are no instances of a module. The module is merely a textual unit.

A typical example of a module is the following:

```
MODULE m;
   IMPORT u,v;
   EXPORT p,q;

   VAR x: ...;
   PROCEDURE p(...);
      BEGIN ... x ... END p;
   PROCEDURE q(...);
      BEGIN ... x ... END q;
BEGIN ... u ... x ...
END m
```

This module owns three local objects: variable x and procedures p and q operating on x. It exports p and q and hides x by not exporting it. The body of the module serves to initialize x; it is activated when the environment of m is activated (created). This example is typical, because it shows how an object x can be hidden and how access from outside is restricted to occur via specific procedures. This makes it possible to guarantee the existence of invariant conditions on x, independent of possible errors in the environment accessing x via p and q. Such is the very purpose of modularization.

The typical purpose of a module is indeed to hide a set of interrelated objects, and the module is often identified by these objects, e.g. a table handler hiding the table, a scanner hiding the input stream, a terminal driver hiding the interface, or a disk system hiding the disk's structure and allocation strategy.

The module concept as described above had been introduced with the language Modula [5]. Modula-2 extends this concept in two important ways, namely by

- qualified export mode, and
- subdivision of a module into two textual parts, the so-called definition and implementation parts.

Qualified export serves to avoid clashes between identical identifiers exported from different modules into the same enclosing scope. If an identifier x is exported in qualified mode from a module m, then the object associated with x needs to be denoted as m.x. The qualified mode is therefore appropriate, if the writer of m does not know the environment of m. This is not the usual case for nested modules; individual members of a programming team more typically design modules that lie on the same level, namely the outermost, or global level (that may be considered as being enclosed in a universal and empty scope). It is this case that is particularly important in the design of large systems, where a better separation of the specification of import and export lists from the description of the actual objects is desirable.

Consequently, we divide a global module into two parts. The first is called a definition module; it contains the export list and specifications of the exported objects as far as relevant for the user (client) of this module to verify the adherence to language rules (in particular type consistency). A definition module also specifies the types of its exported variables and the parameter lists of its exported procedures. The second part is called the implementation module. It contains (usually) import lists and all the details that need not concern the client, such as the bodies of procedures. The notion of textually separate definition and implementation parts was pioneered by the language Mesa [6] and is here smoothly integrated with the module concept of Modula.

Example:

```
     DEFINITION MODULE B;
        EXPORT QUALIFIED p,q;
        PROCEDURE p(...);
        PROCEDURE q(...);
     END B.

     IMPLEMENTATION MODULE B;
        FROM A IMPORT u,v;
        VAR x: ...;
        PROCEDURE p(...);
           BEGIN ... x ... u ... END p;
        PROCEDURE q(...);
           BEGIN ... v ... x ... END q;
     BEGIN ... x ...
     END B.
```

4. Coroutines and processes

With the design of the Lilith computer we did not follow the fashionable trend to design a system consisting of several co-operating concurrent processors, thereby avoiding one certain source of difficulties, namely their synchronization. The consequence for the language Modula-2 was that the concept of concurrent processes played a minor role only, whereas in Modula-1 it had been the major theme. The primary idea had been to distinguish the logical process from the physical processor, allowing implementations to choose their own mechanisms for allocating processors to processes. Logical processes are served by time-sharing the processors, which may well have different characteristics and capabilities. The processes are implemented as coroutines, and transfers of control between them are implied in statements that send signals or wait to receive signals, where the signal is an abstract notion represented as a data type. Each processor executes a sequence of coroutine segments, and the processor scheduling can well be hidden behind the primitive operations on signals. The principal difference between processes (as in Modula-1) and coroutines (as in Modula-2) is that the latter are explicitly identified whenever a transfer occurs, whereas processes are not, since transfers are implied by sending a named signal to some process which remains anonymous.

It is well in accordance with the premise of Modula-2 - namely to make primitives directly available to the programmer - to include coroutines instead of processes, because the latter are implemented by the former. As a consequence, Modula-2 implementations need no "run-time system" and no fixed, built-in scheduling algorithm. There exists no data type Signal, but instead transfer of control from a coroutine P to a coroutine Q is specified explicitly by the statement TRANSFER(P,Q). Here P and Q are variables of the primitive type PROCESS, whose actual values are pointers to the coroutines' workspace and state descriptors.

Furthermore, experience with Modula-1 showed the advisability of separating interrupt-driven from "regular" processes, because an interrupt signals a transfer of service among processors within the same process. A programmer may adopt this advice by supplying his own scheduling program. Modula-2 provides the appropriate mechanism for encapsulating such a user-defined scheduler in the form of its module structure. Naturally, such algorithms may also be provided in the form of library modules.

As an example we list a scheduler reflecting the simple round-robin algorithm. The module exports the data type Signal and the operators StartProcess, Send, and Wait, which correspond to the language facilities of Modula-1. The example excludes, however, the treatment of interrupt-driven processes. (Note that the type Signal is exported in opaque mode such that its structures is invisible to the importer.) Both Send and Wait imply a coroutine transfer. The primitive operation TRANSFER is, like the data type PROCESS, imported from the module SYSTEM, which typically contains low-level facilities. High-level programs should preferrably rely on the process concept as presented by such a ProcessScheduler module, rather than on named coroutines and explicit transfer of control.

```
DEFINITION MODULE ProcessSceduler;
  FROM SYSTEM IMPORT ADDRESS;
  EXPORT QUALIFIED Signal, StartProcess, Send, Wait;

  TYPE Signal;
  PROCEDURE StartProcess(P: PROC; A: ADDRESS; n: CARDINAL);
  PROCEDURE Send(VAR s: Signal);
  PROCEDURE Wait(VAR s: Signal);
END ProcessScheduler.
```

```
IMPLEMENTATION MODULE ProcessScheduler;
  FROM SYSTEM IMPORT PROCESS, ADDRESS, NEWPROCESS, TRANSFER;

  TYPE Signal = POINTER TO ProcessDescriptor;
    ProcessDescriptor =
      RECORD ready: BOOLEAN;
        pr:    PROCESS;
        next:  Signal; (* ring *)
        queue: Signal; (* waiting queue *)
      END ;

  VAR cp: Signal; (* current process *)

  PROCEDURE StartProcess(P: PROC; A: ADDRESS; n: CARDINAL);
    (* start P with workspace A of length n  *)
    VAR t: Signal;
  BEGIN t := cp; NEW(cp);
    WITH cp^ DO
      next := t^.next; ready := TRUE;
      queue := NIL; t^.next := cp
    END ;
    NEWPROCESS(P, A, n, cp^.pr); TRANSFER(t^.pr, cp^.pr)
  END StartProcess;

  PROCEDURE Send(VAR s: Signal);
    (* resume first process waiting for s *)
    VAR t: Signal;
  BEGIN
    IF s # NIL THEN
      t := cp; cp := s;
      WITH cp^ DO
        s := queue; ready := TRUE; queue := NIL
      END ;
      TRANSFER(t^.pr, cp^.pr)
    END
  END Send;

  PROCEDURE Wait(VAR s: Signal);
    VAR t0, t1: Signal;
  BEGIN (* insert current process in queue s *)
    IF s = NIL THEN s := cp
    ELSE t0 := s;
      LOOP t1 := t0^.queue;
        IF t1 = NIL THEN
          t0^.queue := cp; EXIT
        END ;
        t0 := t1
      END
    END ;
    cp^.ready := FALSE; cp^.queue := NIL;
    t0 := cp; (*now find next ready process*)
```

```
    REPEAT cp := cp^.next;
      IF cp = t0 THEN HALT (*deadlock*) END
    UNTIL cp^.ready;
    TRANSFER(t0^.pr, cp^.pr)
  END Wait;

BEGIN NEW(cp);
  WITH cp^ DO
    next := cp; ready := TRUE; queue := NIL
  END
END ProcessScheduler.
```

Interrupts are transfers of control that occur at unpredictable moments. We can regard an interrupt as equivalent to a statement

```
TRANSFER(interrupted, interrupting)
```

that is effectively inserted in the program wherever control happens to be at the moment when the external interrupt request is applied. The variable "interrupting" denotes the process that is destined to service the request, whereas the variable "interrupted" will be assigned the interrupted coroutine. The typical interrupt handler is a device driver coroutine of the following pattern; P and Q are variables of the primitive type PROCESS.

```
PROCEDURE driver;
BEGIN initialization;
   LOOP ...
      start device; TRANSFER(Q,P); ...
   END
END driver
```

The driver process is created by the primitive statement

```
NEWPROCESS(driver,wsp,n,Q)
```

which allocates the procedure "driver" and the workspace wsp of size n to this coroutine, now identified by Q. It is subsequently activated by the statement

```
TRANSFER(P,Q)
```

which assigns the starting coroutine (e.g. the main program) to P. After initiation of a device operation the statement TRANSFER(Q,P), which symbolically stands for that part of the process which is executed by the device (i.e. another processor) actually returns control to P and assigns (the current state of) the driver coroutine back to Q. Termination of the device operation causes an interrupt signal which (if enabled) corresponds, as explained above, to an unwritten TRANSFER(P,Q). This signal again switches control back from the interupted to the driver (interrupting) routine.

Each interrupt signal - the Lilith computer offers 8 of them - is associated with its own variables P and Q at fixed locations. In order that further interrupts remain disabled while the processor executes the interrupt routine, drivers are typically declared inside a module with specified "priority" that causes interrupt inhibition up to that specified "priority" level.

This elegant conceptual unification of coroutine transfers and interrupt handling was made possible by an appropriately designed computer architecture and instruction set.

5. The operating system

The most noticeable aspect of the Lilith operating system Medos is its orientation towards a single user. It is devoid of any protection mechanism against malicious programs that could hamper another user's program. Since Medos is programmed in Modula, it benefits from the safety provided by Modula's type consistency and various run-time checks. Its safety features are "defensive", but certainly not invulnerable, considering the Modula's facilities for low-level programming offered to the brave programmer. In this regard, Medos follows the strategy of Pilot [9]. In a first, superficial look it can be regarded as a collection of modules that are imported by the current program (and its imported modules). Since a number of low-level modules (such as the file system) are used by virtually every program, they form a resident section. This set of modules consists of three main parts:

```
"Program"      - storage allocation, program loader
"Terminal"     - drivers for keyboard and display
"FileSystem"   - disk driver and file administration
```

The module Program exports the procedures

```
Call(name,sharedHeap,status)
AllocateHeap(size)
DeallocateHeap(size)
```

of which the first effectively represents the loader. The module administers the entire store as a stack and loads called programs sequentially. The remainder of the store is treated as data store. In this part, the data stack grows from one end and the heap from the other. The heap is used for variables that are allocated dynamically by calls of AllocateHeap and DeallocateHeap, which merely move the pointer that denotes the separation between data stack and heap. More sophisticated allocators can be programmed which, however, will also refer to these basic procedures.

If a program P calls the loader, the code and data segments of the loaded module Q (and of the modules imported by Q and not already present) are stacked on top of those of P. The set of segments thus loaded forms a new "level", one higher than that of P. The loader operates as a coroutine, and each new level of program is represented as a coroutine too. This slight misuse of the coroutine facility is justified by the convenience in which new sections of data and program (a level) can be administered, if described as a coroutine. Fig. 2 shows the storage layout and the implied transfers of control when a program is loaded from a caller at level 1.

The set of resident modules forms level Ø. Its main program is called the Sequential Executive Kernel. It invokes the loader which loads the command interpreter. This is merely a program that outputs a prompt character, reads a file name, and transmits the file identity to the kernel, which loads this file after the command interpreter has terminated and control is returned to level Ø. Loading of the main program usually requires the loading of further modules that are specified in import lists. Linking or binding of modules is simplified by the architecture of the Lilith computer such that it is performed directly upon program loading. Fig. 3 shows a typical sequence of programs, and how they occupy the store.

Since a program is loaded only after removal of the command interpreter, and because the command interpreter typically has ample time to process the slow input from the keyboard, it can be designed with additional sophistication. It can search the file table for program files whose names match with the input so far received and extend it as far as it is unambiguous. For example, if file names ABCD and ABCE are present, and no others starting with A, it may display both names after receiving "A?" and then allow continuation after receiving either D or E. This is a small but typical example of providing a convenient user interface without additional burden on the user's program.

The entire mechanism for loading and allocating is programmed exclusively in Modula-2; this includes the subtle point of changing our view of a program as data before to code after its loading. In Modula-2, this is possible without resorting to tricky programming and without the escape to small sections of assembly code.

The second principal part of the set of resident modules handles input from the keyboard and output to the display. This module is called Terminal. The input stream fetched by the procedure Read (contained in Terminal) flows through a switch that allows reading from a file instead of the keyboard. Because the command interpreter also calls Read, that file can even be a command file. The output stream, which is fed by calling the procedure Write, is fed to the low-level module TextScreen that simulates sequential writing and generates the bit pattern for each character according to a default font.

The module FileSystem constitutes the third major part of the resident system. Files are used for three main purposes:

- long-term storage of data on permanent, named files,
- communication among programs,
- secondary storage of data on temporary, unnamed files.

We distinguish between the naming and abstract definition of files as extendable arrays of elements (FileSystem) and the physical implementation of files on the disk (DiskSystem). The programmer refers to files through the module FileSystem which in turn calls procedures of the module DiskSystem hiding the details of their physical representation.

FileSystem exports the type File and operations on this type for opening (creating), naming, reading, writing, modifying, positioning, and closing files. Normally files are regarded as streams of either words or characters; writing occurs at the end of the stream only, and if writing is requested at some position other than the end, the file's tail is lost and deallocated. Although it is also possible to modify files, i.e. overwrite them, the abstraction of the stream is the preferred view of files.

The module DiskSystem implements Files on the Honeywell-Bull D-120 disk. It is designed according to the following main requirements:

- fast access, in particular if strictly sequential,
- robustness against hard- and software failures,
- accommodation of a large number of (mostly short) files,
- economical use of storage space.

The following scheme was chosen as a compromise between the various design objectives: Space is allocated in blocks of 2048 bytes. This results in a memory resident allocation table of 392 words (one per cylinder), each bit indicating whether or not its corresponding block is allocated to some file. Each block corresponds to 8 disk sectors, equally spaced on the same cylinder. A separate file, allocated at a fixed place, is called FileDirectory and consists of file descriptors. Every file is identified by the index of its (first) descriptor (= file number), and each descriptor contains a table of addresses of the blocks which constitute the file. Additionally, the descriptor specifies various properties of the file, such as its length, creation date, last modification date, whether it is permanent, protected, etc. Upon startup, the system reads the entire FileDirectory and computes the allocation table.

Unnamed files are released either by closing them or when the system is started. They are used as temporary files during execution of a program. For long term storage of data, a file has to be named. To administer permanent files, the module DiskSystem maintains another file (also placed in a fixed location) called the Name Directory. Each entry consists of a file name and the number of the associated file. The procedure Lookup(f,name,create) is used to search the name in the Name Directory and connects the file (if found) with the file variable f. The parameter "create" allows to ask for the creation and naming of a new file, if the specified name was not found (see Fig. 4).

A fourth, but effectivly hidden part of the resident system is called the Monitor. It contains two auxiliary processes that are used to monitor the third, namely the main process of the user. The auxiliary processes are called Clock and Trap (Fig. 5). Clock is invoked 5Ø times per second. It updates a variable called time, monitors the keyboard by polling, and buffers keyboard input, allowing for typing ahead.

Trap is invoked by various instructions detecting abnormal conditions, such as stack overflow, arithmetic overflow, index out of range, access to picture elements outside the specified bitmap, the standard procedure HALT, etc. The Trap process then may store the state of the main process (essentially a dump) on the disk for possible later inspection by a debugger program, and restarts the main process at the kernel level.

Typing the control character <ctrl>C is detected by Clock and causes an abortion of the main process in the same manner as a trap. Evidently, abnormal situations are here handled by coroutine transfers instead of an additional exception facility provided in the programming language. The auxiliary coroutine then regards the aborted coroutine as data (instead of as a program) and is thereby able to reset it to a state where continuation is sensible.

Fig. 6 shows the principal modules of Medos with arrows denoting calls of procedures. Usually, these arrows are identical to those denoting the import/export dependences among modules. Exceptions to this rule occur through the use of procedure variables.

6. Separate compilation of modules

For reasons of convenience and economy, large system programs need to be compiled in parts. It is only natural that these parts be the ones that from a logical point of view were designed as relatively independent units. The module is the obvious choice for the unit of compilation. Definition and implementation modules are therefore called compilation units.

The idea of compilation in parts is as old as Fortran and even assembler code. In high-level languages with data types the problem of partial compilation is of considerable complexity: we wish that type consistence checking is fully maintained across module boundaries. In fact, experience has shown that this is when it is most needed to avoid catastrophic errors. In order to recognize inconsistencies such as type mismatches, incorrect number or order of parameters, etc., as early as possible, they must be detectable by the compiler. The compiler therefore must have access to information about all imported objects. This is accomplished as follows [7]:

Assume that a module B depends on, i.e. imports objects from a module A. Therefore, module A has to be compiled first. During its compilation, th compiler generates, apart from a code file for A, a symbol file. Compilation of B subsequently accesses that symbol file. More accurately, program B can - according to the rules of the language - refer to information of A's definition part only. Thus, the symbol file is an extract only of the information available during compilation of A. Since only definition modules are capable of exporting, the symbol file is the result of compiling the definition module A, while code is the result of compiling implementation (or program) modules only.

This scheme - in particular the separation of definition and implementation parts - has important consequences for the manner in which systems are developed. A definition module constitutes the interface between its implementation part and its clients. Effectively the scheme forces the programmer to define interfaces first, for, whenever a definition module is (changed and) recompiled, all its importers (clients) have to be recompiled too. However, it is possible to change and recompile implementation modules without that far-reaching and costly consequence.

It should be noted that the consequences of this chronological ordering of compilations are less severe than might be anticipated due to the fact that the importers are usually implementation modules. Hence a change in a low-level module - a module that resides low in the hierarchical chain of dependencies - need not produce a chain reaction of recompilation up to all ultimate clients. The appropriate decomposition of a planned system into modules is nevertheless a most important aspect of competent programming. Often the decomposition has to be decided at an early stage when insight into many aspects of a system are still hazy. Its success therefore largely depends on the engineer's previous experience with similar tasks.

Learning how to deal effectively with a new facility offered by a programming language is a long-term process. The module facility forces the programmer team to make those decisions first that must be made first [8]. One lesson learned so far is that a module typically centers around a data structure, and that it is this data structure rather than the exported operations that characterize it.

7. The architecture of the Lilith computer

One of the challenges in designing a computer lies in finding a structure and an instruction set which yield a high density of code and a relatively simple algorithm for code generation. A premise of this project was that the computer had to be designed according to the language in which it was to be programmed. This resulted in a quite unconventional architecture. No attempt was made to make the instruction set suitable for "hand coding"; in fact, programming in machine code would be quite cumbersone, even if an assembler were available.

The Lilith computer is based on a stack architecture. Stack computers are by no means novel as such. Their history dates back to the early 60s with the English Electric KDF9 and the Burroughs B5000 as pioneers. The Lilith architecture adopts the stack principle without compromise, and its instruction set is chosen to obtain a high density of code requiring only straightforward algorithms for instruction selection. The code is a byte stream. Each instruction consists of one or several bytes. The high density is achieved not only by implicit addressing of intermediate results in expressions, but mainly by the provision of different address lengths and suitable addressing modes. In order to explain these modes, we need to inspect the overall storage organization at run-time. In contrast to earlier stack computers, not only procedures play an important role, but also modules. The underlying premise is that objects local to the location of the present computation are accessed most fequently - and therefore require fast access by short instructions - whereas access to remote objects is relatively rare and requires less efficiency. Fast access is obtained by retaining "intermediate results" of address computations in fast registers (base address), in the expectation that they will be reused frequently, and that thereby their recomputation can be avoided. Several base address registers are used in the Lilith computer.

The origin of all address computations is a table with base addresses of all currently loaded data frames (see Fig. 7). A data frame is a contiguous area of store allocated to the (static) variables of a given module. By "module" we refer here and subsequently to compilation units; this excludes inner (nested) modules. Each loaded module has a number which is used as index to that frame table. The table resides at a fixed location and has a fixed length. The entry belonging to the module of which code is executed currently, is retained in the base address register G. It is the base address of "Global variables" in the sense of Algol or Pascal. G has to be reloaded whenever control transfers from one module to another. Data frames are static in the same sense that they are "permanent" for the duration of a program execution, with the (rare) exception of overlays performed by calls of the loader.

Data local to procedures are allocated in a stack which grows when a procedure is called and shrinks when it is terminated. Each coroutine (process) is allocated an area of the store, called a stack frame, when it is started, and which serves as the coroutine's workspace. The base address of the stack frame belonging to the coroutine currently under execution is stored in the register P, that of the last location allocated in this stack frame in register S, and the end of the workspace is designated by register H. P is used when a transfer from one coroutine to another coroutine occurs, S when a procedure is called or terminated. Each stack frame contains the hierarchy of data segments representing the variables local to the activated procedures. They are linked by the so-called dynamic chain of procedure activations. The base address of the last segment created is retained in register L (for Local data).

Local data are semi-dynamic in the sense that they are allocated for the duration of a procedure activation only. However, their addresses are determined by the compiler as offsets relative to the base address of their owner. Truly dynamic data are those allocated by explicitly programmed statements in an area of the store called heap. This storage area is managed by a utility module called Storage; these variables are accessed via pointer values. As in Pascal, pointers are bound to a given type, providing additional security in pointer handling.

Each loaded module owns a data frame and also a code frame, a contiguous area of store containing the code of all its procedures. The base address of the code frame of the currently executing module is retained in register F. Its value is used when calling a procedure, which is identified by a number used as index to a table containing the starting addresses of all procedures in a given module. This table resides in the header of the code frame. Using such an index instead of absolute addresses contributes to higher code density, particularly since procedure calls are very frequent instructions. The value of register F is changed whenever control transfers between modules. Jump addresses are relative to the F-register value.

8. The Lilith instruction set

Instructions consist of one or several bytes. They can be divided into four basic categories: Load and store instructions, operators, control instructions, and miscellaneous instructions:

The load and store instructions transfer data between memory (stack or heap) and the top of the stack, where they are accessed by operators. The top of the stack, where data are loaded as intermediate results (anonymous variables) is also called the expression stack. Load or store instructions require a single address only bacause the stack address is implicit; they are further subdivided according to the following criteria:

- data size: the transferred data are a word (16 bits), a double word, or a byte (halfword).
- addressing mode: local, global, external, stack, indexed, and immediate mode (the latter for load instructions only).
- address length: 4, 8, or 16 bit address (see Fig. 8).

The presence of different address lengths suggests that variables with frequent access be allocated with small offsets. Our present compiler does not perform any such optimization. The gain to be made does not appear to be overwhelming. The set of directly accessed (statically declared) variables is usually quite small, because structured variables are addressed indirectly.

The various addressing modes are defined as follows (m and n denote instruction parameters, and a the resulting address):

- Local mode: a = L+n, used for variables local to procedures.
- Global mode: a = G+n, used for global variables in the current module.
- Stack mode: a = s+n, where s is the value on top of the stack; mode used for indirect addressing and access via pointers.
- External mode: a = T[m]+n, T is the table of data frame addresses, m a module number; mode used for external variables imported from other modules.
- Indexed mode: a = s1 + k*s2, s1 is the array's base address, s2 the computed index (s1, s2 on stack), and k is a multiplier depending on the size of the accessed data type.
- Immediate mode: a = n. The loaded value is the parameter itself; mode used to generate constants.

The above explanations are given in this detail in order to show that the constructs defined in the programming language are strongly reflected by, i.e. have directly influenced, the design of the Lilith architecture. The beneficial consequence is not only ease of compilation, but simplicity of the linking loader. Whereas our Modula-2 system for the PDP-11 computer for good reasons requires a linker, such is not necessary for the Lilith implementation. A linker collects the code files of all required modules and links them together into an absolute (or relocatable) store image. This task can be performed directly by the loader, because it only has to insert module numbers (table indices) in instructions with external addressing mode.

The second category of instructions are the operators. They take operands from the top of the stack and replace them by the result. The Lilith instruction set includes operators for CARDINAL (unsigned), INTEGER (signed), double-precision, floating-point, BOOLEAN, and set arithmetic. It directly reflects the operations available in Modula-2.

The orientation towards a clean stack architecture also required a full set of comparison instructions which generate a BOOLEAN result. Distinct sets are provided for CARDINAL and INTEGER comparison. The distinction between CARDINAL and INTEGER arithmetic is partially due to the desire to be able to use all bits of a word to represent unsigned numbers, such as addresses. It would be of a lesser importance, if the wordsize were larger. However, our experience shows that it is desirable also from a purely logical point of view to declare variables to be non-negative, if in fact a negative value does never occur. Most of our programs require variables of the type CARDINAL, whereas the type INTEGER occurs only rarely. Although using 2's complement representation for negative values, addition and subtraction are implemented by the same hardware operations for both kinds of arithmetic, they differ in their conditions indicating overflow.

Control instructions include procedure calls and jumps. Conditional jumps are generated for IF, WHILE, REPEAT, and LOOP statements. They fetch their BOOLEAN operand from the stack. Special control instructions mirror the CASE and FOR statements.

Different calls are used for procedures declared in the current module and for those in other modules. For local procedures there exist call instructions with short 4-bit addresses, as they occur rather frequently. Calls for external procedures not only include an address parameter, but also a module number to be updated by the loader. Furthermore, an instruction is provided for so-called formal procedures, i.e. procedures that are either supplied as parameters or assigned to procedure variables.

There also exists an instruction for the transfer of control between coroutines. Various instructions may cause a trap, if the result cannot be computed. Such a trap is considered like an interrupt requested by the processor itself, and corresponds to a coroutine transfer with fixed parameters. The same mechanism is activated by the TRAP instruction (which corresponds to a HALT statement in Modula).

Arithmetic operators generate traps when unable to compute the correct result (e.g. overflow). Traps from CARDINAL and INTEGER arithmetic can be suppressed (masked) upon request; the programmer is then presumably aware that results are computed modulo 2^16. Also, load and store instructions generate a trap, if their address is NIL. This test requires a single micro instruction only. The routines for bitmap handling generate traps, if attempting to access data outside the specified bitmap. All these test are quite inexpensive (but not free).

A test for an array index lying within the specified bounds, or for a value to be within the subrange admitted by a variable, is more complicated. It requires two comparisons with arbitrary values. Therefore, the M-code contains an instruction for an "in range" test. The programmer may choose to omit these tests by selecting a compiler option that suppresses the generation of these test instructions.

These extensive checking facilities reflect our strong belief in designing an implementation (including the hardware) which properly supports a language's abstractions. For example, if the language provides the data type CARDINAL, its implementations should signal an error, if a negative result appears, just as it should signal an error, when a non-existing element of an array is identified. Omissions in this regard are to be considered as inadequacy in implementation. Nevertheless, the argument whether or not the experienced and conscientious programmer should be burdened with these "redundant" checks remains open. Our choice is to give the programmer the option to suppress at least the more expensive checks, at his own peril.

The category of miscellaneous instructions contains operators for reading and writing data on the input/output channels, and four instructions used for operating on bitmaps: The DDT instruction (display dot) writes a single dot at a specified coordinate, REPL replicates a bit pattern over a rectangle - a so-called block - in a given bitmap. The coordinates of this block are relative to the specified bitmap and are given in terms of dot coordinates rather than word addresses. The BBLT instruction (bit block transfer) copies a source block into a destination block. The DCH instruction (display character) copies the bitmap of a character (given its ASCII code) from a font table into a specified place of a bitmap.

The function of these bitmap instructions could well be coded in Modula-2 programs. Instead, they are included as single instructions represented by micro-coded routines. The primary reason is efficiency. The routines include checks against inconsistent parameters, such as blocks that do not fully lie within the bitmap. An essential detail is that they use the same convention about parameters as do regular procedures and operators: parameters are always passed via the stack. Modula-2 for Lilith offers a facility to use these instructions as if they were programmed as regular procedures. This uniformity of parameter passing has proved to be an invaluable asset.

Some analysis of representative programs reveals that M-code yields a significantly higher density of compiled code than do conventional instruction sets. Compared with the code compiled for the ubiquitous PDP-11, we obtained an improvement factor of

3.9. This implies that code for the same program occupies about one quarter of the memory space in the Lilith computer than in a PDP-11. This factor is noteworthy even in times of rapidly decreasing memory prices!

The principal contribution to this result stems from the short address fields. Dominant are the counts of load and store instructions; they address the stack implicitly and hence need only one address field. Access to local variables is most frequent; global variables are addressed about half as often, and external variables occur rarely. Jumps account for about 10% of all instructions, and procedure calls are about equally frequent. The following table displays percentage figures obtained from four programs (of different authors) for the most frequent instruction classes.

1-byte instr.	70.2	71.7	62.8	72.5
2-byte instr.	16.6	17.3	12.6	12.0
3-byte instr.	13.1	11.0	24.5	15.4
Load immediate	15.1	14.2	17.3	15.2
Load local	16.3	21.6	16.3	19.1
Load global	8.2	5.2	3.7	7.9
Load indirect	5.2	6.4	5.5	5.8
Store local	5.8	6.5	5.8	6.0
Store global	2.6	1.1	1.0	3.3
Store indirect	4.2	3.0	1.1	4.0
Operators	5.6	5.7	4.8	5.9
Comparators	3.9	4.4	5.6	3.7
Jumps	7.3	7.7	9.3	6.2
Calls	6.4	8.1	14.5	6.9
Total counts (100%)	11052	7370	7936	2814

Instructions are executed by a micro-coded program called the Interpreter, which may well be expressed in Modula; this algorithmic definition of the Lilith instruction set has proved to be extremely valuable as interface between the micro-programmer and the compiler designer.

9. The Lilith hardware structure

The following requirements determined the design of the hardware most significantly:

- fast implementation of the M-code interpreter, in particular of its stack architecture,
- the need for efficient implementation of the bitmap

instructions which involve a large amount of bit pushing and partial word accesses (bit addressing).
- high bandwidth between memory and display for continuous refreshing.
- the desire for a simple structure with a relatively large, homogenous store.
- ease of serviceability.

The computing power required by the bitmap instructions eliminated the choice of a one-chip processor. An even stronger reason against such a choice was the project's purpose to find a hardware architecture truly suitable for use with code compiled from a high-level language. The bit-slice processor Am2901 offered an ideal solution between a one-chip processor and the complete design of a unit built with SSI and MSI components. It allows for a basic instruction cycle that is about a fourth of a memory cycle (150 ns). This is a good relation considering the average amount of processing required between memory accesses.

The processor is built around a 16-bit wide bus connecting the arithmetic-logic unit (ALU) with the memory for transfer of data and addresses. Also connected are the instruction fetch unit (IFU), the disk and display controllers, and the interfaces to the standard low-speed I/O devices keyboard, Mouse, and serial V24 (RS232) line. Bus sources and destinations are specified in each micro-instruction by 4-bit fields which are directly decoded. The bus uses tri-state logic.

The refreshing of the full screen requires a signal with a bandwidth of 13 MHz, if interlacing and a rate of 50 half pictures per second is assumed. This implies that on the average one 16-bit word has to be fetched every 1.1 us, which implies that memory would be available to the processor about 50% of the time. This unacceptably low rate calls for a memory with an access path wider than 16 bits. It was decided to implement a 64-bit wide memory.

A third candidate for direct memory access is the instruction stream. Like the display, this port requires sequential reading only and therefore can benefit from a wide access path feeding an internal buffer. This organization reduces the average time that the memory is devoted to display and instruction fetching, i.e. where it is inaccessible to the data port of the main processor, to about 10%. The overall structure of the Lilith hardware is shown in Fig. 9. Its heart is the microcontrol unit (MCU) which contains the clock and controls the instruction stream.

9.1 The micro-control unit

The micro-control unit (MCU) consists primarily of a memory for the microcode, a micro- instruction register (MIR), an address incrementer, and some decoding logic. A micro- instruction consists of 40 bits; its formats are shown in Fig. 10. The micro-instruction address is a 12 bit integer, hence the memory may have at most 4K locations. Actually, only 2K are used and implemented as a read-only store (ROM). An additional 2K RAM may be supplied. Approximately 1K is used by initialization routines (bootstrap loader) and the M-code interpreter, and 1K is needed for the bitmap routines and the floating-point instructions.

Fig. 11 shows the structure of the micro-control unit. The next instruction's address is taken from one of several sources:

- the incrementer (normal case)
- an address stack (subroutine return)
- the current instruction (microcode jump)
- a table of addresses of routines which correspond to M-codes
- according to a pending interrupt request.

The addresses are generated by Am2911 bit-slice controllers which contain an incrementer and a short stack for subroutine return addresses. For jumps, the next address is supplied from sources external to the 2911. Conventional jumps take the address directly from the instruction register (MIR). Exceptions are the jumps to the start of the microcode routine representing the next M-code instruction. Here the address is taken from a ROM which maps the 8-bit M-code into a 12-bit address. This exception is signalled by a micro-instruction whose source field value causes the address to be selected from the map ROM. An exception to this exception occurs if an (unmasked) interrupt request is pending, in which case the next address is the fixed number assigned to the requesting line. Thereby the M-code sequence can be interrupted without requiring any additional micro-instructions, and the transition to the next micro-instruction routine is initiated by a single instruction at the end of each routine.

A tag bit of each micro-instruction determines whether it is to be interpreted as a regular or as a jump instruction. During execution of the latter the main processor is disabled. Jumps are conditional upon the state of the main processor's condition code register determined by the ALU's result computed during the previous cycle.

9.2 The arithmetic logic unit

The ALU's heart is a 2901 bit-slice processor. It contains the logic for integer arithmetic (addition) and for bit-parallel logical operations, and a set of 16 fast registers. Half of them are used for global state variables of the M-code interpreter, the others as work registers local to each microcode routine. The 2901 core is augmented by two facilities dictated by the requirements of the stack architecture and by the bitmap routines: a fast stack memory and a barrel shifter (Fig. 12).

The fast stack is a store of 16 locations (16 bit wide) and an address incrementer/decrementer. This memory holds the intermediate results during evaluation of expressions and statements, and must be regarded as logically being part of the (main) stack, but physically separate. Load instructions fetch data from the (main) stack in memory and push them onto the fast expression stack. Store instructions pop the expression stack and deposit data in main memory. As a consequence, each such instruction takes a single main memory cycle only. More precisely, data loaded from and stored into the main stack are transferred to and from a register in the 2901 processor itself, while during the same cycle this T-register is saved (or restored) into (from) the expression stack:

```
Load:   push T onto stack; Bus -> T
Store:  T -> Bus; pop stack into T
```

Operations such as addition, comparison, AND, OR, etc., can also be performed in a single cycle, because both operands are immediately accessible:

```
Add:    T + top stack -> T; pop stack
```

The hardware represents a genuine stack in so far as the current stack top is the only accessible element, and that its address is inaccessible to the programmer. This address is generated by a 4-bit up/down counter and directly fed to a 16x16 high-speed RAM. A slight complication arises because address incrementation for a pop must occur before the data fetch, whereas the decrementing for a push must occur after the store. However, both address counting and data access must be performed during the same clock cycle. The solution is found in using an extra adder and to operate according to the following scheme:

```
push:   DEC(x); S[x+1] := data
pop:    INC(x); data   := S[x]
```

The circuit of the entire stack mechanism is shown in Fig. 13. It may be surprising that the fast stack has a depth of only 16. In practice, this proved to be ample. It should be noted that the compiler can keep track of the number of stack locations loaded, and hence no runtime stack overflow can occur, nor need it be monitored. The stack is empty after execution of each statement. In the case of function procedures, the expression stack has to be saved into the main stack before, and restored after the call. Special M-code instructions are provided for this purpose.

The barrel shifter is prefixed to the input lines of the 2901 processor. It allows the rotation of data by any number of bit positions between 0 and 15. Together with the logical instructions (AND, OR) it provides the necessary speed for partial word handling extensively used in all bitmap operations. It is designed such that it can also generate masks of 0 to 15 bits in one cycle. The shift count (mask length) can either be taken from a field in the micro-instruction itself, or from a special 4-bit shift count register, also contained in the ALU.

9.3. The memory

The memory is built with 16K dynamic RAM chips distributed on four boards, each being organized as a 16K*32 block. For reading, 32 bits are accessed simultaneously from two of the four boards. Multiplexors select 8 of the 32 bits for output to the processor bus via the so-called CPU port. For writing, the same connection is used, and the data are fed to four chips in parallel, of which only one is enabled through the chip select signal. Fig. 14 shows the scheme for two boards; together they represent a 64K*16 bit memory for writing, or a 16K*64 bit memory for reading..

The choice of a 64-bit wide access path guarantees the necessary memory signal bandwidth, but it also poses significant electrical problems that should not be underestimated. Their mastery is an order of magnitude more difficult than the handling of conventional 8-bit microcomputer systems.

Processor and display operate asynchronously. Hence, an arbiter mechanism is needed for controlling memory access. It can easily be extended to accommodate several instead of only two ports. Each port is assigned a fixed priority, and the request from the source with highest rank among those pending is honoured. Fig. 15 shows the circuit used; it contains cascaded priority latches that retain posted requests. Also shown is the circuit used for the synchronization of a requestor (the CPU port as an example) and the memory, which operate on separate clocks. The priority latch is common to all ports, the other parts are individually replicated for each port. Fig. 16 shows the signal timing: If the port requests a memory cycle, the bus data, representing an address, are latched in the memory address register MAR, the port is marked busy, and the request is passed on to the arbiter. Unless a request with higher priority is present, the signal CPU.SEL goes high, indicating that the memory cycle now started belongs to the CPU port and MAR is gated to the address lines. When terminated, the signal CLR resets the busy latch, indicating to the polling CPU that its request has been served.

9.4. The instruction fetch unit

Instructions are fetched via a separate memory port controlled by the instruction fetch unit (IFU). This unit contains its own address registers (PC,F) and an 8-byte buffer. The buffer can be regarded as a small cache memory and is particularly effective because access is mostly sequential. Reloading occurs when either the buffer is empty, or when a new address is fed to the PC by a control instruction. The IFU contains its own address incrementer (the PC register is a counter) and an adder forming the sum of the PC and F values. This adder is 18 bits wide. A byte is fetched from the buffer and the address is incremented whenever the micro-controller executes a jump enabling the map ROM. Fig. 17 is a block diagram of the IFU.

9.5. The Mouse

The Mouse is a device to designate positions on the display screen. It operates on the principle that movements of the operator's hand on his desk are sensed, rather than on the recording of precise, absolute coordinates. A cursor is displayed (by appropriate programming) on the screen, changing its position according to the signals received from the Mouse. Hence, positioning of the cursor can be as accurate as the display's resolution allows, without requiring a high-precision digitizer device. The Mouse is also equipped with three pushbuttons (eyes) and is connected to the keyboard by a thin tail; hence its name.

The movements are transmitted via a ball to two perpendicular wheels, whose "spokes" are seen by a light sensor. The direction of their turning is perceived by sampling two signals received from spokes which are offset. If we combine the two binary signals and represent them as numbers to the base 4, the wheels' turning results in sample value sequences Ø,2,3,1,Ø, ... or Ø,1,3,2,Ø, ... depending on the sense of their rotation (see Fig. 18).

The interface for the Mouse contains two counters for the x- and y-coordinates. They are incremented or decremented whenever a transition of the input signals occurs as indicated by the two above sequences. A state machine registers the signal values sampled at two consecutive clock ticks; a ROM is used to map them into the necessary counting pulses.

9.6. The Monitor

The Monitor is an additional unit which is not present in the computer under normal circumstances, but for which nevertheless a permanent slot is reserved, such that it can be inserted any time. It represents a small computer of its own, and it has the capability to take full control over the Lilith processor. It is therefore used for servicing when the Lilith hardware fails, and it played a most crucial role during the entire development and debugging phases of the Lilith computer.

The Monitor's heart is a Motorola 6802 one-chip microprocessor, augmented by a 2K byte ROM and a 4K byte RAM, interface registers to the Lilith hardware, and a serial line interface to a terminal (UART). Its block diagram is given in Fig. 19. The Monitor can

- read the microinstruction register (MIR)
- supply the next microinstruction (disabling MIR)
- read the micro-program counter (2911)
- supply the next instruction address (disabling 2911)
- read the processor bus
- feed data to the processor bus
- disable the processor clock (halt)
- send clock pulses (single or multiple step)

For debugging and servicing, an elaborate set of programs was developed. In addition to a standard "operating system" residing in the ROMs, test programs can be loaded into the RAM from a terminal. We extensively used an HP 2645A terminal with tape cassettes as our program library store. When a new Lilith machine is to be tested, the Monitor is used to first test the MCU board, then to test the ALU board, thereafter the memory (in conjunction with MCU and ALU), then the IFU, and finally the interface boards. The Monitor not only made a front panel superfluous, but allowed the construction of the entire computer with the aid of only an oscilloscope and, very rarely, a small logic state analyzer.

9.7. The physical layout

The Lilith computer is designed to fit beside or underneath a table on which the 15"-display, the keyboard, and the mouse are placed. The cabinet has a height of 74 cm; it is 43 cm wide and 55 cm deep. The disk cartridge is accessible from the front.

The electronic components are placed on 10 boards housed in a rack with dimensions 42*35*30 cm. One board each contains the microcontrol unit, the arithmetic-logic unit, the processor part and interfaces to keyboard, mouse, and serial data line, the instruction fetch unit, the display interface and the disk interface. Four boards contain the main memory. Another board slot is reserved for a 2K*40 microcode RAM, one for the Monitor, and 5 slots are free for future experiments with other units or interfaces. This makes the computer suitable as an object for experimentation on the hardware as well as the software level.

The remaining space in the cabinet is taken by the disk drive and the power supply. Conventional linear power supplies were built after several disappointing experiments with modern switching power supplies that offer a much improved efficiency. They turned out to be unable to cope with the European 220 Volts.

10. Conclusions

The personal computer leads to an entirely new computing environment. Due to the high bandwidth of information between its user and his tool, a close interaction is possible that cannot be provided by a central, remotely accessed facility. The personal computer is much more than an "intelligent terminal", because it puts the computing power near the user. A particularly attractive feature is its constant availability, and consequently the owner's independence of a computing center's service hours.

Interactive usage is of particularly high value in the development of software, where text editing, compiling, and testing are the prime activities. In our experience, a personal computer increases the effectiveness of a competent software engineer by an order of magnitude. I stress the attribute "competent", for he needs the wisdom to leave his tool and retreat to quiet deliberations when deeper problems of algorithmic design appear. For the less competent engineer, the personal computer amplifies the danger of seduction to programming by trial and error ("hacking"), a method that is unacceptable in professional software engineering.

It has now become a widely accepted view that the software engineer's notational tool must be a high-level programming language. When large, complex systems are the objective, the tool must support modularization and the specification of interfaces. We have designed the language Modula-2, a more modern version of Pascal, with the principal addition of a module structure. Our implementation connects this feature with the facility of separate compilation. Separate compilation, however, is not independent compilation. On the contrary, the compiler must fully check the consistency of the separately compiled modules as if they were written as a single piece of text. The separation of global modules into definition and implementation parts makes it possible to define those aspects of a module that are significant for its clients apart from those that are private to its implementation. It reinforces the strategy of first breaking down a planned system into modules, then to define their interfaces with the goal to keep them "thin", and finally to let the members of the programming team implement the modules with relative independence.

The exclusive use of a high-level language makes it possible to design a computer architecture without regard of its suitability to assembler coding. The resulting architecture is organized around a stack. The instruction set is designed to provide a high density of code, largely due to the use of variable address length.

It is particularly attractive to design such an architecture and instruction set, if no conventional computer must be used for its interpretation. We have therefore also undertaken the design of a hardware system with the purposes to interpret this code efficiently and to accommodate the use of a high-resolution display. The latter requires a high memory bandwidth and bursts of fast computation. The implementation of a microcoded interpreter and the inclusion of a few special instructions for bitmap handling appears to be an ideal solution. These instructions correspond to microcoded routines that perform the necessary bit-pushing with greatest efficiency.

As an experiment to integrate the design of a programming language - the software engineer's notational tool - the development of its compiler and environment, the design of a computer architecture and instruction set, and the construction of the hardware - the software engineer's physical tool - the project has been successful and exciting. The resulting system is, of course, not without its deficiencies. Our consolation is that, if we did not know of items that should have been done differently, we would not have learned through our research. Also, the project had to be conducted with severe restrictions on manpower. This had the benefit that no significant management problems were encountered.

As far as the hardware is concerned, an additional constraint was the limited availability of modern technology. It was therefore decided to rely on commercially available TTL chips only, apart from MOS technology for the memory. The integrated, top-down design from software to hardware outlined by this project, is especially relevant in view of the future role of VLSI technology. Its unlimited possibilities require that the designer obtain new criteria guiding his objectives. The top-down approach crossing the soft/hardware boundary tells the hardware designer what is needed rather than the hardware customer what is available. An aspect of this project that we were unable to tackle was the design of LSI chips representing the essential units of the Lilith computer, incorporating the unconventional aspects of its architecture. The chip count (as well as power supply problems) could thereby have been reduced quite drastically. We hope that someone better equipped for the task will pursue this challenge.

Acknowledgements

I welcome the opportunity to thank all those who contributed to the success of this project, in particular those who suffered through setbacks and lost neither the sight of its goal nor the conviction of its worth. My thanks are due to the team members L.Geissmann, A.Gorrengourt, J.Hoppe, Ch.Jacobi, S.E.Knudsen, I.Noack, Ch.Richner, and W.Winiger at ETH Zurich, and L.Bingham, J.Nielson, and F.Ostler at BYU, Provo. I am particularly indebted to R. Ohran for his untiring enthusiasm and for not giving up even in moments of despair. The idea that such a project would be both worthwhile and feasible originated during my sabbatical leave at the Xerox Palo Alto Research Center in 1976/77, and I am most grateful to its staff members for many inspiring ideas. I thank Ch.Geschke, B.W.Lampson, J.Morris, and E.Satterthwaite for convincing me that complex software was not only needed but possible on small personal computers, and E.M.McCreight for sticking to his belief that it was possible to teach hardware design to a software type and for withholding his plentyful knowledge of all the difficulties to be encountered. Furthermore I am grateful to J.D.Nicoud of ETH Lausanne for his help in the design and for producing the Mouse. Finally I wish to acknowledge the financial support of ETH, making the entire endeavour possible.

References

1. C.P.Thacker, E.M.McCreight, B.W.Lampson, R.F.Sproull, D.R.Boggs. Alto: A personal computer. Xerox Palo Alto Research Center. Report CSL-79-11 (1979)
2. N.Wirth. A personal computer designed for a high-level language. In W.Remmele, H.Schecher, Eds., "Microcomputing", 115-134, Stuttgart, 1979.
3. N.Wirth. Modula-2. Institut fur Informatik, ETH. Report 36, 1980.
4. B.W.Lampson. An open operating system for a single-user machine. Revue Francaise d'Automatique. pp 5-18, Sept. 1975.
5. N.Wirth. Modula: A language for modular multiprogramming. Software - Practice and Experience, 7, 3-35. Jan.1977.
6. Ch.M.Geschke, J.H.Morris, E.H.Satterthwaite. Early experience with Mesa. Comm. ACM, 20, 8, 540-553, Aug. 1977.
7. L.Geissmann. Modulkonzept und separate Compilation in der Programmiersprache Modula-2. In "Microcomputing", 98-114, (see Ref.2)
8. H.C.Lauer, E.H.Satterthwaite. The impact of Mesa on system

design. Proc. Int'l Conf. on Software Engineering, Munich, 174-182, IEEE (1979).

9. D.D.Redell et al. Pilot: An operating system for a personal computer. Comm.ACM 23, 2, 81-92 (Feb. 1980)

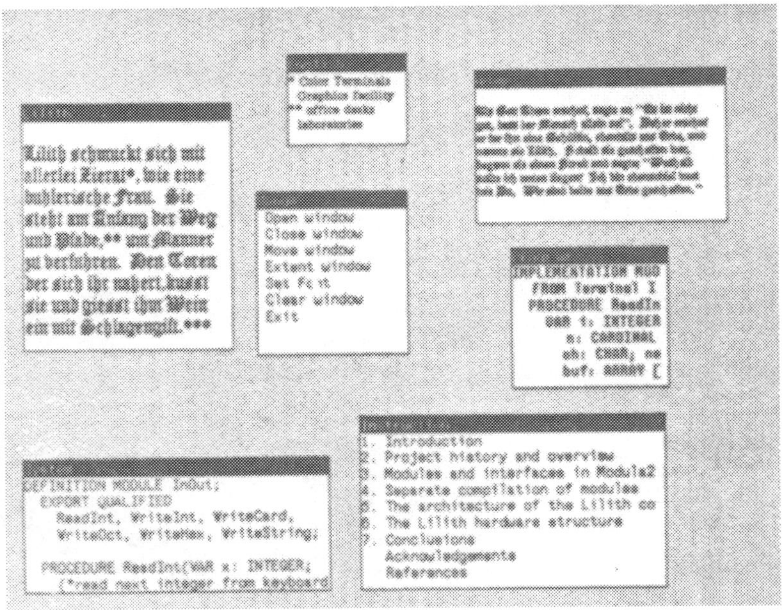

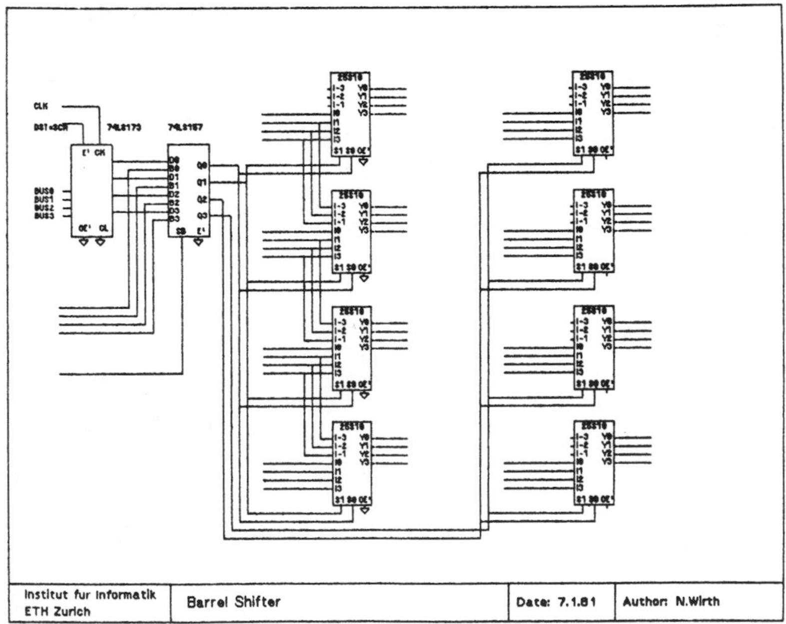

Fig. 1 Examples of displayed pictures in original screen resolution.

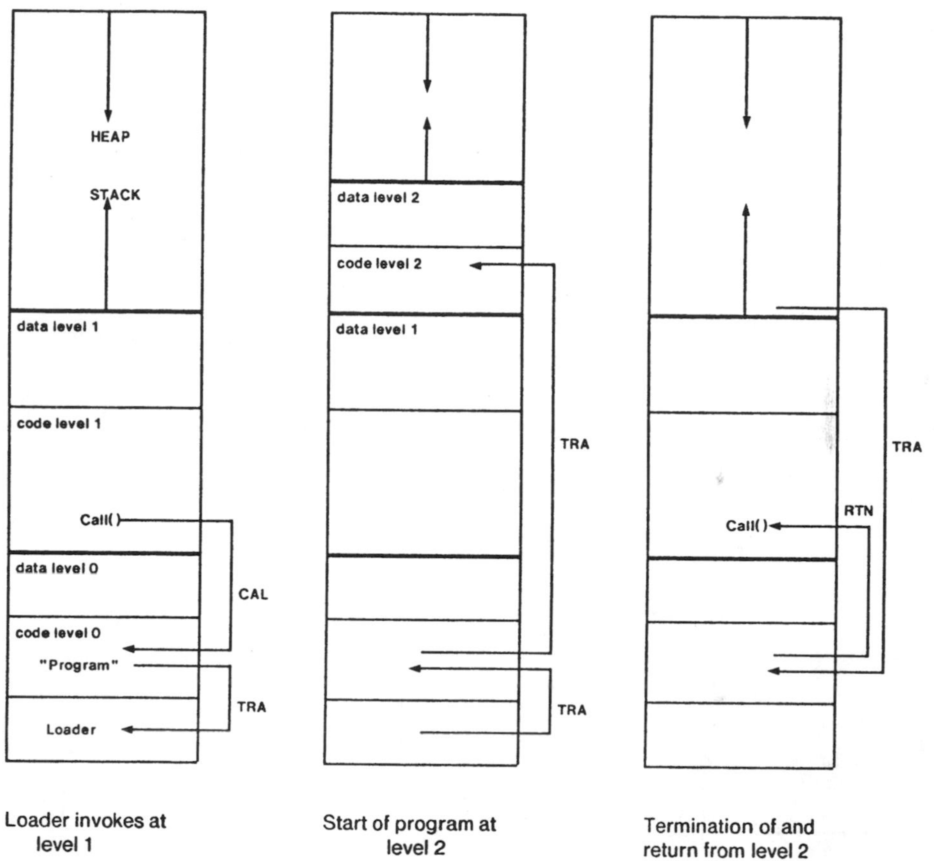

Loader invokes at level 1

Start of program at level 2

Termination of and return from level 2

Fig.2. Loading of program at level 2

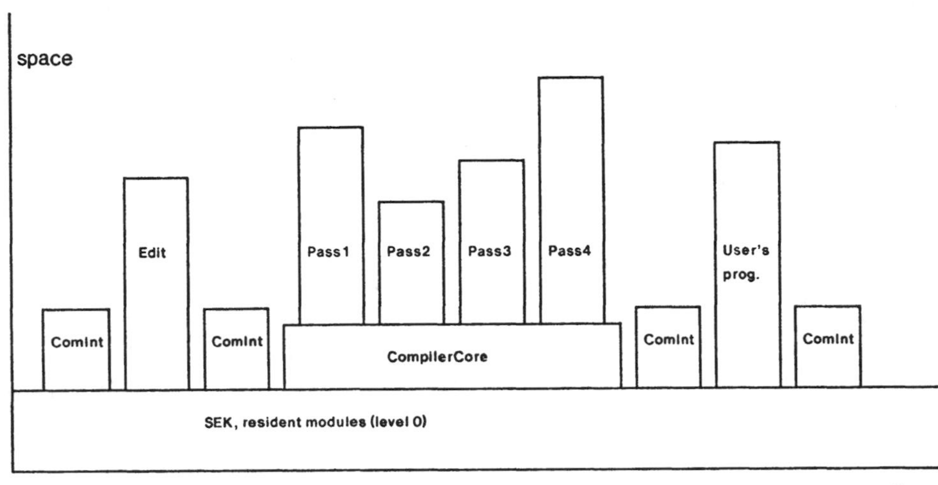

Fig.3. Typical sequence of program loadings

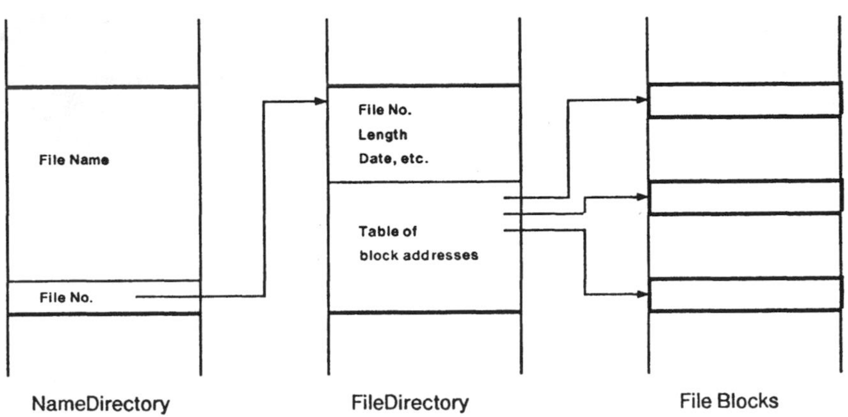

Fig.4. Storage layout on disk

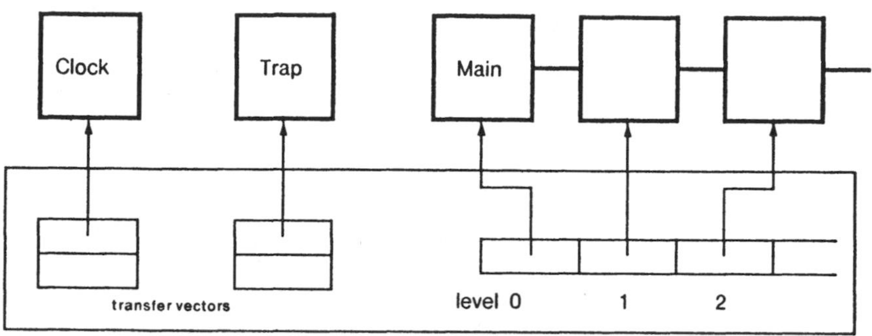

Fig. 5. The three processes of Medos

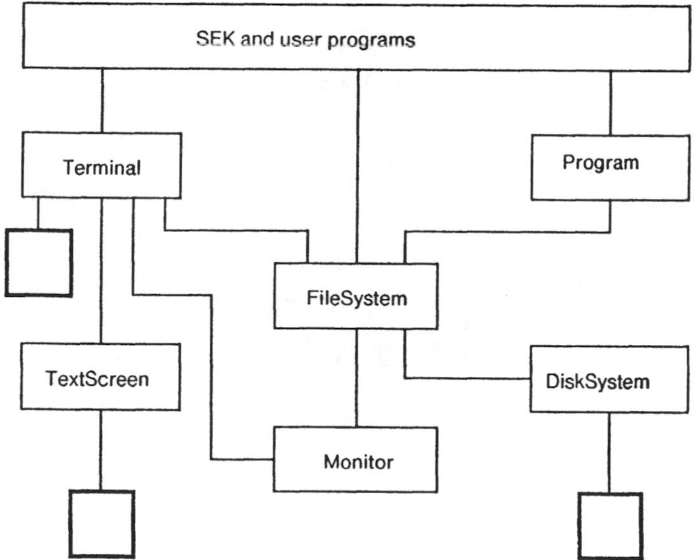

Fig. 6. Procedure call hierarchy

Registers:		
	L	pointer to local data segment
	G	pointer to global data segment
	S	pointer to top of stack
	H	pointer to stack limit
	F	pointer to current code frame
	PC	pointer to current instruction
	P	pointer to current process
	M	interrupt mask

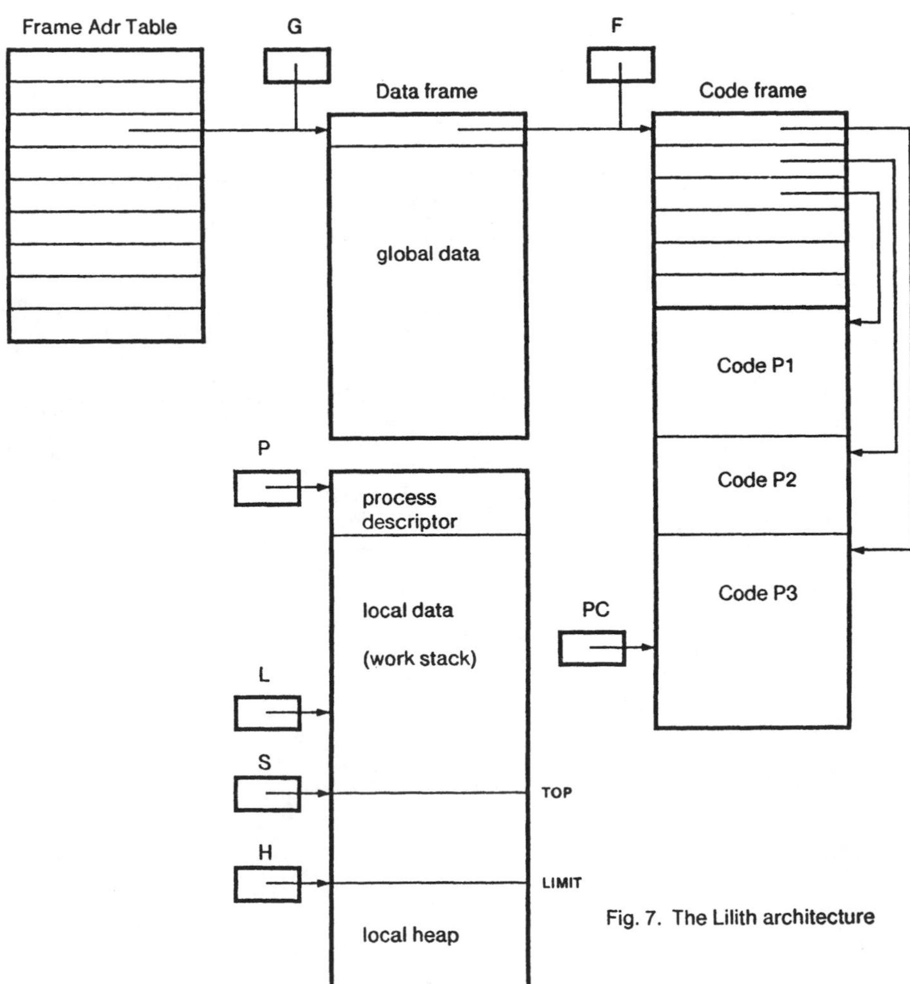

Fig. 7. The Lilith architecture

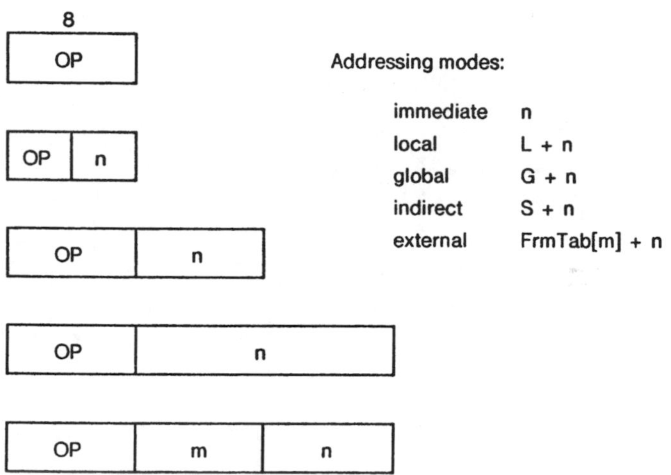

Fig. 8. Lilith instruction formats

Block diagram

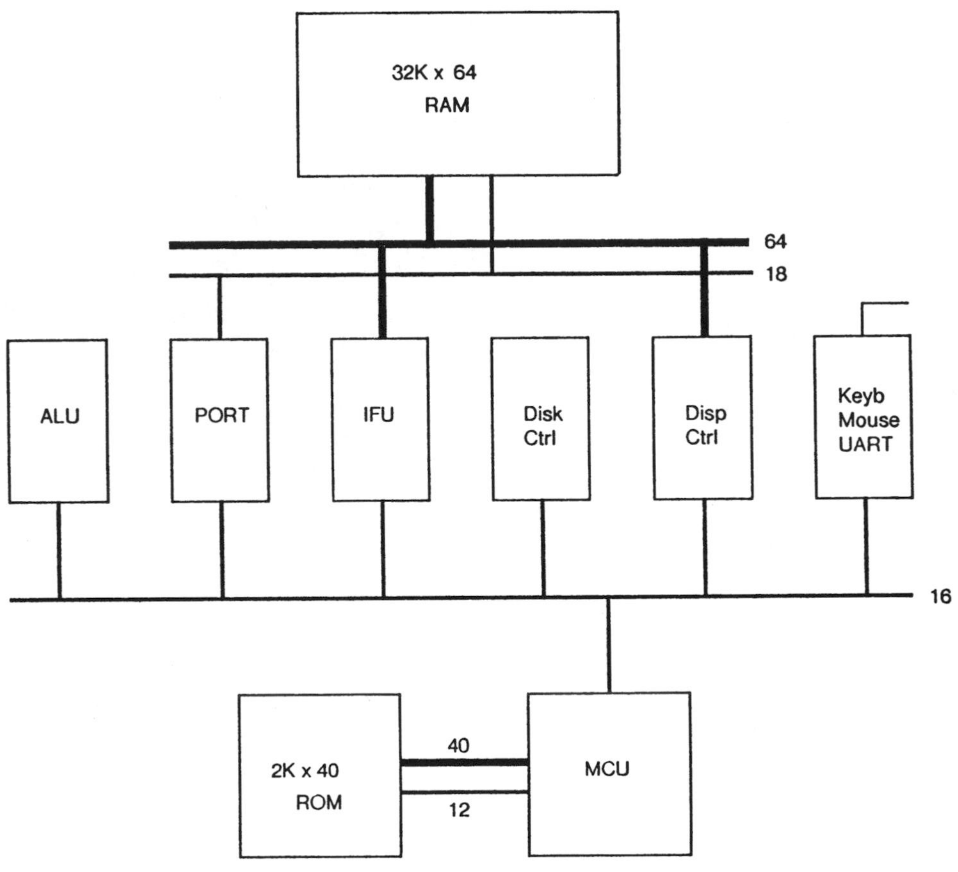

Fig. 9. Lilith hardware structure

1	3	3	3	2	4	4	2	4	1	3	1	1	8
1	Dst	Fct	RS	C	A	B	SM	SC	T	PC	S	1	Constant

1	3	3	3	2	4	4	2	4	1	3	1	1	4	4
1	Dst	Fct	RS	C	A	B	SM	SC	T	PC	S	0	BusDest	BusSrc

1	12	8	5	1	3	10
0	Jump address	CondMask		T	PC	

Dst, Fct, RS, A, B:	2901 control fields
PC:	2911 control field
SM, SC:	Shift mode and count
S:	Stack enable

Fig. 10. The micro-instruction formats

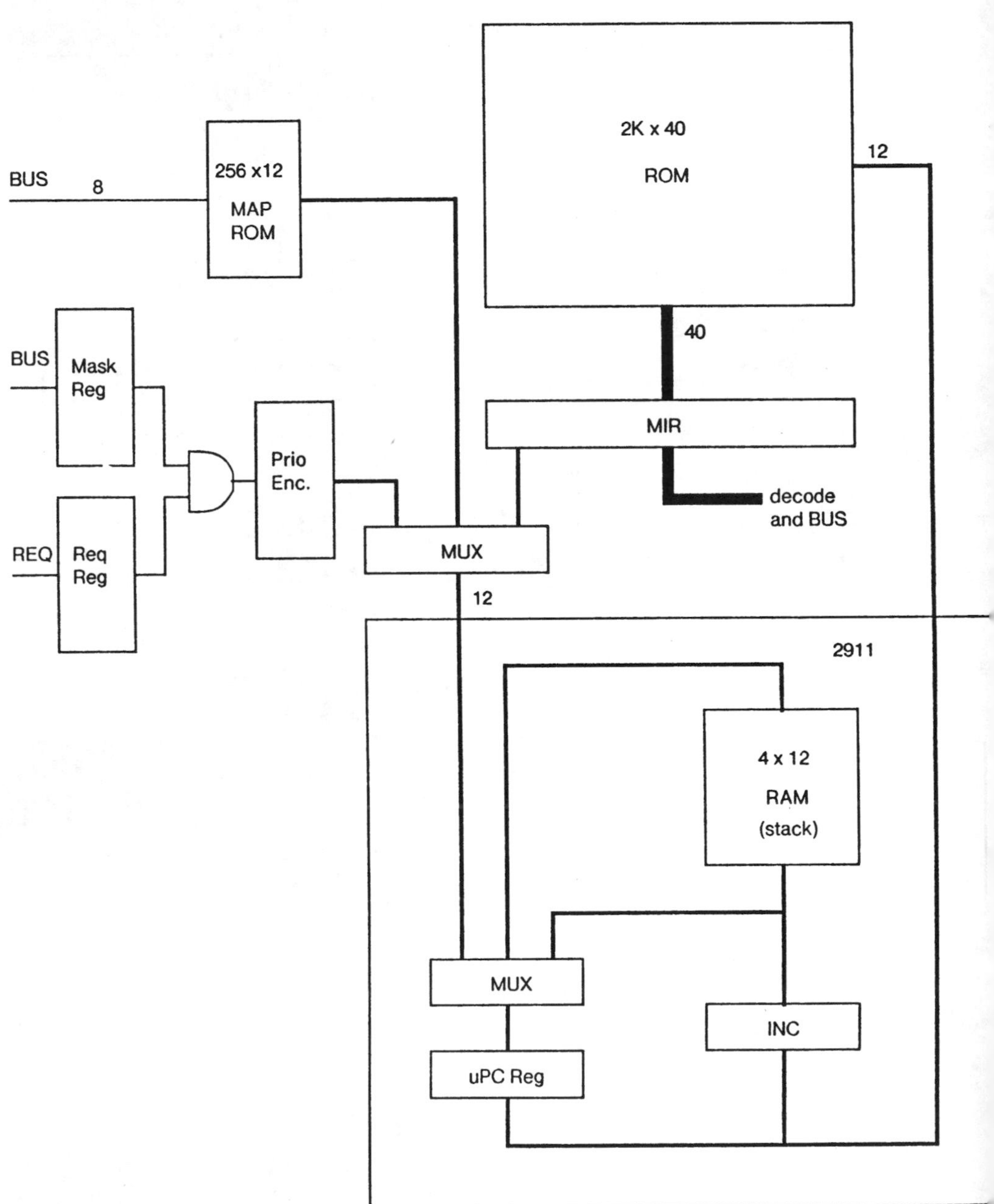

Fig. 11. The Micro-Control Unit

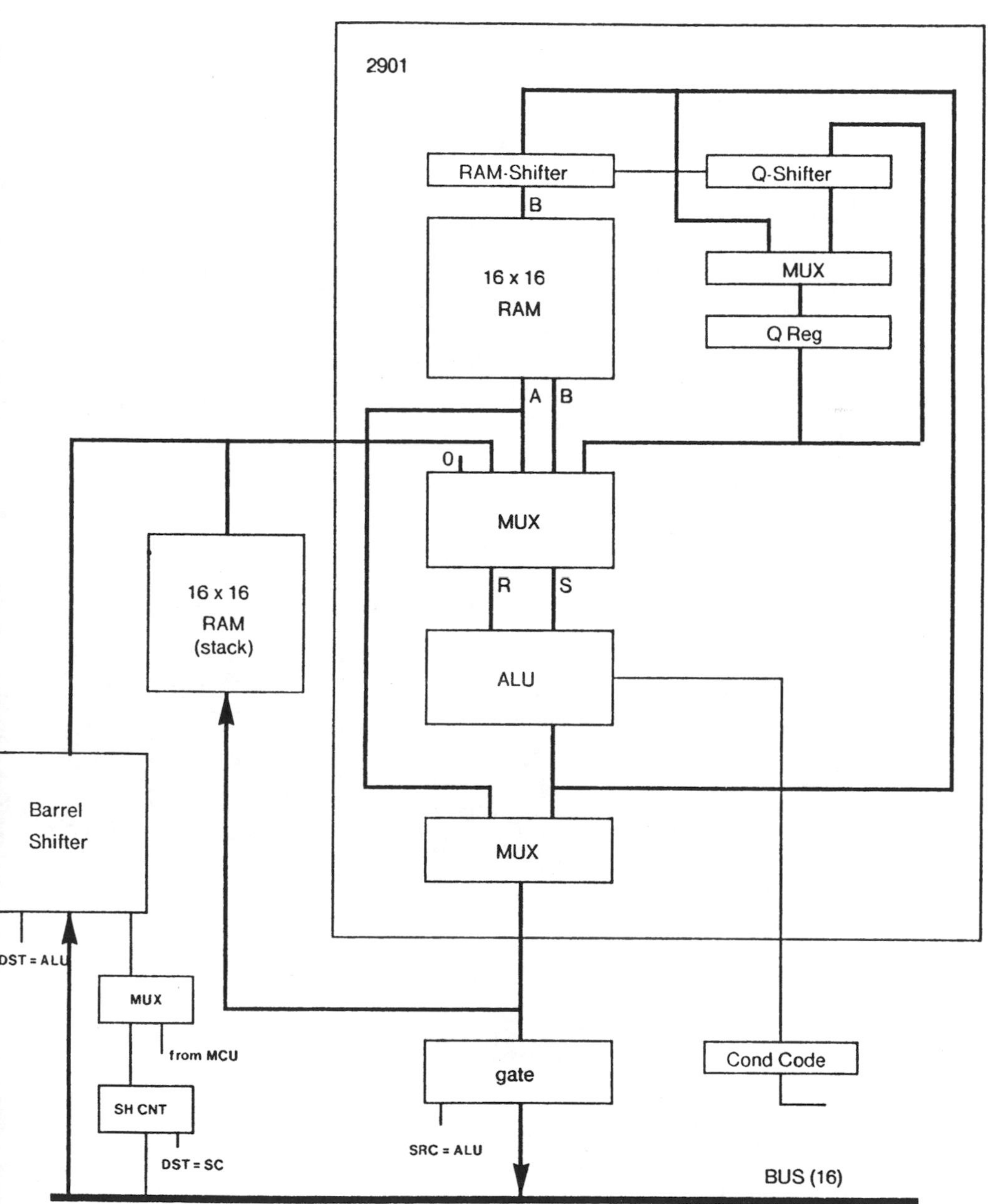

Fig. 12. The Arithmetic-Logic Unit

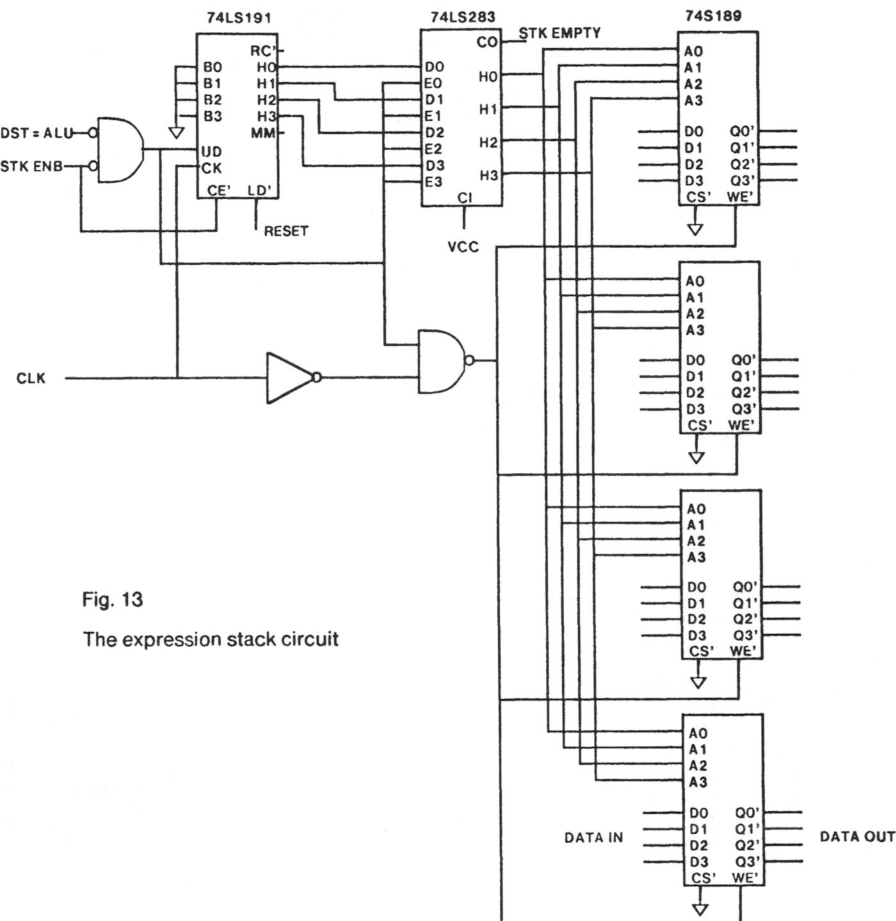

Fig. 13

The expression stack circuit

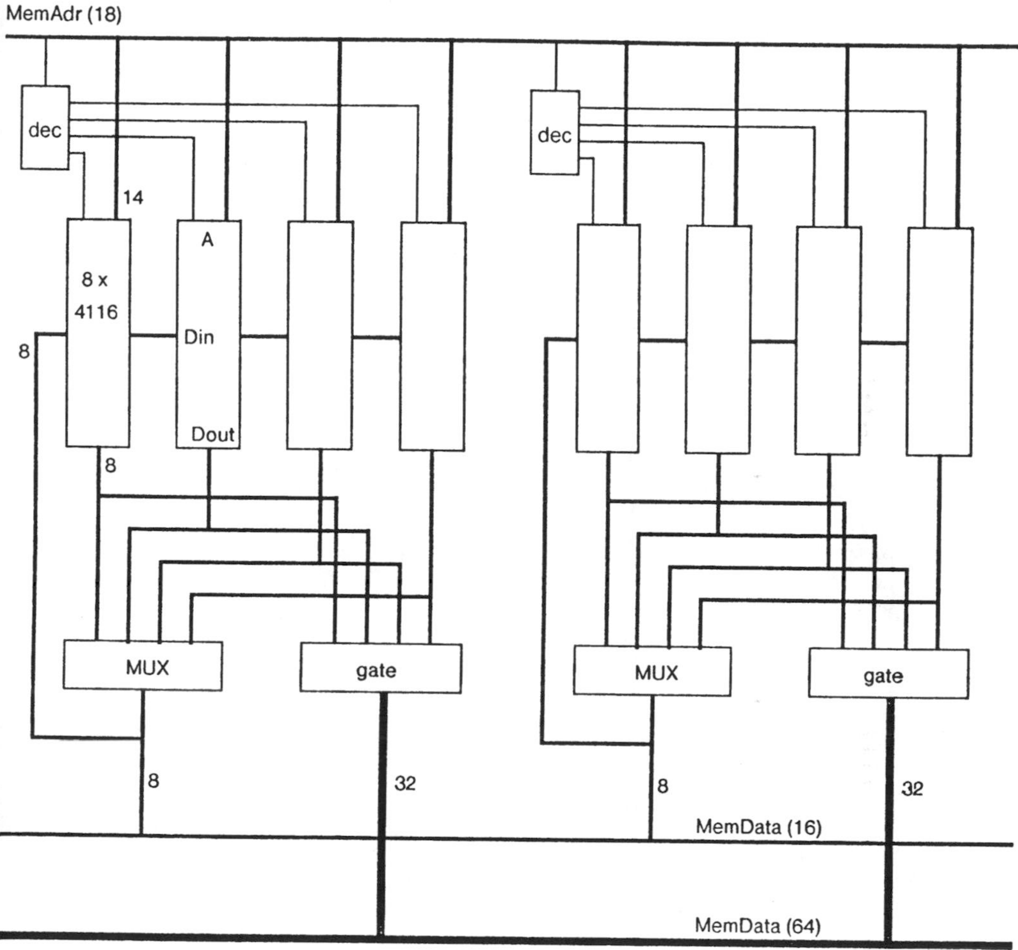

Fig. 14. Memory organization

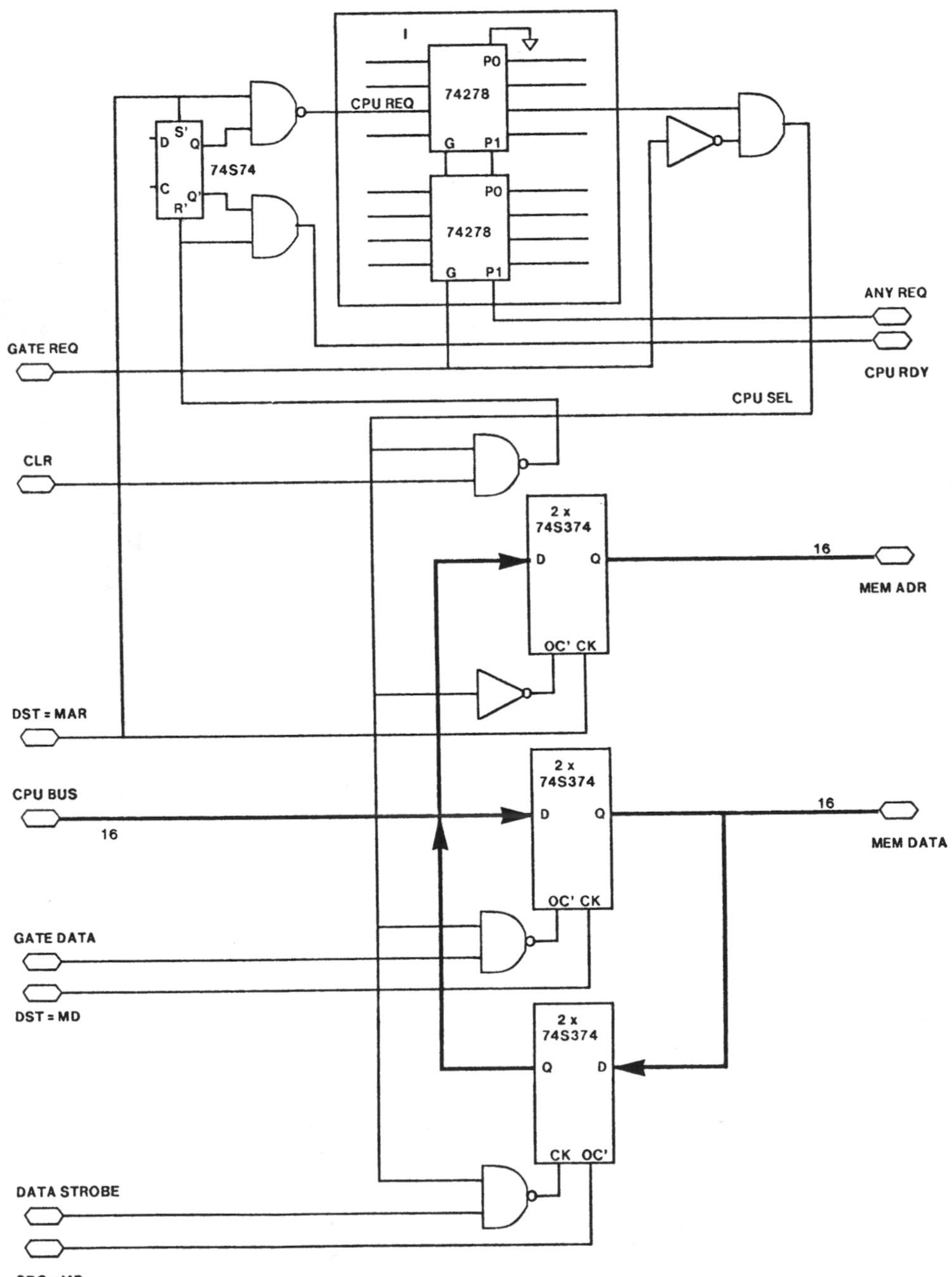

Fig. 15. The bus to memory interface and request arbitration circuit

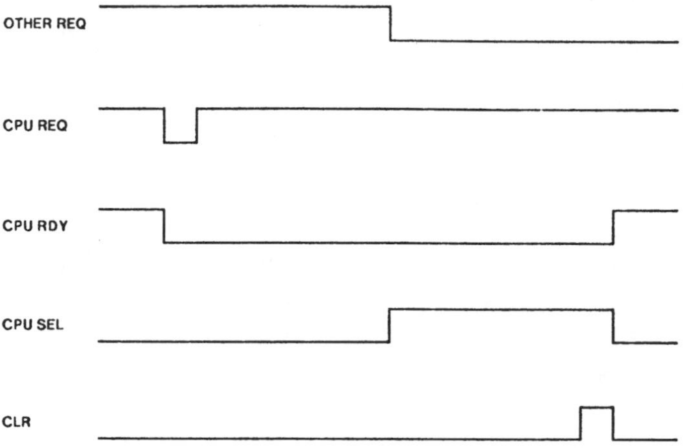

Fig. 16. Memory interface signal timing

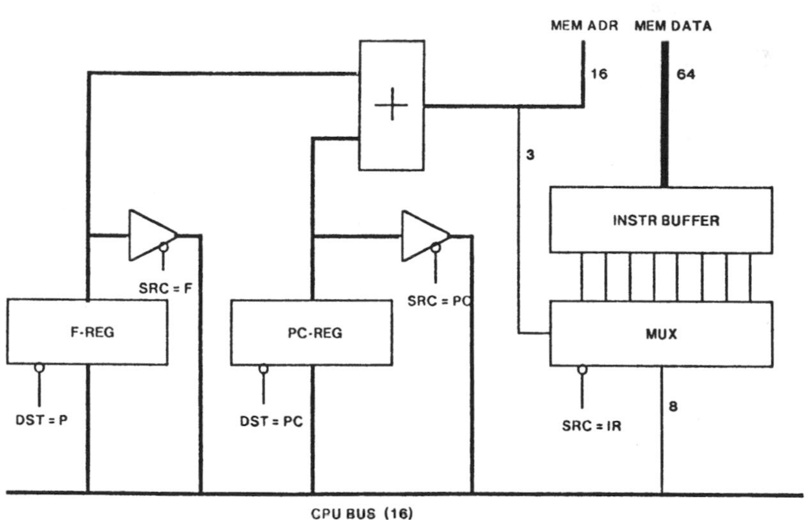

Fig. 17. The instruction fetch unit

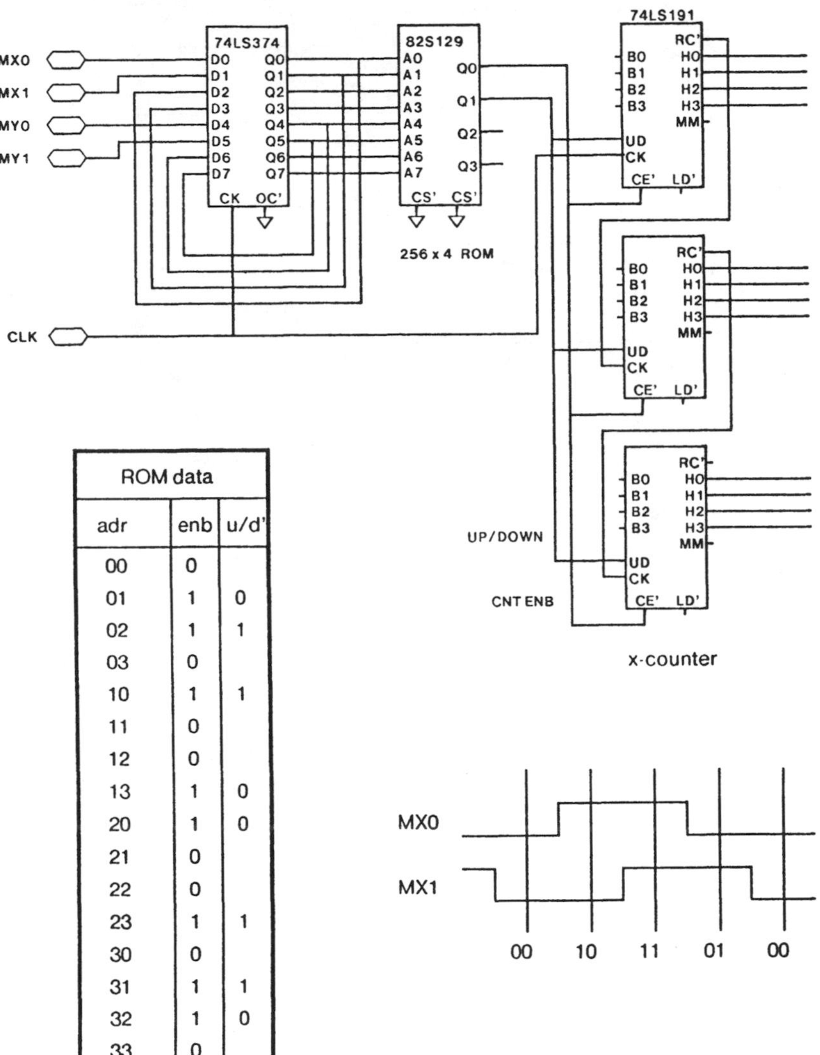

ROM data		
adr	enb	u/d'
00	0	
01	1	0
02	1	1
03	0	
10	1	1
11	0	
12	0	
13	1	0
20	1	0
21	0	
22	0	
23	1	1
30	0	
31	1	1
32	1	0
33	0	

Fig. 18. The Mouse interface with x-counter

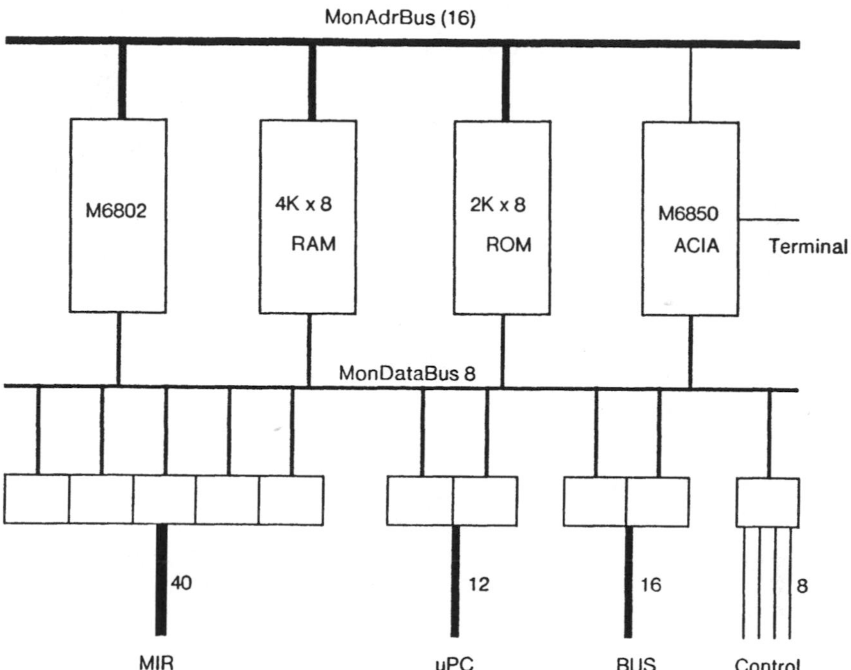

Fig. 19. Monitor with 6802 microprocessor

Vol. 77: G. V. Bochmann, Architecture of Distributed Computer Systems. VIII, 238 pages. 1979.

Vol. 78: M. Gordon, R. Milner and C. Wadsworth, Edinburgh LCF. VIII, 159 pages. 1979.

Vol. 79: Language Design and Programming Methodology. Proceedings, 1979. Edited by J. Tobias. IX, 255 pages. 1980.

Vol. 80: Pictorial Information Systems. Edited by S. K. Chang and K. S. Fu. IX, 445 pages. 1980.

Vol. 81: Data Base Techniques for Pictorial Applications. Proceedings, 1979. Edited by A. Blaser. XI, 599 pages. 1980.

Vol. 82: J. G. Sanderson, A Relational Theory of Computing. VI, 147 pages. 1980.

Vol. 83: International Symposium Programming. Proceedings, 1980. Edited by B. Robinet. VII, 341 pages. 1980.

Vol. 84: Net Theory and Applications. Proceedings, 1979. Edited by W. Brauer. XIII, 537 Seiten. 1980.

Vol. 85: Automata, Languages and Programming. Proceedings, 1980. Edited by J. de Bakker and J. van Leeuwen. VIII, 671 pages. 1980.

Vol. 86: Abstract Software Specifications. Proceedings, 1979. Edited by D. Bjørner. XIII, 567 pages. 1980

Vol. 87: 5th Conference on Automated Deduction. Proceedings, 1980. Edited by W. Bibel and R. Kowalski. VII, 385 pages. 1980.

Vol. 88: Mathematical Foundations of Computer Science 1980. Proceedings, 1980. Edited by P. Dembiński. VIII, 723 pages. 1980.

Vol. 89: Computer Aided Design - Modelling, Systems Engineering, CAD-Systems. Proceedings, 1980. Edited by J. Encarnacao. XIV, 461 pages. 1980.

Vol. 90: D. M. Sandford, Using Sophisticated Models in Resolution Theorem Proving.
XI, 239 pages. 1980

Vol. 91: D. Wood, Grammar and L Forms: An Introduction. IX, 314 pages. 1980.

Vol. 92: R. Milner, A Calculus of Communication Systems. VI, 171 pages. 1980.

Vol. 93: A. Nijholt, Context-Free Grammars: Covers, Normal Forms, and Parsing. VII, 253 pages. 1980.

Vol. 94: Semantics-Directed Compiler Generation. Proceedings, 1980. Edited by N. D. Jones. V, 489 pages. 1980.

Vol. 95: Ch. D. Marlin, Coroutines. XII, 246 pages. 1980.

Vol. 96: J. L. Peterson, Computer Programs for Spelling Correction: VI, 213 pages. 1980.

Vol. 97: S. Osaki and T. Nishio, Reliability Evaluation of Some Fault-Tolerant Computer Architectures. VI, 129 pages. 1980.

Vol. 98: Towards a Formal Description of Ada. Edited by D. Bjørner and O. N. Oest. XIV, 630 pages. 1980.

Vol. 99: I. Guessarian, Algebraic Semantics. XI, 158 pages. 1981.

Vol. 100: Graphtheoretic Concepts in Computer Science. Edited by H. Noltemeier. X, 403 pages. 1981.

Vol. 101: A. Thayse, Boolean Calculus of Differences. VII, 144 pages. 1981.

Vol. 102: J. H. Davenport, On the Integration of Algebraic Functions. –197 pages. 1981.

Vol. 103: H. Ledgard, A. Singer, J. Whiteside, Directions in Human Factors of Interactive Systems. VI, 190 pages. 1981.

Vol. 104: Theoretical Computer Science. Ed. by P. Deussen. VII, 261 pages. 1981.

Vol. 105: B. W. Lampson, M. Paul, H. J. Siegert, Distributed Systems – Architecture and Implementation. XIII, 510 pages. 1981.

Vol. 106: The Programming Language Ada. Reference Manual. X, 243 pages. 1981.

Vol. 107: International Colloquium on Formalization of Programming Concepts. Proceedings. Edited by J. Diaz and I. Ramos. VII, 478 pages. 1981.

Vol. 108: Graph Theory and Algorithms. Edited by N. Saito and T. Nishizeki. VI, 216 pages. 1981.

Vol. 109: Digital Image Processing Systems. Edited by L. Bolc and Zenon Kulpa. V, 353 pages. 1981.

Vol. 110: W. Dehning, H. Essig, S. Maass, The Adaptation of Virtual Man-Computer Interfaces to User Requirements in Dialogs. X, 142 pages. 1981.

Vol. 111: CONPAR 81. Edited by W. Händler. XI, 508 pages. 1981.

Vol. 112: CAAP '81. Proceedings. Edited by G. Astesiano and C. Böhm. VI, 364 pages. 1981.

Vol. 113: E.-E. Doberkat, Stochastic Automata: Stability, Nondeterminism, and Prediction. IX, 135 pages. 1981.

Vol. 114: B. Liskov, CLU, Reference Manual. VIII, 190 pages. 1981.

Vol. 115: Automata, Languages and Programming. Edited by S. Even and O. Kariv. VIII, 552 pages. 1981.

Vol. 116: M. A. Casanova, The Concurrency Control Problem for Database Systems. VII, 175 pages. 1981.

Vol. 117: Fundamentals of Computation Theory. Proceedings, 1981. Edited by F. Gécseg. XI, 471 pages. 1981.

Vol. 118: Mathematical Foundations of Computer Science 1981. Proceedings, 1981. Edited by J. Gruska and M. Chytil. XI, 589 pages. 1981.

Vol. 119: G. Hirst, Anaphora in Natural Language Understanding: A Survey. XIII, 128 pages. 1981.

Vol. 120: L. B. Rall, Automatic Differentiation: Techniques and Applications. VIII, 165 pages. 1981.

Vol. 121: Z. Zlatev, J. Wasniewski, and K. Schaumburg, Y12M Solution of Large and Sparse Systems of Linear Algebraic Equations. IX, 128 pages. 1981.

Vol. 122: Algorithms in Modern Mathematics and Computer Science. Proceedings, 1979. Edited by A. P. Ershov and D. E. Knuth. XI, 487 pages. 1981.

Vol. 123: Trends in Information Processing Systems. Proceedings, 1981. Edited by A. J. W. Duijvestijn and P. C. Lockemann. XI, 349 pages. 1981.

Vol. 124: W. Polak, Compiler Specification and Verification. XIII, 269 pages. 1981.

Vol. 125: Logic of Programs. Proceedings, 1979. Edited by E. Engeler. V, 245 pages. 1981.

Vol. 126: Microcomputer System Design. Proceedings, 1981. Edited by M. J. Flynn, N. R. Harris, and D. P. McCarthy. VII, 397 pages. 1982.

This series reports new developments in computer science research and teaching – quickly, informally and at a high level. The type of material considered for publication includes:

1. Preliminary drafts of original papers and monographs
2. Lectures on a new field or presentations of a new angle in a classical field
3. Seminar work-outs
4. Reports of meetings, provided they are
   a) of exceptional interest and
   b) devoted to a single topic.

Texts which are out of print but still in demand may also be considered if they fall within these categories.

The timeliness of a manuscript is more important than its form, whic may be unfinished or tentative. Thus, in some instances, proofs may be merely outlined and results presented which have been or will later be published elsewhere. If possible, a subject index should be included. Publication of Lecture Notes is intended as a service to the internationa computer science community, in that a commercial publisher, Springer Verlag, can offer a wide distribution of documents which would other wise have a restricted readership. Once published and copyrighted they can be documented in the scientific literature.

Manuscripts

Manuscripts should be no less than 100 and preferably no more than 500 pages in length.
They are reproduced by a photographic process and therefore must be typed with extreme care. Symbo not on the typewriter should be inserted by hand in indelible black ink. Corrections to the typescri should be made by pasting in the new text or painting out errors with white correction fluid. Authors receiv 75 free copies and are free to use the material in other publications. The typescript is reduced slightly size during reproduction; best results will not be obtained unless the text on any one page is kept with the overall limit of 18 x 26.5 cm (7 x 10½ inches). On request, the publisher will supply special paper wi the typing area outlined.
Manuscripts should be sent to Prof. G. Goos, Institut für Informatik, Universität Karlsruhe, Zirkel 2, 7500 Karl ruhe/Germany, Prof. J. Hartmanis, Cornell University, Dept. of Computer-Science, Ithaca, NY/USA 1485 or directly to Springer-Verlag Heidelberg.

Springer-Verlag, Heidelberger Platz 3, D-1000 Berlin 33
Springer-Verlag, Neuenheimer Landstraße 28–30, D-6900 Heidelberg 1
Springer-Verlag, 175 Fifth Avenue, New York, NY 10010/USA

ISBN 3-540-11172-7
ISBN 0-387-11172-7